MT|14

THE STUDY OF
MUSIC THERAPY

This book addresses the issues in music therapy that are central to understanding it in its scholarly dimensions, how it is evolving, and how it connects to related academic disciplines. It draws on a multi-disciplinary approach to look at the defining issues of music therapy as a scholarly discipline, rather than as an area of clinical practice. It is the single best resource for scholars interested in music therapy because it focuses on the areas that tend to be of greatest interest to them, such as issues of definition, theory, and the function of social context, but also does not assume detailed prior knowledge of the subject.

Some of the topics discussed include defining the nature of music therapy, its relation to current and historical uses of music in human well-being, and considerations on what makes music therapy work. Contemporary thinking on the role of neurological theory, early interaction theory, and evolutionary considerations in music therapy theory are also reviewed. Within each of these areas, the author presents an overview of the development of thinking, discusses contrasting positions, and offers a personalized synthesis of the issue. *The Study of Music Therapy* is the only book in music therapy that gathers all the major issues currently debated in the field, providing a critical overview of the predominance of opinions on these issues.

Kenneth S. Aigen is an associate professor in music therapy at New York University. He is president of the Nordoff-Robbins Music Therapy (NRMT) Foundation and the International Trust for NRMT. He is a past president of the American Association for Music Therapy and a recipient of the Research and Publications Award from the American Music Therapy Association.

THE STUDY OF MUSIC THERAPY

Current Issues and Concepts

Kenneth S. Aigen

New York University

Routledge
Taylor & Francis Group

NEW YORK AND LONDON

First published 2014
by Routledge
711 Third Avenue, New York, NY 10017

and by Routledge
2 Park Square, Milton Park, Abingdon, Oxon OX14 4RN

Routledge is an imprint of the Taylor and Francis Group, an informa business

© 2014 Taylor and Francis

Library of Congress Cataloging in Publication Data
Aigen, Kenneth S., author.
  The study of music therapy: current issues and concepts/Kenneth S. Aigen.
  pages cm
  Includes bibliographical references and index.
  1. Music therapy—Research. I. Title.
  ML3920.A173 2014
  615.8'515407—dc23
  2013025941

ISBN: 978-0-415-62640-8 (hbk)
ISBN: 978-0-415-62641-5 (pbk)
ISBN: 978-1-31588-270-3 (ebk)

Typeset in Bembo and Stone Sans
by Florence Production Ltd, Stoodleigh, Devon, UK

Senior Editor: Constance Ditzel
Editorial Assistant: Elysse Preposi
Production Manager: Bonita Glanville-Morris
Marketing Manager: Cedric Sinclair
Project Manager: Kelly Derrick
Copy Editor: Thérèse Wassily Saba
Proofreader: Etty Payne
Cover Design: Lisa Dynan

Printed in Great Britain by TJ International Ltd, Padstow, Cornwall

This work is dedicated to Clive Robbins,
a giant of a man and a visionary whose recent
passing has both cast a shadow upon and
inspired the present work.

CONTENTS

TABLES

PREFACE

In the early 2000s, I was deeply involved in a research project on the use of popular music styles in music therapy improvisation. One central phenomenon that I was examining was the role of groove creation in therapy. My primary focus was how groove is accomplished and what its clinical benefits were.

This interest led me to the work of Charlie Keil and Steven Feld, particularly the explorations and dialogues in their book *Music Grooves* (Keil & Feld, 1994). I found that their concepts which had been generated from ethnomusicological and anthropological contexts—such as Keil's "participatory discrepancies" and Feld's *dulugu ganalan* or "lift-up-over sounding"—were highly relevant to music therapy. These ideas assumed prominent roles in my conceptual analyses. Their usefulness motivated me to dig more deeply into the ethnomusicology literature, something that I had time for once the research project was published.

I asked a few friends from this discipline to recommend one text to provide an overview. Each of them replied that Bruno Nettl's *The Study of Ethnomusicology* (in its just published 2005 revision) would be an excellent starting point. I found the general tenor of Nettl's writing to be highly engaging and its ambition inspiring for a number of reasons: (i) The book was directed to a diverse audience, including ethnomusicologists, scholars in related areas, and graduate students. (ii) The description of issues and conflicting positions in the field was completely intelligible to me as an outsider; it had a clarity that did not appear to come by providing overly simplistic portraits of relatively complex topics. (iii) The book was neither a summary of existing positions nor was it just a statement of personal opinions. Instead, Nettl struck a balance between exploring different positions on issues and offering his own perspective in a non-polemical way.

The value of Nettl's book convinced me to write a book that discussed music therapy in this way. Hence, the purpose of the present book is to address issues in music therapy that are central to understanding its scholarly dimensions, its evolution, and its connection to related disciplines. The approach is guided by the three aspects of Nettl's work noted above. In relation to the first two of these aspects, the work is addressed to music therapy scholars, graduate students in music therapy, and scholars from related disciplines such as ethnomusicology and the sociology of music. While no detailed knowledge of music therapy is assumed, expositions of common knowledge in music therapy are kept to a minimum, providing only that information which is necessary to understand the focus of a given chapter. In relation to the third aspect, the strategy employed regarding the handling of contrasting viewpoints is similar to Nettl's. Each chapter includes an overview of the topic and a description of the different positions and rationales held by various authors. As the different facets of an issue are explored, my own perspective will also be made clear.

Within each of these areas, I trace the development of thinking and provide an overview of contrasting positions with a twofold intention: to provide a broad and detailed view of the scholarly, theoretical, and practical concerns with which music therapists are concerned, while also moving forward the debate on such concerns. In some cases the debate is advanced primarily by gathering the contrasting positions in one place, while examining their underlying rationales. Wherever possible I propose a synthesis that attempts to move past some of the more polarized positions that have been articulated.

By writing in a way that does not assume detailed prior knowledge of music therapy, or of the various related disciplines from which many of the analytical tools will be derived, my hope is that the work will foster multi-disciplinary understanding and collaboration in two directions. This will involve introducing music therapists to perspectives from related disciplines that will be useful in illuminating dilemmas and issues in music therapy, while at the same time the use of these related concepts will provide an entry point to the text for scholars from disciplines outside music therapy.

Given their relative small numbers, music therapists work with an extremely wide variety of individuals across the lifespan and at different levels of functioning. Work is performed from musically-assisted childbirth to end of life care; from nonresponsive individuals in minimal awareness states to fully functioning individuals seeking an alternative form of psychotherapy to pursue self-actualization. Because of the very broad nature of their work, music therapists are confronted with perennial questions addressed in related disciplines such as the nature of music, the meaning of health and well-being, the significance of culture in human development, and the role of context (social and personal) in determining the significance of music.

All of these concerns are indigenous to music therapy, and yet many of them either have strong parallels or are directly addressed in other disciplines. Consequently, music therapists have a great deal to offer scholars in music disciplines. To have a more complete portrait of the contexts in which musicing[1] occurs—whether from an ethnomusicological or sociological perspective—it is necessary to include contexts in which music therapists create music with their clients, whether this is, for example, an outpatient facility for adults with chronic mental illness or a classroom of children with autism. No music discipline can approach comprehensiveness in its efforts unless it considers what happens in music therapy.

Conversely, as my own experience has shown, scholars from other disciplines have generated concepts that can provide insight into what happens in music therapy sessions. After all, music therapy activities—whether they involve composing, listening to, or playing composed or improvised music—are examples of culturally-situated musicing situations. It is thus reasonable to assume that the knowledge base of music disciplines outside of music therapy based on the study of such situations is relevant to music therapy. Because music therapists have tended to draw theory more from nonmusical health-related domains than from non-clinical musical domains, an important focus of the present work is to support the redressing of this imbalance.

Although this book is not a research study *per se*, I did use an analog of a qualitative research method in determining the contents of each chapter and, to some extent, the chapter organization of the book. After articulating a general structure in terms of chapter titles and focuses, I examined the complete contents of all the major music therapy journals and a large number of music therapy books for writings that related to the basic focuses. From this large number of sources, themes within each chapter category were noted, and these themes provided the basic content of the book. So while the specific contents do reflect my interests to some extent, they are firmly grounded in the perennial themes addressed by music therapy authors. In this regard, there are a small number of authors whose writings are referenced in multiple chapters. This is a result of my empirical engagement with the literature rather than merely reflecting my personal preference.

One related issue concerns the central strategy of the book to review various perspectives on areas of debate, while also taking the opportunity to provide some of my own views on these perennial issues. Of course, I have my own set of values, beliefs, experiences, and ideas that undoubtedly influence this book, both in terms of the selection of issues and the way that those issues are addressed. Music therapists familiar with my previous publications will have some idea regarding those commitments; readers without this familiarity will not have this same ability to contextualize my views and the presentation of issues. It is thus important to acknowledge my commitment to creative, improvisational, social, and music-based theories as opposed to the more medically-oriented, scientific, behavioral, and psychodynamic approaches that are also prominent in music therapy.

Because of my commitment to music-based and socio-cultural orientations to music therapy, it is natural that my analyses will critique authors that represent the contrasting medical, purely scientific, and psychoanalytic perspectives. However, my critical analyses also address the work of authors from the former group whose overall programs I generally have greater sympathy for. In critiquing authors across the theoretical spectrum, I hope that the content of my arguments can be evaluated on their own merits, rather than being considered merely as arguments for a predetermined point of view.

I have also provided a counterbalance to my opinions by including a significant amount of quoted material from primary source publications, perhaps more so than is typical of a work of this type. I have done this to substantiate my claims about the perspectives of other authors as well as to offer you, the reader, the opportunity to come into direct contact with their words, in order to be able to draw your own conclusions about how these views are best construed. The relatively detailed citations also provide a guide for readers who wish to pursue more comprehensive investigations of any these issues than can be covered in a broad survey such as the present one.

Because my goal in the present book has been to gather in one place the central issues that constitute the areas of scholarly debate in music therapy, I did not include issues where there is substantial unanimity of opinion. As a result, some of the exploration of issues is inconclusive, although my hope is that in the summaries of opposing viewpoints I am providing a tool for future authors wishing to advance these debates. In some places I attempt a synthesis and offer suggestions for how to resolve conflicts in order to achieve some convergence of opinion. My hope is that the focus on both convergent and divergent writing is balanced and thus provides a rich experience for readers.

As noted previously, I have placed a particular emphasis on the topics that either have analogs in other areas or that may be illuminated with ideas from these areas. The issues addressed have arisen either from clinical practice or from scholarly reflections on such practice. However, there is no claim to provide any type of comprehensive overview of clinical work, nor are any particular methods or models of treatment discussed extensively. What I have tried to do in selecting topics is to favor those issues that I believe would be of greatest interest both to music therapists and to readers from other disciplines. I have also favored issues of conceptual and theoretical origins over issues that are more practical and pragmatic.

Two topics that are not included directly but that are discussed in the context of other issues are the role of aesthetics, and the conceptions of emotional expression in music therapy theory. While these two topics certainly could be included in a book such as the present one, they have been addressed substantially in other publications[2] and the decision was made not to repeat that information here. Additionally, two fundamental areas that are not addressed are those of research and educational training in music therapy. It is not that these areas are unimportant but they do require their own dedicated publications.

If it is not already apparent from this brief introduction, I will note that I am a philosopher by training and by temperament. While this way of understanding the world offers many useful tools in illuminating various aspects of conceptual issues, philosophical writing can challenge the reader to maintain focus on the primary issue as all of its facets are being explored. Additionally, most of the issues explored do not have a clear resolution. This owes to the fact that, more often than not, philosophy does a better job of clarifying questions than of providing answers.

Music therapists tend to be a charitable group when it comes to professional discourse. There is much less published disagreement and very little critique of the writings of others in the music therapy literature compared to other academic disciplines. Part of this is due to the magnanimous nature of the music therapy professional community and part of it is due to the fact that many of the items of discussion in the music therapy literature do not concern matters of fact. Instead, they deal with discussions of clinical frameworks, concepts, and theories that are more or less useful in particular contexts. As pragmatic constructions, these frameworks are used by therapists who resonate with them and are generally not engaged by therapists who work from contrasting positions. While some readers may consider this noncritical professional dynamic as a positive attribute that is reflective of the generally supportive stance therapists assume in their work, it is nonetheless inconsistent with fundamental notions from counseling and psychotherapy that detail how conflict and its resolution are necessary components of growth.

I make these observations because a significant portion of the present book involves a critique of the writings of others. In taking issue with particular notions about music therapy, however, I am not making a case for which of them is correct in any conventional sense of the word. Instead, I endeavor to discern those that are most useful. And although it is not generally articulated in the discussions that follow, my orienting criterion is that music therapy is a service profession that exists solely to enhance the lives of its clients. I have 25 years of clinical experience with a wide variety of individuals. The ideas and perspectives that I argue for are all, at root, motivated by a sense of which of them are best positioned to enhance the lives of clients and which of them are most in line with what I believe clients want from their clinical engagement with music.

My goal in this work is to illuminate underlying problems with some common practices and precepts in music therapy in order to facilitate progress. The largely philosophical exploration of issues contained herein consists of a few different strategies: The various positions and concepts discussed in the book are analyzed for internal consistency and coherence, the presence of unstated and/or unwarranted conceptual assumptions, and the hidden engagement of particular values. This type of work is necessarily critical in nature as it requires articulating the conceptual hierarchy of certain belief systems and showing what I believe their weaknesses to be. However, the value of this transparency is that it really does allow for progress to be made through the collaborative efforts and responses of the community of scholars. Thus, although I do critique the writings of others, I can think of no more rewarding outcome of this work than to have my own work similarly critiqued, so that the progressive determination of how music therapy can best be conceptualized can continue into the future.

Notes

1. The use of the noun *music* as a verb began in music therapy in the mid-1990s. Authors using the spelling *musicing* cite David Elliott (1995) as a source. Authors using the spelling *musicking* cite the work of Christopher Small (1998). Wherever this term appears in the text, the spelling used will reflect the choice of the author being cited.
2. For an overview of the role of aesthetics in music therapy theory, see Aigen (2007, 2008) and responses from Smeijsters (2008) and Stige (2008a). For readings on varying conceptions of emotional expression in music therapy, see Aigen (1995b, 1998, 2005a), Ansdell (1995), Epp (2001), Pavlicevic (1997), and Smeijsters (2005).

ACKNOWLEDGMENTS

Constance Ditzel at Routledge offered constant encouragement and enduring patience as the idea for this book was born and as it came into being. Without her patience and support, it is likely that this book would never have been written. Two anonymous reviewers provided useful feedback that helped aid the organization of the book. I am grateful for their extensive and thoughtful suggestions. For more than 30 years, Carolyn Kenny has provided inspiration in exploring music therapy within a multi-disciplinary framework and I know that a book like this would not have been written (by me, at least) without her efforts as a model. The Boyer College of Music and Dance at Temple University granted a year-long study leave during which the bulk of this writing was accomplished, something for which I am extremely grateful. Darlene Brooks took over my academic responsibilities during this leave, adding immeasurably to her own workload. Without such a supportive and unselfish friend and colleague, I could not have had the uninterrupted time required to produce a work such as this one.

INTRODUCTION

The first issues to be covered in this book center on the nature of music therapy and why this question is the locus of so much disagreement. Before exploring those conceptual issues—and those constituting the remainder of the book—it is important to provide some overview on some of the more concrete aspects of music therapy with which all readers may not be familiar.

Music therapy is a dedicated course of study at the undergraduate, master's, and doctoral level at colleges and universities throughout the world. In some areas such as Australia, Canada and the United States, practitioners can become credentialed with an undergraduate degree[1]. In most other regions, such as Europe and South America, this designation requires a graduate degree. While various types of health practitioners (such as nurses, psychologists, and social workers) may use music in their professional practice, and while various types of musicians may provide music in health care or community settings, none of these individuals are practicing music therapy. That music therapy is a protected professional title, restricted to individuals with the appropriate education and regulatory body recognition, is an important fact to be cognizant of in many of the discussions that follow, particularly those that examine the relationship between this professional practice, and both its historical antecedents and its contemporary parallels in indigenous healing practices that use music.

Although music therapy is a relatively small profession with approximately 5,600 board-certified practitioners in the USA[2], for example, it contains a wide range of clinical applications. Music therapists work with people at every stage of life, from providing services in musically-assisted childbirth to assuming primary care in hospice and palliative care settings; they work in every conceivable type of institution (such as schools, clinics, hospitals, rehabilitation centers, and prisons), in private practice, and in non-institutional community settings; they work with individuals with every conceivable type of disability (including those in the sensory, motor, cognitive, and emotional realms) as well as with individuals who are not disabled and whose goal is wellness and self-actualization; they utilize every possible way in which humans can interact with music, including creating and listening to both improvised and composed music; and they maintain professional identities across the spectrum from those who consider themselves to be medical practitioners working within a predominantly scientific framework to those who consider themselves to be artists working predominantly within a creative framework.

The presence of such diversity in every facet of music therapy is a strength because it allows music therapists to meet the needs of an extremely diverse client base. However, it can also be a problem as it leads to contentious interactions around political, theoretical, and clinical issues because the allegiances of such different individuals with such different ways of working and of conceptualizing their work will often clash. A relatively large discipline that is well ensconced within the structures of society can more easily bear the clashing of diverse interests. Music therapy is in the difficult position of being somewhat of a marginal profession where any social progress necessitates unanimity and the ability to speak with one voice, at least within each national context.

The diversity present in music therapy renders it impossible to make unequivocal statements about the profession, a fact that can be vexing to people trying to understand it from the outside. It also means that the nature of music therapy can often be distorted—or at least represented in an overly narrow way—by authors whose experience causes them to generalize aspects of their own particular clinical approach, work context, or conceptual allegiance to the profession as a whole.

As described in the preface, in writing the present book I have attempted to mitigate some of the unintentional influence of my own preferences through the method used in determining topics to discuss and readings to cite. Nonetheless, readers are certainly encouraged to view the present work as an entry point to an exploration of conceptual issues in music therapy rather than as an exhaustive or comprehensive review of them. The present book is intended to serve as a road map to the more important issues and authors in the field. But the diversity of thought and practice noted above makes it especially important to engage the primary sources in order to gain a reasonably accurate view of music therapy.

Notes

1. Although at the time of this writing, in the spring of 2013, the American Music Therapy Association is considering a proposal to follow the lead of many other therapy disciplines—including all of the other arts therapies—and move to a graduate degree requirement for entry-level practice.
2. This number reflects the situation at the time of this writing in 2013.

PART I

What is Music Therapy?

1

THE IDENTITY OF THE MUSIC THERAPY PROFESSION

Some readers of the present book may come to it with a career-long familiarity with music therapy and other readers may be encountering it for the first time. However, readers in the former group may not be in a significantly better position to provide an unproblematic definition of it than are those in the latter group because the nature of music therapy has been contested throughout its history. As an example of the complexity of defining music therapy, consider that Kenneth Bruscia (1989) devoted an entire book to this task, significantly revising and expanding his work in a second edition (Bruscia, 1998a). Given the quality and quantity of his scholarly work, Bruscia's definition occupies a unique status in the profession.[1] Two of the more prominent, representative, and influential organizations in music therapy are the American Music Therapy Association (AMTA) and the World Federation of Music Therapy (WFMT). Considered together, the following three definitions provide a reasonably comprehensive portrait of how music therapists look at themselves and their work.

Bruscia's definition evokes general conceptions of a health profession in its inclusion of systematic intervention; it references the practice of psychotherapy in the inclusion of the importance of relationship in change processes.

> Music therapy is a systematic process of intervention wherein the therapist helps the client to promote health, using music experiences and the relationships that develop through them as dynamic forces of change.
>
> (Bruscia, 1998a, p. 20)

The AMTA definition is narrower than Bruscia's. Its reference to being evidence-based reflects a more strictly-defined notion of music therapy as a medical profession, not just a health-related one. It adds the claim that music therapy is the province of individuals with specific educational and professional qualifications.

> Music Therapy is the clinical and evidence-based use of music interventions to accomplish individualized goals within a therapeutic relationship by a credentialed professional who has completed an approved music therapy program.
>
> (AMTA, 2013)

As befitting its status as an international organization with pluralistic allegiances, the language of the WFMT expands the focus of the previous two definitions from health to a more inclusive notion of quality of life.

> Music therapy is the professional use of music and its elements as an intervention in medical, educational, and everyday environments with individuals, groups, families, or communities who seek to optimize their quality of life and improve their physical, social, communicative, emotional, intellectual, and spiritual health and wellbeing. Research, practice, education, and clinical training in music therapy are based on professional standards according to cultural, social, and political contexts.
>
> (WFMT, 2011)

The different conceptions of music therapy underlying these three definitions will form the backdrop for the exploration of various issues throughout the present book. But even with their differences, they all represent the views of music therapy from inside the profession. Music therapy is considered to be a health profession that can only be implemented by individuals with specific qualifications determined by governmental, professional, or educational bodies. It has applications in a great variety of contexts, but the predominant social roles upon which the music therapist is modeled after are those of the medical professional, psychotherapist, or perhaps rehabilitation worker such as an occupational, physical, or speech therapist.

In recent years, for the first time music therapy has begun to be investigated by scholars from other areas. The rationale for beginning the present exploration into the nature of music therapy from these perspectives rather than from a detailed look from inside the profession is twofold: First, it will provide a more familiar entry point to the readers who are not music therapists; and second, it offers to music therapists a sense of the issues involved when those outside the field turn their scholarly lenses on music therapy.

The Emergence of Historical Perspectives on Music Therapy

So what is music therapy? Is it a primarily a modern health-care practice that emerged in the post-World War II era as suggested by some writings by music therapists, or is it the contemporary manifestation of the perennial use of music for healing purposes that reaches back to the dawn of humanity as tends to be argued by scholars from related disciplines? Moreover, what is the relation of the primarily Western form of professional practice to the contemporary indigenous models of the use of music to enhance human well-being? Do these indigenous practices represent cultural variations of professional music therapy or are they more accurately seen as something quite apart from it?

In the early 1980s, music therapists began considering the relationship of their work to historical precursors, such as shamanic healing. Since approximately the year 2000 there has been a trend toward more overtly incorporate thinking from fields such as anthropology, sociology, and ethnomusicology in creating music therapy theory. At around the same time, historians, anthropologists, and sociologists began to focus on music therapy to contextualize it, both historically and culturally. These related trends meant that there was a significant expansion in the range of disciplines used by music therapists to find supportive theory outside the medical and psychological frameworks that had been traditionally applied to music therapy.

The attention from outside the field, while potentially valuable for music therapy, has been problematic as some of the initial efforts have confused fundamental issues, as they are seen by music therapy scholars. It is important to clarify these issues so that multi-disciplinary interaction can proceed in a way that is based upon a solid foundation.

The collection of studies edited by Penelope Gouk (2000a), *Musical Healing in Cultural Contexts*, was one of the first publications to reference the modern profession of music therapy from the perspective of "scholars engaged in social, cultural and historical studies" (Gouk, 2000b, p. 1). Gouk's choice of terms has, however, led to some confusion, especially in relation to the words *healing* and *therapy*. Her intention "is to promote interdisciplinary and cross-cultural discussion of the healing powers of music" by addressing questions such as "how do people use music to heal themselves or others" (2000b, p. 1). She acknowledges that the contemporary profession of music therapy involves assessment, treatment goals, and systematic evaluation, while being clear that her book does not cover these activities. However, her choice of the term *music therapy* to apply to any engagement with music for beneficial effect and her portrayal of professional music therapy as not including the notion of "making whole" are both problematic:

> The type of 'music therapy' that this volume *does* take some account of, however, is the general, non-expert kind . . . In this context, the term 'therapy' is being used to denote the general therapeutic effect which can be gained from being involved in any form of musical/artistic performance, either as a participant or audience. The critical difference between this kind of activity and 'proper' music therapy . . . is that it does not need the intervention of a trained therapist, and is chiefly a form of *recreation*: that is, an act or experience selected by the individual to meet personal wants in his or her leisure time . . . Hence the choice of *Musical Healing* as the start of our book's title: this reflects a bias towards thinking of music as a form of healing (i.e. making strong, whole again) rather than just in terms of therapy (i.e. techniques of intervention involving distinct goals and desired outcomes).
>
> (Gouk, 2000b, pp. 2–3)

Gouk's use of the terms *healing* and *therapy* and her means for distinguishing between them does not comport well with contemporary music therapy discourse. She puts the term *music therapy* into single quotation marks indicating perhaps not an ironic but a deliberately vague use of the term, and then says that her historical perspective covers uses of music that predate the modern profession. It is not clear why she uses the term *therapy* when she defines it to mean any use of music not requiring a trained therapist and that focuses on any therapeutic effect, items that distinguish it from what she terms *proper music therapy*. Gouk's presentation suggests that for rhetorical purposes she is taking on the perspectives that contemporary music therapists would hold, but that she may not actually believe in such distinctions herself.

She goes on to explain that she chose the term *musical healing* for the title of her book because she is focused more on "making whole" than on the processes involved in contemporary professional practice. A few problems are present here. First is her use of the term "healing powers of music." While this phrase has been present in music therapy discourse, it is not one in current parlance due to contemporary perspectives that argue against the view that music has essential qualities that transcend context. Rather than promoting the notion that music contains healing properties—such as a medicinal plant—there is a consensus building in music therapy around the idea that humans create the value of music through the way that they engage with it. As Lisa Summer (1995) asserts, "sound has power, but it is a power created and manipulated by human beings when used therapeutically" (p. 60).

Second, there is a whole discourse in music therapy—such as is exemplified in Broucek (1987)—dedicated to including in contemporary clinical practice the very goals that Gouk reserves for healing. These perspectives reflect holistic, resource-oriented, and community practices. Music therapists would generally not accept Gouk's distinction that music therapy precludes a focus on "making whole" for a preference on "distinct goals and desired outcomes." It is not congruent with contemporary thinking to place this type of orientation outside the sphere of music therapy.

Third, the use of the word *healing* is somewhat discredited among scholars in music therapy. Summer's (1996) discussion and analysis of contemporary music healing practices clearly paints as a charlatan anyone using the word *healer* as a self-appellation:

> Practitioners, best described as New Age music healers, have created amongst themselves a philosophy which lacks clarity and logic. It has grown out of myths and legends, converted into 'facts' in a parody of how science progresses. The foundations and axioms of New Age music healing are based upon wishes and fantasies which the practitioners in the field have agreed, perhaps unwittingly, to believe are facts.
>
> (Summer, 1996, p. 7)

Summer's work is an extraordinarily well-researched study exposing how music is the "new age elixir" peddled by individuals seeking to take advantage of their customers' gullibility. However, Summer does not critique shamanic or other healing uses of music used by pre-scientific or non-Western cultures. In fact, the new age healers that are the target of Summer's analysis clothe their approaches in the language of science. What Summer does is expose how nearly every assertion claimed by these healers related to music, vibrations, sound frequencies, the structure of the universe and its supposed parallels with the structure of music, is fundamentally misconstrued or just plain wrong. She debunks these approaches based on the scientific foundations that they claim for themselves.

Thus, for a variety of reasons it will not do to either consider healing as a type of music therapy or to distinguish between the two activities by the types of goals that Gouk suggests. Instead, it would be more accurate to reserve the label *music therapy* for practices and practitioners that stem from the emergence in the second half of the twentieth century of the modern profession with its attendant emphasis on explanation and accountability.

In an effort to establish historical continuity between forms of music healing and contemporary music therapy in the book *Music as Medicine: The History of Music Therapy since Antiquity*, Peregrine Horden (2000a) makes the same fundamental error as Gouk. The subtitle of this edited collection suggests that music therapy has existed for thousands of years and Horden makes clear that he considers any use of music from any place or time "that maintains or restores the health of mind and, even, body" to be music therapy (2000b, p. 1). He says that "the term 'music therapy' is to be understood broadly as a convenient label, rather than in the narrower terms to which modern professionals might adhere" (2000b, p. 2). No rationale is offered for this choice, which would certainly be a problematic one for the modern professionals to whom he refers.

Horden's title notwithstanding, considering "music as medicine" is antithetical to a significant portion of theory and practice in music therapy. And asserting that music therapy has existed since antiquity is not consistent with how music therapists use the term and only serves to add to confusion over the nature of music therapy. Papering over important distinctions like this in the service of establishing historical continuity just does not serve any good scholarly purpose.

Horden's perspective on music in general does not inspire confidence that his analyses will provide a perspective on music therapy which reflects current sensibilities. His critiques of the pervasiveness of music and the attributes of popular music echo the dramatic pronouncements of the end of music that accompanied the birth of rock and roll in the 1950s (as well as the birth of jazz in the 1920s) as he invokes the composer Constant Lambert writing in 1934 to buttress his perspective:

> We live in an age of tonal debauch where the blunting of the finer edge of pleasure leads only to a more hysterical and frenetic attempt to recapture it. It is obvious that second-rate mechanical music is the most suitable fare for those to whom musical experience is no more than a mere aural tickling, just as the prostitute provides the most suitable outlet for those to whom sexual experience is no more than the periodic removal of a recurring itch.
>
> (Lambert, as cited in Horden, 2000c, p. 4)

Horden admires Lambert's anachronistic view, even finding virtue in contemporary theocracies insofar as they protect their citizens from the ubiquity of music:

> Music is omnipresent, and worse—mechanized to an extent that he [Lambert] could scarcely have envisaged. Only within certain fundamentalist Muslim states is there any escaping it dictatorship over the acoustic environment, its unvarying and literally inhuman rhythm . . . With the mechanical beat and harmonic banality of most popular music, profundity, even of the fleeting kind furnished by the latest technology, is seldom in question.
>
> (Horden, 2000c, pp. 4–5)

In opposition to the worthlessness of popular music, Horden juxtaposes "the minority for whom listening to classical music is life itself" (2000c, p. 5). Horden cites a paper that purports to demonstrate that rock music promotes the growth of human cancer cells *in vitro* to make the point that all is not lost in the battle against rock music because as this research becomes better known "the finding that plants or cell cultures have better musical taste than people will presumably lose its shock value" (2000c, p. 7).

In his exploration of the historical use of music to enhance human well-being, it is inexplicable why Horden engages in such gratuitous and anachronistic critiques of popular music. The purpose of his investigation does not warrant this critique and it only serves to cast doubt on his historical conclusions as being fair ones rather than being motivated by a lurking philosophical agenda. He seems to want to use the historical occasion to advance a position that is discredited by researchers in a number of disciplines that include musicological, sociological, and psychological studies of the role of popular music in establishing identity and supporting cohesiveness for individuals and communities.

In considering different domains of practice regarding music and human well-being, Horden introduces a tripartite conceptualization consisting of "the 'heterodox', the 'professional', and the 'historical'. The professional is mainstream music therapy in Europe and America; the heterodox represents a variety of nonmainstream currents; history is the domain to which they both variously appeal for precedent or legitimacy" (2000c, p. 8). Horden's elaborated description of the heterodox renders it nearly identical to the new age healing practices discredited by Summer, and, as such, his consideration of that area is not particularly relevant to the present discussion.

However, in discussing the professional domain of contemporary music therapy Horden goes awry. He claims that rhythm is the fundamental component of professional practice. His support for this claim is a single quotation from Paul Robertson, who is not a music therapist: "Pieces [or music] composed to create specific physiological change . . . are designed to lock into the innate neurophysiological and biological rhythms that underlie the vital functions of the body" (Robertson as cited in Horden, 2000c, p. 12). In his discussion, Horden seems to be referring more to music medicine than to music therapy, a distinction explored further in Chapter 2. Also, it is not as apparent why a single quotation from a person outside the profession would have any bearing in determining the characteristics of music therapy practice.

Horden's argument then makes a dizzying 180-degree turn. After engaging in a critique of the ability of music therapists to provide adequate descriptions, explanations, and justifications for what they do, Horden claims that "the social anthropology of music and healing" (2000c, p. 16) can assist music therapists with issues of evaluation with which they have struggled. Horden criticizes music therapists for not having written extensively about the relationship between their own social function and that of music healers in non-Western cultures, and yet his knowledge of the music therapy literature in this regard is highly deficient, not referencing any of the publications in this area that predated his own, such as Kenny (1982), Aigen (1991a), or Moreno (1995a). Moreover, his stance directly contradicts his previous point that contemporary professional music therapy has inadequate foundations. Does he really assert that applying the worldview of non-technological societies will help music therapists to formulate a more solid foundation for professional practice? His citing of music healing practices in northern Malawi that invoke notions of spirit afflictions and healing trances as potential sources of explanation for professional music therapy serves as his sole support for this highly debatable point.

Horden appears to be arguing both sides of an issue here, so much so that it is not possible to discern his intent. Finally, to make a point about the connection between music therapy and musical healing, Horden makes a claim about music therapy that could not be more wrong. He asserts that "one feature common to music therapists and musical healers is . . . the invocation of history. Both esteem ancestors more than contemporaries" (2000c, p. 19). In fact, I cannot think of a single music therapist who—either in speech, by act, or in print—has expressed such a sentiment. It is the pioneers of the contemporary music therapy profession—people such as Juliette Alvin, Rolando Benenzon, Helen Bonny, Paul Nordoff, Clive Robbins, Mary Priestley, and William Sears—that music therapists cite as inspirations. It is just not true that contemporary practitioners believe that "David, or Pythagoras, can be seen as more or less a founding father of music therapy" (p. 21) in any more than an extremely fanciful sense.

Horden concludes by asserting that "modern music therapy needs a history from which it may derive a sense of its own particularity" (2000c, p. 32). Yet such a history must do two things: it must begin from an accurate portrayal of the current status of music therapy, and it must not create the appearance of continuities merely to establish a coherent narrative. From the perspective inside music therapy, Horden's portrayal commits both of these errors, a judgment with more than a touch of irony as it is both of these errors that Horden accuses music therapists of committing.

Issues in Defining Music Therapy from Inside the Profession

One reason for the confusion in these conceptualizations of music therapy from outside the discipline is that there are a number of definitional issues at the heart of music therapy, some of which stem directly from its name and others from the realm of activities undertaken by individuals who use the label.

Acknowledgments of these problems of definition stem from the mid-1970s. Donald Michel (1976) discussed how music therapists have had to continually engage in clarifying the definition of their field because "the term is not self-evident, that is, it does not refer to a therapy concerned with treating MUSIC (as in speech therapy). It is not as apparent . . . as physical therapy, which implies a physical approach to physical problems" (Michel, p. vii). Michel's view is that the confusion owes to the fact that music therapy draws its name from its mode of intervention rather than from the domain of function in which change is sought, as is the case with other therapies.

Dale Taylor (1997) agrees that "a continuing problem has been the name 'music therapy'" (p. 4). He believes that the profession is unique in being "designated by its methodology—music—which gives no indication of its goals, procedures, clientele, or focus" (p. 4). Taylor views as problematic that basic principles and procedures vary from one clinical setting to another. He argues that there is a "need for a comprehensive basis upon which to explain music therapy" by identifying "a common factor, or a single therapeutic focus that is applicable to *all* areas of music therapy practice" (p. 5). In other words, Taylor sees the definitional problem in music therapy as having an empirical rather than a conceptual basis. Once a comprehensive theory is developed applicable to all clinical contexts where music therapy is employed, the definition of music therapy will be achieved.

Other writers, while acknowledging the definitional problems, have come to different conclusions. Some have seen the definitional problem as reflecting the absence of unanimity on the meaning of words such as *therapy*. Related to this issue is the idea that the term *music therapy* has multiple referents. In these views, it is the way we are using language that causes the definitional problem rather than the absence of unifying theory, as Taylor describes.

For example, Brynjulf Stige (2002a) discusses the name *music therapy* and explores what it means for its identity: "The way the term music therapy has come to use [*sic*] it may be argued that music refers more to the means of the practice than to the ends" (p. 190). Because music therapy is generally not concerned with developing musical skills or sensitivities, the term *music therapy* may be somewhat misleading because related forms of therapy such as physical therapy and speech therapy gain their names from the focus of their interventions, from their goals rather than their means.

A similar point is made by Rudy Garred (2006) who also observes that music therapy is unique in that its name is drawn from the medium of intervention rather than its targeted area of change. Because it is named this way, the implication is that its value is based upon the "qualities of the medium itself as being therapeutic, rather than what it specifically is therapeutic for" (p. 2). While this state of affairs may be blamed for the "chronic identity problems" (p. 2) of music therapy, it may also account for its wide diversity of practice and its constant evolution.

The definitional problem is traceable to two different notions of *therapy*, one with traditional medical connotations and one that is more nonmedical in nature, according to Carolyn Kenny (1982). While the traditional use of the term equates it to medical treatment, contemporary usages have "come to mean any method of healing which seeks to alleviate suffering, develop potential, and encourage rehabilitation" (p. 2). The more broadly-based application underlies some of the conflicts between music therapists and medical professionals as medical practitioners question the ability of music therapists to engage in therapy because they are not sufficiently medical, while music therapists assert that medical professionals "cannot do therapy because [they] are too medical" (p. 2).

That a lack of recognition regarding the variations in how the word *therapy* is used underlies many debates on the definition of music therapy is also attested to by Stige (2003). One common meaning is that therapy involves the treatment of illness and its cure, although "curing illness" is not what many music therapists actually do. This usage is not appropriate because it is not relevant to the palliative, rehabilitative, health promoting, and preventive contexts in which many music therapists work. Because the potential referents of *music therapy* are so broad, Stige suggests that it is a "family resemblances category, with similarities existing between subsets but not necessarily with much core shared" (p. 210). It is not a concept of therapy that provides the shared focus of all music therapists but rather "an inclusive notion of health" (p. 213). As a result, if there were no practical obstacles to instigating a name change, Stige believes that a label such as *health musicology* would be a more accurate descriptor than the current term *music therapy* for encompassing what music therapists actually do.

Both Kenneth Bruscia (1998a) and Stige (2002a, 2003) have identified multiple referents for the term *music therapy* and they discuss how some of the disputes over the nature of music therapy may stem from this lack of unanimity. For Bruscia, music therapy has a dual identity as both a discipline and a profession:

> As a "discipline," it is an organized body of knowledge consisting of theory, practice, and research, all pertaining to the therapeutic uses of music. As a "profession," it is an organized group of people using the same body of knowledge in their vocations as clinicians, educators, administrators, supervisors, etc.
>
> (Bruscia, 1998a, p. 14)

The domain of the discipline is internally defined by music therapists according to their awareness of the therapeutic applications of music and their ability to employ these applications. The domain of the profession is externally defined by the guidelines imposed by the administrative structures of the facilities in which music therapists work and the regulatory guidelines of the political entities in which these facilities are located. And not mentioned by Bruscia, but as was discussed earlier in the present chapter, music therapists run the risk of having their work improperly defined by scholars whose authority is not legislative or vocational, but just academic in nature.

Elaborating upon Bruscia's work, Stige (2002a) identified a four-fold distinction for the referents of *music therapy*: (i) folk music therapy; (ii) music therapy as discipline; (iii) music therapy as profession; and (iv) music therapy as professional practice. By the term *folk music therapy*, Stige refers to all historical practices connected to music and health that predate the birth of the modern profession. This is akin to Horden's notion of the "heterodox" discussed previously. It is unfortunate that Stige says that "there is a prehistory of music therapy going back for centuries" (p. 192) as this claim only muddies the waters, although it is not clear if Stige is just bowing to common usage here, or making a historical claim. In *music therapy as discipline*, Stige refers to a branch of learning for a field of study with a particular tradition of inquiry and discourse. Scholarly efforts as reflected in the present work would belong to this domain. The domain of *music therapy as profession* refers to a particular vocation requiring training with standards of qualification and practical links to formal and informal social structures. Last, in *music therapy as professional practice*, we would consider the actual "interactive process of making music in the service of health and well-being" (p. 193). In a subsequent work, Stige (2003) added a fifth area consisting of "non-expert everyday uses of music for health in modern societies" (p. 217).

Taken together, these five areas comprise all that has traditionally been called *music therapy* but which would more accurately be considered components of the broad area of *music and health*. Because much of what music therapists do does not fit into the conventional meaning of *therapy*, Stige argues that adopting this scheme could relieve music therapists of "the strenuous task of stretching the meaning of the word 'therapy' in all kinds of directions in order to defend the existing diversity of professional practice linked to the discipline" (2002a, p. 199). What music therapists actually do includes therapy, but goes well beyond it to "include other types of interventions, such as primary health promotion, prevention of problems, habilitation, rehabilitation and palliative care" (2003, p. 228). If we reorient our use of terms to use *music and health* as the overarching label, there is room for music therapists not only to practice therapy but also to engage in practices in these other areas, such as health promotion.

How Does the *Music* Relate to the *Therapy*?

One important contribution of the historical studies of Gouk and Horden is the substantiation of the claim that music has always been connected to human individual, social, and ecological well-being. Music therapy can be seen as an attempt to reintegrate the splitting of music from overt health concerns that took place in the history of modern Western society. It is in the reintegration of music and health concerns that the modern profession does have historical continuity with its precursors.

In considering how the two words in its name relate, Bruscia (1998a) observes that there is an identity struggle at the heart of music therapy and therefore at the heart of music therapists: the struggle is both personal and professional. All music therapists articulate some sense that they love music and that they love psychology (or medicine, or people) and that becoming a music therapist has given them the opportunity to combine both interests. Bruscia articulates the psychological truth underpinning the motivations of contemporary music therapists: "It seems as if we are saying: I am this—but not entirely; I am that—but not entirely; and so I want to be and do both—but not entirely" (p. x). While Bruscia acknowledges the value of using integration to resolve internal divisions, the problem is that music therapists "have built an entire discipline and profession by ignoring, crossing, bridging, or integrating the many boundaries within and between music and health care" (p. x).

This division can be seen in the way that music therapy is situated in academic institutions. In considering the North American context, for example, music therapy appears as a music discipline owing both to its being part of departments, schools, and colleges departments of music, and to the fact that 45% of the curriculum for music therapy undergraduate degrees must be in music. And yet it has traditionally been defined by the American Music Therapy Association (AMTA) as a "health profession" (AMTA, 2012). This is another way in which the identity of music therapy is a site of contested claims and this health versus music dichotomy is at the heart of many other issues and dilemmas in the field. These issues include where theory should be derived from, appropriate goals for music therapists to work towards, the appropriateness of nontraditional clinical (but eminently musical) activities such as performing and recording, and the importance of aesthetic considerations within clinical music.

The historical separation of music from concerns of human well-being is a contributing factor in the ongoing struggle to delineate the nature of music therapy. The fact that it is difficult to agree upon the appropriate social or scholarly category in which to locate music therapy is in large degree due to its hybrid nature, combining skills and knowledge from the two domains that constitute it.

It is legitimate to ask whether or not music therapy really exists as a unified entity. Is there anything that all practices subsumed under this label share that would help to define and categorize it? Stige's perspective, that music therapy is an example of a family resemblances category with sub-areas having elements in common but where there is nothing shared by all practices and individuals within it, certainly lends support to the notion that no definition will suffice to accommodate all practices and beliefs carrying the label of *music therapy*.

Thus, there may be no single thing as *music therapy*, notwithstanding the titles of degree programs and professional associations. This might be because "the domains of music therapy practice . . . are so diverse that they belong in multiple general categories" (Aigen, 2005a, p. 21). It is possible that the different areas of practice, such as music psychotherapy or music as medicine, have more in common with psychotherapy or medicine respectively than with each other. The question to consider is whether or not saying that music therapy demands multiple categorizations is actually an argument against the existence of music therapy.

One reason for this existential debate stems from the means–ends dichotomy referred to by authors such as Michel, Taylor, and Stige. It was noted that the descriptor *music* that precedes the word *therapy* holds a different place from what is the case with most other therapies. For disciplines such as speech therapy, physical therapy, and psychotherapy, the descriptor refers both to the target of intervention *and* the medium of intervention. This unity of means and ends is required in a definitional sense. For example, psychotherapy focuses on changes in affect and cognition that are facets of psychological functioning. To practice psychotherapy, it is necessary to focus on psychological goals through a psychological means. Psychiatrists may use pharmacological means to focus on similar ends as psychotherapists but they are not therefore practicing psychotherapy; they are practicing medicine. While their ends are congruent with psychotherapy, their means are not.

Similarly, in speech therapy and physical therapy the media of intervention—speech and muscular movement—are also the domains in which change is sought. Speech therapists intervene through speech to enhance speech and physical therapists intervene through bodily movement to enhance motor function. However, the conventional wisdom about music therapy is different. In it, there is a separation of ends from means in which the therapist intervenes through music to influence other areas of functioning.

A challenge to this conventional wisdom was posed by Gary Ansdell (1995), who simultaneously attested to its character: "Almost every music therapist would deny that their aim is, like the music teacher's, to improve the client's music. Many would, in fact, see this to be the last thing they do—that the music in music therapy is, on the contrary, a means to a non-musical end" (p. 3). Similarly, clients usually come to music therapy "because of a belief that music therapy involves something more than making music" (p. 3). In order to accommodate a therapeutic dimension within their work, some music therapists use the term *music psychotherapy* to imply that their work focuses on the traditional goals of psychotherapy through the medium of music. This strategy is not satisfying to Ansdell (and others) who instead seek to carve out the parameters of a primarily musical music therapy, where the locus of effect is within the musical process itself.

Stige also considers the notion that in music therapy the word *music* "refers more to the means of the practice than to the ends" (2002a, p. 190). He elaborates on the common argument that because music therapy is generally not concerned with developing musical skills or sensitivities, the term *music therapy* may be somewhat misleading. He argues that for individuals whose conception of music therapy is based upon a means–ends dichotomy that a focus on "helping people with developing their music . . . would be a strange description of music therapy, and that it would be more accurate to describe music as means and health as end" (p. 190). However, Stige does not buy into the traditional means–ends dichotomy in music therapy but instead promotes a concept—also developed by Garred—of music as a dialogic medium. In this view, "means and ends are not dichotomies in music therapy, but are aspects of the same process in systems of change, and it may make perfect sense to suggest that music therapists work in order to promote musicking" (Stige, 2002a, p. 191).

Stige's position is that promoting musicking is a legitimate goal of music therapy, if one understands the particular musicking that occurs in music therapy as somehow different from musicking in nonclinical contexts. He says that "the music of music therapy is health musicking, it is the shared and performed establishment of relationships that may promote health" (2002a, p. 190). Stige avoids the commitment of the use of music to a nonmusical end by creating a concept of music in which health concerns are embedded within it, rather than external to it. The crucial point to explore is whether or not this creation of a new— and specifically and uniquely clinical—conception of music is necessary and/or accurate.

Some of these conceptual struggles over identity stem from what Kenny (1996) calls the dilemma of uniqueness. There already exist a number of music disciplines and health disciplines, under which music therapy could potentially be subsumed, although none of them provide a neat fit. Professions go through developmental stages, the same as individuals, and as Bruscia noted, the two processes are often intertwined. Speaking for music therapists, Kenny says that

> we want to be unique as a field, but not so unique that we become isolated, just enough to give us a raison d'être. We want our experiences in music therapy to be unique so that we can offer our clients something different from the other fields; in order to do this we must be distinguished from "the others," have a special identity.
>
> (Kenny, 1996, p. 89)

The need for establishing the uniqueness of all the creative arts therapies—including art therapy, dance-movement therapy, drama therapy, music therapy and poetry therapy—is really a matter of survival according to David Read Johnson (1984). Other, more protected, professions have technologies that only its members can administer. However, music therapists do not have a professional monopoly on the use of music so this strategy cannot be taken in music therapy, thus contributing toward professional identity struggles. As Johnson describes it,

> psychiatrists prescribe medications, psychologists give psychological tests, social workers see families. Regardless of the effectiveness of psychotherapy, these professional groups are required in a setting to perform these activities. There is currently no similar activity for which a creative arts therapist is required.
>
> (Johnson, 1984, pp. 210–211)

The absence of anything unique that requires a music therapist's presence puts the profession in a vulnerable position. The need to be seen as autonomous and separate does meet individual psychological needs for identity, yet it does more than this; it is necessary to create an accurate portrait of a field when what it provides has no precise parallel in society. The challenge for music therapy is to be seen as offering something sufficiently unique to warrant its existence and yet similar enough to other domains in order to be able to fit into social structures.

The Past, Present, and Future of Music Therapy

Returning to some of the historical issues discussed at the outset of this chapter, the critiques of the efforts of Gouk and Horden were not a critique of their intention, which remains important. This is to better place the contemporary profession of music therapy in a cultural and historical context, not because the explanations proffered by non-technological societies for the efficacy of music can be transferred to a contemporary profession, but because there have been many uses of music throughout human history and across a wide swath of contemporary cultures that relate to what modern music therapists do.

For example, music rituals have always been used as an essential part of central life events and transitions, such as occurs in adolescent rites of passage or when music is used to accompany the process of dying. These are two areas in which contemporary music therapists do extensive work. It is important for music therapists to be fully cognizant of the historical precursors of their work because it suggests that there is a perennial archetypal relationship from which music therapists draw and it predates the creation of the music therapy profession.

Being aware of the fact that there is—and always has been—a human propensity to use music in the contexts that music therapists now use it can only assist music therapists in developing effective practices and rationales for their practices. Not because the explanations proffered by these other cultures are appropriated or taken literally as Horden seems to advise, but because they provide insight into the universal aspects of the human relationship to music in a way that can support explanations for music therapy interventions that meet contemporary standards for accountability. The continuity between historical uses of music and the contemporary music therapy is not to be found in the explanations offered by indigenous practitioners but in the functions that music has served in maintaining the well-being of individuals and communities.

A resolution of some of the definitional problems that have perennially plagued the profession requires a more in-depth understanding of the means–ends dichotomy that underlies these problems. In this vein, it seems clear that the traditional notion of music therapy as the use of music to achieve nonmusical ends is deficient in at least three important respects:

1. Because it is based upon the means–ends dichotomy that has been under critique for a number of years, the identity and continuity of music therapy is threatened because music therapy offers nothing unique in this view. After all, if alternative, cheaper, or more easily administered means of achieving music therapy goals are developed, music therapy would have no reason for its continued existence.
2. The traditional notion does not reflect how many music therapists actually practice. This way of thinking cannot accommodate how they understand the most prominent benefits that accrue to clients from engagement in music therapy processes. Supporting this observation is that almost all of the contemporary theoretical frameworks in music therapy—such as those of Aigen (2005a), Garred (2006), Lee (2003), Pavlicevic and Ansdell (2004a), Rolvsjord (2010), and Stige (2002a)—to varying degrees place a greater emphasis on music and musical processes.
3. Because it restricts the focus of music therapy to nonmusical rehabilitative goals, the traditional notion supports the search for explanation that is generally disconnected from any type of social, cultural, or even individual psychological context. If the "real" domain of music therapy is in the brain—as is argued by authors such as Taylor (1997) and Thaut (2000, 2008)—then explanatory mechanisms for all music therapy applications must be couched in terms of neurological structures and processes, regardless of whether or not they focus on impairments traceable to neurological causes. This emphasis on decontextualized explanations that ignore the importance of culturally-situated practices goes against many of the contemporary trends in disciplines such as sociology and musicology. In addition to providing weak explanatory mechanisms, adherence to such modes of explanation runs the risk of isolating music therapy from related disciplines.

Due to the prevalence and strength of the conventional view, the role of music in music therapy has traditionally been decentralized and moved to its periphery. Largely undertaken as a pragmatic step to accommodate to the educational, medical, and psychotherapeutic contexts in which music therapy is practiced, this strategy has contributed greatly to the definitional and identity problems discussed throughout the present chapter.

One publication of the present author (Aigen, 2005a) was devoted entirely to the effort to return music to a more central position in music therapy. Although some critics may have considered its title, *Music-Centered Music Therapy*, to be redundant, many others in the field recognized a need for such a work to remediate the diluting of essentially musical processes that has characterized the conventional wisdom in music therapy.

The analysis of contemporary music therapy frameworks presented in Chapters 16 and 17 shows that most theorists in the field are moving to a position in which the traditional notion is no longer adhered to. Instead of precluding a focus upon musical goals as part of legitimate music therapy work, the new perspectives, to varying degrees, either embrace or at least acknowledge the legitimacy of this way of thinking. Taken together, and from various perspectives, they support the notion that a "legitimate reason to come to music therapy is because of a deficit of music in one's life" (Aigen, 2005a, p. 127).

However, this idea of providing music to people in need of it is not congruent with the role traditionally assumed by music therapists. In searching for role models—and, hence, a vision of what music therapists are, what services they can ethically provide, what goals might orient their work, and what relationships they may maintain with clients—music therapists have most often turned to the fields of medicine and psychotherapy. The discussion in Chapter 2 begins with an examination of the relationships between music therapy and these related disciplines, offers some critique of the strategy of portraying music therapists as akin to both psychotherapists or medical professionals, and then concludes with an examination of some of the alternative identities being developed by progressive thinkers in this realm.

Note

1. In addition to providing his own definition, Bruscia documented 61 different definitions from a variety of individual authors and organizations from every continent where music therapy is practiced.

2

THE IDENTITY OF THE PROFESSIONAL MUSIC THERAPIST

Roles and Related Disciplines

Just as the nature of music therapy is contested, the identity and legitimate role of music therapists is similarly debated. Because the two disciplines most closely related to music therapy are medicine and psychotherapy, the most common roles assumed by music therapists are analogous to the medical professional and the psychotherapist.[1] In North America and Australia, the role of "music therapist as medical professional" has held greater sway; in the countries of Europe such as the UK and Germany, the "music therapist as psychotherapist" construct has been more dominant. However, these observations of general trends do not provide an exclusive portrait of music therapy in any of these regions as there is a great deal of diversity in roles and influences throughout the world.

The present chapter has three focuses, the first two of which examine the relationship between music therapy and the two, closely-related professional domains of medicine and psychotherapy. The identity of the individual music therapist has a strong interactive relationship with the identity of the music therapy profession and exploring these inter-professional identity issues is crucial to understanding the identity of individuals. This topic constitutes the third major focus of this chapter.

Music Therapy and the Medical Model

Music therapy is associated with medical treatment because of its focus on health that is generally in the purview of medicine. There are a number of questions that arise because of this relationship and that will constitute the themes of the present chapter: Is music therapy a medical intervention? If not an actual medical intervention, does music therapy process comport with a medical model? Should music therapists aspire to a medical model or is this a limiting framework to impose on practice? Should the parallels with medicine be limited to the process of assessment, treatment, and evaluation, or should there be a privileging of physiological or neurological explanation and interventions? Is the medical model only relevant in medical settings?

Music therapists work in a large variety of nonmedical and medical settings including hospitals. The focus of clinicians working in hospitals might be medical in nature, for example providing pain relief, or it might be more psychological, for example reducing pre-operative anxiety. However, considering the relevance of the medical model for music therapy means drawing implications for all types of music therapy, not just for the practices occurring in medical settings. Medical doctors assess people, diagnose a condition, prescribe an intervention of specific amount and duration, and attempt to cure a condition or manage its symptoms. In exploring the relevance of the medical model for music therapy, the crucial issue is whether or not these procedures that characterize the practice of medicine will lead to the best care for music therapy clients.

The distinction between music medicine and medical music therapy introduced by Cheryl Dileo (1999) helps to clarify the scope of practice of music therapy. Music medicine is practiced by nonmusic therapists, who primarily use recorded music in a receptive experience; it is not dependent upon a therapeutic relationship for its value, and provides "a nonpharmacological intervention for stress, anxiety, and /or pain for the medical patient" (p. 4). In contrast, medical music therapy is practiced by music therapists, who employ all types of music experiences (including listening, playing, improvising, and composing), and it incorporates a therapeutic relationship as a salient factor. Medical music therapy has a much broader focus than does music medicine as it can involve the whole person and not just focus upon "the presenting medical condition or reactions to the medical procedure" (p. 5).

Dileo (1999) questions "the distinction between medical music therapy practice and music psychotherapy" (p. 6). She argues that because research demonstrates that "mind, body, the social environment, and spirit" (p. 6) are all mutually interactive, classification schemes of music therapy based on a strict division of mind from body produce artificial distinctions that do not hold in actual practice. She acknowledges that "it may be possible to delineate primary and secondary goals of therapy" (p. 6), with a psychological goal and a physiological goal occupying primary and secondary focuses respectively. However, Dileo does not preclude medical music therapy from addressing some of the same goals as music psychotherapy.

In contrast, Kenneth Bruscia (1998a) distinguishes between "practices which seek psycho-social changes in the client . . . to ameliorate the biomedical problem [from] those practices that seek psychosocial changes in the client as an end in itself, quite apart from any biomedical problems the client might have" (p. 193). Whereas, work undertaken with the former focus is medical music therapy, work in the latter area is music psychotherapy. The difference between Dileo's and Bruscia's way of thinking is based upon a difference in what factors are considered relevant in articulating a domain of practice. In Dileo's approach, the work setting and client conditions define the domain of practice; in Bruscia's way of thinking, the clinical goal makes this determination.

In arguing that music therapy must conform to a medical model, authors such as Dale Taylor (1997) and Michael Thaut (2000) do not consider the distinctions made by Dileo. Taylor argues that his biomedical theory of music therapy "systematically and objectively defines music therapy interventions in terms that are applicable to the full range of client populations" (p. 15) with whom music therapists work. The neurological focus of his theory renders it relevant for all music therapy applications, not just those undertaken in medical settings. Similarly, Thaut argues that music therapy treatment must be based upon "objective assessment procedures and . . . objective outcome data" (p. 5). A strictly scientific criterion of evidence is needed for music therapists to be able to have a "systematic clinical method-ology" (p. 5) that will allow them to select interventions that lead to predictable therapeutic benefits within specific contexts.

Music therapists have critically considered the question about whether the medical model is applicable to music therapy. Leslie Bunt (1994) addresses the issue of whether an applied use of music can be considered a form of medical intervention. He asks directly: "Are there any observable causal links between the range of symptoms, the application of specific music therapy strategies and the resultant outcomes?" (p. 30).

Bunt sheds doubt on these claims, first by describing how music is experienced too idiosyncratically for it to be administered as a medication. He acknowledges that music has a more predictable effect on physiological parameters than upon experience. He also speculates that physiological changes cannot be used as reliable indicants of experience as they may only reflect a physical reaction. Bunt considers some limited studies with physiological components, assuming that the medical model requires biological intervention and explanation. He concludes merely that "it is very difficult to be categorical about the use of music and to isolate the physical from the psychological and the emotional" (1994, pp. 33–34).

The idea that employing the medical model in music therapy stems from pragmatic considerations, that may not relate directly to how music therapists practice or to client welfare in general, underlies an extraordinarily comprehensive argument against imposing the medical model on music therapy practice by Randi Rolvsjord (2010). Although they focus on applications of music therapy in mental health, her conclusions are relevant to other areas of music therapy.

Rolvsjord argues that there has been a general trend of pathologizing nonadaptive human behaviors that had previously been considered as actions resulting from personal choice. This "illness ideology" (2010, p. 20) manifests in the proliferation of categories of mental disorder and it focuses the efforts of psychology upon problems rather than on strengths and resources. The therapist's task is "to identify (diagnose) and prescribe an intervention (treatment) that will eliminate or cure the disorder" (p. 21). Because the illness ideology causes people to consider problems of living as psychiatric problems in need of the outside intervention of professionals, therapists are put into an elevated position and clients become disempowered.

Rolvsjord also observes that the medical model is pervasive in music therapy discourse, although its influence is not always explicit. She identifies the evidence-based medicine movement (EBM) as a destructive force in music therapy, not because it asks for systematic investigations of effectiveness, but because it forces music therapists into medical-model thinking. Rolvsjord suggests that even though the hierarchy of evidence employed by the EBM movement "does not necessitate a link between diagnosis and interventions, the medical model is very often taken for granted in the EBM movement" (2010, p. 24).

Taylor's and Thaut's positions are congruent with EBM principles. In their view, not only should music therapy procedures be constrained by the practices of medicine, but legitimate explanation should be similarly restricted to neurological factors. Rolvsjord explains that there is a less extreme position that supports adherence to the procedures of medical practice but that allows psychological explanation that may not necessarily be reducible to physiological terms.

This modified version of the medical model has a number of assumptions that Rolvsjord argues are not warranted: First, while "the therapist, as an expert, identifies the problem and knows what the best procedure is to use in order to change or mend that particular problem or deficit," the client's role "is limited to the provision of information, motivation, and compliance with the treatment" (Rolvsjord, 2010, p. 48). The efficacy of therapy is dependent upon the implementation of an intervention, considered as an action or strategy that is determined by the treating professional and that acts from without upon a passive client. Second, specific interventions must be designated for particular diagnoses in specific amounts and durations. These are the variables that enter into the experimental research investigations that EBM prioritizes in its evidence hierarchy and they originate from pharmacological research. Third, it is also assumed that the treatment effects of interventions are uniform enough so that differences among individuals will not have an effect upon efficacy.

The adherence to the medical model in music therapy has a pragmatic and a conceptual rationale. The pragmatic concern is that engaging in practices and research studies that comport with the medical model is the best way to ensure that the profession thrives and is able to offer a greater number of clients access to music therapy services. As the argument goes, music therapy must be covered by private insurers and government funding to ensure this access. Research according to EBM guidelines is the best way to achieve this goal.

However, the conceptual concern trumps the pragmatic one and for this reason the present discussion will focus on the former issue. Regardless of what the most fruitful social strategy is for music therapy to pursue, any strategy that does not reflect how music therapists practice and how their clients engage with music will be fraught with internal inconsistencies that will render a strict adherence to EBM principles moot. In other words, if therapists do not think in terms of specific interventions, dosages, and durations as a means to cure the problems caused by specific diagnoses, and if clients respond to music in such individualized ways as to render false the comparison to music as a medication, then there is no point in imposing the medical framework upon music therapy, no matter how laudable the pragmatic concerns. And it does no good to answer this argument by saying that regardless of how music therapists have practiced previously, sound scientific principles dictate that they must adapt their practices to EBM principles. If clients necessarily relate to music in ways that are predominantly influenced by their individualized histories, preferences, and interests, then the basic assumption of the medical model is rendered inoperative, and the pragmatic argument for it is undermined.

Are the assumptions that guide medical research appropriate for what happens in music therapy? Of greatest importance here is to consider how people interact with and through music, how they appropriate it for their own uses, and what factors influence these interactions. We will consider the three aspects of the medical model delineated above in light of these concerns.

1. There are a number of limiting assumptions in the conceptualization of the professional medical relationship where clients/patients come to an authority figure (doctor, therapist) who prescribes an intervention to eliminate the illness or ameliorate its manifestations. This model is outdated in many respects: It is based on a pathogenic view of health as a state that one is either in or out of, rather than as a process such as is reflected in a salutogenic view; it preserves a hierarchical relationship and power imbalance between clients and therapists; it ignores the social context and influence of one's environment; and it is based on an outmoded perspective that artificially divides the world into people with and people without disability.

The imposition of a medical model upon music therapy through the demands of EBM runs counter to many progressive social trends and contemporary developments in music therapy theory. Some of the new conceptual frameworks that have emerged in music therapy include community music therapy, culture-centered music therapy, music-centered music therapy, and resource-oriented music therapy. There are some important commonalities among them:

a desire to move beyond psychological thinking to embrace concepts and perspectives from social theory and musicology; a belief in the importance of social context; support for the empowerment of clients; novel formulations that have expanded the boundaries of clinical practice in music therapy; and, to varying degrees, they exist as alternatives to the medical model of music therapy. To argue for the hegemony of the medical model in music therapy unnecessarily limits client and therapist choice by undermining the bases for these new approaches.

2. Rolvsjord (2010) highlights the fact that research in psychotherapy contradicts the idea that interventions are the key element in determining efficacy. Meta-analyses show that most people benefit from psychotherapy and that there is little or no difference among methods. Some researchers therefore argue for a common factors approach that entails "a change of interest and focus from the specific ingredients of psychotherapy to the extra-therapeutic factors and to the factors that are common to all psychotherapeutic models" (Rolvsjord, 2010, p. 46). Common factors are elements present in therapy regardless of the therapist's orientation, and they include bonding factors between therapist and client, motivation, a positive relationship, empathy, and warmth. Also included is the structure of therapy with its rituals and interactions.

Although interventions are the element that is typically tested in experimental research, Rolvsjord discusses how research suggests that it is not interventions that determine efficacy. By decentralizing the importance of interventions, the common factors approach makes a strong argument against the rationale for basing music therapy on the medical model. Rolvsjord's approach is contextual and holistic, has the client at the center, and is based upon a resource-oriented framework focused on client empowerment where the client's own sense of agency provides the main impetus for change in therapy.

To the extent that music therapists work toward similar goals as psychotherapists—such as effecting change in the realms of affect, cognition, and behavior—the common factors approach is as relevant for music therapy as it is for psychotherapy. The typical forms of treatment investigated in music therapy are activities whose specific nature is not pre-determined, whether this involves songwriting or improvisation. Experienced clinicians generally develop the musical contents of sessions from the presenting needs and interests of their clients. The ability to be responsive to clients is absolutely necessary to the efficacy of the approach.

Moreover, even if one were to predetermine that a particular sequence of songs would be played by clients and therapists in a therapy session, in what way could it be said that a different therapist using the same songs would be providing the same intervention? Each music therapist plays in a certain way, employs particular instruments, uses idiosyncratic tempos, voices chords differently, and has a different timbre or phrasing in vocalizing. Unlike a medication in which every lot and administration can be identical, the fact that a song may have a similar underlying common structure based on its lyrics and music in no way guarantees that each administration of it will be identical. It is not possible to ensure the uniformity of music therapy interventions unless one uses purely recorded music on the same device without any response to individual need or clinical-cultural context. But in doing this, one would be engaged in music medicine as defined by Dileo, not music therapy. Such considerations seem to strongly weigh against the possibility of employing a medical model in music therapy.

3. Using complexity science as a foundation, Barbara Crowe (2004) argues against the uniformity of treatment effect requirement because "it is impossible to find any therapeutic intervention, including music therapy, that will affect every client in the same way consistently" (p. 347). The previous section offered an argument against the possibility of creating a music therapy intervention with enough uniformity to be evaluated according to the guidelines of EBM. Crowe's point is that even if this were possible, there are strong reasons to think that music is engaged with and responded to in such a highly individualized way that is just not possible to administer the same music to large numbers of people. The idea is that individual history, preference, interests, motivations, and values all influence how people experience music. The medical model thus conflicts with music therapy approaches where relationship is a central factor, artistic and creative processes are central, individual and social context are relevant, flexibility and spontaneity are necessary, and where there is a belief in the individual nature of musical experience.

Throughout its history, many music therapists have argued that achieving the recognition of the medical profession is necessary to foster the development of the profession. And yet music therapy has survived and developed in the absence of this formal recognition. Of course it is a highly personal decision for each practitioner, teacher, theorist, and research to make: should one attempt to meet the requirements of the medical model and accommodate one's clinical approach to it, or should one maintain the value of creative, improvisational, and context- and relationship-based work in an effort to bring the greatest value to clients? While some may choose the former path for either pragmatic or epistemological reasons, those music therapists who take seriously their ethical obligations to provide the best possible care to their clients are likely to feel more comfortable walking the latter path.

Music Therapy, Psychotherapy, and Music Psychotherapy

In understanding the evolving conceptions of music therapy it is essential to consider its relationship to psychotherapy as well. Many European approaches to music therapy have been developed in a way that reflects an implicit belief of music therapy *as* psychotherapy. This is generally true, although there are important exceptions to this statement, such as among some therapists who work within the framework of Nordoff-Robbins music therapy, those who pioneered work in special education settings, and practitioners in Norway who have worked under a broader social label. In many of the countries of Europe, there has been a tendency to consider music therapy as psychotherapy because the predominance of its applications focused on areas and goals that were psychotherapeutic in nature. The same can be said of South America where the original dominant model—Benenzon music therapy—was strongly embedded within psychiatry.

In contrast, in North America, particularly in the USA, music therapy has had a much more complex identity. Alongside work that was clearly psychotherapeutic in nature, many other applications existed in medical, rehabilitative (non-psychiatric), and educational settings. The situation was described by Helen Bonny (1978a), who bemoaned the fact that music therapy had largely followed the model of music education, and that music therapists generally did not engage their clients in processes of in-depth self-exploration. Music therapists were content to play a secondary, adjunctive role. Moreover, "the powerful evocative effects of music" (p. 3) were largely minimized to fit into the constructs of verbal psychotherapeutic practice.

In an effort to draw a distinction between music therapy with a psychotherapeutic focus and other forms of music therapy, Barbara Hesser (2002) coined the term *music in psychotherapy*, which she later shortened to *music psychotherapy*. Psychotherapeutic applications in music therapy had been present since the 1950s so Hesser's contribution was not in developing this way of working but in, first, recognizing that there needed to be a specialized label because there was a great deal of music therapy practice, in the USA at least, that was not psychotherapeutic in nature; and, second, developing and implementing a concept of music therapy education at the graduate level, focused on developing competency in music psychotherapy.

It is natural that the concept of music psychotherapy originated in a North American context. As was noted above, for many practitioners in other countries all music therapy was psychotherapeutic so the term *music psychotherapy* would have seemed unnecessary. It was only in the USA, where a large segment of music therapy focused more on rehabilitation goals (such as restoring motor and communicative abilities), or educational goals (addressing the teaching of language skills and concepts), that a psychotherapeutic area within music therapy needed to be delineated.

Hesser considers music psychotherapy to be a form of psychotherapy. In an unpublished manuscript written in 1979 and subsequently updated (Hesser, 2002), she uses Wolberg's (1967) definition of psychotherapy and its three levels of practice in which to contextualize music psychotherapy.[2] She indicates that in its focus "music psychotherapy covers all the non-medical problems of psychotic and neurotic individuals" (p. 3). Additionally, music psychotherapists work with children with various types of developmental delay, behavioral and cognitive challenges, such as conduct and attention disorders, as well as "normal and high functioning adults" who may seek therapy for life crises or to develop "more satisfying relationships, more fulfilling attitudes toward their life, and to expand their creative potential" (p. 3).

In contrast to the hierarchical approach of Wolberg, Bruscia (1998b) distinguished four modes of practice within music psychotherapy across a spectrum according to the relative prominence of music and verbal interaction: music as psychotherapy, music-centered psychotherapy, music in psychotherapy, and verbal psychotherapy with music.[3] The first two of these areas are considered transformative therapy and the latter two are examples of insight therapy. In transformative therapy, "the music experience is therapeutically transformative" (p. 4) and does not require verbal mediation for its efficacy; in insight therapy, "the aim is always verbally mediated insight" (p. 4).

In music as psychotherapy "the therapeutic issue is accessed, worked through, and resolved through creating or listening to music, with no need for or use of verbal discourse" (Bruscia, 1998b, p. 2). While Bruscia's point about the primary role of music in this way of working is accurate, he appears to overly minimize the use of verbal interaction. Most practitioners and theorists who operate from this perspective—such as Aigen (2005a), Ansdell (1995), and Lee (1996, 2003)—would find this characterization to be an exaggeration as they all highlight the importance of verbal interaction, although the function of verbalization is not the same as in other approaches where it used primarily to interpret musical experience.

In music-centered psychotherapy according to Bruscia (1998b), "the therapeutic issue is accessed, worked through, and resolved through . . . music. Verbal discourse is used to guide, interpret, or enhance the music experience" (pp. 2–3). The role of verbalization here seems somewhat overstated. In music-centered music therapy the experience of music need not be interpreted for it to be clinically valuable. The presence of interpretation precludes this way of working from being a bona fide music-centered approach and it becomes difficult to distinguish Bruscia's conception of music-centered psychotherapy from "music in psycho-therapy" where "the therapeutic issue is accessed, worked through, and resolved through both musical and verbal experiences . . . Words are used to identify and consolidate insights gained during the process" (Bruscia, 1998b, p. 3). The lack of sufficient distinction between this way of working and music-centered psychotherapy can be seen in the fact that if talking is germane to guiding, interpreting, or enhancing the music, how are these not examples of a verbal experience? In other words, if words are used to determine the therapeutic efficacy in the former, how is this not an example of accessing and resolving clinical issues?

The area of verbal psychotherapy with music is not particularly relevant to music psychotherapy because in it, music experiences may be used but they "are not considered germane to the therapeutic issue or treatment of it" (Bruscia, 1998b, p. 3). What is left unclear here is who actually uses music in psychotherapy without the intent that its use is relevant to the client's process, or further, what the rationale could be for its use in such a case.

Not all music therapists agree that their work should be equated with psychotherapy. Henk Smeijsters (1993) believes that this owes to the fact that "music therapy can be used in more areas than merely in the field of disturbances of the psyche" and "a music therapist who is working on the social skills, the cognitive or motor functions of handicapped people will not care to characterize this work as psychotherapy" (p. 223). Contributing to this reluctance is that music therapists "who contribute to the treatment of disturbances of the psyche are not really trained as psychotherapists" (p. 223). Certainly the first objection is strongly warranted. That clinicians who are working on areas of human functioning not considered to be psycho-therapeutic in nature do not care to identify as psychotherapists is eminently reasonable.

However, Smeijsters indicates that a music therapist working in a psychiatric setting is necessarily working on disturbances of the psyche. His unstated assumption is that work setting and disabling condition dictate the type of music therapy employed. This assumption has been challenged by Bruscia (1998a), who argues that neither setting nor diagnosis can be used to define an area of practice such as music psychotherapy:

> Music therapy with psychiatric patients is not necessarily psychotherapeutic; it is so only when the goals and methods are psychotherapeutic in nature. Similarly, psychothera-peutic practices are not limited to clients who have psychiatric diagnoses; all individuals who seek psychological change are candidates for psychotherapy.
>
> (Bruscia, 1998a, p. 213)

Contemporary approaches, such as music-centered music therapy and resource-oriented music therapy, provide additional arguments against the idea of basing clinical rationales upon areas of disability. In the former approach "viewing music therapy process in terms of categories of pathology or disability does not provide a relevant dimension for analysis" (Aigen, 2005a, p. 121). Music-centered practitioners do not treat schizophrenia, autism, or any other dis-abling condition, "but instead conceptualize their work as discovering how to musically engage with an individual with various universal, human needs" (Aigen, 2005a, p. 121). It is the engagement with music that music therapists can offer to their clients—the ways that clients benefit from the encounter are determined by more universal benefits of music in general, not necessarily by the remediation of a disabling condition. Rolvsjord (2010) argues for a similar perspective, albeit for different reasons. Rather than appealing to the universal benefits of musical engagement, she emphasizes that a resource-oriented approach works with existing client strengths and relationships to music.

Smeijsters (1993) attributes the reluctance of music therapists to consider their work to be psychotherapeutic to a misguided attempt to promote the uniqueness of the profession. He also argues that psychotherapeutic processes are fundamental, inescapable aspects of music therapy, and that music therapists have nothing to fear by describing how their work facilitates these processes.

The fundamental debate here relates to which framework is fundamental (music therapy or psychotherapy), the necessity for music therapy to be autonomous (for either pragmatic or conceptual reasons), and what strategy for developing theory allows a discipline to mature. Smeijsters's position is that music therapists unnecessarily emphasize the uniqueness of their discipline out of a misguided need for professional self-esteem. His view is that psychotherapy theory can fully accommodate music therapy practice and therefore music therapists should use it.

Smeijsters also subscribes to the assumptions of the medical model. He argues that the rationale for music therapy must be based in an illness ideology where the therapeutic qualities of music address specific symptoms of a client's illness. There is no room for existential concerns, the universal need for or relationship to music, or a resource-related rationale. Disease characteristics are the only possible rationale for providing music therapy:

> A number of indications used in music therapy may refer to the person's characteristics, but not to the psychic disturbance. This can be illustrated by the statement that music therapy has been indicated because the client loves music. This quality, the client's love of music, does not say anything about the problems for which the client is in therapy.
>
> (Smeijsters, 1993, p. 225)

Smeijsters's allegiance to the medical model remains, even though the applications he discusses are psychological and behavioral. This is evident in his focus which is to generate research based on criteria for indications that allow for conclusive statements about how much (dosage) of which music therapy treatments (interventions) will lead to a particular extent of amelioration of symptoms (the illness model). He believes that "it is important to gain some insight into methods of music therapy before following the path of the investigation to diagnosis-specific effects" (Smeijsters, 2005, p.4). Smeijsters is not satisfied with merely layering psychological concepts onto music therapy phenomena.

Debates about the relationship between music therapy and psychotherapy have been prominent in the UK. A highly ambivalent relationship between the two domains is described by Kay Sobey (1992): "Whilst other arts therapies seem to have whole heartedly embraced psychotherapy as a model in their training and practice, music therapists seem to treat the relationship with anything from fascination to outright rejection" (p. 19). Sobey argues that music has certain effects on clients and that these effects require a psychotherapeutic framework to be managed effectively. She believes that there are aspects of how music affects people that require psychotherapeutic thinking on the part of the therapist, regardless of whether or not the clinical focus is psychotherapeutic.

In contrast, Lee (1992) sees a danger in using psychotherapy theory to validate music therapy. Lee acknowledges that music therapy has had to cope with problems inherent in attempting to demonstrate its value through extrinsic frameworks. Seeking validation through external frameworks means that music therapists are forced to explain what they do through a nonindigenous paradigm that distorts the nature of the work and diminishes its uniqueness. He questions whether the adoption of the psychotherapeutic model is just the latest in a series of pragmatic choices that inhibit music therapists from more fully developing the musical bases of music therapy.

A comprehensive argument that music therapists must consider psychotherapeutic mechanisms and processes in order to practice ethically, was first put forth by Elaine Streeter (1999). She argues that theory in music therapy that relies more on musical theory and foundations than on psychotherapeutic ones may "prove unsafe" (p. 5) for both therapist and client. She asserts that "psychological thinking is an essential part of providing the necessary boundaries within which the interpersonal relationship between client and therapist can safely develop" (p. 6) and she says that musical experience must be processed through psychodynamic means because experience alone is not therapeutic. She also takes aim at music-centered approaches: "A purely music-centred approach to building theory leaves us dangerously close to an avoidance of the psychological impact a therapist can have on a client, and a client on a therapist" (p. 18). Streeter believes that unless a therapist utilizes the interpretive mechanisms and self-awareness that arise from psychodynamic processes, the therapist will be ill-prepared to help clients.

Some critiques of Streeter's position have focused on the substance of her remarks while others have argued that Streeter is unaware of the unproven theoretical commitments of her own position and illegitimately critiques practices based on irrelevant foundations.

As an example of the latter approach, Sandra Brown (1999) cites the inappropriateness of critique from fundamentally different premises. Seeking to establish hegemony for one way of thinking—in this case, psychodynamic perspectives—stifles diversity and damages the profession, whether the proponents are operating from a traditional psychoanalytic framework or a medical one. Brown decries the "danger of a situation whereby the 'rules' regarding appropriate therapeutic behavior are generated from within a theoretical model itself, whether psychological or musical" (p. 64).

Building upon this line of critique, Ansdell (1999a) claims that Streeter elevates her own theoretical premises to ethical necessities.

> What she attempts to do is to align her chosen theoretical position with an ethical one— that is, to judge other therapists' clinical work by their adherence to her own theoretical premises. Consequently, practice and thinking different from her own is judged both as not good enough and even as 'unsafe.'
>
> (Ansdell, 1999a, p. 75)

Ansdell identifies a trend in music therapy where particular positions are argued for as the only way that one can do ethical or responsible practice. This can be seen in arguments for the necessity of particular theories (such as Streeter's for psychoanalysis) or in the necessity for certain approaches (such as behaviorism or neurological music therapy) as being the only way music therapy can be a real and responsible profession. In contrast, other approaches— such as community music therapy—argue for a plurality of approaches based on client need and cultural context.

Other critiques of Streeter's position have focused more upon the substance of her argument. They have primarily argued against her assertion that psychological thinking can only happen through verbal means, that working with someone's music implies ignoring central aspects of the person, and that traditional psychoanalytic thinking exhausts the possibilities for thinking psychologically. In different ways, they challenge the dichotomy underlying Streeter's position where on one side *thinking* equals words, which imply and require psychological thinking; on the other side, *experiencing* equals music, which is the rationale for music-based concepts.

For example, Mercédès Pavlicevic (1999) argues that psychodynamic thinking can occur in music. One need not leave the realm of musicing to be acting psychodynamically because "musical acts can themselves be psychodynamic" (p. 61). Brown (1999) also shows how working in the music and with the person in music is working with the person, not just the music.

> Therapeutic aims can therefore involve working to free the person's musical limitations, resistances and defences, and . . . building on the structures of his musical elements, components and structures within an improvisational relationship . . . This is not in isolation from the outer world, as Streeter fears, but with an aim of simultaneously working towards healing the other aspects of her or his cognitive, physical, neurological and emotional being.
>
> (Brown, as cited in Brown, 1999, p. 66)

Streeter (1999) presents a caricaturized view of music-based theorists when she says that "expecting the music to contain everything ignores the fact that there is an interpersonal relationship involved" (p. 6). Nothing about working primarily in music with musical rationales suggests that the therapeutic relationship should not be considered. Her arguments also seem to reflect an equating of the more general word *psychological* with the more specific word *psychoanalytic*. Streeter frequently uses the term *psychological*—as in "psychological thinking" or "psychological awareness"—when what she really means to be saying is *verbal psychotherapeutic*. In "equating the 'verbal' with the 'psychotherapeutic', Streeter is assuming what she would like to prove: that music-centered theory and musical interactions cannot possibly bear the full explanatory weight for the theory and practice of music therapy" (Aigen, 1999, p. 79). Streeter does not recognize that her arguments for a psychological awareness are limited to psychoanalytic theory, ignoring the fact that the transpersonal experiences that she criticizes are legitimate facets of other types of psychological thinking.

Efforts such as those by Hesser and Bruscia to distinguish psychotherapeutic applications of music therapy from other forms of practice have been essential to bring clarity to a fairly muddled situation. However, the term *music psychotherapy* may be responsible for creating new areas of confusion. The way that it is constructed raises the question of whether this form of work is a type of psychotherapy or a type of music therapy. While its advocates certainly consider it to be a type of music therapy, it would seem that a simple change to something such as *psychotherapeutic music therapy* would make this clearer. Then the referents for the different forms of music therapy—such as *rehabilitative music therapy*, *didactic music therapy*, and *medical music therapy*—would all have a consistent form and construction.

It is also clear that political differences, the idiosyncrasies of historical developments in different countries, and a lack of clarity in the use of terms have all contributed to some of the professional debates around the relationship between music therapy and psychotherapy. As the situation in the UK demonstrates, when theorists advocate for a narrow view of psychotherapy that is only compatible with traditional psychoanalytic thinking, this causes other theorists to argue, perhaps unnecessarily, against the notion that their work is psycho-therapeutic, even if it focuses on effecting change in the areas of thought, affect, and behavior that characterize psychotherapy. This way of thinking suggests that for music therapy to have a psychotherapeutic focus, clinicians must do things, such as consider the dynamics of transference and countertransference, and formulate verbal interpretations of musical experience and expression. However, as the distinctions drawn by Bruscia highlight, there are noninterpretive, experientially-based forms of work that are legitimately considered to be psychotherapeutic because of their focus on psychological processes and structures. Psychotherapeutic music therapy can occur regardless of whether or not one considers certain theory-specific constructs such as transference.

The limitations placed on music therapy theory and practice by the medical model and its associated illness-based frameworks are not in the best interests of clients and run counter to the ways in which music therapy is developing. First, it is inarguable that music is engaged with and experienced in unique ways determined by each individual's history, preferences, needs, and interests. A medical model for music therapy is just not possible because there is no analog in music therapy to the intervention as it is conceived of in medicine. If the idea of an intervention is untenable, then the idea of linking interventions to specific clinical diagnoses as advocated by Smeijsters becomes untenable.

Second, social trends in many Western societies have focused on the empowerment of individuals with illnesses and disabilities and are supporting the elimination of barriers—both physical and psychological—between individuals with and without disabilities. Some authors go as far as to challenge the somewhat arbitrary division into the fully-abled and disabled world, instead emphasizing that individual differences of all types exist and that nothing is gained by creating an artificial dichotomy. Thus, while the idea of a love for music as an important consideration in recommending music therapy for a client is something that is not accommodated in a medical model, in the empowerment model it is a legitimate rationale. The idea that music enriches all human lives in vital and necessary ways crosses the arbitrary divide of the abled and disabled. While an individual may have autism, schizophrenia, or Alzheimer's disease that person can still gain the same things from music that others do. The medical model—whether applied in medical settings or psychotherapeutic ones—runs counter to these important contemporary social trends and values.

But it is also clear that psychotherapy is generally implemented within a medical model. In the USA, for example, the *Diagnostic and Statistical Manual of Mental Disorders* (DSM) provides categories of impaired psychological functioning and a diagnosis is required for clients to have their treatment funded by public agencies and private insurers. Psychotherapy research proceeds very much along the lines of the medical model with its focus on conditions, interventions, dosages, and outcomes, notwithstanding the research on alternatives such as the common factors approach. So it appears that neither the "music therapist as medical professional" nor the "music therapist as psychotherapist" can provide a comfortable meta-phor or role for what music therapists actually do. There have been a number of alterna-tives to these roles suggested in recent years and it is to some of these proposals that we now turn.

Music Therapist: Musician or Health-Care Worker?

In using an art form to address health-related concerns, music therapy combines two spheres that are normally separate. However, colleges and universities are organized by departments, as are hospitals, clinics, schools, prisons and any other institution in which music therapists practice their craft. A university must decide to locate its music therapy program in a school of music or in a school of applied psychology. A hospital must decide whether the music therapy services should be in a recreational or clinical department. And a professional association must decide if the universities whose music therapy programs it approves should meet the standards for music schools or for the health professions. The choices made by these institutions reflect pragmatic, social, and historical concerns as much as they reflect the actual practice of music therapy, and the identity of music therapists can be strongly affected by these decisions. The hybrid nature of music therapy causes problems however these questions are resolved.

Music therapy is not unique in having a hybrid nature. Many academic disciplines are defined this way, such as biochemistry, psychobiology, and social psychology. In addition, many music-related disciplines have a hybrid nature, such as ethnomusicology and music psychology. But the reason why the identity issue is so prominent in music therapy is because it exists at the intersection of three different types of overlapping dichotomies.

One of these dilemmas is the question of whether music therapy is more accurately considered a music profession and discipline or a health service profession and discipline. The situation in the USA can illustrate the paradoxes that exist in trying to categorize music therapy. In the USA, most academic music therapy programs are in schools, programs, conservatories, or departments of music. All approved music therapy training programs are required to be accredited or affirmed by the National Association of Schools of Music. In addition, 45% of an undergraduate curriculum must be devoted to musical foundations while 15% is devoted to clinical foundations. These facts suggest that music therapy is a type of music study. However, as noted in Chapter 1, the American Music Therapy Association (AMTA) clearly situates music therapy outside the music professions in saying that "music therapy is an established health profession in which music is used within a therapeutic relationship to address physical, emotional, cognitive, and social needs of individuals" (AMTA, 2012). This contradictory situation influences the self-identity of music therapists, which in turn influences how they practice.

While some music therapists may consider themselves primarily as therapists who use music, others consider themselves as musicians who do therapy. The identity of music therapists in relation to this distinction has a profound impact on many areas: their practice with clients, their theories and overall conceptualizations, their view of what makes a competent therapist, and their opinions on the relevant educational standards for music therapy students.

Both types of therapists have different tendencies as well. The therapist who uses music will use supportive theory from nonmusical domains such as psychotherapy, psychology, neurology, and learning theory while employing psychodynamic, neurological, or behavioral treatment models. Treatment goals are formulated in nonmusical terms such as increasing self-esteem, developing insight, facilitating emotional expression, increasing immune system response, or increasing range of motion. In this perspective, the value of music in music therapy is fundamentally different from its value outside music therapy. Whether or not a client's experience is a musical one is not relevant because its value is determined by how well the nonmusical goal is achieved. Practice is modeled after other types of professions such as doctors, psychotherapists, counselors, and teachers. Clinicians of this type will draw more upon the extrinsic features of music such as its ability to function as a projective device, a behavioral reinforcement, a tool for neurological or motoric entrainment, or a means for emotional catharsis.

In contrast, the musician who does therapy tends to use supportive theory from musical domains such as music theory, ethnomusicology, and the sociology of music while employing music therapy approaches such as Nordoff-Robbins music therapy, other music-based models, and community music therapy. Treatment goals are formulated in musical terms and areas such as increasing vocal range or tempo mobility, joining and performing with a band, creating a recording, or composing a song. These practitioners consider the value of music in music therapy to be the same as its value outside music therapy. Their focus is on providing a high quality musical experience for the client that might be quite similar to nonclinical musical experience. It is the supportive context that defines the process as therapy rather than any specific aspect of the experience itself. One's professional role is modeled after other types of music professionals such as composers, music teachers, bandleaders, community musicians, and even music producers. Intrinsic features of musical experience and expression are drawn upon and the basic idea is to bring forth in the client only that which music can evoke.

Each of the two types of professional identity has advantages and disadvantages. The strengths of the "therapist who uses music" conception include an ability to articulate areas of benefit of music therapy, an ability to fit within economic and bureaucratic structures, and the capacity to work in an interdisciplinary way by adopting language and constructs from related disciplines.

Some of the drawbacks of this conception are that the importance of the therapist's musical skills are minimized, which can lead to an impoverished musical experience for clients. Also, the importance of music as a therapeutic medium of experience is not considered. Music becomes a tool to a nonmusical end and the structural properties of music may not be used with clinical focus. The nature of the musical experience for the client is not considered and the potential benefits that stem from clients' needs for what music can uniquely provide are ignored. Last, it maintains the traditional client–therapist role and the idea of meeting musician-to-musician is not considered, something that can inhibit the ability to form relationships based on meeting the healthy part of the client.

Some of the strengths of the "musician who does therapy" conception include an ability to make full therapeutic use of the intrinsic aspects of musical experience, an ability to meet the client musician-to-musician and avoid problematic dynamics that characterize more traditional therapy relationships, and an ability to formulate clinical focuses that are congruent with client aspirations such as to play an instrument, perform in a band, or create a recording.

Some of the drawbacks of this conception include a tendency to attribute efficacy to the external musical structure without sufficiently considering the client's engagement in the music, and a difficulty in engaging the client verbally when clinically warranted.

It is certainly possible that these portraits represent abstractions to some extent and music therapists exist in different places on the spectrum. Yet it is still informative to consider how one's place on the spectrum influences practice. The "therapist who uses music" conception is much more prevalent as reflects a more conventional view of therapy and allows music therapists to fit more easily into the many settings where they work.

However, many of the contemporary developments in music therapy are supportive of the "musician who does therapy" conception, such as is the case in community music therapy, culture-centered music therapy, music-centered music therapy, and aesthetic music therapy. This exploration of the identity of the music therapist will conclude with a consideration from some of the more novel proposals that have been put forward in these models and from perspectives compatible with them.

In the first publication describing the model of guided imagery and music (GIM), Helen Bonny (1978a) does not call the professional responsible for the process a therapist or a counselor, but a guide. Although many of the personal qualities of practitioners are identical to those of good psychotherapists, in selecting the term *guide* over that of *therapist*, Bonny indicates that the latter conceptualization is not sufficient to encompass all that is undertaken by the GIM practitioner.

Many newer conceptualizations of the therapist's role relate to an enhanced awareness of community and cultural contexts. The frameworks of community music therapy and culture-centered music therapy have both crystallized thinking in this area and stimulated new ways of thinking about what a music therapist is.

Because community music therapy is a largely "public and inclusive practice" it naturally incorporates "dual or multiple roles and relationships" (Stige, 2003, p. 434) that have stimulated ethical dilemmas as ethics strives to catch up to developments in practice. Some of the more expansive roles taken on by music therapists in community settings include "counselor, co-musician, advocate, [or] project coordinator" (Stige, 2003, p. 436). As a result of these roles, the ethical rules formed to guide psychotherapy practice are not necessarily applicable in community music therapy. Stige emphasizes that the aspect of *exclusivity* characteristic of psychotherapy— that there cannot be more than one type of professional relationship between therapist and client—should be replaced by a notion of *explicitness*, in which multiple roles are acceptable as long as the various roles and expectations are overt. Stige speculates that as community music therapy grows, music therapists will increasingly see themselves "less as therapists in a conventional sense and more as health promotion professionals" (2003, p. 439).

There is a strong contrast in community music therapy between its conception of the therapist's role and that of the consensus model of music therapy, which operates under the understanding of music therapist as a psychotherapist. According to Ansdell (2002), in the latter approach, the relationship to clients is conceptualized "in psychological rather than social or cultural terms" ("Identities and roles," para. 1) with the therapist taking on a quasi-parental role that includes providing a psychological container or frame in which psychic distress can be expressed and explored. There is also an epistemological dimension to the role as the music therapist aims to learn about the client and assist in the interpretation of symbolic material to facilitate the client's insight.

In contrast, in the community music therapy framework, therapists maintain an equal identity as musicians and therapists. "As a musician the role is to promote music and musicing for individuals and milieus; as a therapist the role is to work with factors which prevent a person's (or community's) access" to music (Ansdell, 2002, "Identities and roles," para. 2). Ansdell says that a "therapeutic musician in residence" ("Identities and roles," para. 2) is an apt description of the music therapist who embraces the broadened role and agendas promoted by community music therapy.

The recognition that music provides experiences of *communitas* means that the strict boundaries and roles maintained in the psychotherapeutic frame are not particularly relevant in the community frame. In this latter area, relationships and boundaries are open to processes of pragmatic negotiation within specific contexts and communities. This might involve guiding or following clients as they discover how to engage with music. While valuing knowledge in all realms, the music therapist's expertise is "primarily musical rather than psychological or medical" (Ansdell, 2002, "Identities and roles," para. 2). The fact that the music therapist can meet musician-to-musician with clients and be related to as someone partly outside the medical hierarchy is also useful.

In order to best meet client needs, some music therapists find themselves moving among different roles. Cochavit Elefant (2010) acknowledges that some music therapists find the constraints of working within a closed therapy room to be unnecessarily limiting and they take their work into more public spheres. Because therapists may maintain group and individual therapy sessions alongside the more public applications, skills are required for the new challenges of public work and in the negotiation of complex and multiple roles demanded by doing both types of work simultaneously.

The matrix model of Stuart Wood (2006) is a supportive framework that assists in negotiating multiple roles and spheres of activity. In Wood's model, all possible modes of engaging with music are arranged in a nonhierarchical fashion, and clients and music therapists move among them. In addition to the traditional individual and group music therapy sessions, Wood's model includes activities such as performance projects, music for special occasions, and participation in musical ensembles. Wood offers a model where clients have the potential to make use of the complete range of musical life. Clients can develop by taking advantage of what different musical experiences offer, and the system can accommodate to each step in client development.

The enhanced mutuality implicit in the expanded roles taken on by community music therapists does more than shift the balance "in the direction of user-led services" (Elefant, 2010, p. 210). It opens up new possibilities for client growth and development because a relationship that embodies "mutuality, openness, and collaboration has the potential to empower on individual and on group levels" (Elefant, 2010, p. 210). The new roles fostered by community music therapists have the power to greatly expand what music therapy can offer to individuals and to communities.

One type of more expansive role supported by the conception of music therapist as general musical resource person is that of music therapist-as-producer. Michael Viega (2012) has discussed how he adopted this role in his work facilitating hip-hop song compositions with adolescents. Viega sees this role as consistent with the combination of humanistic, resource-oriented, and music-centered ideas and values that support his work. This type of therapeutic relationship was established by his clients in response to the way that Viega worked with them in a community music therapy context. Calling him their producer was their way of framing the "therapeutic relationship within their lived experience of Hip Hop culture" (p. 15).

The role that music producers assume in this genre has three strong parallels to therapy work: First, a producer focuses on deepening and enhancing the recording artist's involvement and participation in the music; second, producers help to empower artists by assisting them in discovering new inner resources that help them to achieve their full potential; third, the producer functions as a co-musical creator in helping to achieve an overall sound that functions as "a musical portrait of the artist" (Viega, 2012, p. 16). Viega also discusses how at times he functioned as a music therapist-as-audio-engineer. The role of the engineer is different from that of the producer: the former position deals with the concrete aspects of making a recording, such as handling the equipment and technology; the latter role involves more creative and musical contributions. Both of the roles are essential in any efforts to compose and record music. Viega appeals primarily to music-centered theory in justifying these approaches. When the creation of music becomes a legitimate, self-justifying clinical activity, any roles that the therapist must assume to achieve this goal are not only legitimate but also required.

While many of the novel therapist roles suggested by community music therapists have an overtly musical function, other roles are oriented toward more specific cultural functions. One such function is discussed by Shapiro (2005) as it relates to working with elderly individuals in multicultural contexts. Shapiro sees himself "as a kind of culture bearer, a person who learned their songs and some of their languages" (p. 31). The clinical goals of helping his clients to "lead more active, integrated, and creative lives" (p. 31) are addressed through the way in which he helps them to retain connections to essential aspects of their cultures of origin.

As noted by Pavlicevic and Ansdell (2004b), music possesses a "ripple effect." On a purely auditory level, music overcomes most attempts to contain it as it permeates the physical environments in which it is created. And even as music stimulates people to look inward as a vehicle for self-exploration it simultaneously leads people out of themselves, connecting human beings with each other.

Since the inception of the modern profession in 1944[4], music therapy has been similarly difficult to contain. This is especially true for practitioners whose work is more music-based and who use natural forms of engaging with music. For music therapists who identify with other types of vocations—such as that of the psychotherapist—elements of their practice such as appropriate roles, working contexts, and clinical goals can be adopted fully and without complication. For music therapists who strongly identify as musicians, and who want their work to conform to music itself, the question of self-identity becomes more fluid, challenging, and loaded with potential.

Something that is not often addressed in the professional literature is the question of how clients in music therapy see themselves[5]. For anyone who values the client's perspective and whose focus is client empowerment, the answer to this question is a necessary part of determining the identity of the music therapist. The encounter that occurs in music therapy has multiple participants and facets and a comprehensive and definitive description of the roles and identities of the various parties involved are best drawn in relation to one another rather than in isolation.

For clients who come to music therapy primarily to achieve nonmusical goals, the role of the clinician with whom they are working most likely appears as similar to that of psychotherapist, speech therapist, or physical therapist, depending upon whether the nonmusical goal is emotional, communicative, or motor related. However, a substantial number of clients participate in music therapy out of a primary desire to *music*. This is true whether they are creating music or listening to it; composing music or recreating composed materials; engaged in an individual session in a private room or performing with an ensemble or other type of group in a public location. It is true for people as different as a child with autism who has an affinity for the piano, adolescents with adverse childhood experiences who compose songs in a hip-hop style, or an elderly woman with Alzheimer's Disease singing songs from her youth. The fact that these clients most likely relate to their music therapists as *music enablers* should be prominently considered in understanding the role and identity of the music therapist.

The way that clients see themselves is influenced by the thoughts, actions, and values of the therapists who work with them. A music therapist whose self-concept is that of someone whose primary responsibility is to help fix or remediate a problem in a client will contribute to a client self-image as someone who is primarily in need of fixing. In contrast, a music therapist whose self-concept is that of someone whose primary responsibility is to help someone make music will contribute to a client self-image as a musician, fully participating in one of the most rewarding and eminently human activities in which a person can engage.

Even for a music therapist whose self-identity is fluid and adaptable to the needs of individual clients and particular settings, the two options articulate potential roles. Where one stands on this issue influences everything about a music therapist's practice, including the types of goals considered legitimate, the types of relationships established with clients and co-workers, the types of interventions and activities undertaken as part of the therapy, and the types of explanatory constructs invoked to legitimize their work. And, as will be explored in Chapter 5, the way that the benefits of music therapy are construed is inextricably linked with the nature of the music therapist's identity as well.

Music therapists also have articulated significantly contrasting viewpoints on the nature of music and how it functions in music therapy. Chapters 3 through to 6 examine these views and consider their impact on central questions regarding the basic processes of music therapy. In engaging the issues in these four chapters, it can be helpful to keep in mind this issue of whether one considers oneself primarily as a musician doing therapy or as a therapist using music. It is a distinction that underlies many of the contrasting viewpoints to be explored.

Notes

1. In using the terms *medicine* and *medical professional* I do not mean to restrict the referents of such terms to medical doctors. Instead, I am including rehabilitation professionals such as occupational, physical, and speech therapists in this designation. By *medical professional*, I wish to indicate those professions that are medical in the general sense of utilizing procedures, such as diagnosing physiological or cognitive problems, and formulating specific interventions to remediate such problems based upon scientifically-grounded principles and evidence. While some practitioners would argue to include psychotherapists in this group, my own view is that the process of spontaneous engagement and the use of the idiosyncratically-created therapeutic relationship as an essential curative element in psychotherapy differentiate it from the professions that are more purely medical in nature. However, I do recognize that these distinctions are not hard and fast and there are reasonable arguments to be made on both sides of this issue. Additionally, a third type of role might be stated as "music therapist as educator" for music therapists who work in school settings to address psycho-educational goals. This notion while perhaps prevalent among music therapists in some locales, does not appear in a significant number of publications and thus will not be taken up here.
2. The first published application of Wolberg's levels to music therapy was in Wheeler (1983).
3. Bruscia uses the word *levels* in distinguishing among the four areas, although in the present author's reading, there does not appear to be a hierarchy present in these distinctions.
4. Some authors date the inception of the modern profession from this year when the first academic program in music therapy was established at Michigan State University. Others use 1950, as this is when the first professional association was formed.
5. One notable exception is Julie Hibben's (1999) collection, which focuses on client experiences in music therapy.

PART II

How is Music Considered in Music Therapy?

3

PSYCHODYNAMIC, SOCIAL, AND MUSIC-CENTERED PERSPECTIVES ON MUSIC

In addressing the question of what makes music therapy work, one obvious place to turn is music. However, as Even Ruud (1998) observes, there is a lack of consensus on the nature of music in music therapy because "adherents of various schools of music therapy understand music differently, more or less consistent with the underlying values of their particular theoretical tradition" (p. 70). The different views on this question reflect the different routes people take in answering it. These routes, in turn, are strongly influenced by their metaphysical assumptions about music and how they construe the profession of music therapy and their role in it.

While it is apparent that there is an intimate connection between music therapists' views of music and their clinical–theoretical framework, what is not so clear is which one is more fundamental. Do therapists seek a view of music that supports their clinical approaches, or does the view of music one has serve to establish the nature of one's clinical theory?

Ruud (1998) argues for the former notion, that music therapists "choose a particular concept of music to give music a certain function or to justify a certain practice" (p. 81). His view that the perspective of music held by music therapists is chosen to support the nature of their clinical model is an apt description of approaches based on nonmusical frameworks such as psychodynamic theory, behavioral theory, or the medical model. However, for music-based approaches, this relationship is reversed. Music-centered music therapy begins from the nature of the human engagement with music and pragmatically and empirically builds a clinical practice upon it. The practice rests on an approach to music rather than upon nonmusical theoretical commitments. A third alternative is present in approaches that draw extensively from social theory, such as community music therapy and resource-oriented music therapy. Here, the relationship between the clinical model and the view of music is interactive; the clinical model and perspective of music mutually constitute each other. This tripartite division will be seen throughout many of the discussions in the present chapter.

As was discussed in Chapter 2, in the medical model of music therapy music therapists assess clients and formulate interventions to address the particular conditions revealed by assessment and case materials. Music is akin to a medication and the search is undertaken for exploring how the properties of music as an autonomous entity can lead to desired changes.

is these properties that are primary and they determine the clinical value and efficacy of usic.

In the more orthodox forms of music psychotherapy influenced by traditional psychoanalytic thought, the explanation for the effectiveness of music in therapy must fit with psychoanalytic theory about the personality, human development, and the role of art in human life. In this framework, music is considered a medium for regression, a repository of unconscious emotions, a projective screen upon which unacceptable aspects of one's inner self may be placed, or a representation of objects in the world with which the individual must come to terms in order to become healthier.

The medical and psychoanalytic approaches consider the attributes of music in a relatively narrow way to place its operations within their respective systems. In the medical model, most often it is neurological explanation that is employed and music is examined as a stimulus of quantifiable parameters that is processed through particular systems and pathways in the brain. It is the nature of this processing that determines the clinical value of music. In the psychoanalytic model, it is not the brain but the overall personality structure that is of interest. Nevertheless, there is a strong similarity with the medical model because it is the particular psychological processes that music evokes—such as projection, regression, sublimation—that explain its value.

Both systems offer context-free, mechanistic explanations that do not consider the highly individualized ways that human beings actively engage with music. Because they are not interested in this level of analysis, and because the motivation and engagement of the client toward musical experience is not particularly relevant to their explanations, they confine themselves to looking at "the power of music" to effect personal change, with the properties of music to either affect brain functioning or stimulate the unconscious mind providing the primary locus of effect.

The perspective of socially-based theories is an interactive one as it considers music to be a particular context that humans engage with in ways that are determined in equal parts by properties of music and the desires of people. In this vein, Brynjulf Stige (2002a) invokes J.J. Gibson's notion of *affordances*, which refers to the properties of an environment relative to the characteristics of a particular being. The things that the culture affords exist in an interactive relationship with the organism. They are neither solely properties of the environment nor of the organism; they are properties of the interaction. In this view, to explain how people engage with music to promote their own health, development, and well-being, it is necessary to provide insight into how the properties of music make possible experiences that human beings value and work to engender.

Socially-based theories seek to establish music therapy practice on nonclinical theories of music. Stige (2002a) references the work of Tia DeNora in this regard as someone who "has utilized the notion of affordance in relation to meanings of music in everyday situations, and proposes that it is possible to treat music as situated event and activity without overlooking the meaning potential of the musical material used" (p. 97). In other words, one can investigate the role of music while considering it both in its local conditions and in what may lie immanent in it. Music can be considered in an integrated way, not just as "a stimulus on the one side or a socially constructed sign on the other" (Stige, 2002a, p. 98).

Stige (2003) highlights current thinking regarding musics as a plural construct much as one thinks of cultures. There do not seem to be any universals that characterize what would be considered music (from a Western worldview) through time and across culture. Even if a particular culture does not possess a concept of music, it possesses practices that are music from a Western perspective. Additionally, the notion of "'music in itself' . . . is an abstraction, based on act of taking actions out of context and reifying them in the shape of musical works or traditions" (p. 159). Both of these observations—that music is multivalent and that a construct of music as an isolated entity is an abstraction, and one that may not be so useful at that— militate against looking at properties of music in isolation in developing music therapy theory.

Contrasting Views of Music in Psychodynamic, Socially-Based, and Music-Centered Models

Because Freud's theories were based on the study of neuroses, the psychoanalytic theory of personality is based on the study of dysfunction. One legacy of this practice is that many human activities are reduced to their role in maintaining or reflecting less than optimal functioning. For example, in psychodynamic music therapy, music is often looked at as a medium that enables regressive tendencies and the expression of that which would be better expressed verbally.

This stance leads to two opposing trends in psychodynamic thinking in the creative arts therapies, differentiated by whether one believes that the uses of the arts in therapy are continuous with their uses outside of therapy, or if they are fundamentally different from these uses. In the former view, the creations of artists are seen as symptoms of neuroses or as indicants of unresolved psychological conflicts. The function of art in society is thereby pathologized and the continuity between clinical and nonclinical functions of music is maintained. In the latter view, the function of the arts in therapy is seen as quite different from how they function for people in nonclinical settings; there is thus a discontinuity in the function of music in both domains.

In contrast, music therapy theories from socially-based frameworks (such as community music therapy and resource-oriented music therapy) and music-based frameworks (such as music-centered music therapy) differ from the psychodynamic approach in two important ways. First, they consider a relationship to music as an essential human need that reflects healthy tendencies within the individual. Second, as result of this belief in the positive valence of musical engagement, they seek to establish continuities between clinical and nonclinical uses of music, and they seek to establish music therapy theories based on more general theories of music drawn from ethnomusicology and the sociology of music.

An example of this mode of thinking is Randi Rolvsjord's (2010) use of musicology theory in her discussion of the ontology of music. Her focus is to explore how these ideas "inform the role and concept of music within a resource-oriented approach to music therapy" (p. 60). She acknowledges that such an investigation requires some "understanding of what music 'itself' is" (p. 60), although she recognizes that it not possible to draw strict distinctions between "music as an autonomous object" (p. 60) and how it is employed in various contexts because music only exists insofar as it is "performed, perceived, and experienced by humans" (p. 60).

According to Rolvsjord, the conventional view of music as an autonomous object is problematic for music therapy because it leads to a mechanistic perspective that attributes the clinical value of music primarily to its formal properties rather than to how it is used interactively by people. In contrast, she advocates for the use of musical affordances and appropriations as described by J.J. Gibson and applied to music by Tia DeNora (2000) and music therapists such as Stige and Ansdell.

This view of music fits in well with the resource-oriented approach because "it emphasizes the client's own role in constituting the use of music" (Rolvsjord, 2010, p. 68), something that contrasts with the conventional view where music acts upon the client and it is the expert therapist who determines what music would best induce the desired therapeutic change. Because Rolvsjord does not believe in music as an autonomous object, the therapist must offer a context in which the client can actively appropriate the music in order to create a therapeutically meaningful experience.

Rolvsjord does not advocate that music therapists move from a view of music as primarily a product to a view of music as primarily a process. Instead, she argues for a pluralized view of music that accepts these notions depending upon the particular context being considered. Rolvsjord presents Small's (1998) notion that all people are born musical but the Western specialist view "demusicalizes" individuals. This idea of the innate musicality of all individuals—or rather, the view that all (or most) people are inherently capable of developing a relationship to music where they can appropriate what it affords for their own self-benefit—forms a strong rationale for music therapy in a wide variety of contexts.

As will be apparent in the ensuing discussion, the variety of views of music and the different ways of considering it in relation to music therapy all reflect this fundamental dichotomy: music as a compensatory medium in psychodynamic and medical thinking, and music as more of a value-added medium in social and music-based thinking.

Psychoanalytic Views of Music in Music Therapy

As two of the more prominent music therapists who developed psychoanalytic perspectives, it is important to examine the ideas of Florence Tyson (1981) and Mary Priestley (1994, 2012) about music to gain a complete view of thinking in this area. Although they both employed aspects of traditional psychoanalytic thinking in their theories and methods, they also both worked eclectically and pragmatically. Tyson's practice used unconventional interventions that were inconsistent with a pure psychoanalytic framework and Priestley's writings included music-based concepts that moved beyond pure analytic thinking. Nonetheless, while neither of them wrote extensively about music, what they did write tended to fall more along orthodox psychoanalytic lines and they serve to well represent this perspective.

Tyson believed "that music arose as an audible expression of our internal reactions to sensory, motor and psychological stimuli" (1981, p. 1). As well, she felt that the physiological basis of music as a reflection of biological rhythms provided the foundation for music therapy. She identified the inhibition of, and dissociation from, affect as a pervasive concern for all music therapy work. Because music represents an outflowing from the internal state of the individual into the environment, it is naturally suited to address the core issue faced by clients for whom the lack of capacity for productive emotional expression was debilitating.

Because the focus of Tyson's (1981) approach was to achieve "the freest possible gratification of instinctual aims through the medium of music" (p. 29), her clinical model aimed to facilitate the outflow of emotional tension through music. However, because of guilt, anxiety, or inhibition, she believed that most clients cannot allow themselves the outflow required for relief and regression. Music provides a context in which a scream "incorporated at the apex of an ascending vocal scale" or a "solidly chorded or turbulent forte passage in a piano score" (p. 29) offers the opportunity for a cathartic letting of emotion. The aesthetic elements of the music are clinically relevant, but only insofar as they provide the pretext for the nonmusical release.

Mary Priestley's broader view of music does not fully manifest in her music therapy theory. She locates the origins of music therapy in the idea that music "is a fundamental attribute of all existence" (2012, p. 244) and she recognizes how music therapy is rooted in aspects of its historical antecedents and in concerns of daily life:

> Though music, medicine, religion and magic have long ceased to be one profession, nevertheless the music therapist need not think of his working tool as being an alien art form cultivated separately in the hot-house atmosphere of musical colleges and academies and quite outside the mainstream of the daily round. The elements of music are in all life.
>
> (Priestley, 2012, p. 244)

For Priestley, musicians serve an essential compensatory function for society by providing access to emotional and spiritual experiences from which most people are disconnected. In nonclinical contexts, music listeners adopt one of two stances: First, they become so absorbed in the experience that they resonate to it becoming "a kind of human sympathetic string attuned to its harmonies and melodies" (Priestley, 2012, p. 245); and second, they free their inner censor to allow the projection of "frozen emotions and unconscious images on to the music as a screen" (pp. 245–246) in order to experience aspects of their beings from which they had been disconnected.

In this theory, music functions in a clinical context similarly to the way it does outside of therapy. Providing for the expression of emotions that previously had no other outlet is one of the primary functions of music. This is comparable to an "emotional bloodletting" (Priestley, 2012, p. 247) in which feelings that would otherwise manifest in acts of self-destruction are safely released, sometimes overtly and sometimes through the symbols and images evoked by the self-created music. Musical expression assists in the discovery of one's authentic self, as differentiated from the self-image that had been internalized based upon the views of others. In all cases, music serves primarily as medium through which to explore one's inner world.

In addition to music therapy concepts based on Freudian thought, the thinking of Carl Jung has also been employed by music therapists, although in a more limited fashion. Prominent examples include the work of Priestley (1987), Borczon (1997), Brooks (1998), and Austin (1991, 1996, 2003). In some areas, Jung appears more supportive of artistic processes and of creative activity in general, seeing them not just as fulfilling a compensatory function but also as a positive source of strength and insight.

Jung clearly differentiated between "creative work produced for therapeutic purposes" (Marshman, 2003, p. 21) and creative work that produced art. Any music therapy approach that appeals to Jungian concepts will start from a position that dichotomizes these two types of creations. Jung's use of creativity was oriented toward providing access to the irrational aspects of the unconscious and giving them a material form so that they could be engaged with for the process of individuation.

Within the realm of art, Jung made a second twofold distinction between works that involved a fully conscious intent and those that emerged from the unconscious, more or less fully formed. When artists feel that a work is coming from without, this is an example of the second type of work. Its source is "an independent force in the psyche . . . [known as] an autonomous complex" (Marshman, 2003, p. 22). For Jung, the presence of an autonomous complex was evidence of an imbalance in a normally-functioning person that could be a sign of mental illness. The salient point for the present discussion is that the impulse for what Jung describes as the source of the greatest works of art lies in a dysfunctional process within the psyche.

For Jung, great musical works originate in the collective unconscious of composers. Consequently, when others (listeners, players) engage with these works as the composer did, they can come into contact with the same universals of human experience to which the composer gave voice. What is therapeutic about this encounter is that the individual comes to experience what was formerly a personal suffering as a more universal characteristic of humankind; it becomes depersonalized and identified with something broader and more meaningful.

Creative musicality is implicated in two ways in Jung's thinking: that which serves as the original source of music and that which is involved in receiving its message in a way to access the contents of the collective unconscious. That is where the collective wisdom of humans as a species resides and each individual must come to terms with its contents in order to individuate fully. There does not seem to be a place in Jung's thinking to locate the positive value of creative musicality. There is nothing in it that can make use of the specifics of musical engagement, either with oneself or with others. And as an analytic framework, the source of music still lies within something that is dysfunctional, namely the autonomous complex.

Some contemporary music therapy approaches utilize a psychoanalytic framework to explain the function of music in psychiatry but go beyond the more common notion of music primarily as a symbol of the unconscious. For example, Paul Nolan (1994) uses elements of ego psychology to consider music as a direct manifestation that represents a higher level of functioning than is usual for the person, considered as restored ego function in this psychoanalytic view.

Nolan exemplifies a prevalent approach among contemporary psychodynamic music therapy theorists in claiming that the nature of client expressions and interaction in improvisational music therapy has the same character as mother–infant interactions. It is the universal familiarity with this type of interaction that underlies musical interaction and enables improvisational music therapy as a particularly potent form of psychological treatment. The progress of clients owes to their ability to return to a more primitive form of interaction, prior to the emergence of verbal skills and full ego development. According to the psychoanalytic view, the difficulties experienced by adults with mental illness originate in a preverbal stage of development, and Nolan agrees with this theory as he locates the clinical value of music in its ability to reach into this developmental stage:

> A general theme in the early mother/caregiver and infant research is that musical elements are both by-products and serve as a means of influence on behavioral states . . . It seems that this capacity of the patient to receive musical stimulation from a caregiver and then generate a musical response is especially applicable to the basic foundations and processes of improvisational music therapy.
>
> (Nolan, 1994, p. 89)

Psychodynamic music therapy approaches answer the question about the role of music in music therapy processes in ways that subsume it to existing psychoanalytic processes and structures: music facilitates emotional expression by bypassing internal taboos; it provides a means for temporarily regressing to early stages of development; and it offers a symbol of unconscious contents which must be assimilated into consciousness for the goals of therapy to be achieved. The only way that clinical functions of music reflect the more generalized functions of music outside of therapy is by pathologizing those functions. In taking this strategy, music is treated as a transparent medium, able to be bent to the purposes of psychodynamic therapy rather than as a medium with inherent qualities that suggest clinical practices based in these qualities.

Socially-Based and Music-Centered Notions of Music in Music Therapy Musicing

In music-based and socially-based music therapy theories, the term *musicing* has become a popular one. As noted previously, while European writers for the most part use the writings of Christopher Small (1998) as a reference point and employ his spelling *musicking*, David Elliott's (1995) concept of *musicing*, with its alternative spelling, has been more influential in a North American context. Their shared concept of music as essentially an activity rather than as a thing is based on the notion of "music as action and interaction in social and cultural contexts" (Stige, 2002a, p. 99). The perspective embodied by Elliott and Small counters the traditional view of music as an object whose significance lies in its structures. The new view emphasizes the exploration of contexts of use of music to determine its meaning and significance. Questions about the meaning of music are transformed to questions about the meaning of performance. The meaning of music does not lie immanently in works of music but they "are produced through shared action in context" (Stige, 2002a, p. 100).

Stige argues that because music therapists have traditionally been more focused on process than product, this contemporary view of music provides a very comfortable fit for music therapy theory. He asserts that the concept is not only applicable in live, improvisational uses of music in music therapy but also within clinical models such as guided imagery and music (GIM) that use recordings of Western classical music where the client is in a receptive relationship to the music.

While Small's notion of *musicking* emphasizes that music is a process more than a thing, Elliott's notion of *musicing* emphasizes not only that music is a type of "doing" but that it "is an informed doing, embodying a specific form of knowledge" (Aigen, 2005a, p. 65). For Elliott, "musicing in the sense of musical performing is a particular form of intentional human action . . . To perform music is to act thoughtfully and knowingly" (Elliott, 1995, p. 50).

One of the most important implications of Elliott's notion is that the demonstration of a capacity for musicing "implies that there is intelligence, intention, and consciousness present" (Aigen, 2005a, p. 67), which are profound evaluations to make when a therapist is working with a client for whom the presence of these qualities may be in question. When clients in music therapy are actively musicing, they are exhibiting a form of knowledge requiring the activation of complex cognitive processes that may not otherwise manifest.

Elliott's view of music is as the "diverse human practice of overtly and covertly constructing aural-temporal patterns for the primary (but not necessarily the exclusive) values of enjoyment, self-growth, and self-knowledge" (Elliott, 1995, p. 128). This definition is intriguing for music therapists because its focus on the way that music enriches human life is congruent with how music is conceptualized in music therapy. Working with a definition such as this one suggests that the clinical uses of music in music therapy, construed broadly, are continuous with the nature of music and its use in nonclinical contexts. It embeds music therapy within existing notions of the role of music in society as opposed to setting it apart from these roles.

Music as a Language or an Experiential World

Music shares many characteristics with verbal language: both mediums are temporal and auditory; they both can be represented through visual symbols; and they typically involve a sender, a receiver, and a message. These similarities have led some music therapy theorists to consider music in music therapy as a language, or at least as a communicative medium.

Kate Gfeller's (2012) view represents some of the more conventional thinking in music therapy. In it, music is considered as a language-like symbol system that functions as a form of communication. She cites Owens who describes communication as

> the process participants use to exchange information and ideas, needs and desires. The process is an active one that involves encoding, transmitting, and decoding the intended message . . . It requires a sender and a receiver, and each must be alert to the informational needs of the other to ensure that messages are conveyed effectively and that intended meanings are preserved.
>
> (Owens, as cited in Gfeller, 2012, p. 493)

This view is built on communication theory where the process consists of a producer who sends a message, which is then decoded by the receiver of the message. For communication to occur, the meaning imparted by the sender must be the same as that decoded by the receiver. Moreover, music does not possess strict denotative meaning as verbal language does and so this view often makes use of Leonard Meyer's view on embodied meaning in music.

The view of music as communication with strong parallels to verbal language does not account for developments in semiotic theory and music philosophy during the second half of the twentieth century. In relation to the former concern, in contrast to the communication theory of music, in the semiotic approach, music has three aspects: its configurations or structures; the procedures that have engendered it (acts of creation); and the procedures to which it gives rise, such as perception and interpretation. In this perspective there is no single, objective message or essence of music. Its genesis, its organization, and the way it is perceived all combine to form its nature. In order to fully grasp what music is, all of these levels are considered. Rather than passively receiving a message and decoding the producer's intent through predetermined rules as in communication theory, in semiotic thinking the receiver engages the musical content and actively constructs its meaning based on many idiosyncratic factors.

It is difficult to determine Gfeller's precise stance on this issue. On the one hand, she seems to embrace a more contemporary, interactive view in saying that "communication of meaning is not a function of the stimulus or message alone. Rather, meaning comes from a relationship between the symbol, that to which it points, and the common observer" (2012, p. 493). Yet, she also asserts that "a symbol must have similar meaning for both the originator and the recipient" (p. 493), thus suggesting agreement with the older conception where it is the sender's intent that defines the meaning of music.

The basic framework for this view of music as language is embedded within a behavioral and neurologically-based framework. In terms of the former, the associationist view is invoked to explain the connection between music and its meaning; in terms of the latter, the differences between verbal language and music are explored in terms of varying neurological systems activated by each modality respectively. Faithfulness to the former view and to Meyer's approach leads Gfeller to minimize the intellectual, cognitive processes involved in the experiencing of music. She claims that the absence of referential meaning means that "musical communication is less dependent on rational or intellectual response" (Gfeller, 2012, p. 496) and the appreciation of art in general entails a perspective "in which pressure from reason and rational thought is alleviated" (p. 496).

Gfeller (2012) identifies the clinical value of music as stemming from this minimizing of intellectual capacities: "This reduction of rational response has therapeutic implications for those clients with limited intellectual capacity, as well as for interventions in which intellectualization by the client is considered undesirable" (p. 497). This view offers a stark contrast to music therapy rationales that are based on a cognitive view of music which emphasizes how music necessarily involves complex cognitive processing (such as is illustrated in Aigen, 1995a) and that for many clients of music therapy offers the opportunity to display complex cognitive skills which cannot be demonstrated through other means.

Pavlicevic (1995) also considers music to be a form of communication, particularly when it is used in the treatment of mental illness through clinical improvisation. In her view, "clinical improvisation offers the musical partners the opportunity to apprehend one another directly through the music: they share a sense of themselves in relation to one another, without the intrusion and potential diversion of intermediary objects, such as, for example, language" (p. 168). What she calls "basic communication" characterizes other domains of study as well, such as that of nonverbal communication and mother–infant interaction. Because individuals with mental illness exhibit deficiencies in interactional synchrony, difficulties in engaging in mutualized and spontaneous interaction in music can be seen as a direct manifestation of mental illness. Conversely, the ability to engage in musical communication with increasing degrees of responsiveness and mutuality indicates an ability to overcome the basic problems that reflect mental illness.

However, there is another way of thinking about music that is more broadly construed than that of a mutually-created language. It is the idea that music represents an alternative experiential realm, a different type of phenomenal world for those who can exist within it. Such a broad construct requires more broad-based support than would that of music as language, and yet it holds a greater potential benefit in terms of a broader realm of application.

This notion, if not originating within the practice of Nordoff-Robbins music therapy, certainly characterizes it to a large extent. In reflecting on how the creative and flexible use of improvised music was able to reach and effect profound change with such a variety of children with disabilities, Paul Nordoff observed that "music is an enormous world to live in and to work in. It's the only world we can conceive that can meet the variations of pathology as one sees them in any individual" (Aigen, 2005b, p. 18).

Music therapists who are drawn to the notion of music as an alternative experiential world have generally observed and participated in clinical processes with clients where they have been able to function far beyond the limitations imposed by their disabilities. Consider situations where clients in music therapy can (a) engage in physical motions more fluid and intentional than they are otherwise capable of; (b) establish communication and relationships in music where none others were possible; (c) overcome long-term emotional fears and blocks that had prevented a full engagement with life; or (d) overcome a whole host of cognitive deficits to engage in functional, expressive, and communicative acts that were otherwise unavailable. When clients are able to function "in music unfettered by the barriers imposed on them in nonmusic situations" the medium that allows this to occur is more aptly considered "a novel experiential realm characterized by its own language, value, system, epistemology, spiritual belief system, and metaphysic" (Aigen, 1998, p. 266).

When therapists work with clients who are extremely isolated and who participate in human life in only the most marginal of ways, these clients appear to live another world. In order to establish connections with them, it is necessary to create an alternative experiential realm in which the disabilities are not highlighted. For someone whose experiential world is typically without the comfort of human contact "music can become something rare, evocative or consoling. It can become another landscape for him, one in which he will be able find more than the limits of his own being" (Nordoff & Robbins, 2004, p. 55).

When the very concept of communication has not taken root within a person, when that individual relates to other people more as objects in the environment than as sentient beings, the explanation for why music can awaken a desire to communicate and interact with others must move beyond that of a mere language. It instead is best conceptualized as establishing for each client a unique musical world in which the experiences of the essential qualities of human life can be imparted. Music serves to "establish an intermediate plane of existence in between the normal social world of human beings and the extremely isolated and individualized worlds of disabled individuals" (Aigen, 2005a, p. 147), one in which human relationship can be established, values shared, and dormant capacities awakened.

A similar notion has been put forth by Gary Ansdell (1995) in his description of the "musical between" based upon Buber's concept of the interpersonal realm in which individuals who engage each other as sentient beings interact. This "between" is crucial to the effectiveness of music therapy for Ansdell. His attempt to explain music therapy to someone unfamiliar with it was met with this response: "I see—it's like the difference between being on land and being in water. Suddenly you feel different—freer, supported, you can do different things" (p. 68). Ansdell further developed this response in saying that

> changing the medium you are acting in, whether from land to water, or from words to music, can give a different feeling of both yourself and how you relate to other people. Within this 'musical between' a relationship can come about which is primarily in the music.
>
> (Ansdell, 1995, p. 68)

In a complementary perspective to that of Ansdell, Colin Lee (2003) has reported that clients experience music therapy improvisation as a form of "musical flying" in which the normal bounds of living and dying can be transcended. A client of his reported that "through music I fly. In improvising I leave behind the realities of my illness, my tumor and the degeneration of my living" (p. 72). For Lee, entering the world of music in nonclinical contexts involves entering an altered reality where common logic is abandoned. He sees no reason why the music-making in clinical contexts should be any different.

The profound difference that music therapy can make for some people and the dramatically new types of interaction it affords warrant this broad construct of a musical world. A new language can allow for the communication of an inner state that was previously barred, but "it is the establishment of a new experiential realm which allows for the transcendence of disability" (Aigen, 1998, p. 267) that better accounts for the more global changes seen in music therapy clients.

When people create music together communication happens, but this does not mean that music *is* communication. Consider an activity such as team athletics. Communication among players is necessary for success in this realm and exemplary communication creates perform-ances of beauty in certain team sports. But to consider athletics *as* communication would be to miss the purpose for which the communications were occurring. Similarly, collaborative musicing requires communication, but it is communication for the purpose of creating the experiences of expression, flow, and communality unique to music. Music therapy theory can certainly take into account the communicative facets of music in explaining its value, but to use the concept of "music as a language" as one's fundamental construct would be to ignore the very purpose for which music is engaged in by people.

Many of the aspects of music-centered practice can be understood as facilitating and maintaining participation in a musical realm of experience, such as the minimizing of interpretive verbal interactions and the reliance on session-long aesthetic forms. In this framework, music therapy is most effective when clients are fully absorbed in a musical experience and this motivation is considered to be a property of the whole and healthy part of the person as it activates creative processes connected to the drive for health and well-being. This holistic perspective and its relation to creativity characterize the socially-based, music-based theories more than the ones rooted in medical, behavioral, or psychoanalytic thinking.

Views on Music and Holism in Music Therapy

Psychoanalytic, behavioral, and neurologically-based perspectives on music in music therapy have in common a reductive philosophical stance to explanation. In explaining how people engage with music in music therapy, psychodynamic explanations invoke the interactions of personality constituents; behavioral approaches break down complex musical behaviors into the building blocks of simple behaviors; and neurological approaches consider the neural activity associated with exposure to music. All of these approaches are reductive in the sense that they separate a phenomenon into its components and speculate on how the constituents interact in order to explain what is observed.

However, the idea that adequate explanation results from articulating the structure of an entity and describing the interaction of its parts has been pervasively critiqued in contemporary philosophy of science. It is a tenuous foundation upon which to construct a theoretical frame-work. In contrast, music-based, resource-oriented, and community music therapy frameworks approach explanation from a different philosophical position that considers clinical music something that arises on the level of the whole person. Music is engaged in by human beings, considered holistically, not in isolation as egos, neurons, or aspects of organisms ruled by environmental contingencies. In this view, in explaining the value of music in music therapy, rather than parse human beings into components or sub-systems of organization, the strategy is to investigate how music meets universal human needs such as the need for "meaningful human relationships, a rewarding vocation or avocation, an existential sense of purpose in life, and the ability to expressively relate to others in order to meet those needs" (Aigen, 1991b, p. 269).

The holistic view begins from the notion that "the need to create music is an intrinsic human activity, not necessarily better understood when reduced to, or explained by, other drives, needs or deficiencies. It is fundamental to psychological well-being because of its essential characteristics, not because of incidental, fortuitous, i.e. non-aesthetic benefits" (Aigen, 1991b, p. 269). The process of musical engagement in therapy is not a reflection or symbol of something more basic; it is the actual phenomenon of interest, a point made not only by the music-based and culturally-based theories just mentioned, but even by the contemporary work of Smeijsters (2005) rooted in a more psychological framework.

What the musical and cultural frameworks have in common is considering the musically creative act as a primary orientation point rather than viewing it from an external psychological perspective or belief system. This involves a conceptual reversal akin to that of moving from a geocentric to a heliocentric worldview; the way it conflicts with the conventional wisdom may cause its novelty to overshadow its usefulness.

Music and Creativity in Music Therapy

Musical creativity involves genuinely creative activities in the sense of bringing something into being in the form of an emergent property. "Phenomena embodying creation—like the emergence of life from inanimate matter, consciousness from cells, and the bringing forth of aesthetic experience from raw materials—are all inexplicable solely through reference to the structure and properties of their constituents" (Aigen, 1991b, p. 271). When music therapy incorporates this type of creative process, it is reasonable to accept it as the orientation point from which to view clinical processes, rather than adopting an extrinsic, psychological perspective from which to analyze the creativity at the heart of music therapy. And the connections between creativity (in its artistic dimensions) and the creation of life are also relevant to these speculations. The emergence of life from inanimate matter is the paradigmatic act for all creative acts. Creative activity—whether in the artistic, scientific, or therapeutic realms—is intimately connected with the processes conducive to life, and hence the health of organisms.

Because creativity involves the coming into being of a property not present in its constituents or antecedents, there will always be an unexplainable gap between the phenomenon of interest and its constituents or antecedents. This is why the more reductive approaches to understanding the role of music are of limited utility; they cannot approach the nature of the creative musical experience on its own terms.

Music, even in its most serious manifestations, is a form of play according to Ansdell (1995), and in this playful essence creativity is strongly implicated. The focus of Ansdell's speculations, Nordoff-Robbins music therapy, prioritizes being creative in music and in the interpersonal musical engagement central to clinical improvisation. Being musical is being creative and being creative is inherently therapeutic because it meets fundamental human needs "to find new experiences, new patterns, new meanings; to act freely, flexibly and spontaneously" (p. 103).

Ansdell's view contrasts with Freud's suspicions about creativity, which he saw as a symptom of psychological dysfunction. Although subsequent psychoanalytic theorists held a more benign view, the influence of traditional psychoanalytic thinking in music therapy led to a notion that creativity and play had motives other than artistic ones, even when used in therapy, and the decoding of these motives was an essential part of clinical processes. However, the British analyst D.W. Winnicott is held up by Ansdell as someone who understood the value of play in and of itself (meaning that he understood the value of uninterpreted play) to the extent that his dominant construct for understanding the psychotherapeutic process was as a form of play.

An emphasis on the specific aspects of musical creativity is central to Ansdell. It is not creativity in general that explains the value of improvisational music therapy but rather it is the specific way in which music demands immediacy, interactivity, and trust in the unknown that explains its value. It is the drawing forth of something from nothing, creating an interactive musical entity where none existed previously, that is most valuable for many clients as it counteracts a pervasive self-image characterized by the absence of creativity.

In fact, Ansdell identifies what is commonly called *musicality* as this form of musical creativity. It is an inherent part of being a human being. Music is not a specialized mode of experience but a necessary facet of being human:

> To be musical is a natural part of what it is to be human. And when I say 'be musical' I don't mean to be musically skilled, but a way of being-in-the-world musically. Being musical to me is about this sensitivity to timing, texture, nuance, play . . . Also being in relationship to others musically—trusting that there's a level where you don't need words to understand each other . . . trusting another level of knowing, and being free to move around in that level . . . being confident in it.
>
> (Verney & Ansdell, 2010, p. 48)

This idea is particularly useful for music therapists because it is separate from the idea of musical skill and it can be manifested by individuals with no musical training and in spite of a host of challenging conditions. Music therapists do not necessarily work to enhance the musical skills of clients (although this could be a focus of clinical work) but they do very much work to develop clients' musicality because musicality addresses many of the concerns relevant to music therapy, such as "creativity, flexibility, imagination and a sense of music coming from the whole person, a balance of thought and feeling" (Verney & Ansdell, 2010, p. 108). For many music therapy clients, the clinical process can consist of transforming unmusical playing to musical playing, thereby overcoming self-limiting patterns of rigidity, isolation, and depression.

In contrast to psychodynamic approaches, Ansdell believes this change does not come about by analyzing problems, interpreting music, or through overt or covert suggestions to clients that they change. It is through the type of communication that can occur with a sensitive, listening music therapist that the client achieves a new way of being and from which the client can construct a healthier sense of self.

In a psychodynamic model where the therapeutic relationship is essential to the clinical process, music is considered primarily as a form of interpersonal communication between the two parties in this relationship. While the music-based model supported by Ansdell does consider communication as important, it is only half of the story. The aesthetic value of musical creativity is equally important because within it is contained many of the experiences for which people come to therapy. By valuing musical experience for its own sake, rather than for its instrumental use for a nonmusical purpose, the music-based emphasis on creativity in music therapy serves to establish connections with nonclinical uses of music in society.

Musical creativity takes a central role in explaining why and how music therapy works within the more music-based music therapy approaches. The opportunity to function as creative beings changes how people see themselves and their relationship to their culture and the musical artifacts (styles, compositions, modes of relating, etc.) that constitute this culture. These connections will be explored in Chapter 4.

4

MUSICAL STYLES IN MUSIC THERAPY

Culture, Identity, and the Nature of Change

Sociologically-based approaches in music therapy theory examine the uses of music in nonclinical contexts and apply the findings to clinical work. One of the areas in which creative processes are relevant in clinical and nonclinical settings is the creation of identity. Even Ruud (1997) investigated the nature of identity creation through music. His notion of identity is based upon a postmodern perspective in which identity is not a given but something that we actively construct. Ruud's thesis is that music is a primary arena in which this construction is undertaken.

Ruud examined the musical autobiographies of university students based on the notion that "listening to, performing and talking about music is not as much a reflection of identity as a way of performing our sense of ourselves, our identity" (1997, p. 3). Because music is so central to our identity, its nature influences even how we conceive that a sense of identity is created. Ruud chose a particular notion of identity that is

> rooted within the particular discourse the individual performs when consciousness is monitoring his/her own activities, memories and fantasies. In selecting among the possible life circumstances and memories, and through projecting these towards the future, a concept of the self may be narrated to oneself as a negotiated identity.
>
> (Ruud, 1997, p. 6)

Our individual identities result from the particular discourse that we engage in because the way our life experiences become contextualized is guided by the metaphoric constructs of our chosen discourse. To gain a greater understanding of identity requires insight into the metaphors used to construct it. Through the engagement with music we clarify our values and locate ourselves within a particular culture. The heavily emotional content of music serves to "highlight and position the life events of the person in a significant way" (Ruud, 1997, p. 6).

Ruud's work demonstrates how music and musical experiences serve as an essential touchstone in the creation of identity on many levels and in many contexts. His research revealed four primary locations in which identity construction proceeds through music:

(1) music and personal space; (2) music and social space; (3) the space of time and place; and (4) the transpersonal space. In (1), one finds processes of developing an awareness of feelings, bodily presence, an inner core of one's being not accessible to others, and the notion of an authentic self that requires a melding of socially given musical categories. In (2) are located feelings of belonging to a community, different vantage points from which to consider one's social world that allow for the development of individual values which may be different from those represented in one's family. There is a quest for developing an authentic self that fits into a novel reality embodied in music. In (3), the construction of identity is established within a particular time and place that embodies what one has lived through and to which one feels perpetually connected. The connection to a specific time and place is embedded within musical experiences that provide a life-long orientation point for the autobiographical arc of one's life. In (4), individuals have musical experiences that bring them in touch with something beyond their everyday experience that is not describable verbally. These experiences of energy and power exist outside of the daily experience of time and space and enhance one's identity in the sense of becoming part of a broader reality.

Because of the breadth of Ruud's findings related to music and identity, they have a number of applications in music therapy. The creation of identity is a normal developmental task for all individuals, whether or not that individual has a particular challenge, illness, or disability. Individuals without disabilities are able to negotiate the relevant social structures and engage with music and music communities without the assistance of a music therapist. Those with disabilities have the same needs for identity creation and the same propensity to use music to achieve this developmental task. Thus, establishing a music therapy framework around this use of music is central to notions of community music therapy and to music-centered approaches in which the continuity of clinical and nonclinical engagements with music is emphasized.

The ability of music to play a central role in identity creation is a core principle of music-based approaches such as Nordoff-Robbins music therapy (Aigen, 1998). The artistic work that the client is actively creating is the individual sense of self; the musical work is the external manifestation of the internal work of building a sense of personhood.

The interventions of psychotherapists are supported when the mechanisms proposed to explain the efficacy of treatment are grounded in psychological structures and processes. Explanation in music therapy gains more power when it is based upon a credible, elaborated, and broad-based theory of music. A theory of music thus serves music-based music therapists much as a theory of personality serves verbal psychotherapists.

The internal work in building a sense of self is certainly important. Yet contemporary theorists such as Stige have demonstrated that engaging one's culture is as important as inner self-exploration in maintaining health. Examining the way that culture is contained in music is a necessary part of developing comprehensive music therapy theory.

Cultural Factors and the Role of Musical Styles in Music Therapy

Music can be thought of as preconventional, conventional, and postconventional depending upon the degree to which different style characteristics are present in it. Preconventional music takes the form that it does because its participants have not yet been exposed to or internalized style characteristics; conventional music is based upon the parameters of different styles; and postconventional music attempts to move beyond particular style characteristics. While there are good reasons for challenging such hard and fast distinctions—including the point that in having rules for conventions to avoid, postconventional music is just creating new conventions —they do provide a means for differentiating among the views held by some music therapy theorists about music.

Stige's (2002a, 2003) portrait of music in music therapy includes biological and cultural foundations. While he acknowledges that some aspects of the engagement of clients with improvisational music therapy is preconventional and therefore not dependent on culture— much as is the case for theorists who invoke infant–mother interaction studies as a basis for music therapy improvisation—he suggests that considering the conventional and post-conventional aspects of musical engagement in music therapy will provide a more powerful explanation for how and why music therapy works. This is partly due to the pervasiveness of cultural learning, which means that all forms of musicing will have some conventional elements. As Stige (2003) observes, "even the most spontaneous of acts is channeled through some socially and culturally defined mode or expression in order to be comprehensible as communication" (p. 171).

In fact, the use of musical conventions in music therapy is not just an unfortunate necessity because they may actually explain a substantial portion of the clinical value of music. Because "the path to human individuality goes through social and cultural learning" (Stige, 2003, p. 171) and requires this type of cultural engagement, musical conventions offer access to culture for individuals who do not otherwise have this opportunity. For Stige, preconventional engagement with music supports "individual identity building, while conventional musicking is highly important in the development of sociocultural identity" (p. 171). Thus, the use of musical conventions will vary according to client needs as the necessity for working within musical conventions could also serve to stifle creativity.

Shared conventions and style characteristics of different forms of music are powerful cultural signposts. An essential aspect of any style is its particular groove. Participating in the groove of a musical style implicates the presence of these aspects of a culture as the anthropologist Steven Feld (1994) describes:

> Groove and style are distilled essences, crystallizations of collaborative expectancies in time.
>
> (Feld, 1994, p. 109)

> "Getting into the groove" describes how a socialized listener anticipates pattern in a style, and feelingfully participates by momentarily tracking and appreciating subtleties vis-à-vis overt regularities . . . A groove is a comfortable place to be.
>
> (Feld, 1994, p. 111)

The sense of comfort in social groove is relevant to music therapy applications that use popular music styles in music therapy improvisations. The sense of comfort begins within one's own body as it becomes a source of enjoyment, not just a source of frustration. It extends to the social acceptance of one's peer group, and expands to "the larger culture as one becomes acculturated through participation in the groove" (Aigen, 2005c, p. 36).

As described by Charles Keil (1995), the establishment of groove is a necessarily social activity that takes place in a particular cultural context. Being competent in style characteristics and musical conventions implies a nonverbal, tacit understanding of the culture in which the music is embedded. As Keil has argued, learning how to generate or participate in the groove of any style of music means "learning to be co-cultural with it by doing it" (p. 12).

Clients in music therapy often have barriers to participating in, and establishing a sense of belonging to, their culture. Finding ways to help them to groove musically may be the only means for providing entrée to the culture:

> The groove of a music embodies the ethics, values, aesthetics, and social relationships of culture. The culture is within the music and crystallizes in a specific form that has a necessary, non-arbitrary connection to what it is embodying . . . The constituents of social life lie immanently in music . . . To participate in the culturally and stylistically embedded music is to participate in culture—it is to participate in the attitudes, values, feelings and experiences which define the culture . . . [It] is to find the comfort of a cultural home.
>
> (Aigen, 2005c, p. 37)

The advantages of working stylistically in music therapy are based upon the presence of an existing context in which much idiomatic material—such as typical rhythmic patterns and harmonic structures—has meaning and significance. This shared frame of reference among clients and therapists allows for social connections to be made.

Style characteristics and shared musical conventions often have embedded within them particular types of social interaction as well as cognitive, motoric, and affective challenges. For example, in order to create a groove in rock or jazz it is necessary to maintain a steady tempo along with a degree of responsiveness to the musical contributions of other players. This combination of focused stability and responsiveness demands skills in areas that may be especially challenging for individuals with disabilities. Yet, when an individual can participate in this aspect of a style, there is a circumventing of disability as one is elevated to a higher level of integrated human functioning.

Many of the typical nonmusical goals employed by music therapists in a wide range of clinical applications—such as increasing awareness of self and others, impulse control, expressiveness, communicative skills, motor and sensory coordination–can be addressed "completely within the stylistic characteristics and shared conventions of . . . popular music styles" (Aigen, 2005c, p. 46). Approaching clinical work this way is based on the belief that the authentic realization of musical styles has within it the capacity to address the fundamental conditions that bring people to music therapy.

The idea of deliberately working through particular musical styles is not universally agreed to among music therapy theorists. For example, Mary Priestley (2012) would generally not introduce stylistic elements, such as a 12-bar blues or rondo form, into a music therapy improvisation because doing so would direct clients away from the unconscious contents that constitute the focus of therapy. Exceptions are made for clients whose rigid superego serves as an obstacle to the free expression of emotion because playing in a particular scale, for example, can serve to bypass the mechanism of repression and allow for the "expression of a formerly intolerable emotion" (p. 131). And Mercédès Pavlicevic (1997) says that "the purpose of clinical improvisation is not to generate a particular musical style" (p. 87) because "the stylistic and structural dictates take second place to the interpersonal meaning" (p. 56). In both of these viewpoints, focusing on a musical style detracts from the goals of therapy.

However, working within musical styles is a beneficial strategy "when 1) there is an essential aspect of the feel of a style which holds experiential benefits for the client, and 2) the conventions and characteristics of the style dovetail with areas of clinical focus" (Aigen, 2005c, p. 48). Moreover, it does not seem warranted to set the stylistic dictates of music in opposition to its interpersonal meaning. At times the interpersonal meaning arises as a direct consequence of the shared participation in style characteristics and conventions. When clients with serious communicative or other cognitive impairments participate actively in the appreciation of style conventions, they are demonstrating a level of intelligence and social awareness for which they may have no other means of communicating.

Shared participation in style conventions provides a medium in which connection can occur and relationships built. Moreover, when musical patterns with set meanings are present in the clinical-musical interaction, they can be played off of as well. Qualities such as "humor, irony, and unpredictability can be experienced because there is a 'given' against which the above qualities can be expressed" (Aigen, 2005c, p. 49). An example of this phenomenon would be when clients perceive the humor in the use of atonality in the context of a rock and roll improvisation. In this example from my own work as a co-therapist with Alan Turry (Aigen, 2005c), the client indicated that he understood the unconventional nature of this choice in that particular context. Without the presence of the predetermined stylistic conventions against which to react, it would not be possible for this particular client to have an experience based upon the mutual sharing of his musical awareness and intelligence.

One of the findings from Ruud's (1997) research on the construction of identity through music concerned the relationship between style identity and personal identity. For some performers, a specific style was experienced as being too narrow to accurately reflect their sense of self. Finding music that accurately reflected their authentic selves involved creating hybrid constellations that represented unique, genre-transcending styles such as would occur in mixing folk and jazz music. This trend seems closer to what Stige describes as post-conventional music rather than the aconventional music advocated by Priestley and Pavlicevic because it involves the deliberate combining of previous musical givens to establish something unique with its own conventions, rather than a rejection of musical conventions.

This same dynamic can occur within clinical processes when the music created in therapy begins to stretch beyond elements dictated by a particular style. These style extensions were seen in the case study from Aigen (2005c) when certain novel events began occurring in the mutually-improvised music, such as dropping a straight 4/4 feel in a rock improvisation, introducing departures from an established harmonic form, or altering the standard function of an instrument in a particular style, such as using the bass guitar melodically in the context of rock music. Eventually these "style extensions evolved into a personalized style which blended moods, conventions, and characteristics of other styles in a unique way" (Aigen, 2005c, p. 116). The new musical form, unique to this client's clinical process, was an important step in the client's development of self.

In this new form, the creation of musical groove occurred not as much through the stereotyped dictates of how instruments should function in various styles such as blues, rock, and jazz, but more as a consequence of the unique contributions of the individuals participating in the therapy as individuals. In other words, the "groove was now created more as the product of the unique personal-musical-clinical interaction than through the realization of pre-determined musical parts" (Aigen, 2005c, p. 117). The new style emerged concomitantly with the personal development that it supported and it reflected the client's unique process in the same way that cultural music styles reflect the essence of a culture.

The task of performing one's identity is a life-long venture that has a cyclical aspect as one returns to the cultural forms but with a new sense of self. The creation and performance of identity through music that uses cultural forms and then transcends these forms maintains a person in an ongoing dialogue and engagement with culture.

Interventions *through* Music or *as* Music

The various positions on the merits of working within musical styles in music therapy reflect an underlying dichotomy on the status of music as an intervention. In one view, the music *is* itself the clinical intervention. In creating music, therapists make choices about idioms, styles, keys, rhythms, chord voicing, melodic contours, timbre, touch, dynamics, and the use of tonality. The particular choices made are the clinical intervention. While the use of composed materials creates more constraints on therapist choice, a quick review of the areas of music just listed reveals that there are still a multitude of musical options available to therapists working from compositions. The musicality of the intervention matters because the purpose is to awaken and engage the client's musicality, using it to enhance the client's full capacity to be human.

In a contrasting view, the therapist's interventions occur *through* the music but they are not identified *as* the music. In other words, it is the clinical intent that is most relevant, such as if the therapist wants the music to contain, provoke, stimulate, or support the client, or to use the music with a deliberate intent such as exploring a particular image, feeling, or area of psychological conflict. In this view, the specifics of the music are not particularly relevant in understanding the nature of the intervention; rather it is how the music functions in relation to a particular intervention strategy that matters, and this function is not conceptually connected to any specific musical manifestation. Here, the intervention occurs through music, but there may not be any necessary connection between the detailed musical description of the intervention and its clinical function. The musicality of the intervention is not particularly relevant because it is the nonmusical clinical intent and effect that is most important.

In one sense, it would seem puzzling that music therapists would argue against the position that the music is the intervention. Something that distinguishes modern health-care practices from folk healing is a theory for how the specific biochemical properties of medicines interact with human physiology to produce desired effects on the human body. Given contemporary standards in science, it is clear that "the ability to connect the specific properties of one's means of intervention to a specific outcome is an essential aspect of a modern approach to healthcare" (Aigen, 2009, p. 240). And yet of the thousands of publications of all types in the music therapy literature since 1950, no more than a handful have examined the musical elements of music therapy interventions in an attempt to connect them to clinical intent. Until these types of explanatory connections can be made, it could reasonably be argued "that music therapy itself is operating at the level of a folk-healing practice" (Aigen, 2009, p. 240).

Putting aside the practical problems involved in such investigations, there are three prominent conceptual obstacles in this overall endeavor.

First, in attempting to draw connections between elements of music and verbally-expressed clinical intentions, the traditional problem of musical meaning is encountered. The extent to which specific attributes of music have relevance outside of music has been, and continues to be, an ongoing area of investigation and dispute in music philosophy. Thus, in seeking to establish connections between the specifics of music used in music therapy and their health-promoting functions, music therapists are entering the perennial debate about whether or not music has extra-musical significance and, if it does, how the connections can be systematically established. All of the philosophical arguments against this program in relation to Western classical music, for example, could be invoked against it in music therapy.

Second, one of the strategies taken by the advocates of musical analysis and specificity in music therapy is to examine the tonal construction of music and speculate upon how it influences client experience. For example, Nordoff-Robbins music therapy is built on the notion of musical specificity as of one its foundational elements. In this approach, it is assumed that

> things such as the direction and shape of a melody, the voicings of a given chord, and the tonal relationships of a particular scale, will directly affect the client's experience and hence, clinical outcome. Thus, if we want to understand what elements in the therapy situation helped accomplish clinical goals, then we look to the melodic, harmonic, and rhythmic construction of the music.
>
> (Aigen, 1998, p. 252)

This underlying rationale is manifest in a number of ways: For example, one could contrast two different pentatonic scales: a Chinese form based on the root, second, fourth, fifth, and sixth tones; and a Japanese form based on the root, minor second, fourth, diminished fifth, and diminished seventh tones. The first scale consists primarily of consonant intervals while the second one contains many dissonant intervals, including two minor seconds and two tritones. The presence of these dissonant intervals creates musical tension, which would be relevant if the music therapist had a reason for introducing tension into a music therapy improvisation

However, therapists thinking this way can be accused of adopting an anachronistic essentialist stance as regards the significance of specific elements of music such as scales or intervals. The idea that specific elements of music have an essential nature with broad application conflicts with an anti-essentialism tendency among music therapy theorists that is based on a combination of postmodernism, a recognition of cultural relativity, and a backlash against the unwarranted claims of various types of music healers.

The postmodern position emphasizes that the meaning of music does not lie immanently within it, but can only be ascertained in relation to specific contexts of use. Thus, attributing extra-musical meaning to elements of music cannot be done in an uncontextualized way. Also, the judgments about qualities such as consonance, dissonance, embellishments, tension, and resolution vary among cultures and forms of music. This also mitigates the ability to make general statements. And last, many of the discredited practices by self-appointed music healers are based upon faulty and unwarranted claims about the specific effects of particular scales or intervals (Summer, 1995). Efforts by music therapists to draw connections between elements of music and their clinical uses can be tainted by being associated with the unwarranted claims of music healers in this regard.

Third, there is also a concern that too much focus on musical detail with its attendant claims of the clinical significance of particular musical choices will lead to a prescriptive approach in music therapy. Although the tenets of evidence-based medicine and the medical model support a prescriptive approach where specific musical choices are implemented for specific clinical conditions, there are strong arguments made in music therapy against the desirability and validity of such an approach. They center around the claim that music and human beings are each far too complex and idiosyncratic for music to ever be prescribed in the way the medications are. Moreover, the advocates of musical specificity deny that a prescriptive approach necessarily follows from their basic beliefs.

In discussing the use of styles in music therapy Garred (2006) makes the point that "using an idiom is not solely about knowing a certain scale, and how to apply it technically/musically, but also what it represents, what its qualities are" (p. 270). In other words, particular styles or idioms are not just characterized by their tonal and other technical dimensions but by an essential quality that suggests a particular expressive potential. Garred considers Stige's (2002b) critique that any talk of musical archetypes entails an inherent essentialism and should be dismissed on this basis. Yet Garred's approach is a reasonable one that supports the notion of inherent qualities in particular styles but that simultaneously argues against rendering an overly specific or fixed notion of what those qualities are for any given style. The point is to avoid unwarranted claims and maintain an open mind. He wants to avoid an overly dogmatic adherence to a lexicon of musical meaning without falling into a completely relativistic stance which would be difficult to support given the actual facts of musical styles.

Garred thus articulates a viewpoint that takes advantage of the best of both perspectives on this issue. It is one that acknowledges the facts of music while still maintaining a flexible and responsive stance that characterizes modern music therapy and that distinguishes it from related areas, such as music medicine. The basic argument is that acknowledging that different forms of music have an essential character or some objective elements does not require that the individual character will be experienced in the same way by all people. Instead, it is a unique constellation of factors that determines how different musical qualities are experienced by different individuals at different times. Therefore, the most suitable musical intervention for a particular client in a particular context is something that still must be individually determined. The relevant considerations include a person's musical history, prior experiences with a type of music, the particular dimensions of the therapeutic relationship, and the relevance of the quality of the music for a particular individual's psychological situation.

For example, consider the case of whole-tone music with its absence of a strong orientation point or qualities of tension and resolution. Some people may find these qualities disturbing while others may find a resonance in them with some aspect of their own experience in the world. The important point is that "the variation in perception does not occur in an arbitrary way and is, in any case, limited to, but not determined by the inherent qualities of the music" (Aigen, 1998, p. 259).

Ansdell's view is of music as an interactive medium where its clinical value is determined by what it is and by what types of experiences of self and other it affords. The processes of music therapy and the benefits it provides to clients are inextricably bound with the nature of music:

> We're trying to articulate a role for music in music therapy in which music is neither a "thing" in and of itself, but neither is it some transparent medium, which merely opens the door onto the personal client-therapist relationship. Music is a 'third person' in the room—and it has its own character . . . it gives its own help to the situation

... Music's work is innately personal ... what it does [is] to forge relatedness between people ... in very specific and subtle ways. Something happens in music therapy which is to do with music's ways.

(Ansdell, in Verney & Ansdell, 2010, p. 22)

In this view, the experience of clients, the interaction between clients and therapists, and the nature of clinical processes and change are highly influenced by the nature of music. Such a perspective leads to the idea that changes in the music that constitute the clinical interaction embody substantive changes relevant to the focus of therapy. However, there are varying views on this claim.

Musical Change and Personal Change

An important ongoing area of discussion in music therapy is the relationship between musical change and personal change. A number of questions characterize this area of investigation: What is the relationship between the client's way of being in music and the concerns that bring the client to therapy? Does change in the way that a client engages with music and with other people in music indicate a broader change in the person's being? Will a productive course of music therapy always be reflected in a change in the client's music? The spectrum of opinions on these issues ranges from the belief that musical change is irrelevant to clinical concerns to a position where it is essential to clinical concerns.

In analytical music therapy, there is a strict separation between musical and nonmusical functioning because

the results of successful music therapy should be looked for in the quality of the patient's life and being, and not in the improvement in the quality of her musical improvisation or performance, unless this is her considered life aim. Indeed her music may be the one factor that shows little or no change at all.

(Priestley, 1994, p. 5)

In this perspective, music is a means through which the therapy occurs. The purpose behind music therapy is to effect change in nonmusical areas and the absence or presence of musical change in the client has no bearing on the effectiveness of the therapy.

A less extreme position is argued by Henk Smeijsters (2005) who asserts that "a client changes when his music changes. If an improvisation offers the client the possibility to express himself in music, then a change in music signifies a personal change" (p. 72). Nonetheless, not all changes in music are equal as, for example, "changes in the ability for jazz, pop/rock, and classical improvisation and changes in musical preferences are not indicative of deeper personal changes" (p. 72). The kind of changes that Smeijsters believes that music therapy should focus on are deep personal changes that are not reflected in musical changes based on enhanced technique or altered preference but are only seen in "a change in music that sounds the psyche" (p. 72).

For example, when a client compulsively uses a single motif or rhythm in an improvisation, the music reflects an underlying psychological compulsion that should be the focus of treatment. Or the pervasive use of slow tempi and soft dynamics can express a depressive state of mind. When a client's music changes to incorporate more variety and flexibility the inner being is assumed to change as well. However, Smeijsters would not conceive of this as the therapist teaching "accelerandi, crescendo, variations, and musical structures" (Smeijsters, 2005, p. 73). Instead the music therapist hears the psyche of the client in the music and introduces only those musical changes that have a specific psychological significance in addressing the client's areas of need.

A related perspective is argued by Garred (2006) who does believe that musical change can indicate personal change but that the crucial criterion is the client's engagement in the music rather than an isolated consideration of the music produced[1]. The idea that musical change is personal change is overly simplistic because "a change in the music may be a sign, but [is] not to be regarded as a unilateral measure in and of itself" (p. 245). In considering the relationship between technique and expression, Garred argues that enhanced technique is no guarantor of personal transformation or enhanced capacity for expression. It is the therapist's task to mediate clinical music-making that serves to enhance "the *making of the person*" (p. 245).

At the opposite pole from the position articulated by Priestley is one presented by Rachel Verney (Verney & Ansdell, 2010) which reflects the belief that making music "is a natural part of what it is to be human" (p. 48). Verney's notion of being musical does not necessarily imply being musically skilled but refers more to "a way of being-in-the-world musically" (p. 48). This musical way of being comprises personal sensitivities and a unique way of being with others. In this perspective, music is not a tool for accessing some nonmusical inner core as is the case with Smeijsters and Garred. The way of being in the world musically is the direct focus of the music therapist's efforts because the way of being musically with others is naturally desired by people.

Ansdell's and Verney's position is based on the idea that music is an interactive medium in which the nature of the interaction is influenced by the nature of music, not in a mechanistic way but in a way guided by the intentionality of the participants as they come to terms with music, themselves in music, and how they can relate to others through specifically musical means. The types of relationships formed through music are, if not unique to music, strongly determined by the fact that they occur in music. Because the nature of the interaction is related to specific attributes of music, the enhanced ways in which clients relate through music are singularly relevant to assessing the value of a course of therapy.

Smeijsters critiques this way of thinking as a rationale for treatment in any of the creative arts therapies. First, he asks, if all of the various arts claim to represent the essence of being human, how can they all be correct? Second, he says that arguments built in this way generally appeal to the fact that the individual art domain claims origins in early human development and thus represents an essential area of human experience. He answers that there is no reason to prioritize an activity merely due to the timing of its appearance in human development, and that the only rationale to employ a medium connected to early development is when the client's disturbance originates in that stage of development and can be treated by returning to it. Smeijsters says that there is no reason to believe that a change in a client's creativity will inevitably change the whole person. The basic deficiency in such a claim is the absence of a mechanism for explaining how this global type of change is achieved.

These different positions reflect fundamentally different notions of what music is, in general and in music therapy. If one considers music primarily as a means for achieving changes in nonmusical dimensions of human life, then it is clear that changes in how a person is able to be musical (in Verney's sense of the term) are not of clinical significance. However, if one possesses a view of music that it exists primarily as a medium for the development of the self, then the extent to which a person becomes engaged in it can be used as a gauge of self-development.

The difference that is articulated by Verney—and that does not appear to be acknowledged by Smeijsters and Garred—is that the enhancement of musicality which she and Ansdell imply is different from the conventional notions of musical skill, technique, or knowledge that other theorists consider when discussing the concept of musical change. The change in the client's ability to be in music in a fluid, flexible, interactive way necessarily involves the transcending of limitations that are otherwise active in the person's life.

Conclusion

Because music therapy takes place through a nonverbal medium that is different from how most individuals spend the predominance of their time, it faces unique challenges in explaining its process and value for clients and communities. As a nonverbal medium, it is a challenge to accurately and completely describe in words what occurs during its clinical processes; as an activity that is a highly specialized one in terms of its relationship to the balance of other human activities, it is a challenge to explain how what occurs in it relates to the balance of human life.

The different perspectives reviewed in this chapter and in Chapter 3 are based upon different strategies and answers to these two primary challenges. Psychoanalytic perspectives such as those articulated by Priestley and Tyson employ an approach developed to explain verbal interactions and thereby adopt a fully-developed theory that nonetheless has a role for nonverbal processes. Rather than endeavoring to explain how changes in a person's musical being relate to changes in other domains, the psychoanalytic perspective dissolves this question by asserting that changes in a client's musicing are not particularly relevant to clinical concerns. The qualities of music that explain its clinical value are either not unique to it, for example, it allows for simultaneous participation of both parties, or are framed within psychoanalytic processes, for example, it facilitates regression. Music is merely a means to a nonmusical goal and because it is considered primarily as a symbolic medium its inherent qualities do not have to be considered in explaining its value.

The middle ground perspective occupied by theorists such as Pavlicevic and Smeijsters acknowledges that changes in a client's music are relevant for music therapy purposes and that music is more than just a symbolic representation. It is a medium in which the world of human emotion is activated and lived. People in a state of expressive musicality are not just symbolizing or communicating their emotions; they are becoming them, living in them. Thus, some of the inherent qualities of music as forms of emotional expression are relevant clinically. And it is this stance of moving beyond the idea that music symbolizes emotions, to one where music embodies emotions, that provides the link between musical experience and more generalized areas of human functioning. This perspective does stop short of articulating a belief in the essential continuity of clinical and nonclinical musicing experiences and tends to use other types of psychological theory in order to establish the value of musicing through verbal means. In Smeijsters's case, for example, it is the theories of developmental psychologist Daniel Stern that provide this link.

The music-based ideas of authors such as Aigen, Ansdell, and Verney and the socio-cultural focuses of Stige and Rolvsjord take a fundamentally different approach to answering these questions. First, by arguing that the uses of music in therapy are continuous with those uses outside of therapy, entire domains of theory from areas such as musicology, ethnomusicology, the psychology of music, and the sociology of music become available for use by music therapists, thus helping to address the issue of translating musical experience into verbal theory. This was the reason, for example, why the literature on music therapy and identity could be legitimately applied to clinical music therapy situations.

The continuity of clinical and nonclinical engagement with music also means that the rationale for providing music to individuals with disabilities does not have to be based upon or limited to a remediation of those disabilities. Accepting this continuity means that music provides to these individuals the same things that it provides to other people, and the same rationales used to devote societal resources to providing music in nonclinical settings can be used to provide it in clinical settings. Thus the problem of the generalization of musicing functioning to other areas is, if not dissolved, at least lessened.

Chapter 5 extensively explores the concept of goals in music therapy in relation to this fundamental difference of opinion. Is the use of music in music therapy continuous with its uses in nonclinical domains, thus supporting a conception of it as a medium of experience whose benefits are self-justifying? Or is the music in music therapy specialized in what it affords, thus supporting a conception of it as a means toward nonmusical ends? The way that different theorists in music therapy consider this issue provides perhaps one of the starkest contrasts in music therapy theory.

Note

1. The idea that the client's engagement with the music is of the utmost importance originated in and was central to the development of Nordoff-Robbins music therapy.

5

THE MEDIUM OF MUSIC AND CLINICAL GOALS

The nature of the process of music therapy is a contested area with three central issues. First, is music in music therapy primarily a medium of experience with its own intrinsic benefits or is it primarily a means of accomplishing nonmusical therapy goals in the areas of emotional, cognitive, social and motor functioning? Second, are the processes of clinical and nonclinical musicing different in fundamental ways or are they essentially the same? Third, is music therapy fundamentally an artistic or a nonartistic process? The first issue is taken up in the present chapter; the second two issues are addressed in Chapter 6.

There is a circular aspect to one's stance on these issues stemming from whether one considers oneself to be a musician doing therapy or a therapist using music. A musician doing therapy is more apt to consider the medium as important, to look at aspects of music that make music therapy effective, to consider the benefits that lie within the medium of experience, and to focus on providing an eminently musical experience to clients. A therapist doing music is more apt to look at the music as a tool to achieve nonmusical goals, to consider clinical and nonclinical music as fundamentally different, and to consider music therapy as fundamentally a clinical process rather than an artistic one. Yet rather than yielding to the judgment that there are no criteria for making a determination between these two perspectives, it is possible to examine the effects of these positions on clients, the most important stakeholders in this discussion, and consider which position best serves them.

Music as a Medium or as a "Mere" Means in Music Therapy

The issue of whether music in music therapy is more accurately considered a medium of experience or a means to nonmusical ends was first discussed by the present author in an examination of the theory underlying Nordoff-Robbins music therapy (Aigen, 1995b). I began from the premise that in reflecting on what people gain from music therapy and what makes it work, we must focus on qualities of music that are not necessarily qualities of sound. The only rationale for a true *music* therapy is that music possesses qualities and clinical potentials not possessed by mere sound. Because it is the realm of aesthetic experience that differentiates music from sound, this is where music therapists should look for the efficacy of music therapy.

Aesthetic experience is not only relevant to art. In the domain of philosophy, aesthetics is concerned with issues of beauty, whether this is found in a humanly-created object or in the natural world. Yet much of the thinking over the past 100 years has focused on lessening the distinction between the artwork as a humanly-created artifact and the artwork as something that can be "found"—whether in nature or constructed by humans—and converted to a work of art by its contextualization. A musical composition, such as the oft-cited *4'33"* by John Cage (a piece that is comprised solely of the incidental sounds that occur in the concert hall during its duration), or the monochromatic blue square paintings of Yves Klein, invite the audience to learn to have an aesthetic experience within the sounds and sights of daily life outside the concert hall or museum.

Regardless of where one stands on this issue, and regardless of whether one's definition of music refers to attributes of sound or to psychological processes, aesthetic considerations are relevant in defining music. Music therapists of different philosophical positions on the nature of music could all agree on the importance of aesthetics in determining the "musical-ness" of something, without agreeing on whether the aesthetic elements are properties of the sound entity, something constructed by the listener, or something that only arises within the interaction of sound phenomena and human psychological processes. Moreover, aesthetics could still be considered relevant clinically, even if one acknowledges the centrality of cultural or other social factors in discussing aesthetics.

If music therapy experiences are aesthetic ones for clients, then a challenge for music therapy theorists is to establish connections between aesthetic experience and common music therapy goals such as enhancing "personality development, cognitive functioning, and social interaction" (Aigen, 1995b, p. 237). The agenda underlying John Dewey's (1934) aesthetic theory is remarkably similar: "To restore continuity between the refined and intensified forms of experience that are works of art and the everyday events, doings, and sufferings that . . . constitute experience" (p. 3). In Dewey's view, aesthetic experience has a common ground with ordinary, non-aesthetic experience because the aesthetic aspects of works of art function to "idealize qualities found in common experience" (p. 11).

The fact that Dewey's agenda so closely models the music therapist's task makes it relevant to music therapy. The conventional wisdom in music therapy differentiates clinical from nonclinical musicing. While the former activity must have some nonmusical clinical goal as its purpose, the latter one can be engaged in for its own sake. However, this distinction is only tenable if one accepts that "music making for its own sake is the correct characterization of music experienced for its aesthetic qualities" (Aigen, 1995b, p. 238). For Dewey, this was not correct "because music appreciated for its aesthetic qualities is a music connected to the basic processes of life and nature. Its end is contained in the way in which it serves to enrich the life of listener and performer alike through its capacity to add meaning to life" (p. 238).

It is possible to use music solely as a tool to a nonmusical end; consider how it is used in advertising. However, when music is used to achieve an aesthetic experience, it is more accurate to consider it as a *medium* as Dewey uses the term. For Dewey, there are two types of means in human activity: those where the goals are external to the activity and those where the outcome is incorporated into the activity. In traveling to get somewhere, our trip is a tool or a mere means to accomplish the movement of our bodies from one location to another; in traveling for its inherent pleasure such as hiking in the mountains, the trip becomes a medium, a special kind of means, where the purpose of undertaking it is contained within the activity doing of it. When traveling is a mere means we would gladly do without it if our goal of being transported from one location to another could be otherwise accomplished; when traveling is a medium of experience, we would not do without the trip because its purpose is inextricably bound with the activity of engaging in it.

It should be unproblematic to claim that all music activities are undertaken for some reason, for some purpose. If the idea of music "for its own sake" is another way of saying "for no reason" then this is clearly not a description of nonclinical music and this criterion cannot be used to distinguish between the two types of musicing contexts. What is most likely meant by theorists who advocate that music "for its own sake" describes nonclinical music is that musicing undertaken in nonclinical contexts is done for the appreciation of what is happening while the music is present rather than for any result that endures once the musicing has ended. They are arguing that the only legitimate description of music in music therapy must be that it is done for what is present after the music ends—in other words, what is accomplished through the musical experience—rather than for what occurs during the time the music is present. It then falls to those who believe that music in music therapy is more accurately described as a medium to articulate how what occurs while people are musicing represents legitimate focuses of therapy.

These considerations directly apply to thinking about the rationale for music therapy and the different positions on what constitutes legitimate goals and areas of benefit for music therapy clients. On one side is the conventional thinking in which music is a mere means useful toward a whole host of nonmusical ends. The nature of the musical experience is essentially irrelevant in this mode of understanding because it is not important *as* music; it is only important to the extent that it facilitates the achievement of a nonmusical goal. The goals of music therapy in this view are the same as the goals of any other type of therapy. If a better, quicker, or more efficacious tool can be found toward the nonmusical end, then there is no rationale for the provision of music therapy. This is because the music is merely a tool for an extrinsic purpose.

However, if music enriches human life in unique ways, and if this enrichment is considered to be a legitimate focus of the work of music therapists, then what music therapy provides to people is different from that of other therapies. It provides experiences of music, self, others, and community, within music, that are essential to well-being and that are uniquely musical. The goals of music therapy are unique in this view. They stem from naturalistic modes of relating to music on the parts of clients (construed broadly as individuals or communities of various types and sizes), and music therapy cannot be replaced by other, more effective therapeutic modalities because none of them provide opportunities for musicing in the way that music therapists do. When the aesthetic dimension is valued, music is considered a medium of experience. In Dewey's sense of the term, it is an activity whose goal is embodied within it.

The determination about whether music is being used as a (mere) means or a medium is not an absolute one but is instead dependent upon one's position in relation to the process of music therapy. "In considering whether music is a means or medium in a music therapy setting, one has to specify *for whom* the determination is being made" (Aigen, 2005a, p. 60). Regardless of the theoretical position held by their therapists, a large percentage of clients in music therapy (just how large is an unanswered empirical question) are motivated primarily by the desire to engage in music: this is their goal in participating in music therapy. A strong argument can be made for privileging the client's perspective for ethical, pragmatic, and conceptual reasons. First, to engage in ethical practice, it is important to conform one's activities as a therapist as close as possible to the client's interests, desires, needs and motivations. Second, pragmatically speaking, therapists will be most effective when their perspectives on clinical processes are congruent with those of clients. Third, on a purely conceptual level, the most powerful theory can be constructed when it reflects as closely as possible the phenomena that one wishes to explain. For example, if one wishes to understand how children with autism or adults with mental illness can circumvent communicative and social barriers while engaged in music therapy, it would seem that their perspectives on the nature of their experience should figure prominently in the construction of theory, something that has not been examined in the research literature.

Primary and Secondary Goals in Music Therapy

Another crucial question that has not been explored extensively is how the musical experience is construed by therapists: What are therapists thinking about when they are creating music with their clients? How does the presence of specific nonmusical goals—present on treatment plans that many music therapists employ—affect the quality of their musicing and of the musical therapeutic relationship? Many nonmusical goals are present within musical interactions and interventions, but the crucial question is whether these nonmusical goals are foremost in the therapist's mind at the moment of musical creation, or whether they are added as post-hoc explanations to justify why a particular musical interaction with a client was of clinical benefit.

The research study by the present author discussed previously does explore this issue. In a detailed case study of improvisational music therapy within the pop styles of rock, blues and jazz with a 27-year-old developmentally impaired young man (Aigen, 2005c), the main research finding concerned the clinical value of working within the conventions of various popular musical styles. For the client in this study, there were many gains in the areas of responsiveness, independence, and impulse control. These were most apparent within various style characteristics such as engaging in antiphonal dialogues in jazz ("trading fours" with the client on a drum set and the therapists playing piano and bass) or the use of rhythmic stops such as occurs during the first four measures of the instrumental breaks on a song such as Chuck Berry's *Johnny B. Goode*.

The conventional way of considering the clinical work was that in introducing stops and starts in the music the therapists were working on impulse control and client initiative and responsiveness. The alternative perspective in this study was that the therapy team was "playing jazz, rock or country music in a stylistically appropriate way" (Aigen, 2005c, p. 47), so when the client became able to make predictable stops in the music, "the heightened impulse control came about as a secondary consequence of his involvement in making music" (p. 47). The added benefit is that the therapists conform to the client's perspective that they are all present in order to make music rather than to undergo a clinical process where one party seeks to change another. The client is better able to abide the challenges posed by the musical interaction because he experiences them not as arbitrary decisions imposed by the therapists but as depersonalized challenges that are present in the music. The desire to play stylistically appropriate music helps the client to overcome his limitations without personalizing the challenge in the form of his therapists, something that would have mobilized his pervasive resistiveness.

A vitally important distinction made here is between primary and secondary benefits. In this example, the primary clinical focus—and the primary value of the experience for the client—is the provision of a live, interactive, improvisational band in which the client experiences all of the same benefits of musical interaction that are available to participants who engage in such activities outside of music therapy: musical flow and transcendence, experiencing oneself as a source of aesthetic creation, being in the moment, bonding with peers, experiences of *communitas*, and participating in one's culture through its musical embodiment in stylistically characteristic grooves.

For the client in this study—with severe motor, cognitive, and communicative impairments —the ability to improvise in a sustained, fluid, and responsive manner with his therapists involved circumventing many areas of disability. For example, while he could not focus on a task in an occupational workshop for more than a few seconds at a time, in music therapy he could sustain interactive musicing for many minutes on end. This enhanced focusing was only one of a large number of achievements which he was able to make while in music. Other areas include enhanced motor coordination, tolerating close interpersonal contact, and engaging in a wide range of unpredictable musical events when such unpredictability was extraordinarily disturbing to him in other milieus.

But for the client and the therapists in this work, these nonmusical benefits were not the primary focus. They emerged as a result of the deep involvement in music. They did not provide the orientation for the therapists' efforts nor did they function as the client's motivation. They are examples of how clients who become deeply involved in a personalized musicing experience are able to manifest healthier and more fully-functioning aspects of their being when they are engaged in music. They arise as a secondary consequence of the more primary involvement in music as a medium.

One perspective on this situation that typifies more conventional thinking in music therapy is that the nonmusical goal is the real therapy and the involvement in music is merely an inducement to the client to do something that is challenging and that may otherwise be resisted. In this perspective, the client is fooled into thinking the therapy is in the music when it is really in the nonmusical achievement. Such a view comports well with the thinking of music therapy as essentially a nonartistic, health-related practice based upon the precepts of a medical model. And it might also comport well with the institutional and conceptual frameworks within which music therapists frequently work. However, it is coming into increasing conflict with other contemporary values and movements as embodied in disability theory, consumerism in health care, resource-oriented and empowerment philosophies, community music therapy, and music-centered thinking. And paradoxically, one possibility is that the secondary benefits in the areas of affect, cognition, and motor function are actually better achieved when they are not the direct focus of the therapist's efforts. In other words, there is a plausible argument that clients become more deeply involved in the musicing when this involvement constitutes the therapist's primary focus. And when this deeper involvement occurs, greater secondary gains in the nonmusical areas are achieved.

In exploring the means-medium issue, Rudy Garred (2006) has questioned "whether a strictly and exclusively instrumental perspective" where music is considered as a means toward some other end "actually brings out all the qualities of music as a therapeutic medium" (p. 79). When it is considered in this way, the particular qualities of music *as music* are not of interest because they are not connected to the outcomes they bring about. Of course, certain qualities are relevant, such as when the tempo of music is relevant to gait training. But the music and the experience it gives rise to as a whole are not considered relevant.

Garred raises an important question: If a person does not engage with the inherent qualities of music, will that person gain the full benefit that should follow? A person joining a musical ensemble to enhance social engagement would not do so without having an inherent interest in playing music with other people. One could join an ensemble and then receive social benefits as a result, or as a secondary consequence of the primary interest in musicing. However, unless a person has an inherent interest in communal musicing, the gains associated with it are not likely to accrue. Garred goes on to say that most clients in music therapy will have a primary motivation that is intimately connected to the music itself. This observation becomes an important assumption in building music therapy theory: without the primary connection to music, none of the secondary benefits will follow.

Garred uses the philosophy of Martin Buber as a foundation. He argues that when music is considered purely as an instrumental "It," it is unavoidable to transfer this mode of thinking to clients. In other words, if music is considered to be merely a mechanical tool without inherent qualities, clients are related to as if they are an "it" as well, rather than as willful, conscious, and empowered beings. They become something that can be acted upon by an "it" and their own desires, will, and experience become isolated from the therapist's consideration as to what is best for them. In other words, buying into the notion of music as a mere tool inevitably leads to a dehumanized music therapy practice.

The means–ends issue is also addressed by Gary Ansdell (1995) who explores it from within the perspective of a client who asked him directly "What exactly are we doing here? Are we just making music?" Although admitting that the question would be answered differently by other music therapists, Ansdell concludes that the answer to the client is *yes*, although the implications of the answer are profound as "just making music" covers an enormously rich world of musical experience "from the light hearted to the profound; the entertaining to the life-saving" (Ansdell, p. 221).

Ansdell (1995) frames the issue as "whether music-making is an end in itself or . . . a means to other, therapeutically defined ends" (p. 221). He identifies music psychotherapy "where music-making is explicitly intended to facilitate verbal therapeutic processes" as an approach that contrasts with his in its focus on the extra-musical. Ansdell goes on to say that his focus on "just making music" is not without therapeutic aims as the distinction he is discussing is not an absolute one and relates more to the "emphasis as to where the central locus of the therapy is seen to be" (p. 222).

He also discusses the distinctions between an art and a craft and observes that the goal of a craft dictates its conduct whereas the conduct of art is not governed by any external purpose. The implication is that to the extent that one is focused on the external end (the use to which the craft object is put or the nonmusical clinical goal) the actual conduct of the art will suffer. And, as Garred noted, if the quality of the music suffers, and if the music is the client's primary motivation, then the secondary benefits (the areas of nonmusical growth) will suffer. The paradoxical result is that focusing on nonmusical goals in music therapy inhibits their realization.

Speaking from a music-based perspective, Rachel Verney articulates how her stance as a therapist "is to be present with that person and listening this intently can be a very present-inducing thing—for therapist and client. I aim to be in the here and now as fully as I can . . . The whole point of music is to pull us into the NOW!" (Verney & Ansdell, 2010, p. 8). In this view, music therapy practice consists of a hierarchy or matrix of goals. At the most fundamental level are a set of goals that reflect basic human needs: to be in the now, to experience beauty, to experience transcendence, and to connect with others—just to mention a few examples. These fundamental conditions of musicing form the basis for specific functional goals in areas such as communication, affect, and social and motor functioning.

The difference among music therapy theorists in this regard relates to what level of the process they are focusing upon, both in the moment with their clients and in the post-hoc reflections apparent in theoretical writings. Theorists that are more music-based will focus on the existential, general, non-operationalized goals because they reflect the therapists' consciousness about the process and what they think is of greater value for their clients. Theorists that are more "clinical"—in the sense that for either pragmatic or conceptual reasons they hew closer to the notion that the clinical must be nonmusical—will focus on more specifically articulated functional goals. The present author's work (Aigen, 2005a) is an example of the former approach. In it, the way that people engage with music to meet universal needs for purpose and meaning through personal expression and communal connections are emphasized. The work of Michael Thaut (2008) exemplifies the latter approach, particularly in the way that he critiques approaches oriented toward enhancing well-being in favor of specific goals in the areas of "motor therapy, speech rehabilitation, and memory and attention training" (p. 115).

In music-based approaches, musical goals are clinical goals and this stance is warranted when it "dovetails with the client's agenda, whether this is stated explicitly by the client or is conveyed implicitly by the client's actions, affect, or expression" (Aigen, 2005a, p. 93). When the primary agenda in music therapy is to develop and enhance the client's capacity for musical expression and experience, there may be changes in nonmusical areas as well. As was stated at the outset of the present discussion, though, these changes are secondary consequences of the primary, musical focus. They accompany the primary clinical process but are not the things that justify it.

Underlying this perspective is the idea that music enriches human life in a unique and necessary way. When clients are brought into contact with music in a way where the intention is the enrichment of their lives, they may experience changes in their personality, modes of relating to others and ability to express themselves in other domains. Yet this does not change the fact that it is primarily the client's "capacity for musical acting, feeling, thinking, and being" that orients the therapist's efforts and provides the measure of their outcome (Aigen, 2005a, p. 94).

Justifying Music Therapy on Musical Grounds

Whether or not music therapy can or should be justified on musical bases remains a highly potent issue. Supporters will argue that this stance conforms more closely to the wishes of clients, that it represents a more accepting and pluralistic viewpoint, and that it will advance the maturity of the discipline. It is the only way to build indigenous theory stemming from the specifics of music, and this is necessary to help music therapy survive because it is the only way to articulate the uniqueness of what music therapy accomplishes.

Theorists who oppose this notion argue that the only way for music therapy to survive is to adopt the explanatory mechanisms, standards, and procedures of the health-related contexts and settings in which music therapy is offered. They say that the uniqueness of music therapy requires nonmusical goals and rationales, otherwise music therapy runs the risk of being subsumed to music education, enrichment, or performance.

Assuming for the moment that music therapy achieves both kinds of goals—the primary ones involved in purely musical processes and the secondary ones that come about as an indirect consequence of the music—a fascinating question is what stance will best produce gains of the secondary type? As Ansdell, Verney, Garred, and the present author all argue, even if one does not want to admit the legitimacy of the primary goals, it is still possible that the secondary goals are best achieved by a therapist framework and discourse that puts the primary focus on music-making.

The difference between the two basic positions in music therapy is whether or not it is possible, or even desirable, to develop a musical justification for music therapy that has as its foundation the ability to provide access to musicing for people who cannot accomplish this on their own. To fully grasp the significance of the argument, it is helpful to consider some other domains—such as music education and music appreciation—in which music is provided by society.

Music education exists because it is a benefit to society to have music in it. Without music education there would be no music performance, whether in concerts, rituals, religious celebrations, or sporting events. Education in music performance and composition exists primarily to provide music in society, not to benefit the musicians themselves, the students in these classes or lessons. In other words, music programs in schools do provide jobs for musicians and enjoyment to individuals learning to play instruments, but these benefits to the participants in music education and performance programs are incidental, secondary benefits, and problems arise when people attempt to justify the presence of music education for the musicians (such as in claiming that they improve nonmusical academic performance) rather than for society as a whole. The main point is that in music performance education, people are brought in to active engagement with music-making to bring benefit elsewhere.

In contrast, in music appreciation, society has judged that there is value in its members having a relationship to music and being able to engage with it in an educated way. There may be secondary benefits (educated music lovers provide more work for musicians) but the primary benefit is for the individuals in the classes, something that contrasts with music performance. In music appreciation or general music, the direct participants are the primary beneficiaries.

Arguments for the presence of both areas of music are misguided when they appeal primarily to what are secondary benefits. Listening to Mozart may promote the acquisition of math skills—although most systematic inquiries into this issue have thrown serious doubt on such a claim—but an hour of math tutoring will invariably have a better effect on math scores than will an hour of Mozart.

Music therapy combines elements of both domains in a unique way. As in music performance education, the direct participants are engaged as active music-makers—they are brought into active states of musicing; and as in music appreciation (general music), the primary benefits accrue directly to the participants rather than to society as a whole.

In the nonclinical domain, society has judged that there is value in providing music to itself by training musicians and supporting the activity of composers and in helping its members to access and develop a relationship to music. The central question as it pertains to music therapy is this: Can music therapy be justified on the basis that it provides music to many marginalized individuals who need the special adaptations that music therapists can provide in order to have a relationship to music? Or, must the justification for music therapy be based upon the fact that it achieves functional goals in other areas? The former position erases boundaries between individuals with and without disabilities because it says that people with disabilities deserve a relationship to music and that they gain the same thing from music that people without disabilities do. The latter position maintains divisions—and the distinction between disabled and nondisabled people that is increasingly critiqued as artificial and discriminatory—through the implication that people with disabilities must have their access to music based upon nonmusical criteria that are different from other members of society.

There really is no way to escape the influence of values in answering questions such as what music therapy does for people, what benefits it provides, and what considerations explain these benefits. In one sense, all the answers are correct, or at least they are not incompatible. For example, a person losing motor function due to a stroke may find that range of motion is increased from engagement in music therapy and may also find that musical experiences in music therapy provide social and communicative benefits unique to music, whether or not these benefits are measurable through any nonmusical means. So, the pluralist argument goes, why not just acknowledge that all types of benefits accrue because of music therapy. And perhaps the uniquely musical benefits can be quantified, say through a quality of life scale or some similar assessment device.

However, the question of whether to focus on motor function or intrinsic musical rewards belongs to quite separate belief systems with contrasting precepts on the proper role of the therapist and on the nature of appropriate activities to undertake in music therapy. The differing positions also require particular clinical-musical skills with quite different courses of education and training. In actual practice, it is not so easy for individual practitioners (or training programs, for that matter) to practice in such a globalized, pluralistic way.

Moreover, if a therapist focuses on the quite different approaches of either increasing range of motion or providing intrinsically gratifying musical experiences this will dictate entirely different ways of relating to clients. In reality, it is not possible to pursue both agendas simultaneously. For clinicians operating within a medical model where the therapist is in an authoritative position in terms of knowing what is best for the client and how to best structure the therapy time, there is perhaps no dilemma. For this type of practitioner, the therapist has the obligation to only work toward those goals and through those activities that empirical research has determined will be successful.

But the situation is just not that simple. Again, let us contrast the option of working on range of motion versus working toward providing in-the-moment, intrinsically gratifying, musical experiences. One option would be to ask clients what their preference is and allow this to be the determining factor. The medical model would seem to preclude this approach because clients may opt for focuses whose outcomes would not be guaranteed or measurable in quantitative terms. In contrast, a practitioner whose value system requires the empowerment of clients must of necessity include clients in the determination of the direction of therapy. What should be clear is that both choices are value-laden ones. The decision of whether, and in what way to include client preferences is made by both therapists, even if the choice is to not include the client in such planning.

There are other factors that militate against a more pluralistic approach. Consider a situation where range of motion has been demonstrated to be improved by a particular percentage through implementing a particular mechanical music therapy intervention. It still may not be possible to determine how this enhanced range of motion will transfer into any improvement in the client's quality of life, if the amount of time and effort spent in acquiring the benefit will be considered worth the effort, and if the achievement of the outcome in range of motion would be something that would be more valued by the client than would the intrinsically gratifying musical experiences that another therapist could choose to offer. Thus, in arguing that decisions such as these should be made by the client, it is clear that it is not possible for clients to possess the information required to make a truly informed decision.

Another important issue is how to evaluate the effectiveness of the intrinsically musical experience in therapy. Because its value is self-contained, no external measure can really do it justice. It can best be evaluated by the fact that clients choose it when offered, maintain participation in it on an ongoing basis, and overcome all types of cognitive, emotional, and physical limitations to make it happen. It could be argued that this way of working should be able to be evaluated much as any other approach could. For example, a quality of life scale could be administered that evaluates how rewarding the experiences have been for clients, how much they value it, and how much their lives in general have changed as a result of the experiences.

Assuming for the moment that such self-report was considered a valid tool, this type of evaluation still bears further examination. I would like to ask the reader to perform a thought experiment that involves completing such a questionnaire based upon your own nonclinical experiences with music. Whatever score you achieve, it is possible that there may be other types of human activities you have engaged in that would produce similar or even higher scores on such an inventory. Does that mean that you would willingly give up music for the other activities? I imagine that most readers would answer in the negative because the idea is that musical experience, being unique unto itself, is not the same as any other type of human experience. The evaluation tool can never capture the true value in which one holds music because it is applying thinking suited to a mere means to a medium of experience where the logic of means and ends is different. The only way to determine the value of the intrinsically musical type of music therapy is by the affinity for it and commitment to it demonstrated by participants.

While Garred (2006) is highly sympathetic to music-based thinking, he also believes that it is deficient in some regards. Perhaps, then, his approach represents a type of third way or middle ground between the two approaches. He believes that there are important aspects of music therapy process for which music-centered thinking cannot account and the same is true of psychodynamic-based music therapy theories. Garred's theory, which is similar to Ansdell's as it is also based on Buber's notion of *dialogue* and the type of interaction it implies, is positioned between the two extremes of these other theories as it offers a more comprehensive portrait of clinical processes than can be provided by either one alone.

The fact that music therapy is defined by the medium through which the therapy occurs —rather than its targeted area of change—suggests that the "qualities of the medium itself" (Garred, 2006, p. 2) are therapeutic and therefore explanation in music therapy should be built upon these qualities. However, equally important to Garred is the interpersonal dimension of music therapy processes. In Garred's view, "existing music-based theory does not—and actually can not, because of its philosophical foundation—give adequate attention to this aspect of the process, and existing psychodynamic based theory can not give adequate attention to the musical bases of practice" (Aigen, 2006, p. 48). For Garred, conceptions of music that consider it either as a creative product or as an instrumental means to a nonmusical end are not adequate for portraying how music actually functions in therapy.

Garred observes that music is not merely an alternative language employed in therapy. The qualities of the medium of music attract the user's attention in a way that words in psychotherapy do not. This is another reason why the qualities of the medium are relevant to understanding the process of the therapy. It also justifies a role for aesthetics in clinical theory, although, again this role is not exclusive or even primary but one that exists alongside the interpersonal relationships of therapy.

Garred believes that a more extreme music-based position is not sufficiently clinical in scope and that the claim of similarities between clinical and nonclinical musicing is overstated in music-centered theory. The crucial difference is the orientation toward therapy goals. According to Garred, there is a need to present a theory of music therapy that takes music seriously as a medium but that is oriented equally to the goals of music therapy. The fact that music therapy is oriented to the betterment of the client means that theories of art cannot be applied to music therapy.

All of the writers who argue for music-based theory where primacy is given to the qualities of the medium have the challenge of connecting musical experience to the clinical focus that defines music therapy. To the extent that one emphasizes engagement with the medium of music as being essential to music therapy, one simultaneously creates difficulties in differentiating the world of nonclinical music from clinical music-making. The issue is that in saying that "its qualities are a necessary feature of the clinical benefits it brings" one becomes committed to the position "that it is not used for an instrumental purpose outside itself" (Aigen, 2006, p. 54).

Garred does not address this problem adequately because he is committed to the position that clinical and nonclinical musicing are fundamentally different. He wants to create medium-based theory while maintaining the fundamental difference between clinical and nonclinical music.

When he says, "music is a medium for therapy" what is he actually saying? It appears that his response still relegates music to being an instrumental means. In music therapy, Garred (2006) acknowledges that music's "own qualities are adhered to, but for another end than itself—namely, the betterment, in some way, of the client" (p. 96). But the focus on "another end than itself" contradicts the notion that in engaging with music as a medium one is considering it for itself rather than for an extrinsic purpose. It is not clear that Garred's theory accomplishes the task of describing how one can become "fully engaged with a medium as a medium where the outcome is neither controlled nor directed by any extrinsic agenda" (Aigen, 2006, p. 54).

Some aspects of Garred's argument have to give. If the therapeutic encounter with music relies on the qualities of the medium itself, then either the music is intrinsically therapeutic (which Garred does not want to say in an effort to distinguish clinical and nonclinical music) or the music is being used for therapeutic, that is, nonmusical, ends.

One option developed by the present author (Aigen, 2005a) employs David Elliott's (1995) ideas about the intrinsic value of music. Elliott argues that when people engage with music and the rationale is not a "tangible, biological, or other material reward, then we are engaging with music for the purpose of self-development and this is what we mean by saying 'for its own sake'" (Aigen, 2006, p. 54). In Elliot's view, music exists to promote the development of the self. When individuals engage with music to experience its intrinsic qualities they are of necessity engaged in a process that promotes the betterment of the self. This perspective is an integrative one that brings together the goals of music education and music therapy with the general uses of music in society.

This exploration into the nature of music therapy process and the question of whether the music is more accurately considered a tool to a nonmusical end or a medium of experience with unique, musical benefits does turn on whether or not one believes that music in music therapy functions in a way that is similar to nonclinical applications or fundamentally different from such applications. It is this question that constitutes the focus of Chapter 6.

6

THE RELATIONSHIP BETWEEN CLINICAL AND NONCLINCAL MUSIC

Are Clinical and Nonclinical Music Essentially the Same or Different?

Theorists in music therapy disagree about whether or not there are fundamental differences between music in music therapy and other forms of music. Aside from the intrinsic interest of the question, it is also important for a very practical reason. If the music and musical experiences had by clients in music therapy are similar to those in nonclinical settings, theory from areas such as the sociology of music and musicology can be tentatively applied in music therapy. If the two domains of musical experience are fundamentally different, then theory from other disciplines becomes less relevant to music therapy.

The conventional wisdom in music therapy that music is a means to nonmusical ends supports the notion that clinical and nonclinical music have fundamental differences. The reasoning is that nonclinical music is not meant to be heard, played, or otherwise appreciated as music; it takes the form that it does based on its clinical function. Moreover, these clinical functions can be heard in the music and educated listeners can discern clinical from nonclinical music.

On the other hand, advocating for the notion of music as a medium relies on the continuities between clinical and nonclinical music. In this position, music therapy is most effective when clients are having an essentially musical experience. The necessity for music therapy to be musical in character—and for music in music therapy to be based upon certain considerations that are not uniquely clinical such as style characteristics, and melodic and harmonic patterns and structures—works to dissolve the fundamental differences between clinical and non-clinical music.

A few general observations about music therapy will be helpful before delving more deeply into the nuances of this issue. First, a large percentage of music therapy applications involve music composed outside of clinical contexts, such as popular and traditional songs of all types and classical music compositions. Because the predominance of music used in music therapy originates in nonclinical contexts, it seems inarguable that there is a large area of overlap between the two areas. If there are fundamental differences between the clinical and nonclinical engagement with music, it falls to theorists wishing to emphasize the differences between the two areas to explain why music originating in nonclinical contexts is so useful in therapy.

Consider guided imagery and music (GIM) (Bonny, 2002), an approach in which clients undergo a relaxation-focusing induction into an altered state of consciousness and then listen to recorded programs of classical music while being accompanied by a guide (therapist) who listens to the client's recounting of imagery and sensations while providing verbal and other interventions to support the experience. This method is the most highly developed form of receptive music therapy and engages fundamental aspects of a person's psyche, thus aiming at producing significant personal change and insight.

And yet this most powerful of music therapy methods uses music composed to be heard as music, not for any clinical purposes. Moreover, GIM practitioners emphasize that not all performances of a composition are equal for use in therapy. Only those recordings of the highest aesthetic value that reflect a deep understanding of the piece on the part of the conductor and musicians work well for GIM purposes. What is not clear, then, is if there is a fundamental difference between clinical and nonclinical music and musical experience, why would the nonclinical criterion of aesthetic value be so important in determining the clinical value of a composition? And more generally, if the aesthetic qualities of the medium of music are relevant in any clinical sense, does not this support the idea that clinical and nonclinical music are more similar than they are different?

There are two related questions here that are often conflated but which warrant being teased apart, one that focuses on the music and one that focuses on the experience of music. First, is there any fundamental difference between clinical and nonclinical music that can be discerned from either a score or from listening to a recording? Second, is the experience of the music had by clients in music therapy fundamentally different from the experience of people engaged with music outside of a clinical application? The former issue focuses on the music as a product or artifact; the latter question focuses on the experience of the individual for whom the music is being created.

Considerations on Clinical and Nonclinical Improvisation

Putting aside for the moment the question as it applies to composed music, the issue is less problematically framed in relation to improvisation. In this case, music is being created specifically in a therapy context, so the question is more easily explored. Brown and Pavlicevic (1996) undertook an empirical investigation into this issue. They framed their focus as exploring "the distinction between purely musical improvisation (or improvisation as art-form) and clinical improvisation (or improvisation as therapy)" (p. 397). Moreover, they acknowledge their predetermined belief in this distinction as necessary to support the idea that the skills possessed by music therapists "go beyond the purely musical" (p. 398). In other words, if there is no distinction between clinical and nonclinical music, the claim of a special expertise on the part of music therapists can be challenged and, by extension, so does the legitimacy of the profession.

The authors assert that the differences between the two types of improvisation do not result merely from how they are perceived and described but because there are intrinsic structural differences between them. They also consider Carolyn Kenny's idea that the process of therapy may possess its own type of beauty and conclude that

> the fluid and highly intimate engagement between therapist and client may, therefore, also be an event with a particular aesthetic quality, so that the idea of using art as a

therapeutic medium can perhaps be extended to seeing the therapeutic process itself as an artform—a clinical artform.

(Brown & Pavlicevic, 1996, p. 399)

However, neither the fact that the music of music therapy can possess a clinical aesthetic, nor the possibility that the resulting music can be listened to as an art form should be used to minimize the fundamental difference between clinical and nonclinical improvisation.

The research questions and design in this study address both of the issues described above. The first question considers whether or not there is a difference in the participant's experience of music-making when that individual functions either as a therapist or a client compared to when that individual is functioning as a musician. The second question asks if there is a difference in the music between clinical and nonclinical improvisation sessions as determined by third-party listeners who are not present in the sessions. In the design, the two co-researchers created three duo improvisations: in the first two, they each played either a therapist's role or a client's role and in the third they dropped these roles and played only as fellow musicians. The recordings of the three improvisations were analyzed by the two researchers and by a panel. They conclude that "there is a difference between music-making that is geared simply to playing music with someone else and therapeutic improvisation" (Brown & Pavlicevic, 1996, p. 404).

Although Brown and Pavlicevic can be commended for being open about their commitment to particular answers to the two research questions, this fact does throw doubt upon their conclusions. It is reasonable to assume that they have come to their points of view because of a difference in their own way of musicing when they are alternately clients, therapists, or playing in a nonclinical setting. Thus, their results might be nothing more than a reflection of their own prior commitments. However, putting aside the methodological criticism, it is still possible to reflect upon what such findings—had they been arrived at in a methodologically sound way—would have to say about the fundamental issue under discussion.

Both Brown and Pavlicevic (1996) and Pavlicevic (1997) argue that what makes music therapy improvisations unique and different from nonclinical music is that they are based on interactive and communicative considerations rather than purely musical ones. They claim that in music therapy improvisations it is possible to hear how the music traces the relational contours between the players. While in music therapy the demands of interpersonal relating determine the flow and structure of the music, in nonclinical improvisation the development of the music follows musical considerations rather than interpersonal ones.

One factor underlying the Brown-Pavlicevic argument—although not made explicit by them—is that their frame of reference for nonclinical improvisation may not include popular styles such as rock and jazz, as indicated by their references to "art music" or music as "artform." Improvisation in jazz in particular has been revealed to involve interpersonal communication to a large extent. Studies by Berliner (1994), Hodson (2007), and Monson (1996) demonstrate the interactional patterns that occur in jazz and these patterns have been recently applied to music therapy (Aigen, 2013). Moreover, music therapy improvisations incorporate musical considerations as well as interpersonal ones, just as nonclinical musicing such as in jazz also reflects interpersonal and musical considerations:

Therapists making music with clients are never just concerned with the therapeutic relationship in sound because this relationship is mediated by musical factors. The therapist's choices of instrument, tonality, timbre, harmony, and tempo are all affected by the musicality of the client's expression as well as the clinical needs, the dynamics, and the communicative patterns of the relationship. The same is true of the players in a jazz group. What they play is a combination of what they hear from each other, what they know about each other's predilections, and the relationship dynamics among them, including who is a better listener, who functions more as a leader or follower, and who is a more dynamic personality. In fact, jazz can be as much as music therapy an example of interpersonal communication in music.

(Aigen, 2005a, p. 71)

Of course it is certainly possible—or even probable—that social interaction is more readily apprehended in clinical improvisation and that musical dictates are more readily apprehended in nonclinical improvisation. However, these are differences of degree, not of kind.

It is also important to consider what the results of the Brown and Pavlicevic study actually show. Remember, they want to claim that it is not any particular perspective or mode of listening that revealed the fundamental differences in the two types of improvisation in their study. They want to claim that the findings represent objective claims about the music itself. These claims warrant further analysis because musical performances can be listened to in a number of different ways and with a number of different focuses.

In other words, when listening to any piece of music, one can try to listen just to the sounds as sounds or one can *listen for* the social interaction. And what one listens for will determine what will be heard within these various frameworks. Brown and Pavlicevic claim that just because one can hear artistic value in the product of a music therapy session, and just because an uneducated clinical listener will not hear the therapy dynamics in the music, this does not mean that clinical and nonclinical music are identical. They claim that an educated clinical ear is necessary to hear the fundamental differences that they discuss.

This line of argument privileges the therapist's epistemological position as one that can hear things that others may not, while also endowing the therapist's perceptions with a greater degree of ontological status. In other words, it is not that the therapist's mode of listening develops one (of many) equivalent perspectives on the nature of the music; the therapist's perspective is a privileged one that reveals something about the essence of the music itself that is unavailable to other listeners.

Again, there seems to be a lack of reflexivity here that diminishes the importance of the client's perspective on what is happening in music. Perhaps therapists hear social interaction because that is their focus—it is what they are listening *for*. And perhaps clients hear pure music of expressive value because their orientation is just to make music. Does this mean that the therapist's perspective is somehow more real than that of the client's? To answer in the affirmative would be to adopt a realist epistemological stance that can be particularly problematic in light of the more constructivist approach that therapists typically adopt as a way of honoring the experience of clients.

In fact, Pavlicevic (1995) has elsewhere made an important observation that bears on the central question of the relevance of the client's perspective. In discussing the data collection process she undertook for a study on individuals with schizophrenia, she comments "that none of these patients saw the music therapy session as being anything other than an opportunity to play music" (p. 171). This tendency to "remain at the level of the acts themselves" (p. 171) is portrayed by Pavlicevic as an inability on the part of clients to understand the meaning of what they have participated in. However, if we drop the assumption that the therapist's view has greater ontological status, we could make the opposite conclusion from Pavlicevic. Namely, that the clients' perspective, that what they were essentially doing was playing music, is a reflection of what was valued by them in the experience and the aspect of it that will remain to have an impact on their lives.

Can Music-Making Have an Artistic Purpose in Clinical Frameworks?

Pavlicevic (1997) argues that the construal of music therapy as an artistic process is based upon fundamental misconceptions. It results from not acknowledging that primary creativity (a concept developed by the psychologist D.W. Winnicott) relevant to therapy processes is not the same as artistic creativity. Primary creativity is concerned with engaging with situations of daily life and does not imply any type of processes relevant to creating art. Primary creativity (or emotional creativity, a term used interchangeably by Pavlicevic) is confused with artistic creativity in music therapy because music therapy occurs within an art form. However, she argues that it is essential to be able to distinguish between "creativity that has to do with a work of art—or 'purely' artistic creativity—and creativity that has to do with emotional creativity, or our emotional life" (p. 153).

After going to great lengths to formulate this distinction, Pavlicevic (1997) then pulls back from it, observing that "artistic expression and the artistic act are infused with the artist's emotional life" (p. 153). She goes into great detail regarding how the works of prominent composers (such as Copland and Stravinsky) are "inseparable from the emotional process of the person creating the music: the act of composing offers a new synthesis of the self" (p. 156).

Pavlicevic's observations in this regard undercut her points about the fundamental differences between the creation of music in clinical and nonclinical contexts. The difference is not in the emotional content of the music nor is it in the fact that the process of creation can be transformative. Pavlicevic acknowledges that music created in both contexts can share equally of these attributes. Instead, Pavlicevic identifies two attributes that distinguish clinical and nonclinical musicing: First, the fact that musical creation in therapy occurs within an interpersonal context; and second, the fact that the achievement of emotional form, which is the endpoint of music in therapy, is not the endpoint in nonclinical music with composers in this realm seeking to continue to work with art forms for the sake of developing them further.

Again to her credit, Pavlicevic realizes the close connections between clinical and nonclinical musicing and insightfully articulates the areas of their overlap. However, this leaves her with much less wiggle room in terms of arguing for their fundamental difference, a position to which she is committed. And the two claims that remain for asserting a difference between the two domains can be challenged.

First, it may be that the image of the lone composer working for thousands of hours in a solitary way, isolated from collaboration, is an apt one for the world of classical music. Even granting that point, this context of music creation cannot stand for music composition as a whole. In fact, the creation of music in nonclinical contexts is much more a communal endeavor than it is a solitary one, whether we consider jazz or other popular forms of music. And music composition cannot stand for music creation as a whole either. Music is generally played communally in groups and ensembles of all sorts. Enduring musical ensembles create strong interpersonal contexts that contribute to the form that the music takes, the quality of music achieved, the types of social interaction that occurs in the music, and the esteem in which the ensemble, the music, and the entire experience is held by participants and by audiences. There is too much interpersonal interaction in the predominance of nonclinical musical contexts to use this as a criterion to distinguish it from clinical musicing.

Second, the idea that the endpoint of music created in clinical contexts is that which is merely emotionally satisfying to the client whereas in artistic contexts (popular, classical or otherwise) music is worked with until new forms are achieved also seems to delineate a difference of emphasis rather than kind. Even Pavlicevic acknowledges that emotional forms of composers form the basis of their music. And unless one wants to claim that music in music therapy is a pure cathartic release uninfluenced by aesthetic, artistic, and or musical considerations (which Pavlicevic does not want to assert), then it is clear that the creation of art to some degree is always present in music therapy. The arguments presented for a fundamental difference between the two domains do not seem to be solidly supported here.

Pavlicevic (2000) also takes up this issue in the context of jazz improvisation and its relationship to clinical improvisation. She distinguishes traditional jazz from free and fusion jazz as in the former subgenre she asserts that predetermined musical guidelines—such as playing through chord changes—dictate the course of the music, whereas in the latter, the absence of predetermined musical guideposts means that the music is more inherently communicative and interactive. Putting aside Pavlicevic's misconstrual of fusion jazz—much of which does, in fact, follow traditional structures such as the harmonic use of modes or the rhythmic use of rock-based grooves—her insightful points about the potential connections between free jazz and music therapy are certainly worthy of further exploration. Here is how the parallels are described:

> The musicians' acute sensitivity and responsiveness to one another's rhythmic, melodic, and harmonic nuances, and their ability to express themselves and communicate with one another through music, closely resembles aspects of [music therapy] improvisation: the musical act seems to have an intimate interpersonal basis. Thus, musicians express and communicate themselves in free jazz improvisations, and in MT improvisation, therapist and client (usually nonmusician) form an intimate personal relationship that has a musical basis.
>
> (Pavlicevic, 2000, p. 272)

There are also important differences, according to Pavlicevic (2000), that relate to the purpose behind the creation of the music in the two domains: "The purpose of MT improvisation is not to 'make good music,' as in music improvisation, but rather, to create an intimate interpersonal relationship between therapist and client, through the musical event" (p. 272). As a result, the music in clinical improvisation might sound quite different from music performed to be experienced as music:

> In marked contrast to music improvisation, MT improvisation might, for example, sound rhythmically fragmented and melodically incoherent (i.e., musically "inferior") whilst generating an intimate level of interpersonal communication between the players. Conversely, a rhythmically stable improvisation—which may sound like "good

music," may well be symptomatic of limited engagement between therapist and patient. Good music, it would seem, does not equal an authentic interpersonal relationship in music therapy: the authenticity of the relationship may be generated or portrayed in "unmusical" sounds.

(Pavlicevic, 2000, p. 272)

Pavlicevic's (2000) argument for the differentiation of clinical improvisation from musical improvisation (in this case specifically, free jazz) has two components: First, while music therapy improvisation is oriented toward interpersonal relationship, music improvisation is oriented toward creating quality music. Second, music therapy improvisations might have quite limited artistic value and yet still be valuable clinically, while music improvisations might reflect limited interactivity and yet still be valuable artistically. She concludes that while "improvisation—in the broadest sense—is at the centre of MT improvisation, MT improvisation is not simply music improvisation imported into therapeutic thinking, or into a clinical context: each is a distinctive act" (pp. 273–274).

Pavlicevic's overall program is both important and laudable. She wants to make a case for the application of theory from outside domains to music therapy that takes into account the unique features of music therapy practice. I would like to examine her arguments for the distinctness of clinical improvisation.

The claim that music therapy processes are never oriented to making good music is not something with which all music therapists would agree. Many clients come to music therapy with a desire to make good music, that is, music that they find expressively and aesthetically gratifying. This is no different from musicians outside of therapy. So unless one wants to hew to a position that says the therapist's view on the process is what is "really" happening and the client's more musical view is a mere pretext for the "real" agenda which is a nonmusical clinical one, then it is clear that the most important stakeholders in the clinical process would not agree with Pavlicevic's claim.

Additionally, there are music therapists who work in a client-centered way that allows clients to dictate the agenda of the therapy process and at the same time in a music-centered way that acknowledges that the production of quality music (whether improvised or composed) can be a transformative experience that addresses basic human needs. It may be that a strong interpersonal relationship can facilitate the creation of such music for the client and it may be that such a relationship can amplify the clinical value of the essentially musical experience. Neither of those two possibilities is being negated. But the enrichment of human life that is the core orienting purpose of any type of therapy can occur in music therapy without the type of interpersonal relating in music that Pavlicevic claims is a necessary part of music therapy improvisation. Her assertion that the primary agenda of nonclinical music is musical while in music therapy it must have interpersonal significance will not hold for all music therapy applications.

It is also difficult to also delineate aesthetic qualities that are universally present in nonclinical music and absent in clinical music. Pavlicevic observes that music therapy music might be "rhythmically fragmented and melodically incoherent" in contrast to nonclinical music and thus its status as legitimate music in its own right is challenged. Yet, her descriptions of clinical music are similar to statements that many if not a majority of listeners might use to portray the type of free jazz that Pavlicevic is trying to distinguish from music therapy improvisation. Fragmentation of all types seems to be a defining aspect of some free jazz. It just will not be possible to articulate any particular aesthetic standard that is present in something like free jazz and that is absent in music therapy improvisation.

Garred (2006) has also criticized existing notions in music therapy that draw strong parallels between artistic and clinical processes. He wants to demonstrate that the properties of music and the way that humans engage with it that are suitable for nonclinical artistic contexts are unsuitable for clinical contexts. While nonclinical music—conceived of ontologically as a *work*—has an autonomous life once created, "the music in music therapy is not made primarily to become an end in itself, as a product on its own terms, released, published, or broadcast, and thereby 'sent off' on its own, as an independent entity" (Garred, 2006, p. 77). To determine if Garred is correct in this assertion about the fundamental difference between clinical and nonclinical music, it is necessary to consider if his argument articulates criteria that are unequivocally characteristics of artistic creation while at the same time being unsuitable to the products of music therapy sessions.

Garred asserts that in nonclinical contexts a work is created with the intent that it acquires an independent existence to be experienced outside the context of its creation. In contrast, in therapeutic contexts the music created is not intended to have an enduring life outside of the session, either for the creator or for other potential audiences. However, just considering the modern art world, Garred's assertion is not unproblematic. Whether one looks at performance art, contextual music and sculpture, one-time performances, or dramas created around the real-life circumstances of a single individual only to be experienced by that individual, it is clear that this idea of an enduring work is no longer a universal value. So it cannot be used to distinguish clinical from nonclinical artistic creations.

Moreover, there are at least four situations where music in music therapy does acquire an autonomous existence in a way that is similar to that of the traditional work of music. The first occurs when songs that are either improvised in sessions or composed outside the session for individual clients become permanent works in the form of music books that make them available to be used in other contexts, clinical or otherwise. Second, in the community music therapy framework public performance and the production and distribution of recordings are both seen as legitimate music therapy activities. This new movement that accepts natural forms of engaging with music in music therapy often involves creating music that can be shared outside of its context of creation. The premise is that music originating in a clinical context can have musical legitimacy for an audience, whether in an institutional setting or for the general public. Third, if one admits the relevance of aesthetic factors in music therapy—as Garred does—it is difficult to maintain that the work thereby produced has no value as an artistic creation outside of its clinical importance for the client. Theorist-clinicians such as Colin Lee (2003) emphasize the aesthetic aspects of their work with clients and claim that the music has a musical legitimacy. Acknowledging that aesthetic factors are relevant in clinical music implies that this music would have relevance outside the session, whether this is for the clients who created the music or for an audience not present at the creation of the music. Fourth, researchers such as Trygve Aasgaard (2000, 2005) have explored how songs created in therapy acquire a life of their own as they are propagated throughout an institution or community, thus becoming "works" precisely in the sense that Garred claims they do not.

That clinical and nonclinical music are fundamentally different from each other and that music therapy is not an artistic process are points also argued by Henk Smeijsters (2005). While the second notion is not required by the first, it is strongly related to it. Smeijsters's theory of analogy in music therapy requires that both of these assertions are true. He argues that artistic or aesthetic considerations are not all relevant to clinical ones, and if music that is therapeutically effective happens to have aesthetic properties, this is mere coincidence. It is only the extent to which music sounds the psychological process of the client that is relevant:

> In music therapy it is not music as a cultural/artistic phenomenon that is relevant . . . in music therapy the essence of music is the psychological process it sounds. In other words, not the well-formed as such is healing, but the correspondence of the formed musical process and the psychological process of change of the client. This can be a well-formed musical process or not. I do not believe that the mere aesthetic experience of the well-formed in itself is healing if the musical form does not sound the inner processes and psychological changes of the client.
>
> (Smeijsters, 2005, p. 65)

These beliefs stem from his commitment to the idea that the psychological processes that guide the creation of music in therapy are fundamentally different from those processes that guide the creation of music outside of therapy. According to Smeijsters (2005), the nature of music-making and musical experience is fundamentally different in the two domains:

> What the music therapist and the client are doing when improvising in active music therapy is not just "playing music." Music therapy improvisation is not improvising as in jazz, pop/rock, or classical improvisation . . . Jazz, pop/rock, and classical improvisations are pushed forward by aesthetic rules. Music therapy is not an aesthetic affair. In music therapy, it is not "aesthetic form" but "psychological form" that counts.
>
> (Smeijsters, 2005, p. 71)

Smeijsters (2005) discusses an autobiographical incident in which a combination of stress and exhaustion brought him into a life-threatening encounter with depression. When the most serious aspects of his illness were overcome with medical intervention, Smeijsters realized that he had to make some radical changes in his life. This led him to a Rolling Stones concert where he had a significant, life-changing experience: "While walking away from the stage I felt a wave of strength going through my senses and body . . . [I] looked at the stage and felt as if my whole life were [sic] changing . . . My body felt cool and strong. It was a strength I never had felt before in my life" (p. 147).

Smeijsters described how in his personal listening and playing habits he turned to the style of music characterized by the Rolling Stones and began listening constantly to their songs and similar ones while also returning to the electric guitar and learning and playing these songs. He also accessed the music of Eric Clapton and this connection was equally powerful in facilitating his own self-healing, as he describes it:

> Clapton's music tells me exactly who I am . . . This music is able to contain, it helps to express your strongest feelings, and at the same time is able to hold them for you . . . Clapton's blues sounds sorrow and strength at the same time. It is the paradoxical mingling of the depressive mood and the assertiveness of its expression that makes this music so powerful and, for me, healthy . . . The long tones, sudden fast runs, the vibrati, string bendings, pull-offs, hammer-ons, rough timbres, and timing of the licks sound

power . . . His music is full of emotion, but also 'cool' and assertive . . . From the moment I started playing his solos on my Gibson Les Paul guitar, my existential anxieties disappeared.

(Smeijsters, 2005, p. 149)

Smeijsters interprets his experience through psychological concepts and uses the interpretation to support his notion of music as analogy in music therapy. He wants his personal odyssey to be considered an example of music therapy, although it did not occur with any therapeutic structure. It did, however, reflect how he engaged with music to promote his own well-being.

In my reading of this passage a contradiction emerges. The description of the appeal of the music of both the Rolling Stones and Eric Clapton seems to capture pretty well what most members of their audience experience. In the case of the Stones they become empowered through the music and Smeijsters's words seem to perfectly describe the aesthetic appeal of Clapton's musicianship. But for Smeijsters to acknowledge this overtly would subvert his point about the differences between clinical and nonclinical music, so he calls his responses to the Stones and Clapton "therapeutic."

Smeijsters is so honest in his description of what happened in his personal life that it is not possible to understand what he went through in any way other than as being similar to what others experience. It is just that his theoretical commitments prevent him from seeing that it is exactly the particular aesthetic of rock and blues music that he experienced and that created the therapeutic value of this music for him. So at least in this instance, it would seem that Smeijsters's own experience argues against his fundamental point.

Why should the music of exemplary popular music artists such as Eric Clapton and the Rolling Stones have such powerful clinical value? And why is it that only the highest level recordings of various classical music pieces are used in the music therapy process of GIM? It does not seem reasonable to assert that this is mere coincidence. Instead, it seems much more reasonable to explore the connection between artistic and aesthetic value, just as Smeijsters does in describing Clapton's playing: the wonderful technique, the fluid changes, and the seemingly paradoxical quality of simultaneously embodying strength and vulnerability are all paradigmatic aesthetic considerations, Smeijsters's view notwithstanding.

Smeijsters also argues against the parallel notion that music is inherently therapeutic. While it is obviously true that music therapists use music and thus function as artists, to Smeijsters the artistic is merely a cloak that the therapist wears in which artistic sensibilities are not relevant to clinical work. In other words, the fact that music therapy uses an art form in which to effect human change causes the illusion that the therapist is an artist:

I am not convinced that making music is therapeutic in itself . . . Contrary to the statement that "music therapists are artists," I would say this: "Music therapists are therapists who act like artists." Music therapists are not musicians who listen to and follow the rules of music; they are therapists who listen to and follow the psychological processes, which are sounded in music.

(Smeijsters, 2005, p. 80)

So for Smeijsters, the music emanating from clients is a mere delivery device to convey material of psychological import. The attributes of the medium of delivery are not particularly relevant to the meaning and significance of what is conveyed. In fact, when artistic considerations enter into clinical music-making, the therapeutic value is endangered:

> The client's musical form is different from the work of the artist, because the work of the artist is guided by an artistic point of view, which he wants to communicate . . . The client is not developing art motifs he wants to communicate to others, not using an artistic point of view when expressing his Self. When the client uses an artistic point of view, he withdraws from his self.
>
> (Smeijsters, 2005, p. 83)

Smeijsters makes three fundamental mistakes of generalization. First, in an effort to establish applications of his theory he generalizes from his own clinical approach and argues that this way of thinking and working characterizes all music therapy. He does not recognize that his beliefs may be a reflection of a particular clinical and aesthetic theory to which he subscribes. Second, he conflates the way that he works as a therapist and extrapolates this into the client's experiential world. Just because he chooses to differentiate between clinical and nonclinical musicing does not necessarily mean that this difference is experienced by clients in music therapy. And third, he generalizes from his particular aesthetic theory areas where it may not apply. It is likely that there are artists whose primary focus is self-expression in the way that Smeijsters wants to reserve for therapy. His clinical argument is connected to a particular view of art and aesthetics to which many artists and musicians would not agree.

The idea that the music therapy occurs through bona fide music that rises to the level of art is argued for by Ansdell (1995). The recordings presented along with his text illustrate how clinical music possesses aesthetic qualities and Ansdell's explanation of the clinical processes demonstrate how any understanding of the music's clinical value requires an understanding of its aesthetic nature. The clients who create such music, experience themselves as beings capable of creating beauty, and such a realization changes how they feel about themselves and their places in the world; in some ways, nothing could be more salient from a therapeutic perspective.

The Essential Role of Context

The basic premise of the authors who argue for an essential difference between clinical and nonclinical music is that because making quality music is not the primary focus in clinical situations, the two forms of music must be different. Implicit in this notion is that clinical music does not have the same quality as nonclinical music, that the same standards should apply in determining its value, and that the former would suffer in comparison to the latter.

Underlying this entire line of thinking is the idea that the judgment of quality is universal and not context dependent, a notion that I would like to challenge. And to do this I can only argue from my 25 years of experience as a clinical music therapist working with children and adult clients with a wide range of emotional, cognitive, and physical disabilities. However, my experience with one client—a 27-year-old man named Lloyd, whose course of therapy was detailed extensively in Aigen (2005c) and previously discussed in the present text—best exemplifies my experience in this area. Working within the framework of Nordoff-Robbins music therapy, I participated as a co-therapist in a long course of therapy with Lloyd and his primary music therapist, Alan Turry.

While he had severe motor and cognitive limitations, Lloyd loved to play the drums and many of our sessions involved a musical trio with Lloyd on the drum set, Alan Turry playing piano, and me on bass. Although he had no prior musical skills, Lloyd had a natural affinity and ability in music. When we played in a jazz style, for example, although his playing on the ride cymbal had a basic imprecision, it also seemed perfectly suited to the music in timbre, volume, syncopation and feel. My experience was that the music authentically grooved in a way that was not compromised by Lloyd's limitations. This experience impressed upon me the extent to which the experience of music is context dependent. Whether or not I would have experienced the same music as having groove were it to occur outside a clinical context was irrelevant—the only thing that matters is how we experience music within the particular contexts that we encounter it.

My experiences with Lloyd led to a desire to better understand the phenomenon of *groove*, an inquiry that led to the work of Charles Keil (1994, 1995) and his concept of participatory discrepancies. The basic idea behind Keil's theory is that groove is created by subtle departures from perfect synchrony in the playing of a musical ensemble. On some beats, the musicians' playing lines up in unison and in other parts of a measure, the music is consistently, if subtly, out of synchrony. It is the subtle departures from perfect timing that endow the music with the quality of groove and that serve to invite the participation of listeners.

Building on Keil's ideas, it is likely that different styles of music abide different amounts of discrepancy. In other words, if things are too synchronous, the resultant music is mechanical and lifeless; if it is too discrepant, the music loses its flow and integrity. Musical styles as different as a polka, electronic dance music, reggae, swing, and rock and roll, can all groove with the suitable amount of discrepancy, and the amount of appropriate discrepancy varies among these different styles. That which determines quality in groove-oriented music is clearly context dependent.

Music therapy is one additional context with its own stylistic determinations and expectations. Just as one would not transfer the same amount of discrepancy present in a mid-tempo reggae tune to an up-tempo polka and expect the music to groove, one cannot transfer the same amount of discrepancy from a New York City nightclub with a jazz combo playing be-bop to a music therapy session with nonprofessional jazz musicians and a client with significant global delays and expect the music to groove there as well. But once we accept the fact that all judgments about musical quality—such as whether or not a particular music grooves—are context-dependent determinations, then the fact that music in music therapy may not always reach the same standards as that of the jazz club or concert hall does not weigh against the notion that musical quality is any less important in the former setting than in the latter one.

One way to resolve the differences in this area is to consider that the question "Do clinical and nonclinical music-making differ from one another in essential ways?" is not one that can be answered in that form. The answer might be different for different individual therapists or models of working in music therapy; the answer might differ depending upon the particular style of music in which the improvisation occurs (if this determination can be made); the answer might differ depending upon from which perspective the question is considered, that of the client, the therapist, or some other third party; and the answer might differ depending upon if one is referring to the experience of participants in the process or an analysis of some trace of the music, such as in a recording or score.

What does seem inarguable is that in some contexts there are strong continuities between clinical and nonclinical musicing that greatly outweigh their differences. This is most likely a reflection of the maturity of the music therapy profession in which models and approaches have developed and differentiated to a point where the spectrum of practice is so broad that it is just not possible to make global descriptions of music therapy, even when talking about some very fundamental issues. This makes it difficult to describe the field and to maintain a sense of unity and identity within it. However, the enormous diversity is also healthy as it positions music therapists to meet the needs of an increasing diversity of clients while also being positioned to meet a variety of artistic, political, economic, and social challenges required to thrive as a profession.

PART III

How are the Nonmusical Aspects of Music Therapy Considered?

7

THE ROLE OF VERBALIZATION
IN MUSIC THERAPY

A major theme of the previous four chapters on music was the relationship between music therapy and music in other domains. The present section, comprising Chapters 7 and 8, assumes a complementary focus, examining the relationship between music therapy and other types of therapy domains.

In seeking to understand how and why music therapy works, four areas are typically considered: verbalization, relationship,[1] neurological activity, and music. When the modern discipline of music therapy was first being developed, a great deal of explanatory weight for its effectiveness was attributed to the "direct healing power" of music (Schneider, Unkefer, & Gaston, 1968, p. 3). Such claims about cures resulting from the power of music were problematic because they could not be substantiated. Consequently, in seeking validation for the profession, music therapists "began to deemphasize music activities and emphasize the development of interpersonal relationships" (Schneider et al., p. 3). Abandoning the primacy of music, practitioners began to speak more with their clients, engaging in "too much psychotherapy, for which they were scarcely prepared, and indulged in music activities only as the patient desired" (p. 3). Writing approximately 20 years into the development of the profession, Schneider et al. (1968) observe that clinicians were beginning to implement a more balanced approach in which music, talking, and psychotherapeutic interventions all had a role. The historical progression began from an overemphasis on music alone, the pendulum swung to an overemphasis on talking with music as an adjunct and the relationship as a primary therapeutic factor, and then to an integration of the three elements.

Music therapists still consider these elements to be the factors that make music therapy work, although there are differences among them regarding how much weight is given to each element and if each element should be accounted for in all clinical music therapy processes, regardless of the type of work one is engaged in, or the particular theoretical framework under which one is practicing. Moreover, the profession has advanced significantly in the years since Schneider et al.'s observations and the development they outline has not been unidirectional. As the analysis in Chapter 17 on contemporary music therapy frameworks illustrates, there is a renewed focus on the centrality of music processes in music therapy explanation.

Issues of Verbalization in Music Therapy, Psychotherapy, and Music Psychotherapy

> Once I was questioning a patient about what his chant and drumbeat had meant. Like any good therapist, I found different ways of asking the question. I first asked directly what it meant. He said he didn't know. It just felt good to have done it. Then I probed a little deeper: "Can't you just give us a few words to describe how it felt, what it means to you now?" Then from the group another patient called out to me, "Lady, if he could say it, he wouldn't be singing it."
>
> (Kenny, 2006, p. 31)

The question of the role of verbalization in music therapy is very much connected to the issue regarding the boundaries of music therapy, psychotherapy, and music psychotherapy. Some practitioners argue that while musical experiences are powerful for clients, therapy only occurs when these experiences are interpreted, and when the sources and targets of feelings aroused by music are made explicit through verbal reflection and analysis. In this view, verbalization is necessary for ethical and efficacious practice.

It could be argued that when music therapy is oriented toward any type of functional goal in cognition, motor function, speech, or toward psycho-educational goals—in other words, when the focus of the work is not psychotherapeutic—then the question of verbalization is not particularly problematic or relevant. The idea is that functional, rehabilitative work that does not prioritize the engagement of client emotions to support personality growth does not require verbal interactions of a psychotherapeutic nature.

The counterargument is that because musical experiences are so powerful, therapists cannot control how clients construe or are affected by them. The musical activities introduced by music therapists might evoke powerful feelings, memories, and experiences that warrant being managed in a psychotherapeutic way, even if this was not the therapist's focus or intention. So the claim of some music therapists that their work is not oriented toward psychological functioning does not absolve them of the responsibility for helping clients manage these experiences when their responses warrant it. And interestingly enough, the claim that non-psychotherapeutically-oriented work entails a diminished obligation to manage client emotions through verbalization is made by practitioners from both ends of the spectrum of music therapy: those that emphasize the science of music therapy as represented by behavioral and neurological perspectives and those that emphasize the art of music therapy as represented by more music-based orientations.

There are a number of positions taken by music therapists on this topic. Some music therapists hold that interpretation of experience is necessary for therapy and without verbalization there is no interpretation. Others say that the experiencing of music can be a self-contained therapeutic event not requiring interpretation to be effective. Before exploring some of these differences of opinion it is important to clarify some areas of confusion that have resulted from the conflating of questions that are conceptually distinguishable from each other.

Interpretation is not Identical to Verbalization

Some authors argue that because interpretation of musical experience is required for therapy to occur, then the verbal exploration of the meaning of these experiences in music therapy is necessary. However, if one considers interpretation to involve a conversion of experience from one language or medium into another, then it is clear that there are types of interpretation that can take place other than through words. Sometimes musical experiences are processed (or interpreted) through artwork or bodywork. These are examples of nonverbal interpretations of the experience from the musical domain into another domain of understanding. So to say that verbalization is not always necessary is not to say that interpretation is not always necessary. And similarly, to argue that interpretation is necessary does not automatically establish that verbalization is required.

There are Uses of Verbalization Other than Interpretation

Some authors argue that because verbal relating is a necessary part of a complete human experience, this alone necessitates the interpretation of music experience through a psychological framework. Of course, clients can have powerful experiences in music therapy and it is human nature to want to talk about powerful experiences, especially with those individuals with whom the experience was shared. However, it is not self-evident that the interpretation of musical experience into its symbolic meaning, for example, is always the most suitable form of verbal interaction to follow or accompany powerful musical experiences. Again, one can advocate for a position that musical experience need not be interpreted and this does not imply an anti-verbalization attitude. One can support the benefits for clients of talking about their musical experiences in music therapy, while still maintaining a position that the experience need not be interpreted.

Interpretation is not Necessary for an Approach to be Considered Psychotherapeutic

The confusion here has been accepted by theorists on both sides of the music–words divide. They both agree that psychotherapy cannot happen without verbalized interpretation and insight into unconscious thoughts, feelings and images. The verbal camp uses this argument to assert that therefore music therapy must involve verbalized interpretation. The music camp uses this argument to assert that therefore music therapy is not psychotherapy because it can proceed without verbalized interpretation.

Both camps are wrong for a number of reasons. First, some child psychotherapy models emphasize that children function more naturally within a symbolic realm so that the interpretation of experience is not developmentally appropriate. Additionally, there are experiential and transformative forms of music psychotherapy that do not require verbalized interpretation of musical experience. Bruscia (1998b) juxtaposes "transformative therapy" approaches that facilitate experiential change with approaches that require "verbally mediated awareness" termed "insight therapy" (p. 3). In the former approaches, "the music experience is therapeutically transformative and complete in and of itself" (p. 4). In the latter approaches, verbally mediated insight is required for any important therapeutic or life change. In sum, the absence of verbal interpretation does not bear on the question of whether something is a form of psychotherapy or not.

Music Therapy is not Equivalent to Music Psychotherapy

The verbal camp argues that for ethical music therapy to be practiced, verbalized interpretation must occur. But there are two assumptions here, neither of which is valid: First, that *music therapy* equals *music psychotherapy*; and second, that music psychotherapy requires verbalized insight. We have already seen that the latter assumption is not warranted. But even if it was, it still does not follow that ethical practice could not be engaged in without verbalization because practitioners could claim to be working under the more general label of *music therapy* rather than *music psychotherapy*.

Music Therapist's Dilemma

Before getting more deeply into the issue of the role of verbalization in music therapy it is important to consider the relationship between words and musical experience in general. Music therapy is one type of human experience in music and any thoughts about the relationship between words and music in general are certainly relevant to music therapy.

That problems are encountered when using verbal language to represent music therapy processes is the starting point for Gary Ansdell's (1999b) consideration of this issue. His focus is primarily upon the use of words in professional contexts (publications and lectures) as opposed to clinical contexts (music therapy sessions).

Because he considers music therapy to be fundamentally a musical process, Ansdell (1999b) observed that the problems of music therapy in this regard were merely the latest manifestation of "Seeger's dilemma"—named after the musicologist Charles Seeger—which Ansdell labeled "music therapist's dilemma." This dilemma stems from the fact that using "verbal strategies to talk about musical processes—and, more specifically, to define the relationship between musical processes and the 'therapeutic processes'" (p. 16) unavoidably results in a mismatch between descriptor and what is being described. Ansdell claims that any theory of music therapy must address this dilemma, although the problem is more acute for music-centered practitioners where the musical interaction and experience is the locus of therapeutic effect.

Ansdell says that music therapist's dilemma would not be present if music therapists functioned as practitioners without a need to discuss or present their work in professional forums. And this certainly might be true of the relatively smaller number of therapists who believe that the value of their work is self-evident when recordings of it are played for others. Yet it is likely that a larger number of practitioners would assert that this dilemma exists within clinical practice as well, not just in conferences, team meetings, or publications. Music therapists facilitate musical experiences of a great variety of types and intensity, and the more open-minded among them wonder about the extent to which words should enter the process and how these words should be used. This is just to say that the scope of music therapist's dilemma is clearly wider than Ansdell presents.

Seeger's dilemma arises at the meeting point of speech and music, and it refers to becoming "trapped in a 'linguocentric predicament'" when using speech as an analytic tool to understand musical process" (Ansdell, 1999b, p. 52). Ansdell takes on Seeger's distinction between "music knowledge that operates 'within' musical practices, as opposed to our speech knowledge which is 'outside' of it and about it" (p. 52). The type of knowledge that inheres variously in speech and in music does not necessarily cohere with their means of articulation. Thus, musical phenomena can be misrepresented by the particular type of organization that verbal modes impose upon them. Following upon Seeger's work, musicologists focused upon how people talk about music and how this way of talking interacts with musical experience to constitute it in particular ways. Seeger's dilemma led to music therapist's dilemma because

> music therapists also face the challenge of working with a musical process (and the resulting musical material) which crosses conventional boundaries of musical culture. The music therapist is attempting to reconcile the practice of music therapy (which arguably operates largely within Seeger's "music knowledge") with the need for a coherent system of verbal representation (a "speech knowledge") in order to explain practice, teach or research the work—or simply to feel articulate within everyday clinical communication.
>
> (Ansdell, 1999b, p. 62)

So rather than just a problem of finding the right words for music therapy experience, the solution to this dilemma requires studying the discourse of music therapy and determining how it constitutes the profession through assumptions, modes of thought, and the employment of concepts specific to particular theoretical frameworks.

The two areas of discourse—the professional one among therapists and the disciplinary one between therapists and clients—are strongly related to one another and mutually constitutive. For example, when presenting clinical examples to colleagues, a music therapist might describe a particular musical improvisation from a session as an example of musical countertransference. Countertransference—whether verbal or musical—occurs when therapists relate to clients in ways that reflect their patterns of relating with significant individuals from their own lives. And although it would be unusual for a therapist to use the term *musical countertransference* in verbal interventions with a client, its use in professional forums nonetheless colors how therapists experience clients in the moment and the verbal interventions therapists make. It is because of this mutually constitutive nature that the ensuing discussion focuses primarily upon the use of verbalization with music in clinical music therapy.

Verbalization in Music Therapy and the Psychodynamic Framework

Although Mary Priestley's (1994) ideas on the role of verbalization in music therapy are relevant primarily to her own method of analytical music therapy (AMT), they also embody common thinking in music therapy on this topic.[2] AMT is defined as "the analytically-informed use of improvised music by the music therapist and client" employed to explore the client's inner life in the service of "growth and greater self-knowledge" (p. 3). Because she stresses an engagement with music based upon its nature as a symbolic medium, it is natural that verbalization would be required to unlock the meaning of the music. Her approach contrasts with experientially-based forms of music therapy that consider music as an alternative medium of experience rather than as a symbolic language.

For Priestley (1994), the use of words in music therapy is essential. If the emotional content of the musical experiences is not put into words the session becomes split so that "feelings can either avoid the words and get hidden in the music, or enter the words but leave the music without deeper content" (p. 135). The release of feelings through music without verbalized insight into their causes cannot lead to any type of true improvement in a client's life. Music allows for the expression of acceptable and unacceptable feelings without the risk that others will be able to discern what is being expressed; it expresses that which is taboo for personal or social reasons.

The arguments for the role of verbalization are embedded within psychoanalytic theory. Because music is a symbolic code expressing that which is taboo, language must be used to label the feelings. These ideas have become part of many music therapists' assumptions about their work. They function as filters through which musical experiences in music therapy are understood.

While there is nothing inherently wrong with this stance, problems arise when a rationale, which is embedded within one system, is applied to other models of therapy or contexts of treatment, as is the case when psychoanalytic precepts are used to critique modes of music therapy practice based on alternative foundations. Additionally, psychoanalytic thinking was not created to describe musical phenomena and the ways in which it may distort or not be adequate to musical experience are not considered by users of psychoanalytic discourse.

According to Ansdell (1995), the ephemeral nature of music and musical experience renders it particularly resistant to being spoken about and interpreted. Ansdell questions if it is possible to have a noninterpretive mode of therapy. He draws the broader context for this issue in the aspect of Seeger's dilemma that is concerned with "how we reconcile . . . 'speech knowledge' which is about music (but extrinsic to its process), with 'music knowledge', which is within music (and intrinsic to it)" (p. 171).

Ansdell says that the problem of the music therapist's dilemma is more acute than the dilemma facing musicologists because the music therapist uses music knowledge when creating music with clients, but then is faced with the need to talk about the music. When music therapists use a particular psychotherapeutic framework, the problem is solved because the external framework provides the interpretive lexicon. These systems of thought seek to rationally integrate musical experience into the conscious mind by means of talking about it. But however the music is interpreted, if it is being done through words, the content of the interpretation will be circumscribed by the way that words work. This is highly problematic for music-centered music therapy approaches that are based upon the notion that "music therapy works in the way music works" (Ansdell, 1995, p. 173).

Ansdell identifies two important assumptions that are implicit within the practice of interpreting music and musical experience through psychoanalytic concepts: First, that the music has content that can be rendered verbally, and second, that this content takes the form of an external referent of which the music is a symbol. Although we talk about musical *meaning* and verbal *meaning*, these two senses of *meaning* are quite different from each other. While words gain their meaning from what they point to, music creates meaning within itself:

> Music, rather than "having a meaning" becomes meaningful as one or more people build a structure of rhythms, melodies and harmonies within an overall form. We communicate with words to convey our meaning, whereas we improvise music to find something meaningful between us.
>
> (Ansdell, 1995, p. 26)

Ansdell goes on to acknowledge that therapists who work in music-based approaches are not dogmatic about the use of verbalization, including it when the situation and client needs demand it. However, he does offer a critique based on the limitations of psychodynamic thinking:

> The central issue is that whilst psychodynamic theory may well be one useful way of understanding the nature and problems of the therapeutic situation, it is not an adequate explanation of the central, transformative locus of that situation—the music therapeutic process.
>
> (Ansdell, 1995, p. 177)

In other words, psychodynamic thinking addresses some of the supportive social structures and conditions that accompany the core process. These factors include "issues of relationship, power, dependence" (Ansdell, 1995, p. 177) and others. For music-based practitioners such as Ansdell, there is no denial that these factors can be present and warrant being addressed. The claim is merely that in a music-based clinical model they are secondary issues which can be circumvented through the way that a therapist can draw clients into states of musicing where the most potent meaning lies and personal transformation occurs. This is where the music-based models and the psychodynamic models clash most overtly. The elements that the latter approach asserts are the crucial focus of therapy (interpretations of music and the therapeutic relationship) are seen as nonessential, secondary focuses in the former approach.

Ansdell says that this difference is based upon differing answers to the most fundamental question one can ask about music therapy: What is it that clients fundamentally gain from the experience? Is this "some new knowledge, insight, understanding; or a mostly wordless, concept-less experience which is first and foremost a musical one?" (1995, p. 177). While the former benefit accrues through logical thought, the latter one arises from the type of musical thinking that characterizes music-making in all of its contexts.

In music-based approaches, the focus is not on providing "new insights, knowledge or advice which could be stated propositionally" (Ansdell, 1995, p. 178). Instead, the intent is to create situations of musicing where clients have "a very different experience of themselves—one in contrast to the usual physical and emotional patterns dictated by pathology or habit" (p. 178). This experience is enabled by the process of intrinsic interpretation that is at the core of the music therapist's ability to provide a musical understanding of a client when creating music together. It is a creative, musical response "to the overall musical fabric which is the 'musical between' that includes both the client and the therapist in the music" (p. 179). The therapist creating music with a client makes use of interpretive processes, but these are not ones that are characterized by a translation from one medium to another; instead, they occur completely within one's musical consciousness.

There are three different ways of considering the impact of the perspective developed by Ansdell. The most uncontroversial way to consider it is that he provides a solid foundation for a mode of practice that contrasts with the psychodynamic model, thus contributing to a pluralistic field in which a variety of approaches are accepted and valued.

However, Ansdell's ideas could be taken a step further to ask some fundamental questions about music therapy. Consider that the clients in the music-based approach in which he practices report benefitting most from the way that they are heard and responded to; they forge new ways of being in music based upon the sensitive musical interaction occurring with their therapists. Yet Ansdell identifies this experience as the natural result of music-making. And regardless of the theoretical orientation of their therapists, most music therapy clients are engaged in music-making. It is worth considering if Ansdell's description of client benefit is applicable across different treatment approaches. In other words, regardless of how therapists are conceptualizing their clinical work, and regardless of how much importance they place on verbal interpretation and the secondary factors identified by Ansdell, it may be that what is actually happening for clients is that they are experiencing themselves in new ways in music and it is this phenomenon that explains the benefits of music therapy.

Therapists whose theoretical allegiance includes the primacy of verbal interpretation might not want to acknowledge that the most significant experience for their clients did not result from their interpretive interventions but instead was in the core experience of musicing with a sensitive co-musician trained in the art of sensitive listening and responding. This recognition would challenge some core aspects of a paradigm to which many practitioners have strong allegiances. But it would seem that the experiences of clients should be prominently considered here.

Clients in psychotherapy report quite different memories of the process from their therapists. Whereas therapists offer moments of interpretive insight as being the turning point in therapy, clients instead recall moments of being heard, felt, or responded to in unique ways as being the most important. It is possible that Ansdell's observations—rooted in the common factor of music-making—are relevant beyond music-based approaches and apply in more psychodynamic ones as well. Such a conclusion would challenge the foundations of psychodynamic approaches. It may be that verbal analysis and interpretation serve to convince the participants—clients and therapists—that what they are doing is therapy and not just playing music, although client experience may demonstrate that this is an illusory and unneeded pretext. The descriptions of clinical music-making by music-based practitioners suggest that there are other routes to establishing the legitimate clinical value of music therapy that do not require the adoption of verbally-based psychodynamic theory.

Some music therapists operating in a conventional psychodynamic framework consider the ideas promoted by music-centered thinking to be dangerous for clients and perhaps even unethical. In this view, to advocate that music therapy can be essentially a noninterpretive practice is to ignore some of the most salient clinical factors to the detriment of client welfare. In fact, such advocacy can itself be seen as resulting from a defensive posture against the taboo contents of the unconscious. Ansdell's perspective is considered symptomatically rather than as a rational alternative.

However, it should not be problematic to claim that client experience should have the greatest weight in determining the nature of music therapy process and the elements that bring the greatest benefit. Clients are the most significant stakeholders in the process and they do not have a vested interest in any particular clinical framework. Perhaps music-based practitioners are motivated by their own defense mechanisms to create a theory in which the threatening aspects of the unconscious need not be engaged; and perhaps psychodynamically-based practitioners are motivated by their own insecurities about the nature of their role to create a theory in which the therapist's insightful interpretations are the core factor in what makes the process work. Both states of affairs are certainly possible and it remains to empirical research on the nature of client experience to determine which of these positions is correct. Of course, submitting to this type of judgment requires taking seriously the client's experience of the process, something that will be more easily done in models in which the therapist's role is that of an equal partner rather than a figure of authority.

This issue is considered by Pavlicevic (1997) through the lens of the crisis of language that she says characterizes modern societies. While observing that music therapists are uniquely poised to challenge the primacy of the word and to help people return to more direct experiences of reality unmediated by verbalization, she points to a number of considerations that push music therapists in the opposite direction:

> We seem to feel that unless we can talk about the musical experience, then (1) the non-verbal experience is incomplete; (2) professional colleagues will think that we do not know what we are doing; (3) our clinical grasp of the work will be questioned— we might be seen to be doing "just music".
>
> (Pavlicevic, 1997, p. 11)

A non-polarized perspective in which it is acknowledged that the use of words and music in music therapy enrich each other characterizes Pavlicevic's thinking. This would not seem to be problematic for practitioners in the music-based camp as what they want is the freedom to practice without the necessity for interpretation and not have their work considered unethical or superficial. Yet it might be problematic for some psychodynamic practitioners.

Pavlicevic divides music therapists into those who adopt a psychodynamic frame of reference and those who do not. She claims that within each group there may be therapists who use only music or those who use words and music, so that it is not the use of words that distinguishes between them; instead, it is the adherence to psychodynamic theory that creates the dividing line. Practitioners in the music camp might use music only in their work or they might use words as well, but the words are not directed toward creating psycho-dynamic meanings.

Pavlicevic (1997) identifies two directions in which interpretations occur in music therapy. First, an interpretation is an intervention by the therapist that informs the client about an "understanding or insight that may clarify, for both therapist and client, an undeveloped or unexpressed meaning about an aspect of their work together" (p. 160). Pavlicevic also supports the idea that therapists listen and respond to the client's music in a particular way that is determined by how the therapist interprets the clinical significance of the music. This type of interpretation is not offered to the client verbally, but does influence the therapist's musical intervention.

Pavlicevic argues for a contextual model in determining how and when words are necessary in music therapy. She questions the notion that just because a client does not put words on an experience that the experience is not fully incorporated into the client's conscious awareness. For her, that which is musical should not be equated with the unconscious. In fact, sometimes the drive to articulate an event or experience verbally might even diminish its impact. Playing music in the context of a therapeutic relationship is a way of being with another person that can be complete within itself, not requiring any type of verbal interpretation.

This idea that music experiences can be self-contained clinical events is a central characteristic of music-centered belief systems. And this belief is not connected to a client's disability. It is not the case that words can be dispensed with only because a client has a disability in the verbal area. Instead, music is considered to have a fundamental, nonverbal value in and of itself.

For psychodynamic practitioners, the content of the music must be verbalized because the cathartic release of emotional tension that occurs in music will provide a temporary benefit, but without verbalized, conscious insight, the tension in problematic emotions will only return. However, music-based theorists do not believe that the primary function of music in music therapy is to provide a form of emotional release. Instead, it is "more typically considered as a communal, aesthetic, and/or cultural phenomenon, the creation of which has inherent clinical value" (Aigen, 2005a, p. 119). Thus, the whole issue of verbalization is inseparable from the psychodynamic belief system and one's concept of what music is essentially and what it provides to people generally.

The aesthetic dimensions of music are not particularly relevant in psychoanalytic approaches and spontaneous improvisation in music therapy is considered analogous to verbal free association in traditional psychoanalysis. Music-centered models that draw upon the aesthetic qualities in music differ from psychoanalytic approaches in an important way. In the latter, the music reflects something that already exists, namely, the contents of the unconscious it is representing. In contrast, in music-based models the music involves the creation of something new, something that was not there before. "It becomes an original statement, rather than . . . revealing something already existing" (Garred, 2006, p. 166).

The music created in music-centered approaches has significance beyond being a portrait of psychological symptoms. It goes beyond the individual to convey "a meaning of some kind that can be shared" (Garred, 2006, p. 167). When it is approached as an aesthetic creation, a person can appropriate music to transcend individual limitations. In music-based music therapy approaches the focus is more on the communal meaning of the music rather than on its private meaning. These approaches forgo analytic insight for the benefits of the experiencing of self, other, the music, and the world.

Rudy Garred (2006) discusses some ways of integrating approaches. He cites Alan Turry's (1998) discussion of transference and countertransference in Nordoff-Robbins music therapy (NRMT), suggesting that while Turry works on these phenomena, it is with the intent of preparing the ground for more potent musical interactions rather than as items of insight or value in their own right. They are considered "tools to enhance creativity" (Garred, p. 176).

In contrast, Elaine Streeter (1999) argues that certain psychodynamic practices are not optional but are required for ethical and effective clinical practice. She emphasizes that there is an interpersonal relationship within music therapy that requires monitoring in order for the music to be used most effectively. This relationship comprises a number of types of communication, "conscious or unconscious, emotionally felt, verbally expressed or musically experienced" (p. 6). What Streeter describes as "psychological thinking" (p. 6) must be applied to the therapist's awareness of the relationship in order to ensure that proper boundaries are established and maintained and that client safety is guaranteed. Theory derived from "music alone" (p. 6) is not adequate to accomplish this, although it is not clear what Streeter means by this term.

Psychological thinking is necessary to process the musical experience; otherwise, music therapy is left at the stage of experience without reflection on its meaning. Streeter critiques Colin Lee (1996) because music in his improvisational approach, as she characterizes it, is an analog of free association. In Streeter's psychoanalytic framework, free association reveals the contents of the unconscious which must then be consciously assimilated through verbal interpretation. Lee is also criticized for not considering the "transference relationship"

(Streeter, 1999, p. 9) that reflects the client's unconscious projections onto the therapist. Streeter's basic objection is that for something to be therapeutic it must go beyond the "purely experiential" (p. 10).

Streeter (1999) characterizes the development of music-derived theory as a means of defending the absence of psychological thinking in approaches such as Nordoff-Robbins music therapy (NRMT). By putting it in this defensive posture she attempts to undermine its legitimacy. It is portrayed as reflecting an underlying insecurity or inadequacy that music-based theory is formulated to cover. In the case of NRMT, she states that it is inappropriate to take the noninterpretive approach developed by Paul Nordoff and Clive Robbins in their work with children "into the adult field with articulate verbal clients … without the inclusion of relevant psychological theories to balance and guide that therapist" (p. 11).

Streeter (1999) does not accept the notion of thought in music and juxtaposes musical *experience* with psychological *thinking*. In other words, if thinking is to take place in music therapy, it must do so within psychological theory. However, Streeter appears not bound by psychoanalytic thinking when she says that "a client should expect to have the opportunity to think creatively with their [*sic*] therapist about the music created and its meaning for them" (p. 12). Of course, it is not clear that any music therapist would argue otherwise. She equates psychological thinking with being able to think creatively about an experience in an attempt to undermine the music-centered position. In other words, music-centered practitioners might embrace the idea of reflecting on the music therapy experience with their clients in this way, but would not necessarily want to characterize this as a form of psychological thinking; the reflections would not necessarily take the form of concepts from particular psychological theories.

Certainly there are many ways of reflecting on experience—if one accepts that reflection is needed or helpful—that do not fit under the umbrella of psychological thinking generally, or psychodynamic thinking, specifically. This is not an option that Streeter considers.

While Streeter (1999) says that psychodynamic thinking is only one of many systems of thought in psychology, all of her arguments consider music therapy phenomena as examples of psychodynamic phenomena: there is always a transference relationship, free improvisation is an example of free association, music therapy improvisations are "examples of the transference relationship in action" (p. 13).

Further, practice should be defined by the ability to "match theory to pathology" (Streeter, 1999, p. 13). In other words, the client's diagnosis should be reflected in the theory that provides a guide to intervention. This does ignore the opposite perspective that diagnosis is a construct within a particular framework, not an absolute or necessarily a real or objective judgment. The opposing point of view considers the more universal ways that music benefits human life.

Streeter observes that much music therapy theory was developed from work with severely disabled individuals. She makes the reasonable assumption that it is appropriate to apply psychoanalytic theory to music therapy for people who do not have severe difficulties and who may have no cognitive or language deficits. Streeter also details some of the ways that words and music interact: talking can deepen the impact of musical experience and can provide direct access to affect when clients use music to defend against their emotions. When Streeter advocates that words and music provide alternative means of expression and therapists should be comfortable working in both domains in order to be in a position to meet the needs of clients, her assertions are laudable and uncontroversial. The position which she advocates that is more difficult to defend is that the elements of psychodynamic theory are always present in clinical work and music therapists who do not employ this theory are practicing in an ineffective, unethical, and damaging way.

In contrast, the music-centered position is inclusive of the use of words when clinically warranted. It merely says that words are not always necessary, that the use of words should not be constrained by the concepts of psychoanalysis, and, at times, the experiencing of self, others, and the world through music can be a self-contained therapeutic experience not requiring verbalized insight.

Streeter's assertions meet their limitation when one attempts to include transpersonal, communal, or optimal experiences that can occur in music therapy. Because art in psycho-analytic thinking primarily performs a deficit function—in other words, it compensates for something that cannot be more directly expressed or experienced—the nature of transcendent musical experiences will always be inadequately represented or distorted in psychodynamic theory. Peak experiences in which the boundaries of individual identity are broadened are considered to be examples of regression in classical psychoanalytic thinking.

In contrast, music-centered thinking accommodates to these natural modes of musical experience—*natural* in the sense that they occur when individuals are engaged in nonclinical musicing situations—and recognizes that they can be vitally important clinical events. Rather than force transpersonal musical experiences into concepts from an alien conceptual system, music-centered thinking approaches them on their own terms and attempts to formulate a music therapy theory based on them. To advocate for music-centered music therapy theory "means creating indigenous models, mechanism and constructs derived primarily from music therapy practice. It does not mean avoiding verbal interchange when necessary" (Aigen, 1999, p. 80).

One unstated assumption of the view that verbalization is an essential part of music therapy practice is that music is "something other than itself" (Lee, 2003, p. 56). In contrast to this notion, Lee's model of aesthetic music therapy focuses on creating music suited to clients' immediate needs rather than on creating music to evoke verbal interpretation. Lee challenges the notions that what is expressed musically remains at the level of unconscious thought and that the conscious rationality imposed by words is necessary for clinical processes to reach completion. Instead, he often finds that even verbal adult clients feel that silence completes the clinical experience and he has therefore pragmatically determined that it is not his responsibility as a therapist to impose the necessity for verbalization upon clients.

Lee (2003) does believe that gaining an understanding of clients is helpful but that this is possible purely through musical processes. And this latter qualification is an important one because the stance promoted by Lee is that "music psychotherapy should be able to embrace purely musical expression and AeMT [aesthetic music therapy] needs to include verbal processing when appropriate" (p. 57). In other words, the use of verbalization in individual circumstances should not be determined by an a priori theoretical commitment but instead by the needs of individual clients in specific situations.

In a detailed study of a client with HIV/AIDS, Lee (1996) reports that almost all of the client's musical experiences were the subject of extensive discussions, although none of these talks reflected psychoanalytic thinking, such as interpreting the experience in relation to the client–therapist dynamics, the emotional events of the client's childhood, or the client's relationship to his parents or to any other individuals in his life. Because of this, Streeter does not consider the discussions between Lee and his client to be legitimate processing of musical experience and suggests that his practice borders on being unethical. As I see it, her basic flaw is not in arguing for the therapist's obligation to help clients assimilate powerful musical experiences into their lives. Any responsible therapist should help clients to do this when needed. Instead, Streeter's mistake is in privileging her personal theoretical commitment to psychoanalytic thinking and raising adherence to it into a matter of ethics. In a profession that values diversity of thought, it is destructive to elevate any particular theoretical preference into an ethical necessity.

Verbalization Outside of Psychoanalytic Thinking

There are approaches to verbalization in music therapy based upon a broader framework than that of psychoanalysis. For example, through his use of the word *processing*, Paul Nolan (2005) indicates that he is not talking about the use of verbalization in general—such as using it to identify an issue for musical exploration—but instead is only talking about verbalizations that are undertaken in response to the music. For him, verbal processing "relates to the talking that facilitates the therapeutic process during, and in response to, music making or music listening" (p. 18). It has two primary purposes: First, increasing awareness about internal thoughts and feelings as well as external events in the music and interpersonal relationships— it is essential in linking nonverbal and verbal realms of experience; and second, processing can also provide important information to the therapist about the client that may either confirm or contrast with information gleaned in other ways. As a consequence of these discussions about the music, client and therapist can embark on new musical experiences with greater insight and a stronger therapeutic alliance.

Verbal processing may not always be in the form of discussion as is traditionally conceived. It may involve spontaneous singing as well. Nolan (2005) observes that verbalization is not universally applicable or necessary, and he notes how sometimes musical experiences become described through "intellectualized verbal clichés by the client, thus distancing the client from the spontaneously-mutual affective state" (p. 19). He also cites Austin and Dvorkin's (1993) claim that some music therapists may gravitate to using talking as a defense against the music process, which might be more vague or difficult to understand.

Two research studies have addressed this general issue. First, Dorit Amir (1999) identified three primary perspectives in music therapy on the relative roles of music and verbalization: First, approaches where interventions are primarily musical and any talking during the session is not considered as a psychotherapeutic intervention; second, approaches where music is the primary change agent but talking is also used liberally to share ideas, insights, and interpretations; and third, approaches where equal weight is given to musical and verbal interventions.

Amir's research revealed seven different functions of verbal interventions in music therapy. Three of them are based upon the idea that verbal language is more concrete, logical, and rational than is musical experience. These functions include: (i) to open a space for understanding, awareness and clarity within the client's rational, cognitive mind; (ii) to check issues that deal with content, descriptions and analyses; and (iii) to make an interpretation. Three additional functions are based on the idea that musical experience represents a non-ordinary realm of experience and words can be useful in effecting a transition from this experience and providing distance from it; (iv) to get to the known, natural, and familiar mode of communication [of words]; (v) to be less involved so that one can look at the experience from a different angle; and (vi) to bring clients back from the unconscious to the conscious, from fantasy world to reality, from altered state of consciousness to regular consciousness. The final function is based on the idea that musical experience is ephemeral and talking about it helps to more fully impress it in one's memory; (vii) to acknowledge and give meaning to the experience because sometimes not to talk about it is to suggest that it did not happen. The fact that only two of Amir's functions relate directly to psychoanalytic thinking (numbers iii and vi) suggests that there is a role for verbalization in clinical practice that is not based on the tenets of psychoanalysis.

Other authors have explored the role of verbalization within music-centered approaches. Fraser Simpson's (2000) exploration of NRMT proceeded from the idea that the client–therapist relationship should be based primarily upon interaction in music. Simpson says that this is reasonable given that many of the original clients with whom Nordoff and Robbins developed their method had impaired language skills. However, when second-generation practitioners expanded the work into clinical areas for clients without language impairments, it was natural to explore whether the emphasis on relating primarily through music was still warranted.

In his study, Simpson presented hypothetical scenarios to participant therapists where clients initiated verbal interactions and he asked the therapists to discuss how they would respond. Their responses were categorized into words before, during, and after music. Within each of these areas he identified ways that words facilitated the music therapeutic process and ways in which they hindered the process.

Although all six participants were NRMT practitioners, they differed in terms of the extent to which they incorporated psychodynamic thinking into their approaches. The finding that the degree of adherence to psychodynamic thinking did not indicate a greater preference for using words was quite striking and appears to weigh against the notion that NRMT is anti-verbalization. In fact, it was the length of experience that correlated here, with more experienced therapists showing more comfort and willingness to include verbalization in their sessions. Participants who felt a gap in their skills believed that more emphasis on verbal skills in their music therapy educations would not lead to more verbalization but to more effective verbalization.

Two contrasting positions emerged in the research findings, both related to the idea of wholeness, but with opposite emphases. For one group of participants, the human being was considered a multi-faceted entity through which the whole can be grasped within any one facet, much as in a hologram where the whole is contained within each of its parts. Thus, the whole of a person's being could be apprehended through music if one knows how to listen properly. In contrast was the notion that because speaking is a natural human activity, in order to treat the whole person it is necessary to interact verbally when this is the client's predilection. While both groups of participants valued the notion of relating to clients holistically, they came to differing positions on the necessity of verbalization based on their position on the nature of human beings.

Perhaps this is why the different positions on the role of verbalization in music therapy really are incommensurable. They stem from very different beliefs about the nature of music, human experience, and human values.

In the more conventional view, musical expression exists because clients in therapy are not able to express all that they need to through words. Music substitutes for words initially, but for lasting personal change to take place, words must be placed onto musical experience in order to solidify the nature of this experience, identify it for the conscious mind, and ensure that it can be fully accepted and integrated into all layers of the human personality.

For other practitioners, music provides a unique medium of human experience with its own modes of thought, values, and ways in which it enriches human life. For people whose experiences with music (whether inside or outside therapy) have led them to this position, words at best provide a supportive medium that may lubricate the engine of therapy but which merely function to facilitate the primary forces of transformation. Perhaps there is no better articulation of this position than that provided by Rachel Verney:

> And I think the difference we offer to people in the music therapy experience is that through the struggle, and the coming to new possibilities, a client can learn to trust a different level of themselves [sic], and to value a whole depth and dimension of human relationship that doesn't exist in words.
>
> (Verney & Ansdell, 2010, p. 59)

In this perspective, music offers an alternative mode of human experience that is neither achievable through verbal interaction nor describable through it. Words may be used in a supportive sense but we should not confuse our pragmatic need for words to obscure us from the observation that because of the uniqueness of musical experience and its incommensurability with words, no amount of verbalization can ever fully capture it and no interaction that takes place through words is necessary to enhance the transformative capacities of music.

One of the earliest reflections on the limitations of language in music therapy was made by Carolyn Kenny (2006) whose thoughts appear in the epigraph to the present chapter.[3] Kenny acknowledges that she often struggled with the reflex to bridge a musical experience in music therapy back to everyday life through the use of words. She recounts an incident where she repeatedly prodded a client to explain in words the meaning of his music. After this probing went on and was not effective, a second client called out, "Lady, if he could say it he wouldn't be singing it" (p. 31).

Kenny (2006) took this incident to heart and realized that it was true that the music was self-contained and the experience had gone beyond where words could go: "It was an expression of clarity and communication. Everyone in the group had been moved. I had been moved. He said it had made him feel better. What better occasion for celebration in silence?" (p. 31). Kenny highlights the fact that music therapists often think that they are obligated to either interpret the music or establish its connection to life outside music (or outside therapy) through words.

The underlying issue here is that of generalization, a vital issue in debates about therapeutic efficacy. Traditional thinking asserts that unless the changes that are present in a music therapy session are present outside the sessions, then the work has not generalized and its value is diminished or eliminated altogether.

In music therapy, there is a double generalization challenge (Aigen, 2005a). A truism in music therapy is that clients with disabilities function at a higher level in the cognitive, motoric, social, and emotional domains when engaged in music. Music therapists must demonstrate that the changes that are present in music can transfer to nonmusical functioning and that the changes in the sessions (whether musical or not) generalize to the client's life outside the sessions.

This double challenge is not present for disciplines such as speech therapy or physical therapy because their targeted area of change (speech or motor function) is also the medium of the treatment. They are concerned with how changes in the session are manifested in daily life, but they have no burden of making the cross-modal translation. The conventional notion of music therapy where the music is merely the means for change occurring in other domains—rather than a legitimate focus of intervention itself—is what gives this double challenge to music therapists. It is also what motivates therapists to do what Kenny found herself doing: forcing clients to find words for a therapeutic experience when it might be that words are not warranted. The drive to use verbalization in music therapy cannot be separated from the debate over whether music in music therapy is only a means to a nonmusical end or, alternatively, is it a legitimate medium of experience.

The argument based on the music-centered perspective challenges the necessity for both types of generalization and, hence, the necessity for verbalization. When music is understood as an essential human activity that provides meaning to human life in a unique and necessary way, providing access to it becomes a legitimate clinical focus, thus diminishing the necessity of seeing the transfer of functioning to nonmusical domains. Additionally, when music therapists are able to evoke significantly higher levels of human functioning from clients than they are capable of in other domains, it is not at all clear why this is considered a limitation of music therapy. Instead of critiquing music therapists from not being able to ensure that higher levels of functioning transfer to other milieus, it is possible to turn this question around and to explore why other milieus and domains of treatment cannot evoke these same potentials. Moving toward an acceptance of either of these two views on generalizations minimizes the necessity for the verbalization of experience in music therapy when the musical experience is felt as complete in and of itself.

Notes

1. Initially, *relationship* referred to the therapeutic relationship between therapist and client. In more contemporary formulations, this term can include relationships among clients, between the client and music, and between clients and any socio-cultural context.
2. Contemporary literature on AMT has a more flexible approach to the role of verbalization. The discussion of Priestley's ideas here is not meant to be a comprehensive portrayal of thinking in AMT on this topic.
3. The 2006 publication includes a reprint of a work originally published in 1982, which is being cited here.

8

THE CLIENT–THERAPIST RELATIONSHIP IN MUSIC THERAPY

Music therapy occurs within the context of a professional relationship similar to that of other health and business domains, such as with medical doctors and attorneys. Psychotherapy also takes place within a professional relationship, but the role of the client–professional relationship is somewhat unique in that the quality of the relationship is integral to the effectiveness of the therapy. This situation is different from even closely related disciplines such as speech therapy or physical therapy where an open, trusting, and intimate relationship might facilitate the achievement of clinical goals, but is not necessarily a central ingredient in the efficacy of the therapy.

Music therapists who debate the role of relationship in clinical work either assume the psychotherapeutic stance on this issue or they provide a contrasting option. Although there are scores of schools of psychotherapy, there are three primary positions regarding the role of the client–therapist relationship. They provide a suitable lens through which to understand much of the debate in music therapy on this topic.

Freud's model of the psychoanalyst was based upon that of the medical doctor, a dispassionate scientist who uses the rational powers of the mind to solve the dilemmas of the human psyche. In the original form of psychoanalysis, the therapist is a neutral presence whose real nature as a person is not manifest to the client. What is present is the *transference relationship*. This term refers to the client's perception of the therapist based upon the client's projections. It is not an authentic human relationship, although its examination provides one of the primary focuses of psychoanalysis.

At the opposite end of the spectrum is the person-centered model of psychotherapy developed by Carl Rogers. In this approach, the therapist assumes an authentic, genuine presence in which care and unconditional positive regard for the client are overtly demonstrated. Because the client is fully accepted in a nonjudgmental way, there is no pressure from the therapist for the client to change. It is the quality of this real relationship consisting of genuine care, empathy, and acceptance that, somewhat paradoxically, allows the client to change. The essential point is that the authentic client–therapist relationship provides the major impetus for change.

An example of a psychotherapy approach between these two positions is the rational-emotive-behavior therapy (REBT) of Albert Ellis. In this approach, a warm or authentic relationship between client and therapist is neither "a necessary or a sufficient condition for effective personality change, although it is often desirable" (Ellis, 1995, p. 162). In this approach, there are a large variety of impersonal clinical interventions—such as "didactic discussion, behavior modification, bibliotherapy, audiovisual aids, and activity oriented homework assignments" (pp. 163–164)—and it is this technology that determines the effectiveness of the therapy rather than any aspect of the client–therapist relationship.

In considering functional therapies such as physical, occupational, and speech therapy, with which music therapy can be associated, it is reasonable to assume that although a personal relationship might enhance these activities, it does not seem necessary. Consequently, music therapy that seeks primarily to enhance motor or cognitive skills may not require an intimate, personal relationship, although such a relationship could reasonably be seen as facilitating the work through enhancing client motivation.

Not all music therapists emphasize the importance of the client–therapist relationship according to Pavlicevic (1997). At one end of the spectrum are therapists who operate within a medical model where the focus is on diagnosis and treatment as traditionally defined. In this perspective that can characterize therapists working within cognitive and behavioral traditions, the therapeutic relationship is no more (or less) important to clinical outcome than it is in medical practice. It is important to highlight that this perspective is not limited to music therapists who are working in medical music therapy or who are addressing functional goals. It can be just as prevalent with therapists who are working in mental health care, for example.

But there are forms of music therapy where the client–therapist relationship is of central concern. While some perspectives embrace psychoanalytic thinking on this topic, others reject central elements of it. Pavlicevic (1997) classifies therapists who value the therapy relationship as working within psychodynamic frameworks. Therapists who work from either medical or music-based approaches—while actually differing quite dramatically from each other in many other ways—share this notion of not placing the therapeutic relationship in a central position. For theorists in the medical model, it is the intervention rather than the relationship that is the primary clinical factor, and for music-based theorists, it is the nature of music as an experiential medium that serves this function.

Psychoanalytic and Humanistic Perspectives on the Client–Therapist Relationship in Music Therapy

Florence Tyson (Tyson, 1981; McGuire, 2004) was one of the earliest[1] thinkers in music therapy to apply psychoanalytic thinking in an in-depth manner to clinical processes. She writes primarily about music therapy in psychiatry and her view of mental illness was strongly influenced by the psychoanalytic thinking that dominated the field in the 1940s–1960s, prior to the emergence of organic explanations for conditions such as schizophrenia. She detailed how it was the music therapist's responsibility "to establish an object relationship similar in structure to the primary relationship" (Tyson, 2004, p. 9), that of the infant to the mother. Relying less on interpretation and verbal faculties—something that could be deficient in individuals with severe mental illnesses—she recommended that music therapists in psychiatry provide an "object relationship" where the salient interpersonal interaction can occur nonverbally, much as the mother provides the appropriate relationship that allows for the infant's normal development. Just as normal healthy development in infants proceeds essentially nonverbally with the mother, the music therapist by virtue of working through mu an alternative, age-appropriate, nonverbal medium in which to facilitate the client's ther regression and subsequent development.

Similar to how the healthy infant–mother relationship develops, in the initial stages of the therapeutic relationship, the therapist must be a benign presence who establishes pleasurable, expressive musical experiences without challenging the client. Music becomes the mother substitute and musical instruments become the symbol of the transition from a merged relationship to one of autonomy, just as a child's stuffed animal functions in this role in psychoanalytic theories of child development. In Tyson's approach it is the interactive and nonverbal nature of music that explains its clinical value.

Mary Priestley (1994) also emphasizes the centrality of the therapeutic relationship as "a vital fact for the growth of the patient" (p. 67). Similar to Tyson, she emphasizes its "holding" quality and the fact that it ought to be non-demanding. She appeals to the ideas of Viktor Frankl for whom it was not the therapist's method but the relationship that was the crucial and most significant factor in therapy. Although Priestley's view on the nature of the therapeutic relationship is adapted to the needs of individual clients, she does cite the work of Wilfred Bion for whom the therapist was a container and the client was the contained. The therapist takes on difficult emotions projected by the client and holds these emotions until they can be taken back by the client in a transmuted form.

Priestley (1994) subscribes to the view that there are four levels in which therapists and clients meet: "the working alliance, the transference, the musical relationship and the role-free human relationship" (pp. 72–73). The different levels can be used to assess the stage of therapy that the client is in. The working alliance is a professional relationship that allows the purposeful work of therapy to proceed. The transference relationship reflects interpersonal distortions of each party by the other due to the way in which the relationship evokes feeling responses that originated in early relationships. The musical relationship is a mutually reciprocal one in which feelings from both parties are manifested most overtly; it is the level at which therapist and client "are closest together at the most unconscious depth" (p. 74). When clients are able to function in a role-free human relationship with minimal distortion, the ending of therapy is indicated. It therefore has significance in therapy primarily as a sign that the process has been successful and should be concluded.

Tyson and Priestley represent first generation music therapy pioneers who largely developed their own ideas about music therapy in highly original ways. Some of their ideas have become part of the conventional wisdom in music therapy as illustrated by authors such as David John (1995) who represents a somewhat more updated version of psychodynamic thinking in music therapy. He contextualizes his approach within the psychoanalytic theories of object relations as defined by Melanie Klein and further developed by Bion and D.W. Winnicott. For John, the client's relationship with the therapist is the crucial factor in effecting therapeutic change. Music is, at best, of secondary importance and it only takes the form that it does as "a by-product of the particular forms of relating that occurred in therapy" (John, p. 157). Music as such has no importance save as a reflection of the dynamics of the therapy relationship; it is a sound mirror of the primary clinical processes.

In spite of the consensus in psychiatry that considers mental disorders such as schizophrenia to have organic origins, John appeals to the psychoanalytic explanation for it as a rationale for his ideas about relationship in music therapy. He invokes the psychoanalytic explanation that considers normal infant development as passing "through a psychotic stage of development" (John, 1995, p. 158). The mother plays an essential role in containing the anxieties associated with this stage and this containment allows the infant to move through this stage and achieve normal, healthy development. Although it is implied by his line of argument, John does not directly assert that psychoses are caused by inadequate early development. Instead, he makes the argument that the ways in which the mother helps an infant to negotiate the psychotic stage of development provides a template for how therapists can help adults suffering from psychoses.

For John, nothing specific about music provides its clinical value. Instead, it merely provides a forum through which client and therapist relate to one another in a way that supports the client's return to early stages of development where a symbolic, reparative, re-parenting process can take place. The therapist provides a container in which the client can project "primitive feelings of rage that otherwise might threaten to overwhelm and destabilize a weak and vulnerable ego" (John, 1995, p. 160). In initial stages of therapy, the therapist's music might be more similar to that of the client to provide the client an experience of being merged with. But the therapist's task is to gradually develop more separateness in the music in order to promote the client's ego development. John explains this as analogous to the process of the mother's withdrawal of the breast: it provides frustration that it is necessary to be mastered for development to occur. The music has two functions for John: First, to assist in the management of emotions; and second, to provide a medium of experience through which the client can internalize "the responsive and containing function of the therapist" (p. 166).

To summarize, there are a few important features of the therapeutic relationship characteristic of psychoanalytic thinking. The relationship between client and therapist is not an authentic one built upon transparency, authenticity, or mutuality. It is a contrivance whose artificial nature is necessary to the success of the therapy. The relationship is identical to that of the psychoanalyst who works verbally. There are no special considerations related to the fact that client and therapist relate to one another through the medium of music. None of the unique features of musical experience are considered in determining what the relationship should be or how it functions to advance the processes of therapy.

The humanistic perspective of psychotherapists such as Carl Rogers is also prominent in considering common notions of the client–therapist relationship in music therapy. Edith Boxill's (1985) view is representative of this perspective where a strong client–therapist relationship is necessary for effective therapy. The relationship must be built upon a strong degree of trust where the therapist has an abiding respect for the dignity and personal worth of the client. When feelings of trust and safety are established, the sharing of music creates a special, nonthreatening bond, with the therapist's personal qualities serving "as the living instrument of therapy" (Boxill, p. 89). Chief among these qualities are self-understanding, the ability to project oneself through music, and attributes such as empathy, flexibility, spontaneity, creativity, and intuition.

A warm, genuine, supportive, and open relationship is the central element of therapy. These qualities, along with the therapist's ability to be authentic and to fully accept the client with unconditional positive regard, form the ground from which the client's growth and development proceed. Central to this process is that the therapist relates to the client in a holistic way, not just as a carrier of a particular diagnosis.

In actual practice, a substantial number of music therapists combine elements of psychodynamic and humanistic thinking. However, in a more pure humanistic perspective, the therapeutic relationship, while necessary for therapy, need not be examined in detail by the client and therapist. It does provide the ground for therapy and is perhaps the most crucial element. And there are good reasons for the adaptation of humanistic thinking in music therapy. Primary among these are the focus of humanistic thinking on the client's here-and-now presence rather than upon one's personal and family history of relationships. Musical engagement brings people into the moment, and this can be a highly effective experience for clients whose areas of difficulty prevent them from being fully present in the moment because of emotional or cognitive reasons.

Moreover, in contrast to traditional psychoanalytic models where the therapist is not fully authentic as a person (in order to better facilitate the client's transference or projections), in humanistic thinking it is essential to be a warm, open, and authentic person in the therapeutic encounter. In music therapy approaches, where therapists are fully engaged as music makers, it is natural that more of who they are as people is revealed than is the case in a psychoanalytic encounter. The therapist's musical sensibilities, expressiveness, and limitations are present in the live music-making with clients. A humanistic approach where the relationship is based upon a genuine encounter between two authentic individuals provides a natural fit for what naturally happens in music therapy sessions.

Social- and Music-Based Perspectives on the Client–Therapist Relationship

In the culture-centered music therapy approach advanced by Brynjulf Stige (2002a) the topic of relationship is framed in much broader ways than in approaches based upon psychotherapy models. One of the central clinical goals in this framework is enhanced participation by the client on all levels of society. Thus, in addition to the traditional client–therapist relationship, other types of relationships are emphasized, including the relationship of the client to music and to a whole host of social groups and institutions at all levels of society. Clients who participate within different communities establish "*trajectories of participation* that relate to each other; personal trajectories as well as trajectories connected to specific institutions, communities, and society at large" (p. 215). These individualized paths make possible the creation of new self-identities afforded by the greater variety of social roles and expectations present in various community contexts. Because social context strongly influences the development of self-identity promoted by music therapists, it is essential that therapy take place in the context of as many types of relationships as is possible.

New notions of the client–therapist relationship must be articulated because the music therapist plays a central role in helping to mediate the relationship of client to culture. Stige advocates for a view of the relationship as an egalitarian partnership. Sometimes the relationship is better understood as a consultative one and at other times the music therapist is more of a project coordinator, working to integrate groups of clients into specific music events, cultures, and organizations in the community.

Another notion of the therapeutic relationship that is essentially collaborative is advanced by Randi Rolvsjord (2010). In her resource-oriented approach, both parties are "actively involved in the process of assessment, in deciding the goal for the therapy, and in finding a way to work toward problem-solving, development, or other goals" (p. 214). The therapist's craft is not construed as selecting and executing the correct intervention but as facilitating the client's involvement and overall motivation in therapy.

Rolvsjord believes in the strong value of the therapeutic relationship, citing research in the common factors framework that asserts the importance of various relationship factors in determining clinical outcome. For Rolvsjord, the therapeutic relationship is not just another intervention; instead, the relationship between therapist and client is a real human relationship. She takes Priestley's notion of the "role free relationship" and says that rather than being an endpoint of therapy, such a relationship should be the condition from which therapy proceeds from the outset. The argument for the importance of an egalitarian relationship stems from the belief that many clients of music therapists—including those individuals with mental health problems and learning disabilities—are trapped within power imbalances in many of their relationships in the world. The presence of mutuality is crucial to avoid repeating the problematic, disempowering dynamic which only serves to exacerbate the negative effects of the client's disability.

Rolvsjord considers that music therapy relationships involve something unique: the collaborative creation of music. This is an activity that allows clients to explore resources and problems directly, not just talk about them. There are some unique aspects specific to music that go beyond those of nonverbal mediums in general. The activity of "doing together" contributes to a sense of mutuality where the formal roles of client and therapist are diminished. The sharing of joy and competence in making music together also helps establish feelings outside that of an unequal, purely professional relationship.

Writers from music-based traditions—such as Nordoff-Robbins music therapy (NRMT)— have addressed the question of how sharing musical experience affects the therapeutic relationship. Instead of deriving a concept of the relationship from external, psychologically-based frameworks, these perspectives consider the nature of music and communal musical experience and develop the implications for therapy from them directly.

Central to the practice of NRMT is the idea of "musical meeting, where both players share something of thought, feeling and intention within the purely musical" (Ansdell, 1995, p. 67). Gary Ansdell invokes Martin Buber's notion of meeting in which "each side somehow changes the other, however subtly" (p. 67). The *between* in the Buberian sense is the musical meeting ground where both presences (therapist and client) respond to one another as mutual human intelligences, not as disembodied sounds. The specific qualities of the *musical between* are what allow clients to transcend limitations they face in other media and realms of human experience. Being in music is

> like the difference between being on land being in water. Suddenly you feel different— freer, supported, you can do different things . . . [A relationship is] established in the improvisation from the first time a musical contact is made, and developed through to the point where a true "meeting" can come in the music.
>
> (Ansdell, 1995, p. 68)

Music therapy begins in the musical meeting when clients experience a relationship between their music and that of the therapist. As Ansdell (1995) says of a client, "he hears himself being heard and responds to his being responded to" (p. 69). When this occurs, both parties become involved in a complementary way as they "share one flow of musical experience" (p. 71). Through the therapist's response, the client becomes aware of his own music. Both parties respond to each other in the music mutually constituting a profoundly satisfying human relationship based upon the experience and "feeling of being understood and accepted by someone else" (p. 72). The musical exchange "is a flow of meaning between people which includes physical, emotional and intellectual experience" (p. 72). Consequently, it is more than just an experience of being together; it moves beyond that to a sense of "becoming together" (p. 73).

Is this way of being in music specific to music therapy, defining it to some extent, or is it characteristic of musical interaction generally? Mercédès Pavlicevic (1997) argues for the uniqueness of music therapy in this regard, asserting that it is essential for the music therapist to be able to discern the inter-musical from the inter-personal. In other words, it is essential to know when one is "just" playing music with a client as opposed to making music that has interpersonal significance. The interpersonal significance is necessary for a musical interaction to have implications for relationship, which in turn is necessary for the whole thing to be of value clinically.

Other theorists do not accept this dichotomous framework and do not believe in the differentiation between personal and musical. Just as the idea that *the personal is political* took root in political theory in the 1960s, for music-based practitioners, *the musical is clinical*. For example, in NRMT, the individual aspects of one's musicality and technique are considered to be highly personal representations of the music therapist. They are neither technical nor impersonal but are that person's musical presence in the world. Rachel Verney identifies a sub-personal level of musicality that underlies any type of musical–personal relationship. This level incorporates the fundamental aspects of "gesture and energy . . . which are natural to music-making" (Verney & Ansdell, 2010, p. 18). All of the performative aspects of music that exist beyond notation or dynamic markings—such as the individual's chosen rate of accelerando—are what define the musical inter-relatedness between client and therapist.

This lack of a dichotomy between the personal and the musical dimensions of therapy is central to NRMT. The client is invited into music and is simultaneously making "a relationship *to* music itself and a human relationship *in* music [emphasis added]" (Verney & Ansdell, 2010, p. 20). The client's relationship is always first and foremost to music, but the way that the therapist shapes the client's musical experience ensures that it has a personal dimension. The improvised music is based upon the quality of the client's movements, mood, and overall responsiveness filtered through the therapist's musicality. So there is a personal aspect and a personal relationship, but it is all mediated through the inherent qualities of music as a medium.

This emphasis on musical relating is often considered from outside the framework as indicating a purely musical—read *impersonal*—approach. However, this critique ignores the degree to which the musical is considered to be personal. Gary Ansdell describes it this way:

> This critique assumes that for a child to beat out the phrasing of a song accurately . . . or to stabilize erratic beating is to work for a musical goal only. But as Paul Nordoff said, to order your beating is to order your being—a musical goal is at one and the same time a personal goal.
>
> (Verney & Ansdell, 2010, p. 60)

The type of listening and attention that the therapist must engage in to produce the type of improvised music that serves as a sound portrait of the client's inner being—and to which he or she therefore responds so effectively—results from a focus that allows clients to feel heard and attended to in a unique way. The listening goes beyond that of empathy to the musical between created by the overlap of the client's and the therapist's musical beings. The detailed listening to smallest subtleties of the client's sounds is what allows therapists to respond in a way that clients feel really *heard*, many for the first time in their lives. Therapeutic change comes about from this intense level of *being with* in the music that is dependent upon being fully conscious of one's contribution to the music.

> If you're constantly ahead of your client when you play with them; if you're con-
> stantly (but not consciously) leading them, pushing them in the music . . . this matters
> because these minute details of musical timing, and balance and touch make up how
> you're relating to the client. Actually they are how you're relating—who you are
> together musically . . . This passion for musical detail isn't just a "purely musical" matter
> —it's a concern for exactly what's going on between two or more people in music
> therapy.
>
> (Verney & Ansdell, 2010, pp. 77–78)

In a psychodynamic framework this is considered to be over-listening to the music at the expense of not hearing the client. In the music-based framework, the music is not symbolizing anything more fundamental—such as the contents of the unconscious—so the perception of the music *is* the perception of the client.

Rachel Verney goes so far as to ask the question "is there any such thing as a 'therapeutic relationship'" (Verney & Ansdell, 2010, p. 65)? She notes that in NRMT with children, the client relates primarily to the music rather than to the therapist. It is the attitude of the therapist that determines whether one is working toward a more personal or a more musical relationship.

Ansdell develops the idea that in music psychotherapy the musical relating is a path to establishing the interpersonal relationship and music is merely a means to this end. In NRMT, the observation that children with disabilities related so strongly to the music itself led to this emphasis in both practice and theory. When music therapy work is effective, it draws its power from the strong commitment to music shared by client and therapist. This mutual commitment serves to empower the client and to ensure that the client's willingness to engage in music is not just a matter of being compliant to the therapist.

For Verney and Ansdell, the joint focus on creating music and a musical relationship moves the work beyond that of verbal psychotherapy. The work in music is not at all focused on enhancing the interpersonal relating, although this can often come about as a secondary consequence. Music therapists who consider the music as a vehicle for the interpersonal, work differently from therapists who are more music based. In the former approach, one can see therapists striving to make eye contact and develop more explicit moments of communication. In NRMT, you may not see this same level of physical focus on the other because both parties are focused on playing their instruments. But the real contact is dependent upon listening in a careful way so that the contact is evident in the shared musical creation; the contact is perceptible auditorily rather than visually or physically.

Verney and Ansdell believe that it is a mistake to dichotomize the musical and the interpersonal dimensions. Musicing with another person opens up a different way of being interpersonal, a way that is unique to music. In fact, Verney feels that the *therapeutic relationship* as a reified entity is not a particularly useful construct in understanding a music-based approach to music therapy. Instead of building a relationship, she focuses on developing the client's "qualities of relatedness" (2010, p. 69) through music. There is an interpersonal relationship that builds just from the weekly encounters; spending time with another person builds trust. Yet this aspect of the relationship is different from the musical relating where the real therapy takes place.

For Verney, the reification of the process of musical relatedness at the heart of music therapy only comes about because of the influence of psychotherapeutic thinking. However, because musical relatedness is structured by the music and the way that it is created at any moment in time, the concept of relatedness is both more fluid and vital than that of the therapeutic relationship. The process of relatedness and obstacles to it are what the music-based therapist works on and through, as opposed to the therapeutic relationship with all of its baggage from the client's life that the psychotherapist or music psychotherapist works with.

Clients can engage in vital, flowing, mutually interactive musical improvisations with therapists although the relationship outside of the music may have none of these qualities. The nonmusical relationship can be positively affected by sharing these experiences, but the musical relatedness is the therapy; it is not the examination of the extra-musical relationship upon which the music impacts.

Because the intense relatedness that occurs in music is not necessarily attached to a concrete life event, memory, or person, the process in NRMT is considered to be intimate but not necessarily personal. Music provides the medium through which individuals can experience themselves in freer, more expressive, and responsive ways. It is the liberation from the necessity to attach the musical experience to something outside itself that enables this transformation to occur. Rather than focusing on establishing a relationship, Verney focuses on establishing a type of relating whose goal "is to be in a state of 'meeting'. In music you . . . stay in a constant state of meetingness" (Verney & Ansdell, 2010, p. 72). The purpose of music in music therapy is to be in the present moment and to the extent that one is focusing on the qualities of an enduring relationship, one is not in the moment. "If you're in the now you don't have 'a relationship' . . . you are meeting" (p. 72).

Another perspective on the client relationship builds upon the idea that both parties share the common experience of being co-musicians, and this shared identity provides a connection that transcends the differences inherent in the quite different roles of client and therapist. For example, the idea of the client–therapist relationship having some of the qualities of fellow players in a musical ensemble or band was developed in Aigen (2005c). This feeling of being in a band that endures through time has several important clinical functions as a stable band develops an individual musical profile that can itself evolve.

In this study, the three-member band (therapist, co-therapist, client) was "one in which exploration, risk-taking, spontaneity, and moving into unpredictable emotional realms, were all part of its identity" (Aigen, 2005c, p. 88). To the extent that the client identified with the band, he internalized the values that support transformation by embracing novelty. Enhanced social and psychological functioning is embedded within these health-promoting activities that directly challenge the limitations imposed by client disability. And it is the basic desire to achieve communal experience through music that can help clients overcome their fears and resistiveness.

In this view, the process of therapy—involving a personal transformation that includes a restructuring of one's self image—can be thought of as a cultural rite of passage. As a process of transition between two more stable states of being, it conveys an experience of liminality in which participants share feelings of *communitas* (Turner, 1969). In *communitas*, nonliminal social distinctions are diminished and mutuality, equality and an absence of status differences are promoted. These qualities come to characterize the relatedness between therapist and client in approaches that emphasize the creation of musical *communitas* as an important therapeutic tool.

When therapists establish such equal relationships with clients, and when their theoretical framework goes beyond that provided by psychodynamic thinking to include sociological and anthropological concepts, an entirely new type of therapeutic relationship becomes possible along with the unleashing of powerful social forces that promote individual development. But therapists can only do this when they are comfortable participating authentically in a process in which they are subject to the same transformational forces as are clients. This requires therapists to allow the therapy experience to be meaningful to them to the extent that this is possible within a professional, therapeutic relationship.

Feelings of *communitas* are central components of gaining a sense of purpose in life, and to the extent that music therapists conceive of this focus as being a legitimate part of their work it becomes an important goal in therapy. Individuals who experience musical *communitas* together can develop a strong affinity for both the experience and for the individuals with whom the experience is shared. When this experience is shared in a music therapy setting, it becomes an important component of the therapeutic relationship.

This overall discussion highlights the fact that in music-centered thinking, clinicians think musically as they approach their work. The client–therapist meeting in music therapy is considered as the meeting of two musicians. This can transcend some barriers typically present with clients and help to establish relationships where this is typically quite difficult, such as with children with autism, victims of abuse, or paranoid individuals. The meeting between two musicians supports mutuality and equality in the therapeutic relationship, elements that facilitate the achievement of clinical goals related to developing social and communicative functioning.

In a relationship based upon the opportunity to create music together "the primary message from the therapist to the client is *I am here to help you make music*, rather than *I am here to change you, fix you, control you, or heal you*" (Aigen, 2005a, p. 120). The demands and challenges placed on the client are internal ones that originate in the client's own propensity for musicing rather than being external ones that emanate from the therapist as an authority figure. In this way, the music in music-based theory takes on functions more typically assumed by the therapist in behavioral or psychodynamic approaches.

When the inner dynamics and processes of music are consciously directed by the therapist, the result is to "depersonalize those aspects of the therapy process that might otherwise be more problematic, threatening, or challenging" (Aigen, 2005a, p. 112). Locating the more difficult demands of music therapy in the music preserves the relationship between therapist and client as a safe haven or a resource to be used by the client in meeting the challenges inherent in musicing. The intrinsic gratification provided by enhanced levels of musical functioning motivates the client to overcome the cognitive, affective, and motoric challenges present in the music therapy session.

The Way Forward

Psychodynamically-oriented therapists say that it is wrong for music-centered practitioners to ignore the exploration of the essential dynamics of the client–therapist relationship as this exploration constitutes one of the most fruitful avenues in which therapy can proceed. Music-centered practitioners respond that the way that they use music means that many of the dynamics present in psychodynamic work are just not activated in their approach and, to the extent that they are present, the more fruitful strategy is to use the music in an artful way to circumvent these issues rather than engage them directly. Can these positions be reconciled or at least can some accommodation be reached between them?

A simple answer would be to say that both perspectives have their adherents, they exist within different treatment frameworks, they make sense within those frameworks, and there should be no pressure to either reconcile them or to establish one as more advantageous than the other. After all, the interests of clients are best served by a diversity of clinical approaches and a tolerant attitude supports this diversity. However, to implement such a magnanimous perspective requires a number of professional conditions that are not necessarily present in music therapy:

1. It requires that the elements of any one theoretical perspective are not enshrined in academic or professional standards. This is not necessarily the case in countries where elements of psychodynamic thinking are considered to be essential aspects of legitimate music therapy practice. For example, requiring discussion of constructs such as transference and countertransference to allow one to function as a clinical supervisor, or requiring prospective therapists to have undergone their own therapy, only make sense in a psychoanalytic framework. When standards like these are present in important music therapy cultures such as the UK, adherents of alternative frameworks are at a professional disadvantage.

2. It also requires that—absent unequivocal empirical evidence to the contrary—different approaches are not considered more effective, more advanced, or to work at a more fundamental level within the person than are other approaches. Again, the main issue here seems to be the privileging of psychodynamic perspectives that require the consideration of relationship dynamics as an essential component of the therapy. Because of a belief that this type of work engages the unconscious mind, it is promoted as more profound than other forms of work. Alternative frameworks that are more music-based are considered to be more superficial, less advanced, and more suited to entry levels of practice rather than advanced ones. For a truly accepting profession to exist, it is necessary for psychodynamic theorists to acknowledge that entities such as the unconscious mind and processes such as transference are theoretical entities that exist within some treatment frameworks, but not others. They do not necessarily exist for all practitioners and they should not be invoked to determine levels of music therapy practice or guidelines to ethical practice. This is not to say that different levels of practice do not exist; it is to say that these levels cannot be determined merely by the extent to which psychodynamic thinking is invoked.

3. Enhanced respect for all perspectives benefits clients. It may be that there are psychodynamic music therapists whose theoretical allegiance is determined by their own fears or insecurities about working primarily in the music; and it may be that there are music-based music therapists whose theoretical allegiance is determined by an inability to face their own unconscious fears and blocks. However, neither state of affairs weighs for or against either of these positions. An understanding by psychodynamic therapists that music-based work can be just as important and fundamental to clients as can their

own psychodynamic work should be balanced by a recognition by music-based therapists that there are eminently positive reasons for psychodynamic approaches to be available to clients as well.

One's view of the client–therapist relationship in music therapy is invariably connected to some of the other issues discussed in previous chapters: Is music therapy a form of psychotherapy? Is the identity of the music therapist primarily as a therapist using music or a musician working toward therapy goals? Is music therapy fundamentally a health-care discipline or an arts discipline? Until the answers to such questions acquire consensus in local music therapy communities the best course of action is one that accepts all views of the therapy relationship and that does not use the components of any particular view to legislate guidelines for legitimate and ethical clinical practice.

Note

1. The 2004 publication is an edited collection of Tyson's writings that date back as far as 1959.

PART IV

How Does Music Therapy Relate to Other Uses of Music in Society?

9

MUSIC THERAPY AND TRADITIONAL HEALING PRACTICES

Definitional Issues

Overview

Music therapy as an arena of professional practice emerged in Western countries, first in the USA, followed soon by developments in Northern Europe, South America, Australia, and Asia. It is in Africa that this practice has been slowest to develop and in which the clash between the concepts and practices of music therapy and those of long-existing local healing practices that employ music have been most prominent. The discussion in Chapter 1 considered whether or not music therapy is continuous with perennial healing practices employing music. In contrast to the historical investigation from Chapter 1 where the question of temporal continuity was considered, the present chapter and Chapter 10 take more of a cultural-sociological perspective, looking for geographical continuity in the current day between the modern profession and healing practices as they exist in primarily non-Western cultures.

Two questions form the central focuses of music therapy literature in this area. First, is music therapy a contemporary form of shamanic uses of music or is it fundamentally different from these practices? Second, should music healing practices in non-Western cultures be acknowledged as music therapy? These two questions are similar although they adopt different orientation points in examining the relationship between music therapy and shamanic uses of music. The first question considers whether music therapists perform a social role that fits what is generally understood to constitute the shaman's role. The second question reverses this orientation and considers if what occurs in music healing rituals meets general criteria of music therapy.

In Western cultures, a variety of individuals and systems employ the *sound healer* or *music healer* label, both of which represent new-age practices quite different from music therapy. They do not have dedicated courses of study in accredited universities, nor do they have the same level of professional certification and licensing by regulatory and other governmental bodies. Their practices tend to resemble those of traditional healers more than those of health-care workers and their explanatory rationales invoke contemporary scientific formulations from areas such as physics, acoustics, and physiology, along with more esoteric rationales drawn from Eastern spiritual disciplines. A noncritical overview of these practices is presented by Crowe and Scovel (1996).

It might seem that activities in this area would provide an important connection between music therapy and traditional music healing practices. However, this domain of practice was exposed for its generally confused and fallacious foundations in an extraordinarily detailed study by Lisa Summer (1996). While publications exploring the relationship between music therapy and ritual healing practices with music have been proliferating in recent years, there has been little attention paid to Western-style music healing practices in the music therapy literature following the publication by Crowe and Scovel. Thus, the relationship between these two domains will not be explored in the present text.

Is Music Therapy a Continuation of Shamanic Practice?

In considering the relationship between music therapy and shamanism it is necessary to consider the temporal context in terms of what has preceded music therapy historically and the multicultural context in terms of what music practices exist currently throughout the world. A number of authors cite the historical continuity to argue that Western music therapy is a modern version of shamanic music healing. Moreno (1988a) believes that the modern profession of music therapy is nothing more than "a recent and specialized line of development of the continuing 30 thousand year-old shamanic traditions of music and healing still being practiced throughout the world" (p. 271). Placing the origins of music therapy in prehistory is also done by Winn, Crowe, and Moreno (1989), who assert that the origins of music therapy reach back "20,000 years to the beat of the shaman's drum as he rang his song of curing" (p. 67).

Winn et al. also note parallels in the activities engaged in by shamans and music therapists, particularly in the way that songs are used to convey archetypal wisdom and to develop specific applications to particular individuals' specific circumstances and needs. The establishment of shamanism as the historical precursor of music therapy is warranted because of "how many shamanic parallels exist just below the surface of so much of our usual music therapy practice" (p. 70). An increased awareness of shamanism as the historical antecedent of music therapy should encourage music therapists to make "a more conscious integration of shamanic techniques in music therapy" (p. 70) because doing so will enrich the breadth and depth of contemporary practice.

There is a strong parallel among the client's relationship to the therapist, the shaman's relationship to the person healed, and the listener's relationship to musicians in nonclinical, tribal contexts according to Moreno (1988a). These parallels are used to argue that the professional structure of the creative arts therapies in modern Western society—with strict divisions denoted by disciplines such as art therapy, dance therapy, and music therapy—reflects the overspecialization of modern life. Because shamans used all arts modalities, Moreno argues, so should contemporary arts therapists. Shaun McNiff (1988) also believes that creative arts therapists should be generalists, prepared to act within any artistic medium because this reflects shamanic activity, which in turn reflected natural human needs.

Authors who see the arts therapies as forms of shamanism also argue that they meet religious and spiritual needs in addition to the psychological needs that characterize psychotherapy. McNiff (1988) says that contemporary "concepts such as shamanism, therapy, art, and religion" have a common origin in their constituent "behaviors, rhythms, enactments, and images" (p. 285) and the modern concepts only serve to create an artificial separation among them. In taking this tack, McNiff is also guided by the fundamentally artistic nature of the creative arts therapies and the belief that theory and practice in this domain will be better served when it is informed by "concepts from artistic, religious and shamanic traditions than by psychological theories that have guided mental health systems throughout the twentieth century" (p. 285). The practice of the artist and that of the shaman is a sacred one and "the artist is unconsciously carrying on the work of the shaman" (p. 285). While McNiff expresses caution in the use of the term *shaman*, he employs it because it provides a more suitable and all-encompassing fit for what he does as a creative arts therapist. These activities transcend "conventional psychological constructs" (p. 290) because they meet indigenous religious impulses of people.

One point made by Winn et al. relates to the trance-like effect of music in shamanism. In using music to create trance, the intrinsic qualities of music as a creative, expressive modality are not being drawn upon. Instead, the focus is on the ability of music to occupy a part of the brain that must be stilled in order for healing imagery to emerge. Thus, one challenge that will have to be met by those who argue for the fundamental continuity of music therapy and shamanism is to explain why the activation of the client's expressive, creative, and artistic impulses that are so central to music therapy do not seem to have a parallel in shamanism.

A number of efforts to establish music therapy as a form of shamanism refer to the model of guided imagery and music (GIM), which lends itself to this task due to its use of altered states of consciousness to evoke healing imagery. Kovach (1985) considers the ecstatic state reached in shamanic ritual to parallel the altered states of consciousness reached during GIM experiences. There are a number of additional similarities between the two domains: the common images experienced by the shaman and GIM client; the shared structure of consciousness in both experiences; the four stages comprising each activity; the themes of the narratives that characterize the experiences, such as that of death-rebirth; experiences of ascending and descending through unseen worlds and realms of experience; and, a tripartite division which in GIM is considered to be a division of consciousness and in shamanism a division of worlds.

One important difference between shamanism and GIM is that except for the initiatory rite where the shaman's altered state of consciousness is for self-benefit, the shaman typically enters the altered state for the benefit of others. The person being healed does not typically travel in the shamanic sense. This contrasts with GIM, as it is the recipient of the healing (the client) who enters the altered state. However, arguing against the more prevalent perspective, Winn, Crowe, and Moreno (1989) state that it is not just the shaman who travels but sometimes the music is the vehicle for the patient's exploration as well, such as in "the more serious case of soul loss [where] the shaman's chant may take the patient on a journey in order to locate and return the soul to its rightful place" (p. 68). However, this perspective seems to be a minority one that articulates, if anything, an exception to the general rule.

The fundamental differences between therapy and shamanism owe to fundamental differences about the etiology of illness in the two domains. Shamans believe that illness owes to problems in the world of spirits and the shaman mediates between this world and the everyday world to effect a cure or solve a problem for the recipient of the services. In GIM, the recipient experiences the altered state. The cure is believed to be internal and the healing is self-healing that occurs through accessing inner sources of strength and insight.

In contrast to the notion that all clients can achieve the altered state, the shaman is considered a privileged being who is uniquely able to enter the realms where healing takes place. Even though the acquisition of inner visions is relevant in both practices, the fact that it is the healer who enters the altered state of consciousness in shamanism while in music therapy it is the client who has this experience represents a fundamental difference that militates against the arguments for music therapy being a form of shamanism.

Further supporting this point is the cautionary note sounded by Claire Schmais (1988) who says that to use the label *shaman* is to be aligned "with a mystical, religious tradition and declare that our primary mission is to intercede between man and the supernatural" (p. 287). In contrast, the term *creative arts therapist* suggests alignment with "a secular tradition that links science and art in the interest of healing" (p. 301). For a number of practical, conceptual, and professional reasons, Schmais expresses skepticism about considering creative arts therapists as modern-day shamans.

In articulating the proper relationship between music therapy and shamanic healing, it is important to honor both the similarities and differences between them. The interest within music therapy for exploring parallels with shamanism stems from the realization that "shamanic forms of healing, as well as other ritual uses of music, represent the first efforts to effect self-transformation through music" (Aigen, 1991a, p. 85). It is therefore natural that music therapists endeavoring to help clients transform themselves or their relationships to others through music will see strong connections in shamanic healing. The interest in transpersonal thinking in music therapy is a reflection of the awareness of these historical roots.

All of the authors who describe the connections between these two domains refer to the function of both therapist and shaman in entering an unseen realm and accessing sources of strength, health, and wisdom. One strategy in establishing the connection between music therapy and shamanism is to describe in contemporary psychological terms what the shaman does, such as considering the unseen realm of the shaman as the personal and collective unconscious. It is possible to understand the shaman as an ally who coaxes out and provides manifestations of the hidden parts of the psyche. "The shaman facilitates constructive interactions with these elements, encouraging the 'client' to do battle with and overcome deep fears, to learn from archetypal sources of wisdom representing one's true – and often repressed – self, thereby promoting a healthy relationship among the various psychic structures" (Aigen, 1991a, p. 88).

This strategy does not necessarily require the privileging of the rational, modern worldview. Instead, it describes a translation between two modes of understanding describing the same process. It is not that what the shaman "really" does is manifest "hidden parts of the psyche in the guise of contacting external entities" (Aigen, 1991a, p. 88). The psychodynamic interpretation of shamanic healing is a translation between epistemologically equivalent worldviews. A belief in contemporary taxonomies of psychological structures—consisting of entities such as the superego, id, shadow, anima, parent ego state, inner child—is not inherently more rational than is a belief in the presence of various families of gods or spirits. The psychological taxonomies function as a contemporary mythology; they provide a means to conceptualize and gain mastery over the hidden realms of the human mind. Yet it is not obvious that attributing an individual's actions to the influence of a vengeful superego is inherently more rational than is attributing that same action to the power of a wrathful demon or spirit.

Ultimately, in exploring the connections between shamanic ritual and music therapy, the goal is not to return to a former conceptualization (that of a shaman) that is removed from the cultural context which gave it meaning and efficacy. Instead, the idea is to understand how the contemporary music therapist functions in ways analogous to that of the shaman, in order to develop a more balanced and powerful professional practice.

The efficacy of the shaman's work is intimately connected to the cultural and epistemological contexts in which shamanism developed. That these contexts are not present in contemporary society argues against the maintenance of the archaic role. However, this does not mean that understanding the nature of the shaman's role is without value. A music therapist who believes in the perennial importance of myth, ritual, and creative activity in promoting human well-being is already meeting the social and psychological need that shamanic activity fulfilled.

A therapy client who reconnects with long split-off aspects of the personality is encouraged to integrate them into the present sense of self, not merge with them uncritically. In a similar vein, as music therapists learn more about shamanic and other ritual uses of music in healing, as a result of enhanced cultural and scholarly investigations, the most advantageous tack to take would be to integrate this knowledge into the matrix of rational, clinical beliefs and practices that reflect a modern worldview, rather than merge with this view in what would be, in a psychological sense, a form of regression rather than progression.

The idea that the influence of culture is both pervasive in music therapy and insufficiently considered is argued by Stige (2003). Adopting a perspective that is more cognizant of the effects of culture suggests that there is much to be gained by considering the implications of traditional healing practices for music therapy. The idea is not to import healing rituals into contemporary practice. Instead, Stige highlights three areas in which music therapists can gain from more detailed explorations into traditional healing rituals that incorporate music. First, examining that which is unfamiliar can help music therapists become better aware of fundamental assumptions embedded in their own theories and practices. Second, learning about healing rituals can reveal unexpected similarities with modern practices, which in turn might provide insight into "the shared biological roots for musicking and music therapy" (p. 404). Third, learning about the music healing practices from different cultures can help clinicians to develop greater sensitivity to the influence of culture, something that is increasing in relevance as clinicians work to a greater extent in multicultural contexts.

Are Indigenous Music Healing Practices Music Therapy?

Music therapists are also critiqued by Horden (2000c) for ignoring the social context of their work and he suggests that the "social anthropology of music and healing" (p. 16) represents a body of knowledge that can assist music therapy with addressing the definitional and evaluative difficulties they face. Horden describes afflictions in cultures of sub-Saharan Africa that are conceptualized as being caused by spirits and that are addressed through ritual that includes music, dance, and imagery. He also describes a condition that he labels "socio-somatic" (as opposed to psychosomatic) in that its causes are social and it developed as means to protect the health of this society "from the disease of capitalism" (Prins, as cited in Horden, p. 17).

Horden (2000c) notes, as points of contact between music healers and contemporary music therapists, the similarity in the way that the musical treatment is developed as individualized, improvised, variable, and unique "to both the patient and the healer" (p. 17). Horden laments the current situation where music therapists and social anthropologists have been writing largely in ignorance of each other's efforts and that too often musical detail is absent from the publications that have been produced.

There are some music therapists who have written about non-Western healing practices as forms of music therapy. Moreno (1995a) identifies contemporary music healing practices with Western music therapy. He claims that "music as therapy, without being described as 'music therapy,' is currently a flourishing practice in countless tribal and other nontechnological societies in Asia, Africa, Australia, America, Oceania, and Europe" (Moreno, 1988a, p. 271). To support his thesis, Moreno cites the fact that so much of the world's music has a healing function. He also refers to the performance of polyphonic rhythmic music of sub-Saharan Africa and sees the rhythmic entrainment characterizing this music as representing the common element "that can exist between the shaman and patient and between the music therapist and client" (p. 271).

Moreno highlights how religious belief systems and practices are analogous to therapy through the exploration of the Afro-Brazilian religion of candomblé. He equates religious practices of this type with therapy because they "provide belief systems that assist their adherents in coping with life problems and in providing forms of group support" (1995a, p. 218). Candomblé is of particular interest for music therapy because music is so prominent within it. It is constantly present during the weeks of seclusion that mark initiation rites, it induces spirit possession, and it effects transitions between different stages of ritual.

Moreno establishes a number of parallels between the two domains. First, there is a novice initiation period during which the cult leader becomes familiar with initiates' personality, needs, and areas of difficulty, and then determines the suitable spirits with whom they should bond. This is akin to the psychiatrist's diagnostic procedures. Second, the spirit is chosen to validate the initiate's personality, not to counteract aspects of it. This is like the validation occurring at the outset of therapy, which is important to establishing self-esteem and trust in the process. Third, music has a variety of functions during the initiation process: it maintains the two primary altered states of consciousness; it stimulates possession of the person by the relevant spirits through drumming and song; it initiates dance and acts out the roles of the spirits who possess them; it provokes trance states that may function to alleviate the stress of difficult social realities. Fourth, candomblé provides socially approved forms of emotional release and expression. Manifesting one's spirits can be seen in a Western view as releasing the parts of oneself that would normally be repressed.

Moreno does not support the implementation of Western music therapy with individuals in such cultures because they are already getting the appropriate "therapy" from their culturally-familiar forms. He argues that they would not benefit from Western therapy based on a contrasting worldview; the difficulties that suggest therapy for Westerners are met through the religion. It is religion *as* therapy.

Because the continent of Africa has seen the smallest amount of incursions of modern music therapy practice, it provides a suitable context for examining the question of whether or not ritual musical healing practices should be considered as forms of music therapy. Some of the authors who argue this point suggest that African music as music—not just in its overt healing applications—is inherently therapeutic.

For example, A-E. Mereni (1996) describes what music therapy might be like in an African context, beginning from the idea that healing is part of the natural function of music. The basic philosophy of music is one in which musical force is used to achieve healing or purification. Any approach to music therapy has to incorporate traditional music techniques to take advantage of what is considered effective treatment within any particular African culture. Also, some music is very special in that it allows for divine communion. Some sacred instruments help to connect with the gods and other instruments produce sounds that are considered to be the voice of the gods. But the message of the gods is not something that is understood by all. It requires a special individual to decode it, and this belief "is fundamental to the understanding of traditional music therapeutical practices in Africa" (p. 20).

Mereni equates the various gods/spirits that are given voice and contacted through music with the elements of the psyche in Western terms. To the extent that Africans employ music in healing through indigenous practice, they are already engaged in what would be considered music therapy in a Western framework. Moreover, music is typically used as a primary treatment for what are considered neurotic and psychotic disorders in a Western context, although the disorders are attributed to the actions of spirits rather than personality constituents.

The important uses of music relevant to understanding its therapeutic nature in Africa take place during three different types of occasions: initiation rites, exorcism rites, and funeral rites. Mereni (1997) argues that music is so essential to these events that they can legitimately be described as music therapy sessions used primarily to alleviate feelings of fear, anxiety, and pain.

Participants may receive the healing motion of music receptively and gain from the vibrations of the music or they may be active participants in the music and benefit from the bodily vibrations employed to create music. In each case, the activities are considered as examples of receptive or active music therapy. Treatment may be allopathic or homeopathic. There are no hard and fast rules as the appropriate treatment is individually determined by the practitioner's expertise. In making a comparison between this practice and Western approaches, the basic framework seems to be more psychotherapeutic than medical.

Writing from a Kenyan context, Bernhard Kigunda (2003) highlights a complex issue of terminology. He says that from the traditionalist perspective music itself is generally considered to be healing so there is a questioning of the need for the term *music therapy*, which can appear redundant. What is *music therapy* in the West, might just as well be called *music* in Kenya.

Another issue that Kigunda (2003) discusses is the necessity in Western conceptions for the presence of a professional music therapist for something to be music therapy. In Kenya, Kigunda asserts that there are instances "where music is used for/in therapy without a trained therapist" (Kigunda, 2003, "Related literature," para. 5). Even a liberalized conception of this role is too much for Kigunda. He cites Carolyn Kenny's (1989) definition as being satisfactory for an African context in its general outline but ultimately inadequate because of its reference to the notion of the therapist's role:

> Music therapy is a process and a form which combines the healing aspects of music with issues of human need to move toward the health and development of the individual and society at large. The music therapist serves as a resource person and guide, providing musical experience which directs clients towards health and well-being.
>
> (Kenny, 1989, p. 9)

For Kigunda, the fact that the impact of music therapy on clients resembles the impact of music on ritual participants suggests both the strong link between the two areas as well as the notion that a therapist may not be required for these experiences to occur. However, Kigunda notes that aspects of client experience that may be incidental to the primary focus or intent of the therapist are the ones that are most similar to what happens in healing rituals. Phenomena such as the alteration of consciousness, accessing unconscious material, and mystical, sacred, and spiritual experiences whose significance is typically minimized in clinical music therapy literature are the very things that Kigunda identifies as being most similar to what happens in healing rituals in music. He raises the possibility that while looking at the intent of the therapist might highlight the differences between therapy and ritual, looking at the impact on clients highlights the similarities.

While Kigunda wants to apply the term *music therapy* to traditional uses of music that are not implemented by a trained music therapist, he also believes that the professionalization of music therapy is an important step to be taken in Kenya. He argues that if music is being used with a healing intent then this should be the sole criterion to determine if a particular activity should be considered music therapy. He acknowledges that "this proposal widens the scope in the current meaning of music therapy" but he does not believe that it "hinders [the] growth of professionalism in modern music therapy" (Kigunda, 2003, "Discussion," para. 4).

Kigunda (2003) wants traditional healing to be recognized as a form of music therapy so that the cause of music therapy may be advanced in Kenya. Yet he also acknowledges that within the African academy, the people in positions to make these types of judgments are confused about what direction they should move. Traditional healing methods are familiar, yet unsystematic, practices whose efficacy is not rationally explicable. Contemporary music therapy has a rational, systematic foundation but its practices and rationales are largely unknown. This dilemma explains why "music therapy has remained an unnamed/anonymous therapeutic force in Kenya" (2003, "Discussion," para. 5).

The primary reason for the establishment of a defined profession such as music therapy is for the protection of the recipients of clinical services. Agreeing to the notion that music therapy can occur without the presence of a professional music therapist would go against this basic premise for a regulated profession and it seems like a nonstarter from a Western framework. Just as a lay person can ingest medicinal herbs for self-benefit without being considered thereby to be practicing medicine, the many ways that people engage with music for therapeutic ends should not imply that they are therefore practicing therapy.

Not all descriptions of African ritual as therapy rely on this type of claim. An exploration of ngoma as a form of therapy provides John Janzen (2000) with the opportunity to critique the way in which Western music therapists in Africa have ignored this indigenous tradition. He describes ngoma in ways that suggest a strong connection to therapy in the Western sense as the ritual entails "counseling and support during a lengthy therapeutic initiation" (p. 46). While the word *ngoma* bears multiple interpretations when translated into English, Janzen believes that in its essence it describes the same sequence of activities that characterize therapy processes. Its relevance to music therapy is that it is "an ancient, classical African ritual therapeutic process in which music is central" (p. 46).

Moreover, the very concept of music essential to ngoma is more congruent with the notion of music in therapy than it is with music as a commodity. Janzen (2000) argues that the conventional Western notion of music "suggests performers or players before an audience, rather than music emanating from among the participants" (p. 47). This latter, participatory essence of music that characterizes ngoma is a notion that most music therapists would endorse as well.

Practitioners of ngoma characterize it as a form of medicine rather than as a religion because of its healing focus. Janzen (2000) asserts that the "combination of song, dance and catharsis evocation does not make ngoma any less technically 'therapeutic' than technical approaches to Western music therapy" (p. 47). He adopts a position similar to that of Kigunda in saying that it is the focus on healing that qualifies this ritual as a form of music therapy and he further chastises music therapists for ignoring "African musical [*sic*] therapy" (p. 47). Equally, he critiques ethnomusicologists for not addressing music and medicine or music and therapy in their research. For him, the marginalization of traditional practice comes from both of these directions.

Janzen (2000) considers the writings of Mercédès Pavlicevic (1997, misidentified by Janzen as 1998) who has articulated "a perspective that appears to be compatible with ngoma as musical therapy" (p. 60) while also ignoring the potentials of ngoma in actual clinical practice. It is the emphasis on social and contextual factors in Pavlicevic's theory that Janzen believes makes a comfortable fit for considering ngoma as therapy. However, the ubiquity of ngoma as a social form of music, with purposes other than clinical, weighs against Pavlicevic's consideration of it as therapy.

Her personal experience of participating in African healing rites has led Pavlicevic (2001) to question whether music therapy has anything to gain from them. However, she is absolutely certain that the African worldview and approach to music-making in general has a great deal to offer music therapy. She implies that the supernatural and religious context of music healing practices create an unbridgeable chasm with music therapy, while she recognizes that the basic musicality and forms of expression and interaction in African music can be appropriated within a Western music therapy practice for significant benefit.

Janzen attributes the therapeutic efficacy of ngoma to its all-encompassing integration of music, dance, ritual, healing herbs, family members, community, initiates, and healers. However, it is this totalistic nature, which causes ngoma to be mischaracterized when it is addressed by scholars and governmental agencies. It is considered more primitive when compared to the more specialized approaches that characterize modern Western endeavors in this area. Thus, Janzen (2000) believes that considering ngoma as music therapy only captures one dimension of it, and in fact, "to call ngoma 'therapy' is probably already a distortion" (p. 64).

In its contradictory aspects, Janzen's perspective reflects the ambivalence involved in considering non-Western healing uses of music to be music therapy. On the one hand, he wants ngoma to be considered as a form of music therapy because of its efficacy, the orientation on health, the way in which it is valued by practitioners, and the heightening of emotion through music that it achieves. He criticizes Western music therapists for not considering it as therapy because of their own personal difficulties in coming to terms with how to use and understand it on its own terms. On the other hand, he also claims that ngoma is much broader than the Western notion of music therapy, and to consider it as such is to commit the sin of examining only a portion of it in isolation.

Music therapy is a Western concept embedded within a Western worldview characterized by specialization in training and application. Music therapy is separate from dance therapy, art therapy, drama therapy, and expressive arts therapy; it is also different from music education, music performance, and music education. This type of organization is part of a contemporary, Western worldview. So if ngoma is of a much broader nature than is music therapy, it seems paradoxical and unfair to label ngoma as music therapy and then to criticize music therapists for not adapting their conceptions and practice to the nature of ngoma. Why not just let ngoma and music therapy co-exist as quite different spheres of activity with quite different realms of application?

One possible objection is that the label *music therapy* confers prestige and privilege that does not accrue to indigenous healing rituals. The effort to portray ngoma as music therapy can be seen as an effort to gain esteem for it. However, as Janzen's discussion unintentionally highlights, considering ritual as therapy really does an injustice to both spheres of activity. On the one hand, it forces ngoma into a more narrow conceptualization that does not honor the totality of its practice; on the other hand, it unfairly critiques music therapists for not adapting their notions of therapy to a practice—because of its very totalistic, nonspecific nature—that is at variance with some fundamental assumptions of a modern approach to health care. The integrity of both ngoma and music therapy would be better served by not forcing the fundamentally non-Western healing music ritual into the modes of conceptualization that characterize Western disciplines.

The fundamental question is whether music therapy is a purely Western construct that is answerable to Western contexts and evaluative criteria, or is it something that should change to accommodate considerations from non-Western contexts? In this way, the question *What is music therapy?* is similar to the question *What is music?*. One perspective in gaining a comprehensive answer to the latter question is that it is relevant to consider non-Western music—which would generally be classified as music within a Western view—but not non-Western *conceptions* of music. Ngoma incorporates music but goes beyond it, by including as well movement and the invocation of spirits. Adopting an inclusive, multicultural stance that would refer to these elements in a definition of music would dilute the definition to the point of uselessness.

But while we may not want to incorporate the defining elements of ngoma into our definition of music, we may want our definition to be sufficiently broad to incorporate the elements of ngoma that would generally be recognized as music. In an effort to be inclusive, it is possible to differentiate the inclusion of what would broadly be considered music from a Western perspective from the inclusion of non-Western notions of music. The former strategy can broaden the definition and enlarge its realm of application; the latter strategy can lead to the dilution of the definition to the point where it loses any value.

The former strategy is a useful one to take in considering the relationship between music therapy and indigenous forms of healing that utilize music. It is not necessary for music therapists to consider ngoma to be a form of music therapy to benefit from its examination. Perhaps its public nature has parallels with community music therapy and understanding ngoma might provide insight into the underlying mechanisms of public performance in music therapy. Just as ngoma is a situated cultural practice that should be understood within its practitioners' worldview and value system, so is music therapy similarly circumscribed. To ask that notions of music therapy accommodate practices that define ngoma is no more warranted than it would be to ask ngoma to include procedures that define music therapy.

This is not to say that music therapy should be defined in an ahistorical, fixed way, an issue that Stige (2002a) explores with great insight and sensitivity. However, saying that music therapy should be allowed to change to accommodate to local influences is not to say that any local influence has a claim on this evolution. Stige draws a parallel between the current situation in music therapy and the history of psychology where "Western values have entered the practice, theory, and research of the discipline to a degree that has made the separation of Western values and definitions of the field difficult" (p. 244). The question is whether or not this type of cultural imperialism is problematic. The discipline of psychology (and that of psychotherapy as well) as distinct from philosophy and religion is a Western creation. So the fact that its basic definition and conceptualization is Western-centric should not be surprising and is not in and of itself problematic. The same consideration goes for music therapy.

What can be problematic are the social and political uses to which these professional definitions are put. As Stige (2002a) argues, "if there is not a space for cultural critique some clients will be discriminated against and some countries or regions marginalized in the discourse of music therapy" (p. 247). The real challenge is to balance the natural internal development of music therapy and the right of music therapists to define their field with the processes of accommodation that characterize a benevolent engagement with novel cultures and music practices. Music therapists are obligated to learn about the increasingly globalized world in which we all live and to determine how and in what ways music therapy practices can be implemented and altered within novel cultural contexts. However, this obligation for cultural sensitivity does not carry an obligation for music therapy to be so malleable that it loses connection to its core.

The social and political implications of the encounter between Western perspectives on health and traditional African approaches are addressed by Stige (2008b) in the context of reviewing Gregory Barz's (2006) proposal for the discipline of "medical ethnomusicology." In the negotiation between modern medicine and traditional healing practice it is essential to examine the effects of the power imbalance between the two perspectives, Stige asserts. Because contemporary health practitioners have the institutional support not possessed by folk healers, they acquire the power to define problems and allocate resources.

Stige reports that Barz argues for the value of "a more therapeutic understanding of musical performance" (p. 162) in building his concept of medical ethnomusicology. And yet, Barz inexplicably makes no reference to music therapy, something that is ironic given that Barz criticizes the isolationistic attitudes that keep modern medical practices and traditional healing quite separate. Barz contributes to the very schism that he identifies.

Stige sees the implications of this issue in very broad terms. He acknowledges that music therapists are not the only people, or even the only health professionals, working with music and health concerns. The list includes social workers, psychologists, and general musicians. And the issue of the implementation of Western-style music therapy in the non-Western world is reflective of a much larger issue: that North American and European music therapists have tended not to acknowledge and make use of "the therapeutic potentials of ordinary people's everyday usage of music" (Stige, 2008b, p. 167). The way in which music therapists may or may not engage with indigenous music and health practices is just a localized version of this larger issue. The practical issues faced by practitioners in this regard are taken up in Chapter 10.

10

MUSIC THERAPY AND TRADITIONAL HEALING PRACTICES

Clinical Applications

The present chapter resumes the discussion from Chapter 9 in examining the relationship between contemporary Western music therapy and traditional healing practices using music. The focus moves to issues of clinical application and centers on four questions. First, are adaptations in music therapy necessary when implementing it with individuals from non-Western cultures possessing indigenous healing practices using music? Second, can knowledge of music healing rituals be synthesized with the music therapy knowledge base within a traditional Western medical framework? Third, does music therapy instantiate and reflect perennial experiences of myth and ritual? Fourth, how are the anthropological concepts of liminality and *communitas* relevant in understanding how music therapy works?

Adapting Music Therapy for Individuals from non-Western Cultures

Music therapists with a Western orientation work with individuals from non–Western cultures in the clients' home countries and in Western countries where they may be immigrants or political refugees. Thus, the focus of the present section is divided in these two questions: Are adaptations necessary when importing music therapy into non–Western cultures with indigenous music healing practices? Are adaptations necessary when implementing music therapy with non–Western individuals living in a Western cultural context?

Music Therapy for Individuals from non-Western Cultures in non-Western Contexts

Again, it is within Africa that the question of music therapy with individuals from non–Western contexts within their home cultures has been most extensively addressed. Although the literature on this topic is somewhat sparse, there has been some discussion in relation to South Africa, Nigeria, and Kenya. In spite of the small number of publications in this area, there is a diversity of opinion that ranges from advocating for implementing standard music therapy interventions with only minimal adaptations, to perspectives that argue that music therapy as practiced in Western cultures is not appropriate for African contexts.

As an example of the former perspective, Helen Henderson (1991) describes work in South Africa with an adolescent girl, using traditional psychological terms to describe her areas of need consisting of catastrophic levels of stress and anxiety. Her music therapy approach is characteristic of the Western, consensus model of therapy, comprising elements of music therapy, play therapy, and psychotherapy. The work was client-centered and nondirective, and focused on achieving the freest and safest forms of expression through a variety of modalities including music, artwork, and puppet play. Prior to coming to music therapy the client had been taken to a traditional healer whose inappropriate treatment contributed greatly to her current problems. She had a mixture of Christian and Xhosa beliefs and customs and Henderson acknowledges the importance of these cultural factors.

The therapy process consisted of client initiated songs and stories that were accompanied musically by the therapist who interpreted their contents as reflecting the traumatic events to which the client had been exposed and her beliefs about the use of music to communicate with deceased individuals. Henderson reported no tension between the girl's cultural beliefs and the conventions of music psychotherapy. In this vein,

> the therapy room, with its African drums xylophones, glockenspiels and woodwind instruments has provided Patricia with the tools a Xhosa Diviner uses for expelling evil and communicating with the deceased, while also enabling her to use music as a traditional Xhosa Christian form of worship.
>
> (Henderson, 1991, p. 216)

Henderson's explanation for the effectiveness of the work is based on psychotherapeutic theory in referencing the release of emotions, the symbolic displacement of the true targets of these emotions onto neutral objects such as puppets or instruments, and the revelation of painful personal experiences again through displacement onto story characters.

In articulating the opposite perspective, Kigunda (2003) expresses skepticism that the Western concept of music therapy can be directly imported into an African context. In addition to the issue regarding the redundancy in the term *music therapy*, there is also the problem that scholars in Kenya can be skeptical of the notion that music has any therapeutic value. These complex issues around the notion of music therapy suggest to Kigunda that it will be difficult to establish a Western notion of music therapy in Africa.

As he considers the relationship between ritual and music therapy, Kigunda (2004) works from two complementary positions. First, he puts the cultural ritual at the center and examines how music therapy can enhance it rather than starting from a concept of Western music therapy and seeing how it can be adapted. The orienting question is this: What does music therapy have to offer traditional rituals and health practices? There is no effort to preserve music therapy as it is conceived of in a Western worldview but merely to see what aspects of it can be appropriated in the local culture.

Second, Kigunda also considers what strategies would make the development of a bona fide music therapy more successful. An important one would be the use of music therapy elements that originated in African cultural contexts (such as, presumably, musical styles, forms of musical social interaction, or musical values). He envisions a reciprocally beneficial relationship between a Western-style music therapy and traditional rituals.

Because of the association of music with magical ritual, it may be even more difficult to have conventional music therapy accepted in Kenya than in Western cultures. Nonetheless,

Kigunda details how it is still important to repackage music therapy concepts to traditional ritual practitioners within their worldview because it represents an important health-related resource. In this view, music therapists have an ethical obligation to make available contemporary information to ritual practitioners in order to make the practice of the ritualists more effective.

The situation is similar in Nigeria where music and dance have both been used therapeutically throughout history, but the concept of a modern profession of music therapy is not prominent. Any health related practices employing music are the province of healers, although some authors express a desire to move Nigeria into a more contemporary stance in this area (Aluede and Iyeh, 2008). Whenever music therapy is discussed it is generally thought to be something that is either extinct or that should be in the province of traditional healers, who are the only people using music toward health-related goals in contemporary Nigerian society.

The writings of Mercédès Pavlicevic (2001, 2004) provide the most in-depth and insightful perspective on the implementation of Western music therapy in non-Western contexts, particularly in relation to South Africa where she has lived and practiced. In a project where she worked with disadvantaged home-based care-workers in rural parts of South Africa, Pavlicevic (2004) explored many of the issues involved in working as a music therapist in this cultural context. Moreover, she does not limit the implications of what she learned to music therapists working in unfamiliar contexts; instead, she claims that what she learned is relevant to all music therapy contexts, whether or not they are cross-cultural.

Working with large groups of female health workers in semi-public settings challenged many of Pavlicevic's conceptions of what music therapy must involve. These conditions included the size of the group (32 members), the clients' natural predilections that did not require her guidance or initiative to stimulate music-making, the women's choice to sing conventional quasi-gospel songs with a strong religious identity, the repetition of the songs seemingly without expressive merit, and the natural and organic way in which the women spontaneously began and ended music within daily activities.

In a number of ways, the spatial, temporal, and social boundaries that define conventional therapy were simply not present in this setting: Distressed individuals found support and empathy from the group members as they functioned in daily life outside their formal meeting in therapy sessions, so the therapist's typical function in this regard was not needed; therapists were asked to reveal personal information; group meetings were in a building with open windows so that the proceedings were available to anyone who cared to watch or listen to them; and musicing spilled over into all of the daily activities.

The lack of formal boundaries did not mean that there was an absence of roles. Instead, there was a natural flow from one role to another, which was not dictated by professional convention but by the needs of the moment. Because music, and therefore the possibility for music therapy, could spontaneously erupt during other activities, Pavlicevic had to abandon the sense of control over when therapy would occur. However, in this difficult situation, her music therapy sensitivity maintained its usefulness, primarily in the way that she listened to and felt the music of the group and the way that it represented the members. She concluded that context is as important as conventional theory and practice in conducting music therapy. Additionally, the self-reflection and openness to rethinking one's fundamental preconceptions is something that Pavlicevic says should characterize all music therapy.

Music Therapy for Individuals from non-Western Cultures in Western Contexts

Perhaps because of the cultural variety in the USA, much of the literature on multicultural music therapy has been generated by American authors. Of course, multicultural music therapy does not necessarily have to involve work between a Western music therapist and individuals from non-Western cultures, or even work between a therapist from a dominant culture with clients from a more marginalized one, although in actual practice much of the literature in multicultural music therapy does involve such situations.

In one of the earliest publications in this area, Moreno (1988b) discusses how the presence of a large variety of ethnic groups in the USA necessitates that music therapists become familiar with as wide a range of musical styles as is possible. This is helpful in "establishing effective musical and interpersonal communication with clients from diverse ethnic backgrounds" (p. 19). Moreno does offer one caution: Because music from many non-Western cultures has religious uses and functions, using such music might "elicit more than the ordinary musical and extra-musical associations. The music may reach the client on the deepest possible level of culture and values and a shared world view" (p. 27). Although the use of culturally specific music offers this latter benefit, music therapists who use it should understand its full source and context.

Music therapists have generally acknowledged that multicultural awareness must go beyond just learning the music of a client's culture because the very idea of therapy might be alien to clients from certain cultural backgrounds. As Toppozada (1995) observed, because therapy is a Western concept, it is the therapist's obligation "to make the process relevant for minority culture clients" (p. 72). Moreover, notions of what is acceptable behavior determine clinical goals and these concepts vary among cultures. Therapists must have cultural awareness—of both their own culture and that of clients—in order to provide the best possible care within their clients' worldview.

Within the USA, research has shown that music therapy has lagged other health professions in addressing and engaging multicultural issues in general (Darrow and Malloy, 1998). Music therapists often feel ill-prepared by their academic training in the active engagement of multicultural related issues. This is ironic as Chase (2003) points out that music therapy is a particularly recommended treatment form in multicultural settings, both because verbal psychotherapy may be taboo for clients in certain cultures and because music provides an alternative path of communication where language differences between clients and professionals may be present. Chase asserts that there were still relatively few publications on multicultural issues while it had been extensively addressed in related disciplines including art therapy and music education.

Music therapists have implemented standard music therapy approaches with cultural groups that may not have a concept of therapy involving the treatment of psychological distress by a clinical professional. For example, Wexler (1989) described how grief-related psychosomatic symptoms were addressed through standard music therapy interventions such as songwriting with Native Americans in the USA. The therapeutic approach employed was described as "quite similar to grief music therapy with non-Indian groups" (p. 66). Practical skills in music were combined with empathy, a listening for "the deeper message of the heart" and the reflecting of unexpressed feelings and thoughts back to the client. Song lyrics were composed using images familiar to the White Mountain Apaches constituting the client group. This was done to access deeper feelings and thoughts while the use of song was chosen to "facilitate the expression of unresolved grief, which relieves sufficient stress resulting in a reduction of symptomatology" (p. 66). The standard process of therapy was unchanged to suit the client group, although some specific elements of it were selected according to cultural considerations, much in the same way that a therapist will use a client's preferred music or lyrics whether or not a cultural difference is present.

Clinical work of a multicultural nature with strong political dimensions was described by Oksana Zharinova-Sanderson (2004) working in Germany with refugee victims of torture and political violence. In contrast to Wexler, Zharinova-Sanderson describes the unique challenges and adaptations that were developed. With one client it was necessary for the therapist to accept a third person in the sessions, an interpreter who facilitated communication and whose presence mitigated the client's discomfort about being alone with a young woman, something that was taboo in his Turkish culture. Because the therapist accepted this need, it eventually led the client to agree to stay in sessions when the interpreter was unavailable as the music provided the third presence necessary for his comfort.

The relation among music, culture, and personal identity is an important consideration in this work. Assimilation into the new culture can be a difficult process and music is typically engaged with communally. In activating the desire for musicing, music therapy can help "patients to use this communal repertoire of expression that they are already equipped with by their home cultures to reconnect with their ability to be a creative part of a community" (Zharinova-Sanderson, 2004, p. 242).

Zharinova-Sanderson felt her clinical role shift as a result of cultural considerations. When clients would offer music from their own culture she was not able to accompany them in a stylistically appropriate way. She realized that it was more important to offer her presence as a deeply involved listener than it was to maintain active music-making that was stylistically flawed.

A music therapy project in Australia with adolescent refugees from Sudan (Jones, Baker, & Day, 2004) illustrates how clinicians may report aspects of clinical work as stemming from multicultural considerations when they actually reflect general principles of effective music therapy practice. This clinical program encouraged "students to explore and express their feelings by playing instruments, singing, writing songs, listening to music and talking about song lyrics" (p. 89). The needs of these clients reflected traumatic events in their home country, the difficulties of a forced emigration, and the significant challenge of assimilating into a new country and culture with strong differences of language and custom. Issues of racial discrimination were also present as were the universal difficulties of adolescents making the transition into adulthood.

In addition, the clients and therapists belonged to cultures with very different ideas about health, which, in Australia, is largely considered from "scientific, mechanistic, and individualistic" (Jones, Baker, & Day, 2004, p. 91) perspectives. In contrast, "the Sudanese approach is more holistic and spiritual. While ill health is still considered to be a deviation from normal living, causes are attributed to the mind, the spirit, relationships and supernatural causes" (p. 91). Ensuring health is a community obligation in Sudan and music is used in healing rituals, primarily as a means of communicating with gods to diagnose a problem and to have its cure conveyed. Music itself is not the cure as it functions purely diagnostically.

Clinical findings from this project are couched in terms of cross-cultural issues but they actually reflect clinical considerations that should always be considered, not just in cross-cultural situations. For example, the clients were difficult to engage until the therapists used music with a strongly stated pulse, syncopated rhythms, and an emphasis on beats two and four. These aspects of the clients' indigenous music are also highly characteristic of Western popular music with African roots such as rock and roll, blues, soul, hip-hop, and funk music. However, an experienced music therapist will likely use these elements of music with any adolescent, not just those from an African country. One client is discussed who was musically expressive and who possessed an excellent ear, but whose music "seemed to be self-directed and not at all related to the music therapist's" (Jones, Baker, & Day, 2004, p. 94). It is then noted that "once the music therapist had integrated more 'African' feel into her playing, the music making became more communicative" (p. 94). However, if the client's playing seemed to call for syncopation, pulse, and back-beat emphasis, an experienced improvisational music therapist will be able to discern this need and provide it musically, irrespective of the client's culture of origin.

Another example was in the realization that the use of "imitation and synchrony were more detrimental to the process than helpful" (Jones, Baker, & Day, 2004, p. 94). The authors observe that complementary rhythms were more characteristic of Sudanese music and that therapists were better able to make contact with the clients and promote their expression when their music interlocked with the overall texture of the music and did not imitate that of the clients. But again, the complementary stance of therapist music-making characterizes effective music therapy whether one is considering analytical music therapy, or quite different, music-based approaches such as Nordoff-Robbins music therapy. The present author has made this point in discussing the implications of the study of jazz for music therapy where

> responsiveness is demonstrated by playing in a complementary way, something that is more musically and personally demanding than is pure reflection. The challenge for the therapist is to create autonomous musical statements that reflect the therapist's individual sensibility in a way that is still responsive to the client. Music therapists should use imitation sparingly because it is not characteristic of organic human communication and relationship; vital music-making requires a judicious use of mirroring.
>
> (Aigen, 2013, p. 11)

These observations validate the points made by Stige and Pavlicevic that cultural considerations are present in all clinical interactions, not just those where clients and therapist do not share a common culture. The examples discussed by Jones et al. illustrate not just that one must use music whose character suits the relational profile of the client's cultural music, but that clinical work is best facilitated when therapists can discern the qualities of the client's music and play in a way that complements it, regardless of the cultural considerations involved.

A final example from Jones et al. concerns the work with five pre-adolescent boys, all of whom were described as exhibiting disruptive and aggressive behaviors. Progress was made once the therapists began using age-appropriate pop music such as rap and techno. They conclude that rap was an effective tool to use, not just because it was the clients' preferred music, but also because it was congruent with "the traditional use of song within Sudanese society" (Jones, Baker, & Day, 2004, p. 96) to resolve conflict and it drew upon the boys' natural skills in vocal improvisation. Engaging older children and adolescents absolutely requires the use of their preferred form of popular music. The cultural learning again seems to have steered the therapists to what they ought to have been doing anyway.

One aspect of their conclusions bears some discussion. They propose "that rap music might be used to promote insight, and as a vehicle for both the verbal processing of feelings and the internalising of new societal values" (Jones, Baker, & Day, 2004, p. 99). These recommendations seem to conflict with the nature of rap (or hip-hop) and the nature of the engagement of adolescents in composing, recording, and re-experiencing this music by listening to it. First, developing insight and processing of feelings are an aspect of conventional psychodynamic approaches that are generally less relevant when the composing, recording, and performing of hip-hop music are used as a clinical vehicle with adolescents. It is the way that their inner artistry is developed in a manner that allows them to aesthetically communicate the nature of their lived reality that is more salient. Second, adolescents' use of their favored music serves to challenge societal values and the status quo. Introducing this music as a way to develop compliance with new social values seems to fundamentally misunderstand the social function of the music which is, after all, the reason why adolescents are so drawn to it.

Indigenous Music Healing and the Medical Model

The present section focuses on viewpoints that consider music therapy as a medical practice and examine how concepts from music healing can be integrated into this mode of thinking. A unique perspective on the relationship between traditional healing and the medical model of music therapy is proposed by Moreno (1995b), who develops the idea that an understanding of the use of music in ritual healing contexts can contribute to a contemporary concept of music therapy. He notes that among the many parallels between music therapy and music healing rituals, of particular importance is the special status conveyed to therapists and healers. This is due to their musical abilities and the way music in therapy induces altered states of consciousness with attendant healing images, which he sees as analogous to "the trance state in shamanism and spirit possession" (p. 331).

Moreno argues that music therapists must come to terms with the healing uses of music cross-culturally in order to gain a full understanding of its potential therapeutic benefits. He believes that a universal, general model of music therapy can be created that integrates ritual approaches with scientific thinking to produce a framework applicable across all cultures.

Moreno's thinking is unique in two ways: First, he suggests that the study of indigenous healing is important not just to enrich psycho-social explanations of the value of music therapy, but as something that is relevant for the biomedical level as well. He suggests a new conceptualization called "ethnomusic therapy" that he defines as

> the multidisciplinary study of indigenous music and healing practices with a patient centered focus. Integrating the disciplines of ethnomusicology, music therapy, medical anthropology and medicine, ethnomusic therapy considers the impact of music in ritual performance upon the measured progress of patient-participants with psychophysiological problems of a known etiology.
>
> (Moreno, 1995b, p. 336)

Second, he also advocates for the awareness of music healing practices, not for the purpose of developing cultural sensitivity and the ability to adjust practice to local conditions as is argued by authors such as Stige (2002a), but to integrate knowledge of healing to create a more general, pan-cultural theoretical framework. Such a view would be "culture-free . . . [and] equally applicable to all persons in all cultures without being slanted either toward those persons served by traditional healers or those served by practitioners working within the Western biomedical culture" (Moreno, 1995b, pp. 331–332).

Just as there is scientific research into the value of plants used by traditional healers, Moreno argues that traditional uses of music can be mined to discover potentially valuable curative musical interventions. He uses a traditional scientific, physiological perspective in which the quantitative dimensions of the music have specific effects on clinical conditions. While he acknowledges that some music practices may be too culturally embedded to be applied in different cultural contexts, he does suggest that in analyzing the music used in healing "such variables as their tonal modes, rhythmic patterns, tempi, timbres, dynamics and pitch range" (Moreno, 1995b, p. 332) might be shown to be relevant to the treatment of specific ailments and diseases at specific moments in the disease's progression. This type of knowledge could and should be adapted "into the mainstream of modern medicine and therapy" (p. 332).

Moreno argues against the idea that healing rituals as a whole can be appropriated from one culture and transplanted in another and expected to have the same result. Instead, he believes that certain parameters of the music that will have effects across cultures can be abstracted from the culturally-bound music ritual and transplanted into the new culture.

A fundamental assumption of Moreno's argument is that the abstracted musical elements are the causative factors and that they retain their efficacy when removed from the musical-cultural context in which they are embedded. The approach is a reductive one that conflicts with much contemporary thought in music that argues against this type of essentialism. However, it is one way of creating a more universal, general music therapy approach. Moreno offers general guidelines for how the transplanting of musical ritual might be enacted and he suggests that removing some of the culturally-specific elements is a way of isolating the causative elements of the music:

> A healing song or chant in a modern adaptation might change textual references directed to spirits or other entities to a generic higher power or the closest equivalent in the adapting culture or might even be secularized . . . Unfamiliar melodic configurations could be altered to a style more characteristic of the adapting culture while still trying to retain basic elements of the original song such as tonal range, intervallic sequence in relation to textual implications, meter, emotional character and so on . . . The object of this kind of approach is to isolate the essential musical elements critical in the healing process.
>
> (Moreno, 1995b, p. 333)

A potential difficulty in enacting Moreno's program is that his assumption of universals may not be warranted. That is, even if one can abstract musical elements as he describes, it may be that it is the particular way that those essences interact with the culturally-specific dimensions of the music that determine their efficacy. It may be the interaction of the essences with people and culture that matters and removing the essences and importing them into another culture and with other people does not ensure that those essences will afford the same types of engagement as in the originating culture. Moreover, the abstracted musical elements will likely have other meanings and typical uses in other forms of music. Moreno's approach relies on a universal level of musical organization that will be related to in the same way cross-culturally. There just does not seem to be evidence for this assumption while there are excellent arguments to be made against it.

Moreno acknowledges that what he is trying to do is to apply the framework of experimental research to cultural inquiry. He wants to isolate the independent variable of music from what might be confounding factors. He argues that studying the effects of music when removed from the charismatic power of the healer and the ritual context is the same thing as removing the effect of the human qualities of the individual therapist to better understand the role of the music.

He does recognize that his approach presupposes that the efficacy of the music transcends its specific presentation and context. While existing research does not support this assumption, Moreno says that the psychological and physiological effects of music can be expected to have an effect that transcends cultures because there is an equivalency between Western and non-Western worldviews on the origins of psychological disturbances. He notes that the Western notion of the unconscious does not seem any more rational than that of the spirit world:

> Members of modern Western culture might be likely to describe the belief in the spirit world of peoples from tribal and other traditional cultures as simply a naive reflection and projection of their unconscious. However, if persons from those cultures had the opportunity to examine our own conception of the unconscious, they might also believe us to be incredibly naive and see our idea of the unconscious as simply a reflection of the spirit world!
>
> (Moreno, 1995b, p. 335)

Notwithstanding the fact the Moreno's suggestions have not been acted upon to any significant extent in the years since he proposed them, they still deserve some reflection and critique. While the desirability of general theory in music therapy has been addressed by a number of authors from a variety of viewpoints, Moreno is unique in suggesting that ritual healing be studied for its physiological effects.

However, there are good reasons to think that his program is not tenable. His comparison to the study of medicinal plants is not a particularly apt analogy as physiological similarities shared by all humans are not matched in the cultural domain. There is just no solid reason to assume that elements of music will have similar or nearly identical effects when transplanted from one culture to another if their social and musical context is altered. Also, the very premise of Moreno's thesis is that what makes music effective in therapy is embodied in its qualities as an autonomous object. There is just no support for the idea that the context of music (including cultural setting, therapeutic relationship, personal qualities of the therapist, etc.) are merely background elements whose presence can be controlled. In fact, significant research in the area of psychotherapy at least has shown that the personal qualities of the therapist are essential to its efficacy. However laudable Moreno's goals, empirical research and current theory in music therapy that emphasize the central role of context provide strong reasons for assuming that his would not be a particularly useful program to follow.

Myth, Ritual, and Music Therapy

The present section and the one that follows operate from a broader conception of music therapy where socio-cultural factors have a role in explanatory frameworks. They address how ideas from ritual studies can be applied within a broad concept of music therapy that goes beyond a purely medical framework. Although Moreno's program may not be a productive one, there is a way of thinking about music and what happens in music therapy in which both modes of experience can be honored and integrated. The strategy is not to identify therapy *as* healing but to explore areas of overlap and similarity to gain insight into each realm of activity within each of their own frames of reference.

The idea that music therapy can be a site for the enactment of personally transforming myth through ritual originated with Carolyn Kenny (1982, 1987, 1989, 2006[1]). Her focus was on "how to make a bridge between contemporary music therapy practice and traditional, indigenous healing practices" (2006, p. 166). Beginning from the idea that "music and myth share many purposes" (2006, p. 5), Kenny applies concepts from disciplines as diverse as musicology and ritual studies to argue that music therapy can make a unique contribution to human well-being by providing access to the processes and messages of mythic ritual. The concept of transformation lies at the heart of all ritual and this is the foundation upon which Kenny establishes the "death/rebirth myth as the healing agent in music" (p. 6).

The goal of therapy is to help clients adopt more functional ways of being in the world. One of the difficulties in this process is that people generally fear and resist change because it represents the unknown. Kenny makes the point that letting go of one's self-identity can feel like a type of death of the former self. Ritual that has as its purpose facilitating the processes of death and rebirth can enable the type of transformative process at the heart of therapy.

Kenny identifies the tension–resolution dynamic in music with the death–rebirth myth, both of which represent transformational processes essential to therapy. She cites Chopin's *Prelude* in E minor as a musical example. At one point in this composition, a chord appears that resolves the tension that has accumulated in the previous 15 measures. Death and rebirth are represented in the same moment:

> Music and myth both acknowledge and accept paradox. The point of transformation [the G natural tone in the melody played in measure 17] in Chopin's E minor prelude represents both death and rebirth in the same chord, moment or space. Both exist together and become one another. For at the moment of rebirth, another death has in fact begun.
>
> (Kenny, 2006, p. 33)

Music is a mythic artery according to Kenny because it "is the expression that focuses on the continuity of life" (2006, p. 30). Clients in music therapy access this aspect of music whether or not it is consciously addressed by therapists. It is a necessary level of description and theorizing in all music therapy contexts. The traditional functions of myth to bind individuals into communities and to provide stability and connections among past, present, and future are highly relevant to therapy contexts in which individuals must draw upon the connections to their culture to be reassured that change does not equal a loss of identity. This latter task is addressed in myth through the way in which its contents "balanced constancy and adaptability" (p. 31). At the core of myth is the process of transformation and "with transformation, a type of death and rebirth are always implied" (p. 31). Music used in therapy serves to maintain the needed connection to nature and to the ongoing stream of human existence.

In considering the music therapist as a ritualist, strong connections to the shamanic role are highlighted by Kenny. Yet it is in their shared function within their respective social contexts that binds them together. In this sense, "it is the task of both to help the patient, whether African tribesman or North American stockholder, to mobilize his psychological and spiritual as well as bodily resources" (Kenny, 2006, p. 53) to ensure the health of the community, whether this is considered in its curative or preventative dimensions.

I have previously written about how a modern worldview has rendered much myth and ritual impotent (Aigen, 1991a). Psychotherapy has been created to meet the universal human needs that were formerly met through the power of shared social myth and ritual to access inner sources of power, wisdom, and integration. Psychotherapy allows for the creation of a personal mythology that provides a structure for understanding one's life in more universal terms and that provides guidance for how to move forward.

In music therapy, individuals have the opportunity to create external forms of musical expression and relationship that provide access to their inner world. Because they are individually developed, these forms are powerful agents for transformation as they reflect each person's unique life experience. Conversely, they may "lack the communal energy and impetus carried by social rituals" (Aigen, 1991a, p. 87). There is then "a trade-off in transformative efficacy between the iso-morphism of the ritual form with one's unique psychological reality . . . and the ability to draw from the transpersonal forces present in group ritual" (p. 87).

Music therapy and shamanism work to connect people to hidden sources of insight and growth. In the latter realm, the shaman engages various malevolent spirits bent on destruction and benevolent presences such as tutelary spirits offering healing and guidance. In a psychodynamic music therapy framework utilizing a taxonomy of psychological structures, these entities are alternatively conceptualized as internal presences such as the superego, id, anima, parent ego state, and inner child.

As was argued previously, music therapy should not return to shamanism as a model because it is the specific cultural factors and epistemological framework that determines whatever efficacy shamanism possesses. It would be no more suitable than would be practicing in-depth psychoanalysis with an individual from a non-Western culture. Instead, it is more productive to consider that the music therapist who works in a way that reflects the importance and meaning of ritual and creative activity is already "meeting the social and psychological need that shamanic activity fulfilled" (Aigen, 1991a, p. 95).

Stige (2002a) discusses how the differences between ritual and rational practices are constructed in music therapy. Accordingly, it is possible to study music therapy "as rituals authorized by the society they belong to and developed in order to help people with problems in living" (p. 219). It is not only the efficacy of a ritual practice that warrants it in a contemporary health profession but also the degree to which it is congruent with "other influential rationales in the field" (p. 219). Stige argues that in spite of the drawbacks of comparing music therapy to healing rituals—namely, that one ends up with decontextualized examinations that do not do justice to the less familiar set of rituals—it is still worthwhile to engage in such comparisons.

Stige (2002a) makes use of Arnold van Gennep's concept of rites of passage where rituals are not just archaic patterns, but "conventions shaped and reshaped in evolving cultures" (p. 218). Stige believes that this notion provides a good fit for music therapy as ritual. Although Stige does not make this connection overtly, as van Gennep was most interested in personal and social rituals that mediated the transition "from one place to another, from one age to another, from one social status or position to another" (p. 220), using his concepts to explore music therapy as ritual means that the transitional capacities of music will naturally be high-lighted.

Liminality, Communitas, Music, and Music Therapy

Musical improvisation can be considered a transitional ritual in which participants not only "get from one place to another, but one from one state to another" (Ruud, 1995, p. 93). In this type of transition there is a change in relationship to "other human beings, phenomena, situations—maybe the very relation to oneself" (p. 93). Victor Turner's notion of transitional periods as liminal or threshold states is invoked by Ruud to characterize the experiences of musical transition. Ruud also references Turner's notion of *communitas* as the intense comradeship experienced by people who share the liminal state together. Ruud's basic thesis is that improvisations in music therapy are examples of transition rituals in which *communitas* is established among participants.

The profound change in therapy that involves a restructuring of one's sense of self can be thought of as a rite of passage that mediates between two states of being. Because it involves a transformation of self, "the process of therapy can be a liminal one, something that is apparent in its most intense moments" (Ruud, 1995, p. 94). Liminality includes qualities such as transition, *communitas*, equality, and an absence of status where the symbols and prac-tices of previous positions are abandoned. Other characteristics include a sense of timeless-ness, ambiguity, the transcending of boundaries, a sense of perceived danger, and experiences of flow.

In Aigen (2005c), I described music therapy case material where the most salient episodes of clinical-musical interaction directly embodied these qualities of liminality, particularly through the use of improvisations in groove-based, popular music styles. The transition music included the alteration of traditional client–therapist roles to be more equal and mutual, the transcending of client limitations, an ever-increasing sense of flow in the music, enhanced spontaneity, and even danger as the enhanced level of functioning the client exhibited was also threatening to his established sense of self. In addition, there was a sense of musical camaraderie established among the therapy team members and client that embodied *communitas*.

There were also important elements in the therapy process of what Turner labels the "status system" that directly contrasts with *communitas* and that complements it in a necessary way. The elements of the status system include structure, status, and technical knowledge. These elements of structure were present in the making of concrete decisions, overcoming obstacles and challenges through applied work, "and the restraining of impulses or other personal desires in the moment" (Aigen, 2005c, p. 97). Applying technical knowledge and working on concrete musical skills were emphasized in the musical interactions representing this complementary mode of being.

In describing how the development of the human engagement with music is recapitulated in music therapy, Barbara Hesser (2001) notes that "each music therapy group is a miniature society" in which "the uses of music for healing and therapy will be organically discovered by the members of that particular community" (p. 56). It is natural that music therapy groups will create the means for experiences of liminality and structure, as well as vehicles for productively moving between the two states of being. When music therapy clients identify with a social structure that embodies both modes of being, they internalize and solidify a more complete sense of self.

Accepting that the forces of myth and ritual can be accessed in music therapy and used for establishing liminality and *communitas* provides a connection to earlier, more archaic uses of music—such as in shamanism—in a way that does not require the abandoning of a modern worldview. It does place unique demands on therapists to engage in mutual experiences guided by the exigencies of transcendent music-making as opposed to consciously direct-ing and controlling the nature of the musical interaction with clients. This is similar to the expansion of boundaries noted by Pavlicevic. In developing explanations for what accounts for profound changes in clients during music therapy, what is gained in considering some of the most powerful musical experiences in music therapy as liminal experiences is accessing "a cultural force which has as its nature the power to support such dramatic changes" (Aigen, 1991a, p. 98).

Although they have the same needs as others in this area, individuals with disabilities face numerous obstacles in participating in the social structures and rituals used by most people to mediate the transition from one stage of development to another. The use of ritual theory as an explanatory framework in music therapy establishes a sense of equality between clients in music therapy and other people. It allows the consideration of "music therapy not as a specialized service or mode of interaction fundamentally different from normal social processes, but as a medium for providing essential opportunities for personal development sought by all people" (Aigen, 2005a, p. 98). Arguing that improvisational music therapy can function as an individually tailored rite of passage demonstrates the value of going beyond clinical theory based on disability to show that individuals with disabilities gain the same thing from music that all people do.

In the context of discussing enhanced mutuality in music therapy, Stige's (2002a) consideration of the social relations involved in ritual offer an important cautionary perspective. Because ritual represents the larger society that sanctions it, the therapist represents this society and is in a more powerful position than clients. Thus, the therapeutic "interaction will probably hardly ever lose all elements of mediated communication and guided participation" (p. 224). And, although Stige does not make this point, perhaps this consideration owes equally to the fact that clients with disabilities may not always be in a position to determine the nature of their own therapy process. But as Stige does observe, experiences of *communitas* are usually developed among initiates rather than between initiates and ritual leaders. This does not preclude the establishment of *communitas* between clients and therapists in music therapy and it also points out the importance of quality of the relationships among clients themselves as powerful forces in therapy, particularly in the community and culture-centered approaches that Stige presents.

The importance of *communitas* as an explanation for the value of music therapy is becoming more prevalent, particularly in applications using improvisation, popular music, and com-munity music therapy (Aigen, 2005c; Wood, Verney, & Atkinson, 2004; Ansdell, 2004). Ansdell (2004) posits *communitas* as an important link in developing a comprehensive theory of community music therapy and cites its prevalence among many authors writing from a community music therapy viewpoint. Rather than thinking of "community as place or ideal, or even an enduring association" (p. 86), Ansdell's notion is of community in context that can provide a "graceful but prepared happening of mutual experience within a social and cultural context" (p. 86). In this way, ritual theory is being applied in music therapy, not in an uncritical, non-reflexive way, but in a way that reflects the broader contexts of understanding provided by the discipline of music therapy and by the local social and cultural contexts in which musicing takes place. These new developments around community music therapy and the various issues raised by it form the focus of Chapters 11 and 12.

Note

1. Kenny's publications in this area date to 1982 and include major works published in 1987, 1989, and journal articles and book chapters written throughout the past 30 years. Because the two original books are out of print, all quotations from her work in the present chapter have been taken from an anthology published in 2006 that includes the out-of-print works and the balance of her other publications.

11

COMMUNITY MUSIC THERAPY

Origins And Definitional Issues

Historical Context

A major impetus for the creation of the modern profession of music therapy was the response of people in hospitals to music that was provided for recreational purposes. Many of these activities occurred in veterans hospitals in the USA during and immediately after World War II. Music therapy, therefore, developed from a naturalistic engagement with music, similar to what happens outside of health-related contexts.

Consequently, the ways that early music therapists used music resembled that of nonclinical settings and included activities such as singing or playing songs and other compositions, listening to live or recorded music and possibly discussing one's experience of it, and engaging in therapeutic instrumental or vocal music lessons. Music therapy was considered an adjunctive and recreational therapy, not a primary treatment modality. Music therapists provided music for the institutions in which they were employed, and their clients, patients, and students often participated in events meant for the institutional community.

In the late 1950s, this situation began to change and throughout the 1960s and 1970s a small number of music therapy models were developed with indigenous music practices that had a limited connection to nonclinical musicing contexts. Four of these approaches drew clients into active music-making, primarily through improvisation: Nordoff-Robbins music therapy (Paul Nordoff & Clive Robbins), free improvisation therapy (Juliette Alvin), Benenzon music therapy (Rolando Benenzon), and analytical music therapy (Mary Priestley). A fifth approach, guided imagery and music (Helen Bonny), was a receptive method in which clients listened to specially created programs of classical music in an altered state of consciousness. The approach of psychiatric music therapy (Florence Tyson), while important, primarily made use of existing forms of interacting with music.

Because music therapy began to distinguish itself from other forms of musical engagement—such as music appreciation, education, and performance—by developing specialized practices that were identifiably clinical in nature, its identity began to be connected to these new practices. Additionally, music therapists were asserting that the potency and efficacy of their work warranted consideration as a primary treatment form for a variety of clinical conditions.

The presence of specialized methods became connected to the argument for the recognition of music therapy as a primary, rather than an adjunctive, therapy.

For music therapy to be practiced in an in-depth way that made the best use of clinical practices to advance the health and welfare of clients required the same things possessed by similar clinical modalities: regularly scheduled meetings in a space that provided privacy and confidentiality; the freedom to work with individuals and small groups in order to tailor treatment to the specific needs of particular clients; and essential tools such as quality instruments and audio equipment. All of these elements require the devotion of fiscal and material resources that are often competed for in institutional environments.

The provision of quality care thus demanded the delegation of resources, the allocation of which was dependent on demonstrating the advanced and in-depth possibilities for practice developed by music therapists. Because the practice of psychotherapy engendered the institutional resources that music therapists needed for their work, advanced practice in music therapy (and in some cases, music therapy itself) became identified with the concept of music psychotherapy, an area of practice with a number of specific characteristics: a focus on intra-psychic determinants of thought, affect, and behavior; an emphasis on therapeutic process as opposed to the generation of a musical product; and, a consideration of the relationship between therapist and client as a primary focus of treatment. The development of the profession of music therapy appeared to necessitate a move away from naturalistic modes of engaging with music in public venues to specialized ways of engaging with music in private spaces.

In spite of this general trend, there were some exceptions, even within the advanced music therapy models noted previously. For example, within Nordoff-Robbins music therapy, group work originally comprised the learning of compositions designed for therapy that could be performed for public audiences. And the Creative Arts Rehabilitation Center (CARC) at which Florence Tyson developed her in-depth method of reconstructive music therapy included weekly groups for individuals wishing to play jazz or rock music or to work on issues related to performance, as well as bi-annual musicales in which clients wishing to do so could perform for other clients, therapists, and invited guests. So in spite of the pressures to minimize the role of activities such as music lessons and public performance, these natural modes of relating to music were still maintained to some degree, both in entry-level, generalized music therapy practice as well as within models that characterized advanced levels of practice.

Three other social trends relevant for the present discussion were occurring during the 1960s and 1970s.

First, there was a drive toward deinstitutionalization in which individuals, who for reasons of psychiatric illness or developmental delay had been housed in large, state institutions which were often segregated from other members of the community, became integrated into small group homes and residences within their own community. Quality care was increasingly being seen as something that could be better accomplished within a community rather than apart from it.

The impetus behind the creation of CARC by Florence Tyson reflected this trend. Working in hospitals Tyson noted the profound gains made by clients in music therapy who were then released to the community, only to return months later when the cycle of their illness reached an acute phase. She reasoned that music therapy would be much more effective if implemented in the community on an outpatient basis as a means for preventing or mitigating the effects of the patient's symptoms in order to maintain the person in the community and thereby prevent rehospitalization with its attendant human and financial costs.

Second, the discipline of psychotherapy, which originally had an intrapersonal focus and was considered apolitical, acquired a social conscience with the recognition that it was not possible to be apolitical. To assert that one was apolitical was in effect to endorse the status quo, itself a political stance. In the 1960s, psychotherapists from a variety of orientations took on a framework in which they could become socially active. In music therapy, this was reflected in the establishment of the group "Music Therapists for Peace" in 1988.

It was in this context of the evolution of music therapy and the political nature of psychotherapy that community music therapy emerged. In it, the concept of a client was expanded "to include a community, environment, ecological context, or individual whose health problem is ecological in nature" (Bruscia, 1998a, p. 229). The basic premise was that the health of communities and the health of the individuals constituting those communities were inseparable, so that therapeutic efforts that focused on one party—either the individual or the community—naturally affected the other. Moreover, enhancing the relationship between individual and community had a mutually beneficial impact on both parties:

> In Community Music Therapy, the therapist works with clients in traditional individual or group music therapy settings, while also working with the community. The purpose is twofold: to prepare the client to participate in community functions and become a valued member of the community; and to prepare the community to accept and embrace the clients by helping its members understand and interact with the clients.
>
> (Bruscia, 1998a, p. 237)

Third, developments in musicology began becoming influential in music therapy and Ansdell (2004) positions the emergence of community music therapy as consistent with these developments. He highlights the fact that ethnomusicological concepts are relevant to music therapy and ought to apply to it as well as to any other social context of musicing. Important aspects of the new musicology that were relevant to community music therapy include the notion that music is a socially-embedded activity rather than an autonomous object; that its meanings are constructed by its users rather than lying immanent within it; that music is as much a product of material bodies as nonmaterial minds; that music constructs and enacts emotions rather than just expressing them; and that music is naturally a social activity (pp. 68–69). Additionally, musicality is "a core human capacity" that functions to "attract participation and create relationships" (pp. 68–69).

The first writers on community music therapy acknowledged that while community practices had proceeded throughout the period 1970–2000 they were without a theoretical foundation. Ansdell (2002), in one of the first publications to articulate the theoretical framework, described the conditions that provided the impetus for it:

- Therapists working with clients from cultures without a concept of therapy (such as indigenous peoples in Australia and South Africa);
- Therapists working with clients whose most central need was for connection to a community;
- Therapists working in settings such as hospice care where their work addressed the needs of individuals not formally identified as clients such as family members and clinical staff;

- Therapists working with traumatized war refugees where the treatment issues had social and political dimensions;
- Therapists whose clinical work incorporated performing or creating recordings with clients.

The irony in the development of community music therapy is that "while music therapists have advocated for individualized treatment, small groups, and closed environments in which to work, the natural modes of relating to music favored by clients have led in the opposite direction" (Aigen, 2012, p. 140). Some of the practices engaged in under the banner of community music therapy conflict with the psychodynamic approach that some authors argue represents the maturity of the profession. Even some of the music therapists sympathetic to the focus of community music therapy express caution regarding the dangers involved in embracing it as it could represent a regression for the field. Consequently, this has been somewhat of a contested area of practice in the professional literature.

Critiques of community music therapy have ranged from the assertion that there is no need for the label *community music therapy* because its precepts articulate what some practitioners already do under the general label of *music therapy* to the notion that it represents a destructive regression to an earlier stage of development in which ethically-questionable practices—such as performing publicly with clients—are engaged. Proponents of the model range from those who suggest it as a new paradigm replacing conventional music therapy to those who think it provides a necessary complement to existing practices.

In considering the five conditions noted by Ansdell that led to the creation of community music therapy, it has been the focus on performing and recording that has been the most controversial and that has generated the most literature. Consequently, the present chapter will cover some general issues surrounding community music therapy while the more specific focus on issues of performance and recording will be taken up in Chapter 12.

Contested Notions of Community Music Therapy

The variety of meanings and origins of the term *community music therapy* were explored in detail by Stige (2002c), who provides a comprehensive historical overview of the term in German, Norwegian, and North American contexts. Rather than placing its origins in the period 1998–2002 as I have done, Stige (2004) discusses roots and uses of the term going back at least 30 years prior to that time, although he acknowledges that it was dormant for a while and then experienced a resurgence.

Community music therapy weaves together many strands of thinking and practice from music therapy and related domains from throughout the world. Stige (2004) identifies its roots in various music therapy pioneers such as Schwabe and Seidel in Germany, Ruud and Aasgaard in Norway, Tyson and Kenny in North America, and Alvin, Nordoff and Robbins, and Priestley, all of whom had influence internationally. There were also community-oriented traditions in Australia and Canada, and Stige believes that contemporary developments throughout Africa and Asia are relevant as well (Stige, 2004, "A history of community music therapy," para. 2). Stige agrees that Bruscia (1998a) presented the first published definition of the term, although he characterizes it as continuous with older uses, seeing it as "not his [Bruscia's] own creative innovation, but a sub-tradition to music therapy with some quite old roots" (Stige, 2004, Appendix, para. 4). Stige's characterization notwithstanding, Bruscia's conceptualization seems more like the foundation of a new concept rather than a mere summation of historical functions. It includes the notion of the community as client, a novel idea at the time.

Moreover, while Stige is correct that the term was present earlier, in some of its uses it referred to the implementation of traditional individual and group music therapy sessions offered on an outpatient, nonresidential basis rather than as an inpatient or residential service. It was not considered by early practitioners to be fundamentally different from traditional music therapy, as evidenced by the fact that it neither generated nor required any novel theoretical foundations. The new foundations that were offered by Ansdell (2002) and Stige (2002a) himself, attest to the fact that something new was happening in music therapy that was fundamentally different from what had preceded it.

Stige is correct that some of the individual elements that currently characterize community music therapy were present throughout the period from 1960 through the late 1990s. The question is the extent to which the presence of individual threads existing in isolation can characterize the presence of an overall perspective, and the extent to which early appearances of the term indicate what is currently meant by it. This is not to say that community music therapy has been given a clear definition by its proponents, yet there does seem to be a consensus emerging around certain characteristics.

Ansdell's (2002) initial formulation emphasizes that community music therapy involves new practices, not just the importation of existing practices from institutions into the broader community, thus differentiating the new approach from older ones:

> *Community Music Therapy* is an approach to working musically with people *in context:* acknowledging the social and cultural factors of their health, illness, relationships and musics . . . *Community Music Therapy* encourages Music Therapists to . . . help clients access a variety of musical situations, and to accompany them as they move between 'therapy' and wider social contexts of musicing. As such, *Community Music Therapy* involves extending the role, aims and possible sites of work for music therapists—not just transporting conventional Music Therapy approaches into communal settings.
>
> (Ansdell, 2002, "Defining community music therapy," para. 3)

Stige (2002a) cites a number of factors that characterize a community music therapy approach:

1. The community "is not only a context *for* the work but also a context to be worked *with*" (p. 113) as it involves "social and cultural mainstreaming."
2. Social and cultural isolation is considered "a potential health threat" and the health promotion approach undertaken focused on the "development of social networks and of personal experiences of quality of life as main goals" (p. 113).
3. The process of music therapy moves outside the therapy room to include other contexts and people such as "teachers of the community music school, musicians in local bands and choirs, social workers and nurses of the homes of the clients, and local politicians" (p. 113).
4. Public performances are included in therapy processes.
5. Overall, the approach embodies "a way of working that is more public and political than what is conventional for music therapy" (p. 113).

Ansdell (2003) soon critiqued his own original definition as too prescriptive and insufficiently context-sensitive. He introduced the following, more succinct, version: "Community Music Therapy is an anti-model that encourages therapists to resist one-size-fits-all-anywhere models (of any kind), and instead to follow where the need of clients, contexts and music leads" (p. 4). In this view, community music therapy is not something defined by specific theories or practices, but by the process of human beings as they engage with music and develop their own directions of growth from this musical engagement.

The role of performance is a central, essential value in Ruud's (2004) notion of community music therapy. He believes that none of the other aspects of community music therapy are unique to it, as "culture and context are crucial aspects of all forms of music therapy" ("Performance-based music therapy," para. 1) and not all music therapy approaches are psychotherapeutic in nature, suggesting that defining it in contrast to Ansdell's consensus model is not adequate.

When these elements are eliminated, it is the performance aspect that remains. Because many contemporary music therapy approaches make improvisation and music listening central activities, the importance of performance and product have been minimized. However, according to Ruud (2004), community music therapy makes a performance-based approach more credible; it even becomes necessary because "without the public performance, there will be no exchange with a community" ("Performance-based music therapy," para. 2).

Although Bruscia (1998a) identifies community music therapy as only one of a number of ecological practices, Ruud says that the ecological character of community music therapy is distinctive and requires systems thinking as a supportive theory. With the ideas of performance and systems thinking in hand, Ruud (2004) defines community music therapy as "*the reflexive use of performance-based music therapy within a systemic perspective*" ("Definition," para. 1).

In Stige's (2004) comprehensive review of definitions of community music therapy he includes an appraisal of the strengths and problems of Ruud's definition. He agrees that the focus on systems theories and reflexivity are essential, but believes that the focus on performance is problematic. In particular, he takes issue with Ruud's notion that without performance there is no community engagement. Stige says that it is not the fact of performance that is essential; instead it is the forging of new ethical and practical boundaries in which "the role of clients and music therapists (in relation to each other and to society at large) is being negotiated in new ways and within new contexts" that should be at the center of conceptions of community music therapy (Stige, 2004, "Some thoughts on Ruud's definition," para. 7).

Moreover, Stige objects in principle and in fact to the notion that any type of activity—such as performance, listening, or improvisation—should be designated as specific to a particular area of clinical practice. He observes that activities other than performance could build feelings of community and be employed in community music therapy. Additionally, there are contraindications for the use of performance with particular clients and Stige does not want to say that community music therapy is therefore inappropriate for such individuals.

Stige (2004) believes that it is nonetheless important that community music therapy is bringing the value of performance to the foreground although it is more fruitful to think of performance in a more general, sociological sense of the term that connects to "performance as presentation of the self in everyday contexts" (Stige, 2004, "Some thoughts on Ruud's definition," para. 10). It is this broader sense of performance that has more to offer the theory of community music therapy, although this assertion does not minimize the importance of the narrower conception.

In contrast to Ansdell's notion of community music therapy as an anti-model, Stige (2003) recognizes particular beliefs and practices that characterize it. It is a participatory approach focused on client resources and collaborative ventures that can promote health through projects in nonclinical and public settings in the community. New types of roles, where therapists function in multiple ways, which are different from the conventional notion of a therapist, offer new avenues in which to not only promote health but also suggest that new ethical guidelines are needed. A possible framework to understand this approach is through the notion of rituals: conventional therapy is a closed ritual with designated individuals having prescribed roles; community music therapy is more of an open, inclusive ritual with more flexibility in terms of who participates and what their participation consists of. In addition to the flexibility of location, there is flexibility of time in that the ritual occurs when and where it is needed, not necessarily according to a predetermined schedule as in conventional therapy.

Is the Construct of Community Music Therapy Necessary?

Critiques of community music therapy as a construct have been undertaken from three positions with varying degrees of sympathy with its overall program. First, some authors suggest that there is not even a need for the label because the precepts and practices that constitute the perspective are already a common part of responsible music therapy practice. Second, some authors accept the need for the label and do not challenge its premises but argue that the approach should be limited in application and merely complement existing practices. Third, some authors argue that practices at the core of community music therapy are either not therapy or represent areas of ethical conflict.

In the initial, detailed exploration of community music therapy, Ansdell (2002) established the need for a concept of community music therapy by contrasting it with what he termed the "consensus model" that had established hegemony in many areas where music therapy was highly developed. Thus, exploring the various arguments for and against the necessity of community music therapy necessitates considering it in relation to this model.

Ansdell was motivated by a recognition that the work of significant numbers of music therapists seemed not to match how music therapy was traditionally defined:

> [Music therapists] are no longer always sure whether they know *what Music Therapy is*. Or, rather, whether the diversity of practices and theory they find themselves engaged in can comfortably come under the disciplinary umbrella of "Music Therapy" any longer. How many times have we heard our colleagues and students describe novel aspects of their work—which have followed from client needs—followed by the caveat "But I'm not sure *this* is Music Therapy!" What they mean is that what they find themselves doing does not seem to fit into the current theoretical model which describes "what Music Therapy is"—and "is not". They are sometimes under the impression their work is professionally unsound or ethically questionable.
>
> (Ansdell, 2002, "What flag is music therapy sailing under," para. 3)

Ansdell anticipated that his conceptualization of community music therapy as a new way of thinking about music therapy would be criticized as unnecessary. His defense was that the consensus model of music therapy was based on precepts about professional identity and appropriate clinical focuses that clash with practices in which therapists were engaged because they were desired by and benefited clients. Therefore, a new label with a supporting theoretical framework was necessary. Ansdell detailed four central areas where community music therapy is incommensurably different from the consensus model:[1]

Basic Aims

In traditional music therapy, individual clients are supported in exploring their inner emotional lives and music is considered a psychological phenomenon, not a socio-cultural one. Community music therapy recognizes that musicing leads people inward and outward; internal exploration is not the sole focus of the music therapist. The drive to commune with others through music is as important as the drive to self-expression and self-knowledge. Therefore, community music therapists support their clients' desires in both directions.

Mode of Intervention

In the traditional conceptualization, music therapy is distinguished from other music domains—such as education, performance, and music appreciation—not just by goals but by means as well. The importance of activities such as learning an instrument, composing, or performing is minimized. In community music therapy, clinical and nonclinical musicing are considered to be similar and music therapy can involve musicing formats that are similar to those outside of therapy. These natural modes of relating to music are encouraged.

Professional Identity and Role

The traditional role of a music therapist is clearly different from that of a music educator or performer. The nearest role model is that of a psychotherapist, who has insight into clients and can decode symbolic meanings. In community music therapy, the music therapist's expertise is primarily musical rather than being primarily psychotherapeutic or health-related. The goal is to promote music and musicing for individuals and milieus by removing obstacles.

Location and Boundaries of Therapy Processes

In the traditional approach, music therapy occurs in closed private spaces to ensure confidentiality. The work is primarily intrapersonal, and its main context is the therapeutic relationship, either between client and therapist or among clients. Activities occurring outside the session are generally not taken up. In community music therapy, the music therapist takes musicianship wherever it is needed: this could be in a private room, or it might be in more public spaces such as corridors, waiting rooms, or shared group recreational spaces. In contrast to the traditional approach, the therapeutic frame is more fluid and permeable. The therapist's job is to work with the entire context of a client's life with the overall goal of increasing the musical spirit of a community and enhancing the quality of life of its individual members.

The practice of community music therapy is based on what Pavlicevic and Ansdell (2004b) identify as music's "ripple effect." The idea is that music radiates from its source in concentric circles, much like a pebble dropped into a pond. These ripples radiate spatially as the music permeates its physical location and temporally as it establishes connections between a person's past and future. In the spatial sense, it "calls to others, attracts, gathers, connects people together.

It creates community" (p. 16). In extending outward, it brings those who create music out into the larger community at the same time as it brings the community into the source of the musicing. This bringing together of self and community emerging from the natural essence of music is why community music therapy has strong socio-cultural implications and is also why it is considered to be music-centered.

The conceptual foundations and rationales for community music therapy have been developed for legitimating practices that music therapists had created but which were thought to be outside the realm of their proper responsibilities as music therapists. These included performing and recording with clients, as well as engaging with larger institutions and social bodies outside the direct community of care in which the music therapist was employed. Community music therapy offers a vision of music therapy that can encompass these practices and a platform to develop new ones. But at its core, it is a flexible, context-based approach, not something to be defined in narrow or rigid way. This means that its nature could be continually debated and discussed.

Pavlicevic and Ansdell (2004b) also consider the issue of whether community music therapy represents a new development in music therapy or if it is a mere rebranding of existing practices that may be Eurocentric and ill-informed as some critics have charged. Although they acknowledge that there are streams of development dating back to the 1960s, because there has been very little evidence of this work being presented, written about, theorized about, or researched, it has been at best a marginal tradition until around 2002 when it began being overtly discussed. While they point to their own independent formulation of the label in 2000, they do acknowledge that others have come to the formulation independently. This realization of the need for a label formulated by different people in different cultures itself is evidence that the new conceptualization is needed.

Community music therapy is based on the idea that the needs of clients should come first and that conceptual and ethical guidelines must evolve to reflect effective practice. Pavlicevic and Ansdell (2004b) make what to some may seem a radical suggestion: Practitioners of community music therapy should "throw theoretical concerns to the wind when appropriate, to follow the needs of people and circumstances, asking not 'what is music therapy?' and 'what is a music therapist', but 'what do I need to do here, now?' They dare to follow where people and music lead" (p. 30).

While he does not emphasize such radical changes in ethical guidelines, Stige (2002d) does agree that sensitivity to culture and social context is a hallmark of community music therapy. He also addresses the question of whether community music therapy and the consensus model are complementary and can co-exist or if they are contradictory and mutually exclusive, as Ansdell suggests. He clearly comes down on the side of the former notion:

> Conventional music therapy and Community Music Therapy could reciprocally support and challenge each other, that is, they could support and remind each other about the continued relevance of some of the established insights in the discipline and profession, and challenge rigid dogmas or attempts of reifying the old ways as the only ways. This will represent a different future than the vision of Community Music Therapy as something that should replace conventional music therapy, or as something that could exist as a separate area of practice with no bearings on how conventional music therapy is understood.
>
> (Stige, 2003, p. 386)

Skepticism about the need for a new term for music therapy, particularly one that employs the term *community music* within it, was expressed by Jane Edwards (2002a). She has two objections. First, she says that as a music therapist, she already considers clients in the broader social and cultural contexts that characterize community music therapy. Second, she has endeavored to differentiate what she does as a music therapist from community music and believes that employing the new label will only create more confusion.

Edwards (2002b) also asserts that the professional obligation of music therapists prohibits a role akin to that of a community musician. It is a misnomer to add the word *community* to music therapy in order to describe this work because it inappropriately implies a connection to community music which she asserts is fundamentally different from music therapy. In contrast to music therapy, community music can happen without designated practitioners present and it may not have any repeatable features. The idiosyncratic approach taken by community musicians is part of its nature according to Edwards, and this basic fact precludes any connections to music therapy practice. She believes that these basic differences render music therapy and community music incompatible, even within a hybrid area of practice such as community music therapy.

Ansdell (2003) does address the question of whether community music therapy as a separate area of practice is a warranted construct only within the British context or if it has a more global relevance. He considers the possibility that what he is calling *community music therapy* is just general music therapy as practiced throughout the world, while the predominant type of music therapy in British contexts—that is, the consensus model—might be better described as *clinical music therapy*.

This special situation in the British/Irish context is partly due to the fact that it is the only one with a dedicated academic area of study for community music. Stige (2002c) suggests that Ansdell's retrenchment is not necessary because Edwards's points are relevant only in this context and therefore are not valid as guidelines internationally. The increasingly international use of the term suggests that it would be problematic to preclude its use solely due to problems that it causes in one cultural context. Moreover, Stige nowhere makes the suggestion to replace *music therapy* with *community music therapy* as Edwards's critique of him suggests. He merely is arguing for the delineation and description of an area of practice in a way that accurately summarizes its nature and differences from other existing areas of practice.

While much of the literature on community music therapy focuses on whether, how, and in what ways it is defined and differentiated from other forms of music therapy, O'Grady and McFerran (2007) consider the other end of the spectrum in examining how it is differentiated from community music. Their empirical examinations consisted of interviews with community musicians and music therapists doing community-oriented work. The basic differences that emerged between the two types of practitioners reflected the focus and rationale of their respective work efforts.

According to O'Grady and McFerran (2007), music therapists prioritize the needs of individual participants for self-expression as opposed to the focus on aesthetic value or social change that characterizes the work of community musicians. Music therapists express greater fealty to existing ethical guidelines while community musicians depend more on an internal sense of what is appropriate. Also, music therapists work with clients "along the entire health-care continuum whereas community musicians do not work as frequently in the acute illness/crisis or rehabilitation stages" (p. 21). The authors say that, at the risk of oversimplifying things "'good' music in CoMT is a tool for the individual whereas the individual in Community

Music is sometimes a tool for social change or for 'good' music itself" (p. 21). This does not imply that the community musician ignores the individual but that the benefits of the work stem from feeling part of something larger than oneself, not necessarily from feeling oneself as a central focus of the music.

There are two assumptions in these conclusions that may not be warranted. First, for the community music therapist, the community itself can be the client. So to say that social change is being focused on is not to say that the client's needs are being ignored, just that the community as a client is more important than is any one individual as client. One issue in this regard is that these results may reflect the particular sampling of this study—a possibility that the authors acknowledge—and they may not say anything in general of the difference between the two domains. Second, there is an assumption in the conclusions of O'Grady and McFerran that is based upon maintaining a dichotomy between aesthetic value and self-expression such that aesthetic value is discussed as something apart from any essential human, therapeutic interest. This formulation is also not warranted given the argument in Aigen (2005a) that music for its own sake means music for the sake of human development and that it has a strong role in human development and well-being.

The idea that music in general is undertaken for the development of the self is central to music-centered music therapy. Also key to this approach is that the human engagement with music within music therapy is continuous with its engagement in nonclinical contexts; it is thus supportive of naturalistic engagements with music in therapy such as is embodied in performance and product orientations. Stige (2004) considers community music therapy to be music-centered and Ansdell's (2003) strategy in defining community music therapy clearly locates it as a music-centered form of practice. It begins from and answers the question of what music and musicians can provide to communities:

> The central question that comes to me from these varying definitions is this: Can a Community Music Therapy model help bring about a more fruitful match between what musicians are best equipped to do, and what society in the coming generation will need from them?
>
> (Ansdell, 2003, p. 4)

Regardless of where the different theorists in community music therapy stand on the centrality of performance, they all recognize that it plays an important role. Additionally, for those authors who critique community music therapy, the notion of performance is the most controversial element as it includes a number of elements that clash with the consensus model: a product focus, the loss of anonymity, the absence of clearly defined boundaries, and the engagement of multiple roles between therapists and clients. Its centrality to the concept of community music therapy and the differences of opinion regarding its value and appropriateness are both items of continuing debate, much of which is addressed in Chapter 12.

Note

1. This summary is from Aigen (2012).

12

PERSPECTIVES ON PERFORMANCE IN COMMUNITY MUSIC THERAPY

General Thoughts on Performance in Music Therapy

Music therapists have been engaging in performances with their clients since the inception of the profession. They have variously considered public performance to be part of music therapy process, an outcome of it, or unrelated to their work as clinicians. Alan Turry (1999) makes a number of points regarding performance in the early years of music therapy that suggest it was undertaken for reasons other than therapeutic ones: Some music therapists conceived of their work as recreation or instruction that had performance as a natural focus; some administrators pressured music therapists to provide performances to increase the visibility of the music program; therapists were given such large groups to work with that group performance was the only option for a focus of their work; and behavioral frameworks employed by many therapists supported the use of instruction with music serving as a form of reinforcement. None of this is to say that these activities were not beneficial for clients, but it does highlight how performance was used to reduce options for therapists and clients, not to enhance them.

The activity of performance is particularly susceptible to being implemented in a way that client welfare becomes secondary to other concerns. When the agenda for performing originates with the therapist or administration, "the focus on creating a finished musical product appropriate for performance can exacerbate the problems of clients" (Turry, 1999, p. 2). This is a particularly pernicious situation when the quality of the client performance is considered a reflection of the efficacy of the therapist's work.

Music therapists are musicians with their own needs for expression through performance. When less experienced therapists who are not sufficiently self-aware about these needs engage in performance, client welfare may be compromised. Turry detailed a broad range of concerns of this type, including therapists using performance for professional self-promotion and recognition, as a means to act as a type of savior for clients, as a way to have their own music heard and recognized, or to work on their own issues around performance. In spite of these dangers, performance done consciously, ethically, and professionally holds significant benefits for clients because it can "create hope and raise the self-esteem for clients who . . . gained a sense of mastery and confidence in presenting themselves publicly" (Turry, 1999, pp. 2–3).

Feelings of support, camaraderie, and community are engendered through performance in a way that enhances the self-worth of clients.

As music therapy developed advanced levels of practice and a concept of music psychotherapy, performance became associated with entry-level, supportive work. The practice of music psychotherapy requires authentic self-expression. In using music for self-expression in music psychotherapy it is important that clients not be concerned with how the music would be judged aesthetically by an audience. In this advanced work, music therapists focus on developing client authenticity, self-reflection, and the ability to discover meaning and self-worth from an inward search, all of which led them away from performance.

Turry's thoughts on these topics are particularly instructive because he discusses how to embrace a focus on musical products through performing and creating recordings while working on an advanced level of music psychotherapy. He does not consider the focus on product to be antithetical to psychotherapeutic concerns when the potential issues are handled in a psychologically sophisticated manner. This entails fully examining the effects of the performance focus upon the relationship between client and therapist. Turry emphasizes that performing and recording music can bring legitimate benefits for clients by engendering feelings of accomplishment and self-worth. Yet, even acknowledging these benefits, therapists must be cognizant of the fact "that successful performance or product does not equal successful therapy" (1999, p. 10) because clients may have many and varied reactions that must be explored fully to further the goals of therapy.

While the idea of performance as taking on a role is antithetical to the tenets of therapy that value authenticity, other notions of performance are more congruent with these tenets. For Ansdell (1995), although the Romantic notion of performance as "the self-expressive artist projecting his ego through the music" (p. 217) is antithetical to therapy, there is an older concept of performance from the sixteenth century that is more congruent with the goals of therapy "where getting yourself out of the way allows the music and the dynamics of the performance to channel what is potential, unexpected, and, ultimately, spiritual" (p. 217).

In this view, "performance is a natural context for music-making and a natural part of musical experience" (Ansdell, 1995, p. 218). Performance does not conflict with a therapeutic focus because "a good performance is, after all, not an inauthentic 'show', but something where the conditions have given rise to an enhancement of the performer's ability and inspiration" (p. 219). Ansdell considers creative music therapy to be an artistic pursuit rather than a treatment of symptoms. It is not artistic in the sense of pure emotional expression but in a broader sense where musical expression provides experiences of oneself beyond the limitations imposed by disability.

Rather than being something false, performance can be construed as something that helps a person contact his more authentic self. Ansdell (2005) explores the various paradoxes about performance that directly relate to its value as a clinical tool within the context of community music therapy: "Performance can allow you to be yourself through 'being someone else'; can enable you to do what you 'can't do'; can be naturally 'unnatural'; can allow you to reflect on the real through the unreal; can be personal yet public; can be shared yet different for everyone" (2005, "Introduction," para. 7).

Ansdell notes four objections that underlie the belief that the goals of therapy and performance are antithetical to each other. First, the common notion of performance is connected to the idea of not being authentic by playing a role. This is the very thing that therapists want to treat rather than support. Second, some critics assert that public performance for individuals in exacerbated states of need because of physical, social, psychological, or political reasons is contraindicated and ethically questionable because of their vulnerability. Third, the focus of therapy should be on its process, not on any particular product. Fourth, therapy requires privacy and confidentiality with clear spatial and temporal boundaries.

In contrast to these considerations, Ansdell's notion of community music therapy provides a multi-faceted rationale for why performance can be appropriate in music therapy. First, performance does not involve the artificial contrivance of a false self but is instead integral to healthy psychological and social functioning in daily life. Second, process and product are not necessarily dichotomies and music therapy processes can incorporate both types of focuses. Third, performance is integral to establishing the types of relationships necessary for healthy individuals, institutions and communities. Fourth, sometimes the well-being of clients requires flexible ethical guidelines and permeable boundaries.

Ansdell reviews a number of conceptions of performance congruent with the goals of therapy. Two of them in particular are relevant for the present discussion. First is the sociologically-based idea that the performance of self is the primary goal of therapy. Rather than thinking of therapy as a process of *discovering* one's inner self, clients are instead *creating* a new sense of self. They learn how to perform themselves in ways that go beyond existing constraints to enact new ways of being.

Second, musical performance engenders the cultivation of mutual respect among participants. Many music therapy clients exist in relationships with therapists characterized by an imbalance of resources and prestige in which the establishment of mutual respect is difficult. The collaborative relationships required by performance establish respect where each party is an equal contributor. This produces benefits in enhancing the self-respect and dignity of clients.

Performance has two faces, according to Ansdell, and it is the tension between them that explains the ambivalent status of performance in music therapy. There is "performance as pressure" (Ansdell, 2005, "Conclusion: Returning to the paradoxes," para. 3) as reflected in performance situations characterized by expectations, competition, and judgments. There is also "performance as epiphany" ("Conclusion: Returning to the paradoxes," para. 3) as reflected in performance situations characterized by peak experience, hope, the building of identity, and musical *communitas*. Ansdell speculates that community music therapy practitioners utilizing performance have the task of reconciling these opposing forces.

Jampel (2006) further supports the idea that there is no tension between performance and the value of authenticity crucial to therapy. In his work researching the benefits of performance in a rock band for adults with mental illness, he noted that in order to gain the most from the experience and to "experience a deeper resonance, the performers needed to feel more closely connected to an authentic sense of self" (p. 196). To achieve this, it was necessary for the performer-clients to not only connect to their chosen music but to understand why they had chosen a particular composition for performance. For Jampel, authentic expression rather than degree of skillfulness is what distinguishes artistic efforts when performance is used as therapy.

While the popular notion of performance implies entertainment of an audience, there are functions of performance in a music therapy context unrelated to the concept of entertainment. There is a way of considering performance that sees it as continuous with daily life rather than as something apart from it. David Ramsey believes that "a public display of one's self is an important part of being a human being, whether it's on stage or it's just in the hallway" (Aigen, 2004, p. 189). For Ramsey, who provides opportunities for real-time performance of music for people with physical and communicative disabilities, the benefits of an artistic performance provide essential human experiences for individuals who need the artifice of a performance in order to demonstrate that they have something of value to offer their fellow human beings. When they perform, individuals who are severely compromised due to physical disability are looked at with more esteem by, for example, workers charged with their daily care, because music performance is so culturally idealized. For individuals who cannot demonstrate competence or even their basic humanity in any other way, the ability to perform for others—whether in an institutional setting or outside of it—can serve to achieve this.

Performance within an institution can have goals that alter fundamental social relationships within it. At Ramsey's "Happy Hour" medical and administrative staff can serve alcoholic drinks to patients and other employees of lesser status can have an opportunity to perform. Because it is a performance framework, certain rules are suspended and the alteration of roles functions to change the community, particularly in the way that patients are perceived. When the patients perform in this venue, they come to experience themselves as successful and "as somebody who can captivate and engage others, and express themselves in a way that draws people in to them" (Aigen, 2004, p. 194).

Performance and Psychodynamic Thinking

Much of the critique of performance in music therapy comes from psychodynamic perspectives such as that of Elaine Streeter (2006). She asserts that "music making and audience response to music can both be experienced as therapeutic, but neither has a therapeutic goal as such" (para. 3). The reaction of audiences is unpredictable and not limited to what performers themselves may judge to be helpful. Audiences may be so distressed by a performance "that they attempt to escape the auditorium (as happened in the first performance of Stravinsky's *The Rite of Spring*)" (para. 3).

Streeter (2006) draws a parallel between Stravinsky's audience and clients in music therapy who may "also need to escape the boundaries of therapy when staying within them is too much to manage" (para. 4). The desire to bring one's music into the public sphere is not seen as a natural, growth-promoting aspect of a therapy process but as the expression of resistance to recognizing difficult or painful aspects of the therapy process. The therapist should not collude with the client's avoidance by participating in the fantasy of "running away together" and instead should maintain the appropriate psychotherapeutic stance within existing boundaries.

While Streeter's perspective may accurately reflect standard psychotherapeutic thinking, it does not provide an argument against performing and recording with clients. A number of assumptions underlie Streeter's argument that may not be warranted. First, she assumes that audience response is the only reason to perform and the only part of performing relevant to therapy concerns. This ignores the fact that, as artists, many musicians pursue their craft without any significant public recognition. Instead, the performance of music in public can be its own reward regardless of any acclaim thereby gained. Similarly, for music therapy clients who follow their musicing desires from a private, closed session room to a more public sphere, it can be the act of moving into the public realm that is of significance more than any particular audience reaction.

It is not clear why the desire to move into a public sharing is construed solely as a type of escape. While this could be the case for some clients, for many others moving into a public realm is a highly significant growth step involving the overcoming of all kinds of emotional or physical limitations. It can be a major achievement and highly relevant to therapy goals. Streeter's analysis takes no cognizance of this aspect of performance.

Streeter's view is dependent on projecting the standards of psychotherapy practice to all forms of music therapy. She does not consider that the demands and opportunities of music psychotherapy warrant standards and ethical guidelines that are different from those of verbal psychotherapy because of the role of creative musical engagement that characterizes the former area. There is also a great deal of music therapy practice that does not claim to be psycho-therapeutic in nature and it makes no sense to apply standards from psychotherapy practice to these domains.

Moreover, there are music therapists who embrace psychodynamic thinking—for example, Turry (2005) and Maratos (2004)—who embrace performance while operating within a music psychotherapy framework. Streeter, however, does not take up Turry's (2005) argument that "it is vital for music psychotherapists who are psychodynamically oriented to avoid limiting one's understanding of performance solely as a compensation or sublimation. The desire to perform can be driven by natural, healthy impulses" ("Strategies on performing with a client," para. 3). The fact that the desire to perform and its enactment can embody client growth is not addressed by critics of performance.

Turry's (2005) numerous precautions and detailed contraindications demonstrate the awareness with which this activity is undertaken. He describes a course of music therapy with a client that involved public performance. The client, Maria Logis, was a woman with cancer whose course of therapy involved the spontaneous creation of songs and song-like structures that were eventually shared publicly in a variety of settings. Turry cautions that therapists from community music therapy and music psychotherapy orientations might critique his work, the former due to his invoking of a psychodynamic focus within performance and the latter due to his use of performance. However, the way that this course of therapy developed in a pragmatic, experimental way, guided by the exigencies of music-making is fully compatible with the community music therapy precept of following where the music leads:

> I did not undertake the therapy with the idea of applying a particular model or a theory. On the contrary, I was discovering a unique path that was being set by each step that the client and I took together. We veered into unknown territory, and the path we took was not pre-determined in any way. It is only with hindsight that I explore theoretical considerations in attempting to contrast ideas and at some points integrate the models relevant to work inside and outside the music therapy session room.
>
> (Turry, 2005, para. 4)

The way that the work evolved illustrates the ripple effect described by Pavlicevic and Ansdell. It originated in a closed music therapy session room, expanded to being shared with close friends and family, extended to professional circles in small clinical presentations and then larger professional conferences, and eventually widened to include performances open to the general public and the generation of recordings with professional musicians of songs that originated in therapy. The process of recording music was an extension of the live performance. It introduced Logis to a different circle of people (musicians) from those therapists, family members, and fellow cancer patients who attended her live events. It also extended the reach of her story to people other than those who attended her live events. In recording the CD, Logis found that "it was not easy facing her own inner critics and trusting her judgment in making decisions" (Turry, 2005, "Creating a musical product as a way of developing trust and confidence," para. 1).

Turry (2005) suggests that there is a way of considering performance that positions it as part of a psychotherapeutic focus. By accepting the "authentic self-expression" that is a natural part of this work, "the therapist can help the client to accept aspects of his personality that he previously rejected or felt shame about" ("Music psychotherapy and community music therapy: Bridging two streams of music therapy practice," para. 2). When the client's self-expression and emerging process of development call for public performance or the recording of music, the music therapist can help fulfill this role while still working within a music psychotherapeutic framework. Just as with any clinical intervention or strategy, the choice to engage in performing or recording with clients has to be undertaken with care as there are pitfalls. Turry offers contraindications for these activities that include the possible damage that can occur and the types of personality attributes that weigh against performing with clients.

A psychodynamic perspective is also used by Diane Austin (2006) to analyze issues involved in performing with clients such as in Turry's example. She recognizes that meeting the authentic needs of clients can be beneficial when done ethically. However, therapists cannot take at face value the needs expressed by clients, such as when clients state a need to have a sexual relationship with a therapist to address intimacy issues. While it is true that performing with clients does bring up ethical concerns—such as whether it establishes a dual relationship that is proscribed by ethical codes—this is not the same as engaging in a sexual relationship with a client, which, unlike performing with clients, is in and of itself unethical. There is nothing about having a sexual relationship with a music therapist that can be construed as a natural outgrowth of the way in which music therapy taps creative resources in the service of personal development. Consequently, it cannot be taken as a critique of performing with clients that it establishes an unethical, dual role, not originating in legitimate client needs just because having a sexual relationship with clients would do so.

An important issue raised by Austin is that of confidentiality and anonymity. Clients in therapy have the right to know that what happens in therapy is confidential, and that if they provide permission for details to be revealed publicly that they will remain anonymous and not connected to the clinical materials discussed. However, as Austin notes, when recordings from sessions are played publicly the promise of anonymity cannot be granted because a client's singing voice may be recognized by audience members. Austin writes that neither she nor the client were aware of the client's unconscious ambivalence about the clinical recordings being played publicly and that neither of them imagined that feelings of regret over being exposed in this way would surface.

However, in Austin's example it was not the revelation of personal material that was ultimately upsetting to the client (the loss of confidentiality); instead, it was the attaching of the material to the individual in question (the loss of anonymity), which was unexpected. This is not a concern with performing or releasing recorded material by music therapists and their clients because in the very act of public performance, anonymity is forsaken. While it may be a significant step for a client that should certainly be undertaken with great care and preparation, again Austin's example does not seem particularly relevant as a counterargument.

For many clients who may engage in performance, it is the issue of anonymity rather than confidentiality that is crucial. In Turry's example, the client performed songs that were intimate reflections of her personal struggle with cancer and her life-long struggle about feeling emotionally constricted. This material was clearly personal. However, other performing contexts growing out of music therapy may not involve personal material, such as when individuals with mental illness perform as a band playing cover songs. In cases like this, it is self-identifying as a person with mental illness that is the crucial variable, thus showing how anonymity is generally more of an issue than confidentiality.

Austin (2006) also raises the point that clients often have a need to feel special in the eyes of their therapists, to be their favorite client and "to extend the relationship beyond the therapeutic frame" (para. 6). They may engage in behaviors that do not reflect their self-interest in an effort to curry the favor of therapists and to be special. According to Austin, performing with clients brings unique challenges because "the client is indeed special because of the contributions he or she makes to the therapist's career, in the form of articles, presentations, fund-raising" (para. 6). Austin goes on to note that these benefits may compromise the therapist's best judgment as both parties collude to support the performing relationship at the expense of a deeper examination of the dynamics of the therapeutic relationship.

But again, none of these issues is unique to performing or recording music with clients. The contribution of the client's permission to share clinical materials in the form of articles, books, conference presentations, or participation in research studies is something that is always present. And while these activities are therapist initiated, performing and recording music is usually client initiated. This latter recognition suggests that performing and recording music with clients is at least as ethical as is sharing their clinical processes through professional forums, if not more so.

An important topic of discussion is where the therapy lies in performance-oriented music therapy. Is it in the processes involved prior to and subsequent to the performance, in the quality of the performance, in the process of performing, or all of these things in combination?

An interesting perspective is provided by Maratos (2004, 2005), who employs the performance of original dramas in her work in an inpatient psychiatric setting. While her psychodynamic framework would seem to clash with a performance focus, she effects an integration of the two. In contrast to Ansdell, Maratos says that performance-oriented work need not be antithetical to psychoanalytic thinking and does not require a music-centered view. This dimension of community music therapy can be implemented within a variety of other clinical frameworks and does not "necessitate a shift away from analytically-informed practice" (Maratos, 2005, "What theory would support a community music therapy model?" para. 4).

Ansdell, however, does not accept the idea that because Maratos claims that the rehearsals were therapeutic that this shows the ability of a psychoanalytic framework to accommodate performance as a valid treatment focus:

> Her point that "It was 'therapy' partly because the rehearsals were as important as the performances' I don't understand. Under this logic the choir I sing with is doing covert therapy! Indeed I smell some desperation to preserve the notion of "therapy" here!
> (Ansdell, 2005, "Throwing out the (analytic) baby with the bathwater," para. 2)

Ansdell argues that Maratos's rationale saves the psychoanalytic label at the expense of the core aspects of psychoanalytic thinking. He believes that the two approaches are incompatible, as evidenced by the ways in which even Maratos asserted that psychoanalytic thinking clashed with ideas about the value of performance for her clients:

> My thought is that in terms of music therapy as *practiced* it's not what psychoanalysis *is*, or believes, but how the model is *used* in any circumstance that matters—that is, what possibilities of action it admits or frustrates. For [Maratos] this model seemed as limiting as it is for many music therapists in terms of its normative 'rules' concerning sites, roles, boundaries and attitudes. Her working around these and her excuses for them lead me to ask how far you massage a theory and its basic assumptions before you've preserved only the name?
>
> (Ansdell, 2005, "Throwing out the (analytic) baby with the bathwater," para. 3)

Ansdell's critique of Maratos's argument that performance is consistent with psychoanalytic thinking does not extend to a critique of the value of the preparation for performance in general. In fact, while arguing for the legitimacy of performance in community music therapy, Ansdell further says that it is not performance as an isolated phenomenon that matters but rather how performance relates to what happens before and after it that is most salient. His research revealed

> that it is in the relationship between the performance and non-performance aspects of the group that its identity (and effect) lies. The therapist also works skillfully with individuals, parts of the group and with the context and surrounding structures of the local community. It's somehow the network of these various interactions that characterises the group.
>
> (Ansdell, 2005, "Just add performance?" para. 2)

A similar point is made by Jampel (2006) for whom "performance is a path and not a particular destination" (p. 217). A significant part of his research findings detail the interpersonal interactions, roles, and chronological process of what occurs in the preparation for public performance. In considering how roles are formed and how the interactions recapitulate problematic family dynamics of group members, Jampel shows how traditional group therapy theory can be applied to performing. The process of preparing for performance becomes the setting and context in which a typical group therapy process occurs and is revealed.

In addition to the process of preparation is the process of the performance itself. Jampel notes five different types of connection as the primary clinical benefits of performance: connection to self, to other performers, to the audience, to the world beyond the audience, and to the spiritual. The relationship to the audience is a reciprocal one in which the musicians give of themselves to enliven and engage the audience members, while audience members give interest and support to performers in a way that makes the performance more meaningful.

Any focus on creating a musical product (whether conceived as a recording or a performance) is considered by some clinicians to be antithetical to the process nature of music therapy. In light of some of the actual examples of performance in music therapy, this objection has embedded within it two assumptions that can be challenged:

1. Focusing on the creation of a musical product in therapy is antithetical to client needs because it moves the focus away from the client and onto the creation of an object guided by extrinsic aesthetic or commercial purposes. This assumption is not always warranted because (a) sometimes the client's health-related needs can best be met by the creation of a musical product, and (b) the criteria guiding the creation of a musical product in therapy may be other than commercial or aesthetic. Consider how the public performances and recordings created by Maria Logis led to the implementation of public performance events for fellow cancer patients or the ways in which the play described by Maratos served as a socio-political critique of the institution where it took place.

2. Music therapy is essentially a process-oriented practice and any focus on performance or recording necessarily changes this to a product-oriented practice antithetical to therapy goals. Even granting the assumption that music therapy should be solely a process-oriented practice, it does not necessarily follow that incorporating a product focus precludes or inhibits the primacy of process. The process of making a product can be very valuable clinically. This recognition underlies practices that are as different on the surface as Nordoff-Robbins group work with children and work with adults with mental illness in rock or jazz bands, such as in Jampel (2006).

In product-oriented work there is still a therapy process (as traditionally defined) that involves clients interacting with each other and learning things about themselves that are similar to what happens in traditional therapy guided by the tenets of group therapy theory. But there is another type of process that involves work on a creative product, where the actual work is an essential part of the clinical value. In other words, creating a product for public sharing is its own unique process with its own unique clinical benefits. Again, this is essential in Nordoff-Robbins group work where the focus is on learning compositions, whether made for therapy or not. So even in therapy with a product focus, there are still two types of processes present: one that includes traditional therapy considerations involving working on personal issues and group dynamics, and one that is unique to the communal creation of a creative product.

The process-product issue is taken up directly by Maratos (2004) in the context of describing her drama project for adults with chronic mental illness. It involved the creation, rehearsal, and performance of an operetta called *The Teaching of Edward*, "a fictional account of the English composer, Edward Elgar's 'discovery' of music therapy through being persuaded by the patients at the asylum where he was employed to go beyond his usual musician's role of performing to patients" (Maratos, 2004, p. 136). In the story, Elgar is unsuccessful in generating interest in performing his music, yet when he inadvertently begins a spontaneous composition with the patients, they participate enthusiastically and with a confidence that belies their psychological difficulties. The drama was performed within the institution where it was created and for outside audiences. An important implication of the work was how it caused productive re-examinations of the relationship among certain staff and patients, and of how power was used among the former group in less than benevolent ways.

The principles of music therapy were active throughout the preparations for the project performance. Events that occurred during the preparations were discussed as if they had occurred in a therapy group and the process involved in preparing and implementing the project was as important as the performance itself. Moreover, the creation of the dramatic project was not a strictly delimited, self-contained process without precursors or consequences.

The project itself resulted from client relationships to the therapist (Maratos) that had preceded the performance by many years and that continued, albeit in a changed form, after the performance. Thus, the product itself was only one stage in a long-term process.

The Necessity of Performance in Client Empowerment: Performance for Closure in Therapy

Whether or not one embraces the idea of performing is based on how one looks at the music in therapy. For Garred (2006), music can either be considered as aesthetic expression or as "symbolically projective of psychic content" (p. 283). He argues that as aesthetic expression, it invites community participation because its meaning is embedded within communal contexts. Conversely, when it is a symbolic projection of inner conflicts it should be a private, confidential matter in line with ethical guidelines that protect clients.

In addition to community music therapy, many of the other contemporary frameworks in music therapy are based upon the former conception of music, including feminist music therapy, music-centered music therapy, and resource-oriented music therapy. This embrace of music as an aesthetic vehicle rather than as a psychological symptom or clinical tool is one of the prime forces behind the drive to include performance in music therapy. The processes that therapists activate and support within their clients require performance to reach completion. The change in theory is to see the act of aesthetic completion via performance as within the music therapist's professional activity rather than outside of it.

In the exploration of alternative notions of performance consistent with the former view of music, Ansdell (2010) considers the roots of the word *performance* that offer an important component to the examination of its role in music therapy. He builds upon Victor Turner's view of its origins as indicating not "the structuralist implications of manifesting form, but rather the processual sense of 'bringing to completion,' or 'accomplishing'" (Turner as cited in Ansdell, p. 178). Ansdell goes on to reason that "this sense of performance as completion assumes then that something needs completing, both in the cultural form, which is the performance vehicle, but perhaps in the personal and social life of those who participate in the performance event" (pp. 178–179). This is the sense in which Maria Logis engages in her community talks, workshops, and performances.

It is also relevant in Elizabeth York's (2006) study (discussed below) in which women survivors of domestic violence engage in community performances as the culmination of their therapy. The evolution of the therapy process and its completion requires the public manifestation; these public performances complete the individual, health-related processes begun in music therapy. As Ansdell (2010) remarks, when clients in music therapy engage in public performance, they are not just communicating the form of musical compositions; instead, they are completing "both the songs and themselves in the course of performance" (p. 184).

The presence of an audience is a crucial factor in understanding the role of performance in therapy. Of primary importance is how the audience serves to intensify the musical experience in a way that has intrapersonal and social consequences. It can lead to a new, more potent level of engagement with music from which the client develops an enhanced sense of self. Moreover, the contact with the audience can represent the enhancement of the client's social connectedness. This is an especially important consideration in Garred's (2006) dialogical approach to music therapy as it represents an "increased relationship capacity, accompanied by a change in the sense of self" (p. 287) that occurs in a two-way, interactive process.

York's (2006) research study examined "the efficacy of a feminist approach to music therapy and creative arts interventions on the self-esteem and empowerment of female survivors" (p. 251) of domestic violence. Clients initiated the idea of creating a performance based on the material that emerged in their therapy sessions. York employed the research construct known as an "ethnographic performance piece" through which the research findings were organized and presented. This type of performance piece was a way for the clients to share their experiences in therapy with others. Their desire to do so was considered by York to be a breakthrough because it indicated "a level of ownership, trust, and empowerment that was unanticipated at the beginning of the project" (p. 256).

Given the physical danger posed by their domestic situations, the issue of anonymity was of paramount importance for the participants. It was addressed in a number of ways: some women chose to participate openly; others participated in hidden ways through the use of masks, costumes, and pseudonyms in the performance program; some participated only as support staff, such as being a prop manager or set designer; others allowed their materials to be used but did not personally participate in the performance; and some chose to leave the project and not participate in the performance aspect. The choice was left to each participant and the structure of the program allowed for these varied levels of participation and anonymity.

Similar to the situation with Turry and Logis, the performance was not just reporting about a therapy process but was an essential continuation of it. The transition "from victim to advocate, from client to singer, dancer, and creative artist" (York, 2006, p. 258) so central to the goals of the therapy process was only made possible by the way that the performance gave a public voice to the women's experience. Performances began in the safe environment of the agency supporting the initial therapy work and gradually moved into the outside community. It encompassed an audio recording of the entire performance that enabled the fruits of the work to be shared with an audience beyond those who were able to attend a live performance. One thousand copies of the CD were used to raise funds for the original agency and for music therapy services. This last issue seems to be one open for debate as some see a conflict of interest when materials generated by clients are used to fund positions for music therapists.

In music therapy performances, clients can perform non-original compositions (Jampel, 2006), original compositions intended as art or social commentary (Maratos, 2004), or they can perform pieces that grew from a therapy process and that deal with highly personal concerns (Logis & Turry, 1999; O'Brien, 2006; Turry, 2010, 2011).

As an example of work of the last type, Day, Baker, and Darlington (2009) describe music therapy with women who had been abused as children and in marriages, and who were experiencing relationship and parenting difficulties as a result. The original clinical project involved creating and recording songs that dealt substantially with private material and painful, traumatic emotions and memories. Although the clinical program was initially conceived as just including the composing and recording of the songs, the participants requested the opportunity for a public performance "to educate others about the long-lasting effects of childhood abuse" (p. 20). The public performance was an essential way in which the participants were given a voice with which to relate their experience. This giving of voice through public performance was especially relevant as a clinical focus "given the silence and secrecy that had surrounded their experiences of child abuse" (p. 20).

In addition to providing its own intrinsic benefits—something noted by almost all of the authors who discuss performance in music therapy—the performance functioned to extend the therapeutic process into a broader realm, something that also characterized the work of Turry and Logis (1999). In contrast to psychoanalytic approaches used in the treatment of adults who have experienced childhood abuse that stress the confidentiality and private nature of the process, this project demonstrates the value of the opposite strategy of the public acknowledgement of the experience through a creative art form, when it is initiated and desired by the client.

The importance of completion through the performance of compositions as a concluding phase of the therapy process is demonstrated in Felicity Baker's (2013) research. The composing of a song in therapy starts an important process but its benefits are limited. For these benefits to carry over to the person's life requires public performance. Part of the way it does this is by helping the client-composer in "experiencing more fully the emotions attached to the lyrics and music" (p. 23). The public performance of the song can represent a consummation of the creative-clinical process and the client can then move on to other concerns in the therapy process.

Baker's work empirically investigates the topic of performance in music therapy, illustrates its benefits, and discusses its contraindications when the following conditions hold: First, clients have a life-long experience of being judged; second, clients have insufficient inner sufficient resources to manage the performance context; third, clients are not well supported by the context (e.g. degree of audience support is unreliable or unknown); fourth, performing in public is outside clients' comfort zone.

Baker (2013) also discusses how some of the greatest needs of clients can only be met through community-oriented, public performance. When clients' life experiences resonate with those of their audiences, they experience a sense of self-worth that is coupled to the ability to convey their emotional reality in a way has a "clear impact and meaning for the audience" (p. 24). It is through this type of performance that clients are able to demonstrate "their intellectual, creative, and musical capabilities that transcend disability or disadvantage" (p. 24) and be looked at as whole human beings, not defined by their areas of need. Identity is not something that emanates from solely within the person; it is instead created in social interaction and the essential goal of creating a healthy and complete sense of self requires the type of social interaction that performance can provide.

Questions about the propriety of therapists performing music with clients outside of therapy sessions may be less relevant in non-Western contexts. For example, with a Kurdish client from Turkey, Zharinova-Sanderson (2004) discusses how "musical performance was not seen as an imposed task" (p. 243) but rather considered as natural consequence of the musical explorations that had taken place in their individual sessions. In this client's culture, music is for the purpose of connecting with other people, and there is almost no concept of music apart from its public sharing. To only work in the context of a closed, individual session is to not take advantage of a client's musical cultural resources. In this example, occurring with traumatized political refugees, the public performance was essential in re-establishing the client's self-worth, something that is often lost by the experiences of trauma and exile. To not offer performance as a focus of therapy would deny the client an essential resource.

PART V

How are Psycho-Biological Concerns Addressed in Music Therapy?

13

EARLY INTERACTION THEORY AND MUSIC THERAPY

The present chapter and Chapters 14 and 15 address three concerns that are not always linked in the professional literature: the musical aspects of mother–infant interaction and analogs in music therapy, the proper role of brain science in music therapy, and evolutionary perspectives on the nature of music and the implications for music therapy. While the first two topics are of interest in their own right for music therapists, they are also invoked in arguments for the adaptive value of music in evolutionary theory and its implications for music therapy theory.

In the evolutionary literature, two general perspectives are present: one that considers music to be of survival value and something that emerged from natural selection, and an opposing view that music has no survival value and that it emerged from a combination of human capacities developed for other purposes. For theorists who argue that music is of evolutionary value, there are two primary forms of evidence. The first is related to the musicality of early interaction. Establishing bonds between mother and infant clearly has survival value. If it can be shown that the processes that establish this connection (a) have a musical character, and (b) are precursors to the later development of actual music, then two things are accomplished: music is demonstrated to be of survival value and a target of processes of natural selection, and a strong rationale for music therapy is provided that is rooted in biological science. The second form of evidence for arguments supporting the evolutionary value of music relates to brain science. If it can be demonstrated that there are dedicated neurological networks specific to music, this supports the notion that music was an object of natural selection and therefore necessarily possesses survival value. This line of reasoning can be used to support the primacy of neurological phenomena in creating explanatory theory in music therapy. The first of these forms of evidence is addressed in the present chapter; the second is considered in Chapter 14.

The present chapter begins with a review of thinking in music therapy on the musical dimensions of mother–infant interaction—hereon referred to as *early interaction* as a more general term—and its implications for music therapy theory. While some of this material is primarily relevant for understanding theories underlying the effectiveness of clinical improvisation, some of it will also be drawn upon in the discussion of whether music has evolutionary origins or not.

Colwyn Trevarthen and Stephen Malloch (2000) have constructed a comprehensive theory of mother–infant bonding based on the musical qualities of early interaction. Following the discussion of their theory, applications to music therapy will be taken up. The music therapy theorists Mercédès Pavlicevic and Henk Smeijsters have considered early interaction theory in great detail and have used it as essential pieces of comprehensive approaches to music therapy. The close analysis of their thinking will reveal some of the basic conceptual problems that must be solved for early interaction theory to be effectively applied in music therapy.

Trevarthen and Malloch's Communicative Musicality

In their concept of communicative musicality, Trevarthen and Malloch (2000) extend the observations about the musicality of early interaction to create a notion of human relationship-building that centers on these protomusical capacities. They propose that the musical dimensions of early interaction reveal in a relatively pure form the capacities and parameters that underlie all human relationship. Consequently, the communicative musicality that characterizes early interaction can explain the therapeutic efficacy of music in applications where establishing relationship is paramount.

Trevarthen and Malloch (2000) cite John Blacking to the effect that people who belong to different "affective cultures" can nonetheless "sense what underlies a person's actions and experience" in music (p. 4). This occurs in spite of belonging to different musical cultures with different musical conventions. While some may find this claim surprising and not consistent with common knowledge on the topic, this ability is attributed to the fact that the rhythmic and melodic movements of the body and the voice, respectively, are linked to expression with which all humans can sympathize.

> Research on how infants attend to and stimulate intuitive music in parents' vocal play, and how they can imitate and reciprocate intricately co-ordinated expressions, strongly suggests that we are born like this and the infant's sympathy arises from an inborn rhythmic coherence of body movement and modulation of affective expressions . . . We believe that underlying acquired musical motor skills and perception of cultivated musical forms is an intrinsic "musicality."
>
> (Trevarthen & Malloch, 2000, p. 4)

Trevarthen and Malloch believe that whatever capacities are necessary for music are present at birth and specific to musical interaction. Whether or not one wants to consider this early musicality to be a form of protomusic depends on one's view of its function. The belief that musicality exists to facilitate healthy interaction between infant and adults before verbal means of communication are available suggests that musicality is preverbal (even if music is not) and that musicality could have a survival value in the way that some theorists deny. Music as we know it then becomes the extension of infant musicality into the artistic realm.

A central question raised by their theory is which function is essential and which is secondary. In other words, does musicality exist primarily to support the subsequent development of music, which then enriches human life in a unique way, or does music exist as a secondary outgrowth of musicality, which had an essential developmental function prior to the existence of what we now call *music*? In the former case, music as such has no unique or original function in an evolutionary sense; it is more like an accidental consequence of musicality without unique implications for human development and well-being. In the latter case, music could have unique evolutionary value and the suggestion is that theory in music therapy should focus as much on the phenomenon of music as on the processes of musicality that predate it.

Trevarthen and Malloch (2000) hold music in great esteem and argue that an understanding of both early interaction and clinical music therapy requires seeing what music is on its own terms, not just in contrast to verbal interaction. As with early interaction, the authors note that responsiveness to musicality noted by music therapists is also not dependent upon the learning of musical skills. Consequently, they believe that music "is a uniquely human motivation, part of our psycho-biological endowment" (p. 4) and therefore an innate capacity.

Moreover, they argue that the parameters of human communication that exist outside words warrant being defined in their positive function, not just in relation to what is absent. This is why the term *nonverbal* does not do them justice. The synchrony of voice and body found in conversational analysis underlies all human relating and it is achieved through these other modalities. Because "bodily and vocal expression is [*sic*] so powerful in the management of human relations" it warrants the designation *communicative musicality*. However, their use of the term *music* harks back to more archaic origins that "applied to all the temporal arts together" (Trevarthen & Malloch, 2000, p. 5) so what they are proposing is not specific to what we understand as music in a contemporary sense.

Communicative musicality is necessary for healthy emotional and cognitive development and its principles provide the rationale for a therapy treatment regardless of age because "humans, of all ages, not just infants, need to have the impulses of sympathy attuned. They need to share experiences in order to help make sense of them" (Trevarthen & Malloch, 2000, p. 7). The same functions and capacities that underlie music also support the development of the self, the building of healthy relationships, and the acquisition of a sense of purpose in life.

Trevarthen and Malloch consider early interaction primarily in its antiphonal aspect regarding vocalization, examining temporal responsiveness, imitation, and embellishment that take place in temporal information segments. They conclude that "the elements conventionally represented in music appear to be an intrinsic part of spontaneous human communication" (2000, p. 11) so that with individuals for whom verbal communication is impaired or not possible, the musical interaction provides a nonverbal means for contact.

Although it builds upon psychoanalytic traditions, their rationale does not depend on classical psychoanalytic thinking about childhood trauma causing all problems and the need for adults to regress to an early, preverbal stage of development to repair the trauma. They describe how humans need healthy relationships at all stages of the lifespan. A person who was well adjusted as a child could experience problems later in life. Difficulties in meeting the challenges of new developmental stages can emerge from problems brought on by things such as substance abuse, psychiatric illnesses with an onset in late adolescence or early adulthood, medical problems, accidents, and progressive/degenerative diseases. All of these things cause problems in communication and therefore all of them are susceptible to being effectively treated by music therapy. None of these applications require a theoretical rationale dependent on psychoanalytic meta-theory.

However, Trevarthen and Malloch can be critiqued for their emphasis on imitation in musical interaction. Strict imitation is not musical but is a parody of musical interaction. Music therapy practice that employs imitation excessively does nothing more than mechanically reflect back to a person the musical manifestations of disability or pathology. What is missing in such a conception of music therapy is the contribution of the motive to relate to another person that is necessary to true dynamic communication. This perspective is asserted by Garred (2006) in his application of Martin Buber's philosophy to music therapy and in much of Nordoff-Robbins music therapy theory as well (Ansdell, 1995; Aigen, 1998). Thus, one deficiency of music therapy practice based on this foundation is an over-reliance on imitation, perhaps extending this aspect of communicative musicality inappropriately in the artistic domain of musical creation that fuels the most potent music therapy interactions.

To be fair to Trevarthen and Malloch, they do make the point that the type of communication they refer to must go beyond imitation to include a commentary or personal input into the communication, even if the early interaction processes they refer to do not make significant use of other interactional dynamics beyond imitation:

> To mimic an other implies we are attentive to his or her behavior. However, to abstract a communicative motive from that movement and to relay it back to the initiator in a changed yet emotionally appropriate form implies we are not simply mimicking, but creating an attitude or evaluation of what has been given to us by the other. In responding, some of one's inner emotional life is added to the relationship.
>
> (Trevarthen & Malloch, 2000, p. 12)

They also make use of Stern's notion of affect attunement and agree that it is a "trans-modal phenomenon, in which the affect of a vocal and/or bodily gesture is attuned to by another and expressed in a different form from the original" (Trevarthen & Malloch, 2000, p. 12). For Stern, the transfer to another modality is a necessary aspect of conveying that one has attuned to the quality of an expression, presumably because it necessarily involves more than just a mechanical imitation.

But one clear problem in applying this theory to music therapy is that client and therapist are both responding in music; they are not crossing a modality which seems to be a necessary feature of Stern's theory. In fact, this is a serious confounding problem for any music therapist that wants to apply early interaction theory to clinical processes. Most authors in this area do not indicate that they are cognizant of this problem, with the notable exception of Henk Smeijsters who attempts his own solution for it, discussed later in the present chapter. Nonetheless, Trevarthen and Malloch (2000) attempt to provide a firm foundation for music therapy by supporting the notion that music is unique and necessary, and that music therapy "is based in the life-long human trait of creating companionship with another by structuring expressive time together" (p. 14).

Pavlicevic's Concept of Dynamic Form

In an effort to explain the processes and effectiveness of clinical improvisation in music therapy, Mercédès Pavlicevic developed the notion of dynamic form, a construct that she has been refining and elaborating upon for over 20 years. A relatively brief article (Pavlicevic, 1990) is one of the earliest, most detailed and conceptually coherent expositions of the rationale for applying studies on mother–infant interaction to improvisational music therapy. In it, Pavlicevic claims that clinical improvisation is best explained by using concepts from early interaction.

She draws primarily from the ideas of Daniel Stern and Colwyn Trevarthen in describing the empathic connection established between mother and infant through the processes of affect attunement (Stern) and inter-subjectivity (Trevarthen). This interaction occurs vocally (although nonverbally) through facial expression and through body movement. These various expressions are formed in ways that evoke the forms through which music is expressed:

> When the relationship is inter-subjective, both infant and mother initiate, complement and respond to one another in a highly fluid and intimate dance, within which their internal states resonate with one another through their apprehending of one another's dynamic forms. This "dance" has all the complexities and subtleties of a musical improvisation duet, and includes expressive features of tempo (e.g. *accelerando, rubato, ritardando, allargando, ritenuto*); of dynamics (e.g. *sforzando, crescendo*); of timbre (e.g. changes in voice quality) and of pitch (melodic contours and harmonic colour).
>
> (Pavlicevic, 1990, p. 6)

These dynamic forms characterize the communication between mother and infant because they are forms of our emotional lives, a claim that also explains their pervasiveness in music. The dynamic shifts characterizing these forms of expression are called *vitality affects* by Stern and the forms common to a variety of expressive modes are "intensity, shape, time, contour, motion and number" (Pavlicevic, 1990, p. 6).

These abstract forms are mental constructs not bound to a particular mode of perception or experience and their presence serves to unify our perceptual world. Conceived of as amodal properties, they are thus recognized through any of the senses. Pavlicevic uses the example of "a child bursting with energy, a burst of temper, . . . bursting into tears" (Pavlicevic, 1990, p. 6). In all of these instances, the "bursting is the dynamic form of the action or feeling, irrespective of whether it is a positive or negative emotion, or of whether there is any feeling component at all" (p. 6). In saying that "it is the dynamic forms of actions, rather than merely the actions themselves, which enable the mother and infant to know one another intimately" (p. 6), Pavlicevic seems to be arguing that the form of the expression is much more important than its content, in this case the specific emotion that might be communicated between mother and infant.

The concept of *forms of feeling* originated in the aesthetic theory of Susanne Langer. One of the primary problems of Langer's thought is inherited by anyone using a derivative of it. Langer was criticized because her approach cannot account for the way that the particular emotions and feelings are differentiated and conveyed through music because many contrasting emotions can share the same dynamic forms.

Pavlicevic appears to get around this difficulty by saying that is not the emotional content of the improvised music that is relevant but the shared play and interaction within the dynamic forms that matters most. This answers one problem but raises another. If the mother (in this case) is not attuning to the content of the specific emotion but just connecting to the form of its realization (a form shared by quite different contents) it is not immediately clear if this is bona fide attunement or not. It seems more sensible to argue that people feel a stronger empathic connection when another person attunes to the content of our feelings, not just the form or the intensity of their expression.

In considering what happens when client and therapist improvise music together, Pavlicevic likens the situation to what occurs when mother and infant improvise within their relationship.

In creating music with clients, therapists perceive the dynamic forms of their clients' music and respond musically with the intent of "moving towards an inter-subjective musical/emotional relationship with them" (Pavlicevic, 1990, p. 6). The music does not symbolize the client's emotional state, or if it does, this is not its salient element from a clinical standpoint. Instead, the improvised music is the modality through which the client presents and tries out different dynamic forms in the context of a supportive relationship.

Establishing this type of communication and the relationship that builds from it is dependent upon the active intention of both parties. Its clinical value lies in the manner in which it enacts the aspects of early interaction:

> Where the music therapist and patient are able to create a shared musical space between them, within which both players can express themselves, then a highly intimate and dynamic inter-subjective relationship is possible. For this to happen, the therapist needs to enable the patient to express himself through the music; she needs to apprehend the dynamic forms of his or her expression and give meaning to these by responding dynamically in a way which the patient himself apprehends, i.e. the two players need to share a reciprocity of intention.
>
> (Pavlicevic, 1990, p. 7)

Pavlicevic's proposals solve some problems and create others. She articulates a perspective different from the traditional psychoanalytic view of music in music therapy as an expression or symbol of unconscious feelings. This can be seen in her focus on the form of the music rather than on its content, unless one wants to designate the various dynamic forms of the music as its content. In either case, the music is more than just a vehicle for conveying non-musically-based emotions and Pavlicevic asserts that the specific emotional content of the music is not particularly relevant, even if it is present.

Although the ideas from early interaction originate in psychodynamic thinking, Pavlicevic makes a stronger case for a music-centered approach to clinical improvisation than a psychoanalytic one. She does not overtly contextualize her remarks within this latter framework but indirectly does so in leaning on the concepts promoted in Nordoff-Robbins music therapy (NRMT). Her ideas would be at variance with those theories promoted by any of the primary approaches in psychoanalytically-oriented music therapy.

Pavlicevic may go too far in eliminating the emotional quality of the music as an important aspect of the client's music in clinical improvisation because of her desire to highlight the role of the dynamic forms. Even in NRMT, it is more than just the intensity or form of the client's music that matters. Its quality is relevant as well in determining clinical-musical interventions.

Certainly the dynamic forms of the client's music are relevant and the therapist will work from them. But within the basically generic qualities of tempo and dynamics, the therapist also has available for use the more specific and uniquely musical tools of style, scale, melody, and harmony. These specific components of music may have no direct counterpart in the amodal forms of feeling. Moreover, the therapist's music may not always express the client's emotion, but it will generally take account of it in some way, such as expressing it on occasion, commenting on it, offering transformed versions of it, or presenting an opposing expression to it. In other words, just because the therapist is not conforming to a conventional psychoanalytic approach in which the client's emotion expressed in the music is of primary consideration, this does not mean that the client's emotional content is irrelevant. To ignore this completely would certainly be an example of lack of attunement. What is not clear, then, is the role of the client's emotion in forming the music. In NRMT, the therapist's musical contribution can take place within the context of the client's emotion without becoming merely a vehicle for its manifestation or reflection.

Pavlicevic continued to develop her ideas about dynamic form subsequent to its initial presentation. While her emphasis remained on the observation that the ability to form human relationships is based upon innate skills possessed by infants that are musical in nature, there was a shift in the role of emotional expression in this process that results in some inconsistency in the overall theory. She builds upon the innate skills of infants related to dynamic forms to suggest a stronger role for personal expression:

> Infants are neurologically predisposed to identifying, and responding to, musical patterning, and are extremely sensitive and responsive to contours and rhythm of movements, gestures and vocalizations; subtle shifts in vocal timbre; tempo and volume variations in their mothers' gestures vocal sounds and facial expressions. In other words, infants receive, elicit, and respond to their mothers' movements, gestures and acts not as musical or temporal events, but rather, as personally expressive and communicative; that is as the basis for forming human relationships.
>
> (Pavlicevic, 2000, p. 274)

Here, Pavlicevic uses the phrase "in other words" to equate two different assertions that are not actually interchangeable. She seems to be claiming that just because infants have perceptual sensitivities of the types that she describes, this in and of itself suggests how they are construing these perceptions (as personally expressive). First, if true this does seem to contradict some of the earlier formulations of her theory that specifically de-emphasized the personally expressive contents of the shared communication. Second, it is not at all obvious that sensitivity to the form of movements, gestures, and vocalizations necessarily suggests that these expressions are perceived as personally expressive.

It could just as easily be construed that it is merely the activity of musical play together that forms the relationship rather than the fact that it is personally expressive to any extent. This would be an alternative way of looking at the situation, especially if in moving to the realm of music therapy one would like to argue that it is the act of musicing together that is most valuable clinically rather than the contents of the shared music. Pavlicevic seems to offer contradictory notions on the role of emotions in these activities—mother–infant interaction and clinical music therapy improvisation—on the one hand saying that the music does not have to be personally expressive and on the other hand arguing that emotional expression is primary and that the musical quality of clinical music therapy improvisation is not relevant:

> Not unlike mother and infant, therapist and client in improvisational music therapy present themselves through spontaneous soundform, whose constant shifts of tempo, dynamic level, intonation, phrasing, rhythm, and melody suggest a constant negotiating of themselves in relation to one another—nonverbally. Although this improvisation

may be heard as musical—and indeed, may be aesthetically pleasing and musically engaging—the primary agenda is for the therapist to elicit and directly experience the client's emotional experience of the world.

(Pavlicevic, 2000, p. 275)

Pavlicevic is committed to the notion that clinical and nonclinical musical interaction are fundamentally different, primarily because the former is guided by non-interactive musical considerations while the latter is solely guided by relational, interactive considerations. In basing the clinical theory of dynamic form on early interaction, Pavlicevic must portray this developmental form of relating as containing the same interactive parameters as clinical music therapy improvisation. This need to preserve the differences between the two types of musicing seems to force a situation where the role of personal expression is construed in two different, mutually exclusive ways in the theory.

Pavlicevic acknowledges that her approach does diminish the musical value of the music in music therapy where it becomes a means to establish relationship, not music as it is commonly understood outside of clinical applications. She challenges music therapists to accept that it may not be music as such that is the salient aspect of what they offer to clients but merely the amodal parameters that are nonspecific to music that explain the underlying processes of clinical improvisation:

> Like MT improvisation, mother–infant interaction is not a "musical" event, in the sense that free jazz improvisation is. Rather it is a communicative event that has a musical basis. We might posit that mother–infant communication is pre or quasimusical, in the sense that the very foundations of the act are the (unformed and unsynthesized) ingredients of music: those of tempo, rhythm, contours of voice, gesture and act, volume, timbre. Does this mean that MT improvisation, too, by its emotional, interactive emphasis, is pre or quasimusical (and can music therapists cope with this idea)?
>
> (Pavlicevic, 2000, p. 277)

The music-like aspects of early interaction are further claimed to have survival value by Bunt and Pavlicevic (2001) because they allow the infant to communicate its needs, some of which are biological such as hunger, and others that are more psychological such as distress and frustration. The implication is that these music-like communications are available before language and thus musicality is of biological significance. These expressions are expressive of inner states; they are strictly functionally communicative and it is the communication of needs and the understanding of the communication and the response to them that allows them to form the basis of a relationship. The fact that communication occurs through music-like expressions is not particularly relevant except insofar as this is what is available to the infant. The implication is that this communication does nothing that could not be better achieved verbally if words were available.

The communication of needs stemming from physiological considerations is a common, persistent theme in the literature on music in early interaction, brain science, and evolutionary theory. Many theorists of all types seem to be compelled to articulate how music can function to support biological survival. To anticipate a theme further developed in Chapter 15, the opposing view is that music is valuable primarily because it is not required for biological survival. From this perspective, it can be argued that the meeting of physiological needs is not the only way to construe what happens in early interaction. Another way to look at it is to consider the interaction as a joint musical creation in which the bonding occurs because of the shared expressive, creative activity. Thus, it is not the communication and satisfaction of needs that is most salient in building the relationship; rather it is the interactive, jointly creative musical activity that forms the relationship. This would be one of way of using mother–infant interaction as a basis for understanding music therapy improvisation that is adequate to music as a creative, aesthetic, fluid modality and not only a symbol of inner states to which it is constrained in psychodynamic theory.

Construing personally expressive communications as the only basis for personal relationship precludes a role for the non-agenda-based, joyful sharing of sounds and gestures as an essentially human and vital activity. What is most puzzling is that this latter construal of what is happening in early interaction—and in some improvisational music therapy contexts—is one that actually seems most consistent with the initial presentation of Pavlicevic's theory. Perhaps this ambivalence about the musicality of early interaction and music therapy interaction can be seen in the claim not to be "denying or diminishing the *musical* basis of the therapeutic event in music therapy" (Bunt & Pavlicevic, 2001, p. 194). However, this sentiment does seem to be at variance with the arguments that they present in which there is nothing inherently, essentially, or uniquely musical in the function of music in their construal of improvisational music therapy.

Pavlicevic's approach in drawing upon developmental infant literature in understanding clinical improvisation is based on the conceptualization of music as communication. However, while communication may take place in music, this does not mean that music fundamentally *is* communication, or that communication among its participants is its primary focus, function, or the best way of understanding what it is. Looking at music as a form of communication is a common perspective in music therapy. For example, Tønsberg and Hauge (2003) make use of shifts in communication theory to a more musical foundation in their discussion of the musical nature of human interaction:

> As the literature in modern developmental psychology shows, a process towards a paradigmatic shift in theories concerning the development of communication in children started in the 70's. This includes a shift of attention, and, as described in Nadel and Camaioni (1993) the theories developed from an *emit/receive/answer telegraphist model of communication*, towards an *orchestra metaphor model*. The latter model focuses on harmonisation, improvisation, joint activity and co-regulation as prominent qualities. The orchestra metaphor invites the use of musical terms as rhythmicity, harmony, theme with variations, shared beat and musical improvisations and leads our attention to certain qualities in co-creation of non-linguistic human interaction.
>
> (Tønsberg & Hauge, 2003, "Introduction," para. 4)

While the authors focus on communication, this may not be what is most salient from a clinical perspective, or perhaps not is what is most salient from all clinical perspectives. It is interesting that the shift in metaphors used in communication theory moves toward a more musical one, but again, the implications of the musical metaphor are not carried through completely. The joint cooperation in the creation of a communal product or process is what is most important and it does require interaction. Yet to look at it purely *as* interaction without an understanding of what is actually guiding the interaction and how the necessity to create music together requires certain kinds of interaction is to miss one of the most important dynamics of music therapy.

People playing music with each other are being in a particular way that enables them to create something. Communication facilitates the joint creation—much as in any cooperative human activity—but this does not imply that the nature of the activity is best understood as a form of communication. The issue comes down to this: because communication happens in music, some theorists see music as communication. For theorists who see the agenda of music therapy as making music—with all of the benefits that this entails—the communication that happens within it is just a tool to the primary focus. Thus the focus on communication is missing the primary purpose for which people engage in music. This purpose is the way that they feel about themselves, other people, and the external world when engaged in music, a singular human experience.

In more recent publications, Pavlicevic acknowledges that the psychobiological approach may have to be reframed in light of cultural critiques of it, although the reframing has less to do with the fundamental metaphoric understanding of music as communication and more to do with complementing the developmental constructs with considerations that are more culturally-based.

> Many music therapists, myself included, continue to find the psycho-biological descriptions of human communication and its musical roots fundamental to understanding how music works as communication and—of course—how communication works as music. These empirically based concepts were helpful to me in conceptualizing dynamic form in the late 80s, in order to make sense of improvisation in music therapy (Pavlicevic, 1990, 1997, 2000). In the twenty-first century, shifts in discourse, practice, and in the social world, demand a revisiting and possibly a reframing of this work.
>
> (Pavlicevic, 2006, p. 88)

Awareness of the essential role of context and culture has led Pavlicevic and Ansdell to account for these elements in making a more complete theory than can be achieved from the elements of psychobiology alone.

Collaborative Musicing

The theory of communicative musicality developed by Trevarthen and Malloch represents what Pavlicevic and Ansdell (2009) consider the most mature elaboration of the psycho-biological narrative of early interaction. While asserting that this overall narrative "has been a rich and influential one on music therapy theory, training, research and practice" (p. 358) the authors claim that its impact on music therapy has been mixed rather than unequivocally beneficial because it does not sufficiently allow for the influence of culture and context.

Although not stated so by them, part of the impact of culture originates in the identity of music as a process and mode of interaction in nonclinical and clinical settings equally. Thus, to enlarge the context in which the psychobiological ideas can be considered in music therapy means necessarily accounting for how music, as music, facilitates the goals of clinical music therapy. This task requires moving beyond considering music as just a communicative medium to considering it as an artistic one as well. No theory of music therapy will be complete without an accounting of its artistic dimensions and culturally-situated meanings.

To supplement the ideas from early interaction, Pavlicevic Ansdell (2009) propose the concept of *collaborative musicing*. As a foundation for socially-based approaches such as community music therapy, they say that "communicative musicality provides a necessary, but not sufficient, theoretical platform" (p. 358). While lauding the contribution to music therapy of Trevarthen's and Stern's work, Pavlicevic and Ansdell note problems as well. They discuss how this theory was used to promote a view of music therapy as psychotherapy, a notion that was described as contested in Chapter 2, and that the theory put an overemphasis on the dyadic relationship as a salient factor in the therapy process. They also indirectly indicate that looking at music in music therapy through the lens of communicative musicality puts undue emphasis on certain interactive factors that may not be crucial to musical interaction.

> Many music therapists' initial use of Stern and Trevarthen's work tended to reduce music in music therapy to 'just' preverbal protomusic. This was linked with a project of redescribing music therapy as a form of psychotherapy, in which the purely psychological relationship between therapist and client was privileged. Musical communication was seen as just a means of establishing this psychological therapeutic relationship, which was seen as the key healing agent. This use of early interaction theory emphasized the nature of music-therapeutic dyadic relationships, at the cost of attention to groups and communal events in music therapy.
>
> (Pavlicevic & Ansdell, 2009, p. 359)

Music therapists who have used communicative musicality as a basis for music therapy are critiqued because "for them music in music therapy seemed to stop with protomusic" rather than considering the maturation of protomusic in a bona fide music. Pavlicevic and Ansdell (2009) provide a conceptual framework for understanding the different types of musical faculties possessed by people. Their hierarchy is presented as an inverted pyramid with "musicality" at the lowest level relating to a capacity, "musicianship" just above it denoting a facility, and "musicing" at the top reflecting an activity. The lower attributes are necessary for the higher ones, but the influence flows in two directions because "musicing stretches musicianship, which stimulates musicality" (p. 362).

They also see the necessity to move beyond notions derived from purely dyadic communication—or even communication at all—as an exhaustive description of the function of music in music therapy. More than just communication, collaboration characterizes how people generally interact within music. To complement the idea of communicative musicality, Pavlicevic and Ansdell (2009) propose the notion of *collaborative musicing*, considered as "the outward and audible sign of musical community" (p. 364). The new construct is based on the fact that community-situated music therapy practices consist of modes of interaction that cannot be accounted for merely as an accumulation of dyadic communications. These communal activities are sufficiently unique to warrant their own theoretical constructs.

Collaborative musicing is built upon naturalistic modes of engaging with music within music therapy contexts that are quite similar if not identical to nonclinical musical engagement. This clearly contrasts with Pavlicevic's earlier theory where the discontinuities between the two domains of musicing were emphasized. What is not clear is whether Pavlicevic's own ideas have shifted in this way, or if the more naturalistic engagement with music that is proposed as essential to community music therapy practices is specific to it or also applicable to non-community related practices that provided the area of application for her earlier ideas about dynamic form.

Smeijsters's Forms of Feeling and Analogy in Music Therapy

All of the literature applying early interaction theory to music therapy locates the mechanisms of music therapy improvisation within innate capacities present in early interaction. Part of the motivation for doing this is to identify the salient clinical properties of music in something other than its aesthetic or cultural value. The theorists who employ early interaction theory, such as Pavlicevic and Smeijsters, believe that musical experience in music therapy is fundamentally different from musical experience in nonclinical settings. Consequently, they have to identify causal mechanisms for its efficacy outside the sphere of music's identity as a cultural, social, artistic, or aesthetic object or process. The argument for the value of early interaction studies is tied into broader concerns about the nature of music and musical experience in music therapy. This is why theorists who argue for the cultural-artistic value of music as relevant for its clinical use have critiques of the developmental and (by extension) the ethological arguments.

Henk Smeijsters (2003) employs Stern's concept of vitality affects in establishing the legitimacy and value of music therapy, particularly in its psychotherapeutic applications. He believes that Stern's theories can establish the link "between a person's inner experiences and his expressions in music" (p. 72). Smeijsters argues that the amodal characteristics of Stern's theory "can explain the connection between the musical expression and the person's intra- and interpersonal processes" (p. 72).

According to Smeijsters, from the study of mother–infant interaction Stern concludes that infants possess a means to represent qualities of sensory experience in a way that allows for the transfer of the same quality among different senses:

> [Infants] are able to represent tactile, visual, and auditory forms without words and symbols. The transposition from one modality to another modality is possible because the baby has an abstract *a-modal* representation of the *physical form*, *intensity*, and *temporal form*, which acts as an intermediary bridge from one to another modality.
>
> (Smeijsters, 2003, p. 73)

As mentioned previously, it is not the reflection in the same modality that is the basis for human relationship; instead, it is the ability to communicate recognition of expression across modalities that achieves the type of response required for human relationship:

> When a baby experiences joy (form of feeling) he will express this joy in a smile on his face (visual modality). The mother then can answer by smiling too (same modality). What Stern found out is that mothers are used to answering in different modalities. For instance, they make a sound (auditory modality) that lasts as long as the smile and goes up and down like the baby's lips and cheeks. The baby *understands* that mother's sound is an empathic answer to his smile and thus his joy. Stern tells us that it is this

cross-modality and not the imitation in the same modality that communicates empathy to the baby . . . The infant experiences this as empathy not knowing the denotative meaning of his mother's behaviour. The baby does not interpret the mother's behaviour.

(Smeijsters, 2003, p. 73)

Smeijsters's commitment to Stern's theory requires him to identify the connective tissue of human relationship in the mutual sharing of vitality affects which are "the dynamic, kinetic qualities of feeling, like 'surging', 'fading away', 'fleeting', 'explosive', 'crescendo', 'decrescendo', 'bursting', 'drawn out', which should be distinguished from categorical affects like being happy, sad, or angry" (p. 74). In other words, just as was emphasized in the discussion of Pavlicevic's theory, it is not the specific quality of emotion that is shared and reflected back that is salient but more the form in which the feeling emerges that is relevant and shared. Additionally, these forms are not just aspects of human emotions and art forms such as music and dance, they are characteristics of the natural world as well:

It is not the referring signal or symbol which signifies categorical feelings that counts, but the "way of feeling" which is expressed in a pattern in time and intensity. What is more, these patterns in time and intensity are everywhere; they are psychological as well as non-psychological. This makes it possible to grasp the sameness of time and intensity patterns in different types of processes and different modalities of expression. For instance: you can experience a form of feeling in the dynamics of weather conditions. Because a person is able to perceive these patterns in different processes and modalities of expression, it is possible to express and perceive intra- and interpersonal forms of feeling in patterns of music.

(Smeijsters, 2003, p. 74)

A number of issues are present in Smeijsters's theory. He is committed to the idea that it is the form of emotions that is shared in the establishment of human relationship rather than the quality or the specific emotion. Presumably this is because the specific emotion—referred to as the *categorical affect*—arises on the level of style or culture and Smeijsters does not want to attribute efficacy to this level of the music, preferring to identify the non-stylistic components of music as where efficacy in music therapy lies.

Smeijsters is pushed to this point because in adopting Stern's thinking he incurs the obligation to argue that it is the cross-modal transfer which generates attunement, connection, and empathy, such as when an infant expresses an affect bodily and the mother responds auditorily. But in music therapy, the therapist and client are responding in the same modality, namely through music. This would seem to preclude the transfer of Stern's ideas to music therapy. Unlike other music therapists who have taken on Stern's thinking but have ignored this fundamental contradiction, to his credit Smeijsters is fully aware of it and attempts to meet this challenge.

Smeijsters's (2003) argument has as a basic premise that client and therapist are "not just playing music" (p. 75). Aesthetic concerns as such are irrelevant in music therapy and it is only psychic form that matters.

What is essential for music therapy is that it is a psychological affair. The musical processes in the intermediary musical space are experienced and interpreted as expressions of the

> psyche . . . In music therapy the client in the music sounds his Self, how he behaves, how he feels, and how he expresses his conflicts . . . It doesn't matter whether it sounds like an artistic form. What is important is that the music sounds as the client's psyche.
>
> (Smeijsters, 2003, p. 75)

Smeijsters is arguing that there is a cross-modal transfer from psychic form to musical form. He has to make the argument that the salient characteristic of the music is its form because he needs to locate a cross-modal transfer to preserve that aspect of Stern's theory. This is not to say that Smeijsters is acting in a post-hoc way just to preserve the phenomenon. He clearly believes that music in music therapy is only relevant to the extent that it is a reflection of vitality affects, forms of feeling, or the structure of the client's psyche.

Similar to Pavlicevic, Smeijsters inherits other problems from his foundations in Stern and in Langer whose term *forms of feeling* he uses interchangeably with Stern's *vitality affects*. Because many different specific emotions share the same forms of feeling, Langer's ideas tell us nothing about the connection between specific elements of music and their affective content. Additionally, Langer's views can only account for the intellectual appreciation of music and not the profound emotional engagement people have with music. As a consequence, they are not taken particularly seriously as accounts for the value of music by contemporary philosophers of music. In music therapy, these two elements are at least as important—if not more so—than they are in nonclinical domains so applying Langer's ideas in music therapy is very problematic.

Also difficult to understand is what these amodal parameters really are and how they differ from what is commonly understood as a symbolic representation. Central to Stern and Smeijsters is that infants can encode and recognize sensory and emotional experience in a way that is not verbal or sensory-based. Tactile, visual, and auditory forms can be represented in the infant's internal world without words and symbols because there is present an "abstract amodal representation of the physical form" (Smeijsters, 2003, p. 73). But what exactly is an "abstract representation" if not a type of symbol? This aspect of Stern's and Smeijsters's theory seems contradictory.

A common critique of Langer is that the musical expression of contrasting emotions can share the same form, so that looking at the form really does not tell us anything meaningful about the specific emotion expressed in music. Smeijsters's approach inherits this problem as well. It is a tough argument to make that it is not the specific content of the client's emotion that the therapist responds to and that explains the feeling that the client has of being heard and responded to in music.

And last, there are reasons to doubt the aspect of Stern's theory and Smeijsters's appropriation of it that claims a direct perception across modalities unmediated by complex cognitive processes including that of symbolic representation. Recall the example of the infant who smiles and the mother who responds vocally with a sound that has the same duration of the smile and that ascends and descends in pitch in a way that reflects the shape of the facial expression when smiling. This example is presented as an example of cross-modal perception and response. However, pitch change of the mother's vocalization is only vertical in a metaphoric sense[1]. In music, there is no object that moves up and down in physical space. So if the infant perceives verticality in a tonal expression, this requires the presence of metaphoric cognitive processes. It is the only way of explaining how the infant can draw a connection between an ascending tone and a smile that ascends at the corners of the mouth.

Yet this requires the notion that cognitive metaphoric processes mediate the cross-modal transfers—and thus mediate the process of interpersonal bonding—something that both Stern and Smeijsters argue against.

The Value of Early Interaction Theory for Music Therapy

The recurring theme in the present chapter is that the theories employing early interaction as a basis for music therapy must explain the value of music in something other than its identity as an aesthetic-cultural artifact. None of the theories proposed so far have done so. Yet this does not mean that they are not without value.

The study of early interaction is certainly relevant for therapy of any type. To the extent that music therapy involves the establishment of relationship—either as a primary clinical goal or as a vehicle for other types of goals—an understanding of how early relationships are formed can be invaluable. Many clients of music therapists may never have had the experience of creating satisfying human relationships, whether with family members, peers, work colleagues, or any other members of a shared community. The study of early interaction reveals processes essential to the establishment of human relationships. As noted by many of the authors already discussed, this is particularly true for music therapy, which overtly employs some of the temporal and auditory dynamics that characterize early interaction.

One of the important dynamics of early interaction that has received a fair amount of attention in the music therapy literature is that of attunement. It is a phenomenon noted by many of the authors discussed in this chapter with contributions by, among others, Pavlicevic (1997), Aigen (1998), Garred (2006), Pelletteri (2009), and Ruud (2010). My own exposure to the concept dates to 1981 through the work of Judith Kestenberg (1975) who posited "that a primary mechanism of normal developmental and interactional processes is comprised of a rhythm of attunement and clashing in relation to the mother's and infant's mutual perception of, and reaction to, tensions levels in each other" (Aigen, 1998, p. 181). Establishing trust and empathy depends upon each party's ability to perceive and adjust to these changing levels of tension. Kestenberg used the analogy of a musical instrument with a vibrating and a resonating component to describe the infant–mother dyad:

> At times, the resonator and the vibrator are out of phase, working against each other. A resonator may refuse to be the slave of the vibrator and may produce interference. In the language of mother-child interaction, we speak of clashes between them. However, clashing is part and parcel of the interaction in which a mother calms the baby or vice versa. A clash occurs, for instance, when the mother lowers her tension while the infant's remains high. If the mother lowers her tension gradually, there comes a point at which the baby follows suit, and a harmony between their tension qualities can be reestablished. A feeling of sameness is re-created that is an intrinsic aspect of empathy. Clashing that is not followed by reattunement creates battles between mother and infant.
>
> (Kestenberg, 1975, p. 141)

Music therapists using improvisational approaches of all types learn how to attune to their clients and to create music that in some way relates to aspects of the client's being. This can be done by attuning to tension levels or other aspects of a client's emotional life. It can also be achieved by relating to the timbre of a client's expression (vocally or instrumentally); the rhythms, tempi, and dynamics employed by the client; the stylistic and attitudinal qualities of the client's music; or the melodies or other tonal phenomena generated by the client. These activities of attunement can be similar to what happens in early interaction. However, the therapist's task is not just to attune to the client and match what the client does, but to complement and offer something greater. A therapist who only reflects what the client does will be limited to providing the client no more than the limitations of his or her own being; development in therapy is built upon processes of attunement but also requires the type of clashing that characterizes early interaction.

In addition, music therapists such as Even Ruud (1997) and the present author (2005c) have also made use of the concept of participatory discrepancies as developed in the ethnomusicology literature by Charles Keil and Steven Feld. This concept describes how quality music in a great variety of cultures and genres is enabled by subtle departures from synchronous timing and tuning. These "imperfections" are actually the human element in music that makes it come alive. They are present in clinical and nonclinical music and can be understood as a subtle form of clashing in the sense that Kestenberg discusses.

In making these observations, it would be an oversimplification to say that the dynamics of attunement and clashing explain what happens in clinical music therapy improvisation. Drawing the connection between clinical processes and developmental processes demonstrates that music therapy is congruent with a particular theory on the development of human relationship. It can also suggest directions for more detailed theory and clinical interventions depending upon how far one can justifiably extend the analogy between the two spheres of activity. Yet music is so much more than just a process of attunement and clashing. It is a culturally situated phenomenon with all types of affordances related to the creation of identity, the transcendence of limitations, the enabling of aesthetic experience, the creation of community, and the overall establishment of a meaning in human life. To explain the value of music by any theory not created to explain music—such as is done in the employment of early interaction and evolutionary theory—is to miss the very things that define and characterize music as music and that differentiate it from related spheres of human activity.

And this really is the problem caused by the overreach in much of the biological theorizing in the present chapter and Chapters 14 and 15 that follow. Theories that attempt to explain the fundamentals of what makes music therapy effective—by arguing that all that is relevant in understanding music therapy is: First, showing how clinical music therapy processes can be explained by nonmusical developmental process; second, explaining what occurs in the brain; or third, demonstrating how musicality has contributed to biological survival—all possess the common fault of reducing music therapy processes to something that is not recognizable as the artistic-cultural artifact that we acknowledge music to be. Taking this extreme position invites a complete rejection and dismissal of such theory by theorists whose clinical experience has demonstrated that music is much more than can be accommodated by biologically-based theories alone. This is equally unfortunate because it goes without saying that any form of human knowledge, properly contextualized and delimited in terms of the contributions it can make, potentially has great benefits for music therapy theory and our understanding of what happens in clinical processes.

In a sense, the challenge for music therapy theorists seeking holistic and pluralistic theory that accounts for the action, benefits, and affordances of music *as music* in music therapy is to first demonstrate that the biologically-based theories are inadequate as foundations for general theory in the field, but then having undertaken this critique, to demonstrate what its true benefits are. It is unfortunate to have to use time and intellectual energy in the critique, but this is an important activity to undertake in response to such claims. And in so doing, the more productive work of spelling out the appropriate role for biologically-based theory can then be articulated.

Note

1. See Aigen (2009) for a discussion of the metaphoric aspects of music perception in music therapy based upon Lakoff and Johnson's schema theory

14
NEUROLOGICAL SCIENCE AND MUSIC THERAPY

Early Perspectives

One of the first music therapists to write about music, aesthetics, the development of the brain, and the survival value of music was E.T. Gaston (1964, 1968). As important as Gaston was to the early development of the music therapy profession, contemporary perspectives on his theoretical writings reveal contradictions in them and the present area of discussion is no exception. While Gaston understood and argued for the role of music in bringing aesthetic enrichment to human lives, seeing in it one of the primary values of music therapy, he also argued for the supremacy of a scientific, medical approach that supported the reduction of psychological phenomena to descriptions in biological terms. This can be seen in his earliest pronouncements related to neurological concerns: "The neural mechanisms are the same whether a patellar reflex is elicited, a beautiful sunset enjoyed, a symphony listened to, or the fragrance of a rose scented. In the final analysis of mentation, we have only biochemistry and physics" (Gaston, 1964, p. 4).

Although Gaston's point was to support the primacy of biologically-based explanation in music therapy, it could also be used in the opposite way. From the observation that all variations of human experience and behavior are based upon neuronal activity, it is possible to "conclude that if such different mental experiences share common mechanisms, then studying the mechanism will be of limited use in understanding the experience" (Aigen, 1991b, p. 158). In other words, because brain states are not isomorphic with psychological states, it is reasonable to conclude that "the laws of psychological organization will function independently of biological or neurological ones" (Aigen, pp. 158–159).

Gaston believed that aesthetic appreciation of the world is an essential aspect of human nature and that the need for it is physiological. However, because humans are biological entities functioning within biological constraints, any explanation for the function of aesthetic experience must have a biological rationale. He further narrowed his focus by arguing that biological explanations must inevitably have an evolutionary explanation. That is, the presence of any human behavior must be explained by how and why it evolved and how its presence conferred enhanced survival value. Gaston speculated that "it may well be that aesthetic endeavor or experience may be one of the best devices man has found to enable him to adjust to his environment" (1964, p. 5). For him, sensory experience and the neurological development that it precipitates are the precursors of music. The value of aesthetic music experience in music therapy must therefore be explained in terms of these origins.

Gaston highly valued music and the aesthetic experience it engenders, noting that "all mankind has need for esthetic expression and experience" (1968, p. 21). This need is so essential that it can form the foundation for a clinical theory of music therapy: "Sensitivity to beauty and the making of beauty comprise one of man's most distinguishing characteristics (Dobzhansky, 1962, p. 214). Without beauty, man is less than Homo sapiens; and when this is so, he is sick or handicapped" (Gaston, 1968, p. 22). However, Gaston also argues forcefully for the idea that as a behavioral science, all explanation in music therapy ultimately has to rest upon sound principles of biology. Gaston created a legacy of paradox for music therapy where the investigation of aesthetics is both necessary and yet proscribed (or at least severely limited) by the extrinsic constraints imposed by behavioral and biological constructs.

The flexibility and potential of the human nervous system allows "some margin beyond that necessary for adaptation to life" (Gaston, 1964, p. 5), something that supports a view of aesthetic experience that does not rest on it bestowing a functional, evolutionary advantage. And yet Gaston also speculates that "it may well be that aesthetic endeavor or experience may be one of the best devices man has found to enable him to adjust to his environment" (p. 5). Gaston points out that aesthetic experience is valuable because it motivates activity that is beyond that needed for survival, and he contradicts this position by noting the potential adaptive value of aesthetic experience.

In supporting the two mutually exclusive points that music is valuable because it rises above biological necessity, and music is valuable because it provides biological advantages, Gaston reveals the two contradictory tasks that motivated much of his professional writings. These are: First, to carve out a unique role for music that recognizes it as essential to the notion of what it means to be a human being, meaning that it goes beyond biological necessity; and second, to firmly locate the origins and rationale for music within biological considerations.

It seems inarguable that humans do not need music for biological survival. Rather than seeing this as a limitation of music, it can be used to help explain why it is so highly valued by people. It is an activity that helps us move beyond the mere meeting of biological needs and helps us to experience ourselves as beings concerned with more than just survival. But biological explanations for the value of music are committed to making the opposite point: that music is only present because it confers some type of biological advantage that translates into enhanced survival value. The contradictions present in Gaston's original publications also characterize much of the ethological argument in music therapy and they will be returned to at the end of the discussion of evolutionary perspectives and music therapy in Chapter 15.

Advocates for the Primacy of Brain Science in Music Therapy

In seeking to understand the mechanisms of how music therapy works, one of the historical legacies of Gaston's ambivalence in this area is an ongoing difference of opinion over the locus of effect of music therapy. Theorists disagree on not just the content of specific theories but on fundamental questions regarding what level of organization those theories should address. The situation is not unlike that of psychology throughout the twentieth century with disagreements between cognitive psychologists focusing on unobservable mental processes and behavioral psychologists focusing on observable acts of behavior. In music therapy, we see a difference primarily on whether the fundamental area of investigation should be on the physiological (primarily neurological) level or the level of the whole human being.

Theorists such as Dale Taylor (1997) and Michael Thaut (2008) argue that the brain is the fundamental focus of music therapy interventions and that all interventions in music therapy have to be explained by their ability to positively influence brain functioning. Taylor (1997) argues that his bio-medical music therapy approach is applicable to people with any type of need or disability because all areas of disability can be conceptualized in terms of brain functioning. The brain is the central focus of music therapist's efforts because sounds must be interpreted by the brain before they are even heard as music. Further, in invoking a biological explanation for the beneficial effects of music, Taylor says that "it should no longer be necessary to refer to the therapeutic influence of music as magical, mystical, or unexplainable" (p. 19). He asserts that reducing music therapy explanation to brain science is the only way to put it on a sound, rational foundation, thus seeming to dismiss the legitimacy of explanations based upon psychological, sociological, or musicological foundations:

> Investigations of music/brain relationships provide the means for describing therapeutic influences of music in terms that explain objectively a basic domain, a single theoretical framework, that applies to all music therapy applications . . . Matthew Lee . . . advised [music therapists] to "Forget all this psychology stuff and get on with music as medicine." . . . Music therapists should find a medical basis for musical interventions.
>
> (Taylor, 1997, p. 18)

In Taylor's view, neurologically-based theory does not complement psychosocial theory but is a replacement for it. He adopts this position from a belief "that literally all of the work that music therapists do is primarily and ultimately aimed at changing the functions of specific biological structures of the human body. Such change begins with the brain" (Taylor, 1997, p. 18). There is no place for a conception of music therapy as a form of psychotherapy, community building, identity creation, a contributor to general health and wellness, or a means for life enrichment. All of these ways of conceptualizing music therapy are proscribed in favor of a strictly medical conception of music therapy.

Thaut (2008) similarly positions his neurological music therapy approach as a new paradigm in music therapy developed to replace social science and interpretive models. This is accomplished by showing "how music perception and music production engage the brain in ways that can be meaningfully translated and generalized to nonmusical therapeutic learning and training" (pp. 61–62). In Thaut's view, it is "the brain that engages in music [and that] is changed by this engagement" (p. 62). Therefore, there is no discussion of the whole person and no need to consider individual goals, meanings, histories, fears, resources or any other attribute that arises on the level of the whole person in determining clinical interventions and in explaining the value of music. Thaut asserts that music considered in its aesthetic dimensions or as a cultural object "does not initially contain any direct and obvious therapeutic attributes" (p. 116). Because the sound waves that constitute music are processed in the brain, and because this processing is the antecedent of any psychological or social engagement with music, Taylor and Thaut argue that the psychosocial level of explanation is just not warranted in music therapy.

According to Thaut (2008), studying the way that music is processed in the brain reveals a great deal about generalized brain function, especially in regard to the perception of complex auditory sound stimuli, time, and rhythm processing, differential processing of music and language as two aural communication systems, biological substrates of learning versus innate talent in the arts, and processing of higher cognitive functions related to temporality and emotion.

(Thaut, 2008, p. viii)

In saying that music "is a biologically deeply ingrained function of the human brain" and that it contains "neural circuitry that is dedicated to music" (p. viii), Thaut articulates a position that evolutionary biologists suggest is consistent with the idea that music has emerged from forces of natural selection.

However, Thaut does not seem to believe in this common implication of this position. For him, "the human brain is an arousal-seeking system rather than a system that operates on simple stimulus-response interactions," a position that he believes is the only way to explain why human beings have demonstrated "progress beyond evolutionary constraints" as seen in "the development of culture, science, and technology" (2008, p. 23). This way of characterizing some of the grander achievements of humankind suggests that humans have motivations beyond that of mere survival, something consistent with humanistic and transpersonal psychology.

Thaut seems to be saying that evolutionary pressures cannot explain the existence of music; rather it is some aspect of the brain—desiring certain forms of arousal, independent of the value of that arousal in promoting survival—that explains music. To some theorists, this makes music trivial; to others, it demonstrates that the existence of music owes to aspirations beyond mere survival; to still others, it is not possible because a dedicated neuronal pathway and area of brain function is only something that could arise through natural selection, and natural selection only acts upon survival enhancing structures and processes.

Thaut claims that artistry emerged more or less suddenly in human development without evidence of incremental progression, something that challenges the notion that the arts are merely "the 'icing on the cake' of human brain development, after the basic needs of survival in culture and civilization are satisfied" (2008, p. 25). Instead, such data suggest that engagement in the arts is a fundamental aspect of brain function. It is the way that music creates brain systems useful for other tasks that explains its existence, according to Thaut.

> The brain engages in the arts because the arts, including music, create a particular type of sensory input, a specific perceptual language that is necessary for the appropriate regulation of arousal and activation states. The brain needs to engage in combining forms of lines and colors, creating horizontal and vertical layers of sounds of different timbres, building physical shapes and movement of human body in dance, in order to build, sharpen, maintain, and create order in its perceptual machinery as an essential aspect of brain function . . . Artistic expression may exercise fundamental brain functions and may create unique patterns of perceptual input that the brain needs and cannot generate through other means in order to keep its sensory, motor, and cognitive operations at optimal levels of functioning.
>
> (Thaut, 2005, p. 25)

In this description of music, rather than being something that manifests aesthetic, spiritual, or communal aspirations, music is nothing more than an exercise system for the brain, something to keep it at an optimal functioning level.

Thaut's proposals just do not seem to match the facts of the human engagement with music. He does acknowledge two essential aspects of music that must be accounted for in explaining its presence: "music as an art form has existed in all known cultures throughout human history [and] . . . music is not connected to direct material and biological necessities of survival of the human organism," (2008, p. 114) instead functioning primarily to provide pleasurable experience. From these two observations, Thaut concludes "that there is a biological and neurological basis of music in the human brain that plays a role in shaping brain and behavior function considerably beyond general concepts of musically induced well-being" (pp. 114–115). This argument is further used to support his call for a move away from a social science basis for music therapy to a neurological-medical one.

There are a number of problems with Thaut's argument and his overall agenda. First, in spite of his facile linking of the phenomena, there does not appear to be any logical connection between Thaut's premises that music is ubiquitous and not contributing to survival and his conclusion that neurological analysis is the only way to reveal the fundamental importance of music to people. In fact, just the opposite case can be more easily made, that both in the absence of conferring enhanced survival value and in the presence of the extra-ordinary psychological allegiance that humans have to music, any explanation for its value in music therapy must at the very least place psychosocial factors in a prominent position.

Second, it just does not seem reasonable that the extraordinary amounts of resources that humans dedicate to both producing and consuming music can be explained by the fact that it is fundamentally no more than a glorified workout for neurological systems. This just seems like a highly inefficient way of achieving optimal brain function. In dismissing the entire realm of psychosocial explanation, Thaut dismisses anthropological, psychological, and socio-logical research findings into how music functions to build individual identity, relationship, and communal connection; how it satisfies inherent spiritual and aesthetic desires; and how it provides a means for facilitating engagement in cultural rituals of all types across the entire lifespan. It just does not make sense to dismiss all of these realms of human engagement with music as having no central implications for its value in therapy.

There are three contradictions in Thaut's perspective that would have to be addressed for his overall program to be more strongly supported. First, he simultaneously claims that music represents human aspirations that go beyond the need for mere survival, while concluding that biological considerations can fully explain the presence of music in human culture. These two beliefs are mutually inconsistent. Second, in a related way, Thaut argues for dedicated neurological structures for music, a claim that other authors use to buttress the notion that music has emerged from processes of natural selection. But when he emphasizes the independence of music from survival factors, his position conflicts with the claim that music was selected for by evolutionary forces. It would seem that Thaut has to either give up the idea of dedicated brain structures for music or the idea that music was not selected for. Third, if music is merely what Thaut says it is—a mechanism for exercising brain functions needed for other tasks—then it would seem to be something that was selected for as enhanced brain function would presumably confer enhanced survival potential. It appears contradictory for Thaut to argue that music enhances brain function while also arguing that music was not a target of natural selection.

None of this critique of Thaut's perspective should be taken as a critique of having a neurological understanding of how music is processed or produced in the effort to understand music and build music therapy theory. In terms of music therapy, it would seem that treatment of people whose conditions stem from neurological damage or malfunction would be particularly helped by the knowledge gained about how music and brain interact. Instead, the critique of Thaut's program has two purposes: First, to demonstrate the flaws in his particular argument for elimination of social science theory in music therapy in favor of neurologically-based theory; and second, to demonstrate that the reductive approach in general is a flawed one that cannot account for the ubiquity of music in human culture and the voluminous findings about the human engagement with music generated by a large number of scholarly disciplines. Any understanding of music and human beings can only gain from the employment of multiple perspectives and the effort to elevate any one over the others should be rejected as antithetical to general goals of knowledge acquisition.

Alternative Perspectives on the Relevance of Neuroscience to Music Therapy

The application of a purely medical model in music therapy limited to biologically-based considerations is not warranted according to Gary Ansdell (1995) because of the resulting explanatory gap. It is not the purely quantifiable, physical components of music that explain its efficacy, but it is music as psychosocial phenomenon with ritual and aesthetic qualities that must be considered as well:

> There will always remain an ontological gap between the two phenomena: music and physiology. In the same way as music cannot be explained by its acoustical properties alone, so too its influence on people is more than just its ability to induce physiological effects. There are in fact many diverse stimuli which cause much the same physiological patterns of arousal or relaxation as music does.
>
> (Ansdell, 1995, p. 82)

For Ansdell, the psychological aspects of the human engagement with music have to be considered along with the physiological effects of sound because music is "a locus of meaning and feeling within and between people" (1995, p. 82). Music cannot be separated into its constituents in order to have its therapeutic value understood. It is the phenomenal experiencing of music that is of value, and this is something that only exists when perceived by the whole person.

According to Ansdell, it is the artistic-aesthetic dimensions of music that explain its value, not just in psychological applications where this might be a less contentious claim, but even in areas such as neurological and motor rehabilitation where clients are helped to regain physical capacities through music. Musical motion has particular qualities and it is precisely these qualities of motion that activate physiological processes that facilitate the achieving of rehabilitative goals. It is not that music *is* motion that makes it therapeutic; instead it is the particular *qualities* of its motion that account for its efficacy. And these qualities are necessarily aesthetic and psychological in nature. Thus, these levels of description and explanation are indispensable in music therapy theory.

Much of music's effectiveness across a wide range of clinical applications owes to its dynamic qualities, which we experience as motion. This sense of motion is appropriated by the person on both a physical and emotional level, and these two levels interact and mutually constitute each other. According to Ansdell (1995), "music works therapeutically not by giving a mechanical stimulus but by somehow lending some of its qualities of liveliness and motivation to both body and spirit" (p. 81). Music acts not through a mechanical stimulation of brain processes that result in physical movement but through enhancing human motivation. The key to understanding the therapeutic action of music is to realize that "to move us physically it must also move us emotionally" (p. 82).

Motion in music is not mechanical or physical but metaphoric and therefore cognitive in nature. Metaphor is a property of minds, not of brains. Therefore, any explanation of the way in which musical motion facilitates emotion and physical motion has to begin with the way that the experience of motion is created in the mind from a source that involves a change of state rather than a change of place. Ansdell grounds his analysis in Victor Zuckerkandl's philosophy of music. Zuckerkandl described how in hearing tonal motion the listener experiences this motion as his own. "To hear tones in motion is to move together with them" (Zuckerkandl, as cited in Ansdell, p. 83). Ansdell (1995) notes that in contrast to common belief, it is melody more than rhythm that embodies movement in music, in spite of the fact that there is no physical object that literally moves through space in tonal motion:

> Rather than a tone moving through space like a ball, melody is really one tone continually making a relationship to another tone, handing on its impulse like a relay-runner to the next man. Though melody is, empirically speaking, a succession of separate tones in *time*, not in space, its subjective musical effect is to create a sense of musical space— of directions, resolutions and phrased shapes.
>
> (Ansdell, 1995, p. 85)

Effective human movement that originates in human will and intentionality is not mechanically repetitive. Instead, effective human movement has certain qualities which, to Ansdell (1995), are musical in quality, such as "flow, continuity, coordination, purpose and direction" (p. 83). There is a similarity between the way that music and the human body "organize themselves as moving forms in time" (p. 83) so that when the body becomes impaired in its capacity for movement, through music therapy it is able to appropriate these qualities to enhance its motion.

The dynamic–aesthetic qualities of music central to its efficacy in stimulating motion are most apparent in the tonal-melodic dimension. Rehabilitative music therapy that focuses on rhythm (because of its temporal nature) to the exclusion of melody is missing a key component of what makes music effective in this domain of practice.

Just as it is true that brain activity is part of the picture in understanding music therapy but not the whole picture or even the most salient part of the picture at times, the purely physical description of music is relevant to explaining its value but may also not be the whole picture or even the most salient part of it. The way that music is contextually perceived by individuals who belong to a particular culture (or cultures) and who have idiosyncratic tastes and prior experiences with music will always have to be taken into account in explaining music therapy. These artistic-social-individual considerations can be the most prominent elements figuring in explanation. The bottom line for Ansdell is that while neurological considerations are relevant in gaining a full understanding of music therapy in the rehabilitation of physical movement, music ultimately works in therapy because of the way it can motivate individuals to want to participate in the world.

In order to fully understand the role of brain science in music therapy it is necessary to consider trends in the larger context of research in social and biological sciences and the politics that underlie them. Legrenzi and Umiltà (2011) discuss the proliferation of disciplines utilizing the prefix "neuro" and they argue that what is happening is an attempt to supplant the concept of mind and replace it with that of the brain. Part of the motivation is to take advantage of funding for brain research by governmental agencies. Moreover, the program of eliminating discussions of mind in favor of their neurological correlates has a particular social effect:

> We must not forget that today the definition of the relationship between mind and body, psyche and brain, can involve choices in the realms of social politics and well-being. If the body, or more precisely that part of the body which is the brain, becomes the system of reference . . . cognitive processes must take a back seat and consequently social politics and well-being will also have to take a back seat.
>
> (Legrenzi & Umiltà, 2011, pp. vii–viii)

The values underlying the privileging of explanation couched in the terms of neuroscience are part of its appeal. And just because it is a form of science does not render it immune from the influences of the values held by its advocates. For example, neurological music therapist Michael Thaut (2008) has expressed an antipathy to explaining the value of music therapy in terms of a generalized sense of well-being, disparaging it as relevant only to social science understandings of music therapy. The approach that eliminates psychological and social under-standings of the minds of human beings in favor of exclusive reliance on neurological analyses is motivated by a particular type of scientism with its own values and rhetoric.

The rhetoric of neuroscience can influence nonscientists who are influential in public policy. For example, neuroscience is cloaked with a certain type of presentation that lends the appearance of a measure of credibility that is not always warranted. Legrenzi and Umiltà (2011) explain how the rhetoric of neuroscience works:

> Newspapers and magazines often carry articles reporting that one research institute or another has found the area of the brain which governs falling in love or resisting temptation, illustrated by a picture of the human brain with a coloured section. The article explains that the coloured section is that part of the brain which becomes active when participants in the experiment see the face of their loved one or look at a cigarette they know they shouldn't smoke. The reader is led to believe that, by using complex and sophisticated equipment, neuroimages will give a direct view of which parts of the brain are active while the person thinks about a particular object or desire . . . Readers do not know that many steps are needed to produce that simple picture of the brain with a coloured area, and that each of those steps is based on assumptions which are not always sound.
>
> (Legrenzi & Umiltà, 2011, pp. 14–15)

The authors describe how assumptions about the latency of changes in blood flow in relation to external stimulation are assessed through statistical probabilities. It is these probabilities that are used to create neuroimages. The engaging color pictures that represent neurological activity are actually the result of a whole set of assumptions that are based on statistical probabilities that can be challenged. Using this this type of visual presentation has an underlying rationale related solely to the way that it can endow assertions with a greater degree of credibility.

> A diagram of the brain covered with numbers is not the most effective way to get the message across to the public; attributing colours to the various levels of chance probability is much more efficient. The idea of being able to see the brain at work, which so greatly appeals to the layperson, is misleading. What in fact is represented is simply the result of a graphic device which transforms chance probability into colour and is then superimposed on a drawing of the brain . . . The use of attractive colours in neuroimaging has probably played a crucial role in their appeal to the public . . . Our brain is predominantly visual and, as in the other primates, contains a large number of areas with neurons that respond to visual stimuli. We are very susceptible to the impact of visual evidence.
>
> (Legrenzi & Umiltà, 2011, pp. 26–27)

It is not only the general public who can be seduced by the aesthetics of the presentation of neurological data. Scholarly journals are also susceptible to overlooking some of the problems and challengeable assertions of neuroscience research because of its mode of presentation.

> Highly prestigious scientific journals, which normally reject out of hand papers with even slightly dubious statistical inference, have published articles concerning neuro-imaging studies with more than dubious statistical inference. In other words, even expert reviewers assessing scientific papers for publication can be 'blinded' by fascinating neuro-images and fail to apply sufficiently stringent criteria.
>
> (Legrenzi & Umiltà, 2011, pp. 28–29)

Ultimately, it is possible to acknowledge that all music therapy processes require and take place through neurological processes without accepting the notion that neurological explanation exclusively can account for what happens in music therapy across a broad range of applications. To state that there is no engagement in music without a brain is trivial; to take this trivial observation and use it to argue for the primacy of neurological explanation is to do no more than assume what it is one would like to prove.

While there is no musicing without a brain, this does not imply that an understanding of the neurological correlates of musical experience will explain the mechanisms of music therapy across a wide spectrum of practice. Saying that all music therapy theory has to be based on brain science is like saying that it is necessary to understand the atomic properties of the circuitry in a computer in order to understand how a word processing program operates. Insight into the functional aspects of the word processing program is provided by the codes written by its programmers, not through an understanding of the material properties of particle physics. Similarly in music therapy, neurological information, while an important tool to corroborate the effect of music therapy on certain psychological processes, cannot alone provide all the information necessary to fully understand clinical processes when one is concerned with human motivations, intentions, and experiences.

15

EVOLUTIONARY THEORY AND MUSIC THERAPY

The Argument against an Evolutionary Rationale for Music Therapy

A central issue running through all the discussions on evolutionary theory, music, and music therapy is the question of whether or not music is an adaptation. Different authors provide different answers to this question and it can be useful to consider what agendas and unproven assumptions support both possibilities. Moreover, each position has different implications for music therapy.

Research in evolutionary cognitive neuroscience is used by Leif E.O. Kennair (2000) to undermine the use of early interaction and psychodynamic theory as a basis for adult treatment in music therapy. He identifies the underlying rationale as having these conceptual steps: First, adult pathology originates in problems in early, preverbal stages of development; second, the nature of these problems originates in a deficit in the type of communication experience that music provides; third, music and music therapy provides access to this stage and to the impaired communication processes; and fourth, musical interaction as an adult repairs the problems and heals the pathology.

Kennair uses contemporary thinking in psychology as well as an evolutionary argument to criticize many stages of the psychodynamic rationale and singles out theories such as those of Daniel Stern for criticism. He critiques in equal measures the notion that music is preverbal and that adult pathology originates in early experience. While acknowledging that childhood experiences can influence the adult personality, he claims that resilience is a more typical response to early difficulties. He also says that to consider music as a preverbal phenomenon—as opposed to merely nonverbal—is to suggest that it is an infantile medium.

While Kennair's formulation of the psychodynamic rationale accurately characterizes older thinking in psychoanalytic music therapy, such as that of Florence Tyson (1982), it is not an accurate portrayal of the beliefs of contemporary music therapy theorists who use Stern and other early interaction theorists. What they say is that some of the parameters of music that enable it to be communicative and expressive are similar to parameters that allow for communication and expression on a preverbal level. This is not to say that music itself is preverbal, just that it shares structures and dynamics with other nonverbal modes of communication and expression. Kennair's assertion that the logic of treatment based on early interaction theory requires music to be a preverbal phenomenon is not correct.

Kennair (2000) extends this argument in saying that it requires "the existence of music in a pre-verbal mind (the child's)—this seems theoretically unlikely" (p. 35). However, saying that "music can access preverbal memories" is not the same as saying "music is preverbal." Kennair is drawing the psychodynamic argument into a more extreme form in order to be able to criticize it. Meanwhile, his statement that the presence of music in a preverbal child's mind is theoretically unlikely is itself very dubious. Certainly children can hum, sing, and express themselves musically prior to the development of verbal skills.

The appeal to early interaction theory as a basis for music therapy treatment requires that the client's problem originates not just in a preverbal stage of development but that it is somehow connected to a deficit or problem in communication, according to Kennair. So music is merely a reparative medium for impaired communication processes. This does not seem to comport with psychodynamic rationales that consider the content of the communications as well as the quality of the relationship in the mutual musicing. Psychodynamic theory does not rely on the particular rationale as Kennair describes it; instead, the deficit is not in a particular type of communication but in a particular type of relationship. The nonverbal aspect of music is what allows it to provide an analogue of the quality of relating that was not provided early on and that caused subsequent problems.

In addition to undermining psychodynamic treatment theory based on the idea that music precedes verbalization in an ontogenetic sense, Kennair is equally interested in critiquing the notion that music precedes verbalization phylogenetically and that there are dedicated cognitive structures for music that would have allowed it to be a target of evolutionary processes. Kennair claims that there can be no special adaptations that have emerged through natural selection to account for music because it is a recently emerging phenomenon for the species. All of the mental mechanisms that process music must have evolved to process other types of information.

In using these observations to undermine a rationale for music therapy in evolutionary thinking, Kennair is putting the potential client solely into the position of a listener of music. However, music is a medium that one lives in and through, and that one helps create; it is not just an external, ecological scene that one perceives and processes. Any examination of the evolutionary origins and value of music has to consider the human being as music-maker, not just music-receiver. And even if Kennair is correct that neurological networks that process music did not arise directly through processes of natural selection, this does not necessary imply that they do not exist. It is a meta-theoretical assumption that only those capacities arising from natural selection (a) exist, and (b) are unique and irreducible to combinations of other capacities.

In considering ideas about how music might have emerged, Kennair (2000) claims that "music is still most likely not a human adaptation and thus the existence of music most likely is due to an interaction of adaptations" (p. 31). He reviews six types of mechanisms proposed by Steven Pinker that are involved in music perception: language mechanisms, auditory scene analysis, emotional calls, habitat selection, motor control, a "spandrel of the mind, or a right hemisphere counterpart to the left hemisphere's speech mechanisms—which creates the synergy effect" (p. 31). His point is that musicing cannot be something selected for because it involves no specific or unique adaptations.

Another consequence of Kennair's (2000) perspective is that "there can be no (from a functional, adaptational neurocognitive perspective) specific disorders of musicality as there does not exist any original state that was not adequately stimulated musically" (p. 33). Impaired musical ability can occur as has been documented in the literature, but when such a deficit appears it can only result from impairments in systems designed for nonmusical functions; its cause must lie in one of the six domains of capacities implicated in music experience. For this reason, Kennair does not consider the primacy or uniqueness of music to be a scientifically justified claim.

To review, Kennair says that music is not innate and that it involves no specific, dedicated cognitive processes. This is certainly a questionable claim given the presence of deficits that impair the engagement with music but that do not appear to impede any other functions, and the presence of unique musical capacities in individuals with areas of disability (such as autism, dementia, and traumatic brain injury) that exist in stark contrast to the levels of functioning in nonmusical areas. Musical skills and sensitivities certainly involve cognitive functions also relevant to other areas such as those involved in sequential or simultaneous auditory processing. And perhaps it can be argued that the auditory skills necessary to discern and differentiate the specific sounds of a predator or prey from the background of other sounds in a forest environment are similar to those that allow a musically-gifted individual to discern individual tones in a polyphonic musical environment. Yet just because simultaneous auditory processing occurs in both domains does not imply that the skills that allow one to discern separate tones when they are combined in a chord are derived from, or less unique than, the skills that allow one to discern footsteps on the ground from the rustle of leaves caused by the wind. The two types of judgments are so different that to equate them to each other or to reduce tonal differentiation to the mere differentiation of sound not involving tonal differentiation appears unsupported by the facts of the human engagement with music. The nonmusical auditory capacities of sequential and simultaneous processing may be necessary for musical competency but this does not mean that they are sufficient to explain them.

Moreover, the psychological problems that bring people to therapy are not necessarily musical problems. Their etiology does not necessitate a particular treatment as Kennair himself argues. He says that just because music works with someone to help that person, it does not imply that the etiology of the problem is musical. True enough, but similarly, just because an alternative explanation can be proffered, this does not diminish the musical qualities of the effective treatment.

Language and music are fundamentally different, according to Kennair (2001), in the sense that "language is probably an adaptation, music is probably not" (p. 58). However, in examining this issue it is clear that the rhetoric of evolutionary thought puts advocates for music in a defensive posture. The language of adaptation suggests that music is a purely reactive phenomenon—it is a solution to a problem posed by the relationship of an organism to its environment. It is an organismic behavior that stimulates pleasure centers in the brain to control behavior in certain directions. There is no room in this way of thinking for music to represent the meeting of a higher human need for connection, meaning, or purpose. It cannot represent a creative achievement devised to meet human aspirations. While "adaptation" is something that reacts to a given, "creation" is the fashioning of something that did not previously exist in a way that cannot be reduced to the solving of a problem related to material survival. Considering music purely as an adaptation to extrinsic circumstances does not well explain the extraordinary lengths to which profoundly disabled people go to in order to engage in it.

A reductive philosophy of science is present in Kennair's advocacy for the primacy of biology. No particular argument is presented for this perspective, which precludes the presence of fundamental processes on a psychological or sociological level, but which also stops reduction at the biological level. After all, if the reductive philosophy is a correct one, why would one stop at the level of biology and not attempt to explain music based on principles of biochemistry or even physics? The fact that reduction stops at one's chosen discipline perhaps reveals the conceit of such an approach.

> The ability to perform music behavior has to be based upon a biological human nature that allows music behavior to be performed . . . The 'origins' of music must be sought in the biological human musical nature. And this human nature is only properly investigated through the convergence of the biology of music and the art itself.
>
> (Kennair, 2001, p. 58)

In contrast to Kennair, I would observe that perhaps the interesting thing about music is that it was created, survives, flourishes and becomes essential to a satisfying life *in spite of biological considerations rather than because of them*. It is trivial to say that humans cannot create anything not allowed by their biology—the more interesting consideration is whether or not the existence of a human activity can be explained solely by biological considerations. The conceit of some evolutionists is the unproven assumption that all human activities either confer a biological advantage or they exist as incidental benefits of other processes that do confer biological advantages. Such theorists cannot truly explore the question of how to explain the existence of something unrelated to biological considerations. If the best explanation for the role of music in human life in society is actually independent of biological concerns, then the biological assumptions will not allow this to be discovered.

The Argument for an Evolutionary Rationale for Music Therapy

In contrast to the positions held by theorists such as Kennair, other authors have argued for the evolutionary value of music, creating explanations for how the capacities involved in musicing relate to considerations regarding survival. Bjørn Grinde (2000) takes the position that music enhances language skills, which gives it survival value and Ellen Dissanayake (2001, 2009) makes the case that the musicality of early interaction means that music has survival value in assisting mother–infant interaction in a way that enhances biological functions.

Music, Language, and Evolutionary Selection

The rationale for an evolutionary value for music and its relevance for music therapy was first made by Bjørn Grinde (2000). He begins from the premise that because the capacity to respond to and enjoy music appears innate, its presence should have an evolutionary explanation that explains how music enhances survival value. The fundamental premise of Grinde's proposal is that the brain offers pleasant sensations to influence human behavior to focus on sounds. Focusing on sounds improves human abilities to hear and to vocalize. In light of our dependence on language, enhancing these skills benefits survival.

> Due to the evolution of language, auditory signals are particularly vital for humans. Consequently, it is to be expected that the human brain is designed to offer particularly strong rewards for attending to sounds. According to this hypothesis, our appreciation for music was designed by evolution primarily in order to improve brain structures involved in language.
>
> (Grinde, 2000, p. 21)

This argument presupposes that verbalization completely preceded music because music only exists to enhance skills used in verbalization. Logically, then, the development of music could not have preceded the development of words, because if music is a language-enhancing medium, language had to first exist. But this means that language developed without the presence of music, so why would it be needed in the first place? Grinde's chronology is also criticized by Erik Christensen (2000) who believes that the premise of Grinde's argument that the human "preoccupation with sounds is mainly related to behaviour associated with our dependence on language" is incorrect because "the ability of listening to sounds and producing sounds precedes the acquirement of language, not vice versa" (p. 32).

Grinde's perspective removes from music as a primary rationale for its existence what it intrinsically provides: it becomes merely a support system for language. It takes from music anything unique to it. Rather than becoming a complement to verbal interaction and experience, its reason for being is subservient to verbal interaction and experience.

As with Kennair, Grinde focuses on the receptive relationship to music. Thus, Grinde's approach may explain why humans listen to music but not why we create it. But it is the experience of creating music that is primary and that must first be explained because if the creation of it did not have profound rewards, we would never get to the listening of it. Also, in relation to music therapy, it is the creation of music that is more relevant because most music therapy involves clients in actively creating music.

Another criticism of Grinde's approach is that the creation of highly complex musical forms seems to be an extremely inefficient strategy for training auditory and vocal skills. If the purpose of music is to train and enhance skills related to verbalization, it would be more direct and efficient if the brain rewarded verbalization itself with highly pleasurable sensations. It makes no sense to require humans to go through all of the effort it takes to produce music (acquiring instruments, composing materials, years of practice, etc.) if music is merely a vehicle for enhancing skills related to verbalization. Think of all the premusical and nonmusical effort and time spent here, whether one is thinking ontogenetically or phylogenetically. Certainly all of this time would be much better spent verbalizing if music existed primarily to enhance verbalizations. This argument was also made by Björn Merker (2000):

> One might ask why language evolution took a round-about via music, that is: why would music be needed as a language teaching device in the first place? Why not attach the emotional (hedonic) valences assumed by Grinde in the case of musical structures directly to the language sounds themselves, rather than that to a substitute structure which in many ways differs from language?
>
> (Merker, 2000, p. 29)

Grinde also makes a number of claims related to the nature of music to support the idea that music exists to train and prepare the brain for language. However, some of these claims seem somewhat dubious if not outright incorrect, thus undercutting the basic position for which he argues.

In considering the complexity of music, Grinde (2000) observes that "a single, pure tone is not that interesting to explore, it is to be expected that a measure of intricacy is required to excite human curiosity" (p. 21). But if it is neuronal activity that governs music, why would not the brain reward these single pure tones with the pleasurable sensations Grinde claims underlie music? This would be a much more efficient use of scarce human resources, especially when music was originating in prehistory as Grinde claims. His response is that "music requires similarities to language, such as complexity and melody, in order to be valued, because only then does it utilize the brain resources involved in processing the spoken words" (p. 21). In other words, music takes the form it does because of the language systems thereby activated.

How then to explain polyphony which has no counterpart in language? How to explain minimalistic music? How to explain any of the myriad qualities of music that do not have counterparts in verbalization? Why would music be intimately linked to emotional expression? A brief consideration of the predominance of attributes of music reveals the difficulty that the language hypothesis has in explaining music.

Grinde also claims that "several authors have suggested that preference for purity, and possibly for consonance, is innate . . . One reason why these qualities are favoured may be because they enhance oral communication" (2000, p. 22). First, the premise of this particular strategy contradicts Grinde's previous assertion about tonal purity not being music. It also runs against the facts of Western music that have traced an evolution to dissonance. Third, it seems naïve in terms of multicultural considerations. What is dissonant in one culture may not be dissonant in another. If this judgment was innate, we would not expect to see such differences.

In relation to the resources devoted to the production of music, Grinde (2000) observes that "it is not an expected evolutionary strategy to encourage a certain type of behaviour in excess of what is adaptive. A person who is preoccupied with song or music pays less attention to other tasks or possible dangers" (p. 22). This is correct and it is exactly what happens with music. People spend lifetimes enjoying the creation and appreciation of it in a way that takes them away from the concerns of daily life. How can this possibly be explained in evolutionary terms? How could musicality ever have evolved and flourished if one is limited to explaining either its origination or ongoing presence purely in terms of enhancing adaptation? The evolutionary perspective that must reduce explanation to this agenda just cannot account for the facts of music.

Ignoring much of the research on the use of music to create identity, facilitate social ritual, build community, provide aesthetic gratification, and offer a means for transpersonal and other spiritual experiences, Grinde (2000) asserts that "the language connection and the relaxing quality are the most important factors responsible for the human devotion to music" (p. 24). It is not clear if Grinde's entire argument is in terms of development of the individual, of the species, or both. Also, the "relaxing quality" is clearly not the primary reason that people engage with music. The energizing quality is at least as important as are all of the various functions music has in the psychological and social spheres. Grinde considers these areas to represent secondary functions and claims that the evolutionary perspective does not preclude this. Grinde elevates what are most likely incidental, secondary benefits to the position of primary function because of his evolutionary commitment. He claims that the secondary benefits embodied in the various social functions of music can also have adaptive value.

Christensen (2000) also critiques Grinde's "pleasure explanation" as being only half the story, and draws upon the fact that humans employ more than just relaxing sounds in the production of music. He agrees that "musical sounds arouse immediate and strong emotional response, but noisy, startling, disturbing and dissonant sounds are no less important for musical experience than pleasant, relaxing, gentle and consonant sounds" (p. 32). Christensen goes on to detail all of the musical styles and compositions in which negative emotions are expressed, sounds are penetrating, clashing, dissonant, chaotic, threatening, noisy, and otherwise the opposite of being pleasant, relaxing, gentle, and consonant. He also notes the types of music that contrast with Grinde's position are especially important in considering the applications to music therapy that form the orientation for the entire discussion.

Grinde could make two possible responses here. First, he could claim that music of the type referred to by Christensen provides the pleasure sensations, and that pleasure is not connected to the qualities of relaxation and consonance. Second, he could also claim that the origins of music when it served as a language training device were associated with pleasure and that the type of music referred to by Christensen results from secondary causes, not the original function of music.

Grinde does claim that an appreciation for music could be fostered through processes of natural selection even if music would not have any demonstrated value for the species survival. For him, "it is definitely conceivable that sexual selection spurred the evolution of musical capacities, that is, mate choice could depend to some extent on musical ability" (2000, p. 24). However, this observation appears to contradict Grinde's main point. He is saying that humans have an innate predisposition to appreciate music that exists apart from its survival value. People enjoy and chose mates based on its presence, so it developed further from selection. This begs the question of why this occurs. The only logical answer is the intrinsic appreciation of music apart from any practical use or value, exactly what the evolutionary perspective that Grinde is operating from does not want to allow.

It does seem that Grinde is aware of some of the unresolved or contradictory aspects of his position. Contrary to what one might think given the primacy of language preparation in this theory on the origins of music, Grinde (2001) nonetheless realizes that it is the fact that humans possess language and do not require music for communication that makes the human devotion to music particularly interesting. While it is true that "song and music certainly can serve communicative purposes, this does not seem to be their primary function" (2001, p. 101). It is the fact that humans can appreciate music in the absence of communicative intent that "requires an evolutionary explanation" (p. 101).

Grinde (2001) accuses Christensen of confusing phylogeny and ontogeny. Grinde agrees that in individual development "musical appreciation is present prior to language in infants" but that "the capacity of musical appreciation evolved along with, not before, the capacity for language in our evolutionary history" (p. 101). So here Grinde seems to place music and language as contemporaneous phenomena without one preceding the other.

The necessity to provide an evolutionary explanation for all human activities is an unproven assumption that not all theorists are obligated to have. It certainly is possible that significant human activities such as music have non-evolutionary explanations. Contrary to the assumptions of biological thinking, this does not mean that there is no explanation.

Music, Early Interaction, and Evolutionary Selection

In the view of Ellen Dissanayake (2001), an ethological perspective on music can provide a comprehensive foundation for music therapy as well as other creative arts therapies and it can do so in a way that is supportive of basic psychodynamic theories. Her belief is that insight into the original purpose of music can provide an enhanced understanding of its contemporary clinical applications. In other words, music promoted survival and the ways that it promoted biological survival should explain why it helps people with disabilities today. A challenge for Dissanayake's position is to explain why an activity that promoted biological advantage would be relevant in the psychological realm.

A fundamental premise of ethological thinking is that "behavior, like anatomy and physiology, has arisen and changed (evolved) over time to better suit an animal to a way of life in a particular environment" (Dissanayake, 2001, p. 161). While Dissanayake presents this notion as unproblematic, it is possible to challenge it in a number of ways, particularly in considering its application to concerns relevant to music therapy theory. First, just because some behaviors can be explained as evolved adaptations does not mean that all behaviors can be explained this way; second, conceptualizing music as a behavior does not reflect other ways of thinking of it as embodied, intelligent action; and third, there is no reason to assume that a human realm of activity first must be proved to not be adaptive in order to not consider it an adaptation. In other words, it might be adaptive even though this is not its reason for being, just as hiking in the mountains promotes biological cardio-vascular benefits but this is not why we do it. We crave aesthetic experience independent of its biological benefits.

Here is the general outline of Dissanayake's (2001) ethological approach: Music is a phylogenetic antecedent of early interaction that emerged "as an evolved or adaptive behavior that contributed to the fitness (survival and reproductive success) of ancestral humans" (p. 159). The antecedents of music are the "ritualized vocal, visual, and kinesic components of mother-infant interaction" (p. 159) that gradually took on artistic elements and evolved through their employment in ritual ceremonial practices to what we now call music. The motivation to create music originated in concerns regarding the uncertainties of human life addressed through communal ritual. Music functioned to relieve individual anxiety and coordinate communal efforts through ritual.

Central to this theory is the specific nature of mother–infant interaction with a number of visual, motor, and auditory characteristics. Through a process of ritualization, these behaviors acquired unique meanings that served to more intensely bond the mother–infant dyad, which in turn increased the potential for the infant's biological survival. The various expressions that constitute early interaction are not music but antecedents of it. Dissanayake (2009) considers mother–infant interaction as musical because it is

> organized in bouts (phrases) over time and in time, using such musical features as melodic vocal contours, rhythmic and regularized vocalizations and body movements, and expressive dynamic contrasts and variations in space (large-mall, up-down) and time (fast-slow, short-long) with behavioural "rests" or silences between bouts.
>
> (Dissanayake, 2009, p. 22)

The elements of communicative musicality, as present in early interaction, are identified by Dissanayake (2009) as "simplification or formalization, repetition, exaggeration, elaboration (and for older infants, manipulation of their expectation, or surprise) of simultaneous vocal, visual, and kinesic expressions" (p. 23). In this early interaction are the origins of those capacities necessary to subsequent interactions with music. Because these capacities had as their primary function the intimate bonding of mother and infant, Dissanayake suggests that "the capacities for eventual music originate . . . in *love* or 'mutuality'" (p. 23).

In order for the precursors of music to develop into music some external situation or motivation was required. Dissanayake believes that the "universal use of song-like vocalization (often with percussive timekeeping, dance and mime) in human ceremonial contexts to mark importance" (2001, p. 166) suggests that the original motivation for music "may have developed as a response to uncertainty or anxiety" (2001, p. 166). Music evolved gradually from the repetitive movements and sounds constituting rituals related to hunting, fighting, and rites of passage.

> By joining with others in music and art-filled ceremonial behaviours, individuals may have felt more of a sense of coping with the uncertain circumstances addressed by the ceremony and thereby effects of the stress response were better ameliorated . . . The physiological and neurological effects of entraining brain and body with others—through the vocal, visual, and kinesic behaviours and aesthetic operations that evolved to establish communicative musicality and ultimately music/art in ceremonial practice—require and establish a sense of behavioural control and actually could enable our ancestors to cope emotionally with uncertainty.
>
> (Dissanayake, 2009, p. 25)

The rationale for music therapy is that music originated as an antidote to unpleasant emotions that are often a focus of therapy. In some ways, this rationale highlights the whole contradiction of the evolutionary approach. The presence of unpleasant emotions is created by the brain to induce people to avoid certain behaviors that threaten survival. Yet the brain also provides pleasant emotions induced by music to mitigate the unpleasant emotion it itself creates. This line of argument portrays a brain at war with itself that, if not illogical on the face of it, at least suggests a highly inefficient use of resources that should throw some doubt on the basic approach.

Dissanayake's theory of early interaction is different from that of Pavlicevic and Smeijsters because it offers a foundation for music therapy theory based on early interaction that has a phylogenetic rationale rather than an ontogenetic one. One strength of Dissanayake's approach is that it posits two original motivations for music in areas highly relevant to two prominent therapy goals: 1. reducing anxiety, and 2. enhancing social functioning. Her strategy is based on the argument that music is similar to other human activities that would not have emerged had they not provided some evolutionary advantage:

> These universal human predispositions—to speak, to make music, to join with others in meaningful collective practices—can be viewed as evolved behaviors. Like other complex behaviors, they must have been biologically useful or they would not be so widespread, even universal, in individuals and societies. They were *adaptive*: they helped those who did these things to survive better than individuals who did not speak, make music, or join with their fellows.
>
> (Dissanayake, 2001, p. 160)

Dissanayake's premise is that any common behavior or practice must have contributed to biological survival. It is a fundamental assumption that might, in fact, be wrong. Certainly Kennair and others do not agree, calling music an exaptation or spandrel to indicate that it arose from a combination of capacities that were adaptive. The rhetorical device of Dissanayake is to combine music with language and social behavior. However, this is an assumption. If music is fundamentally different from language in terms of facilitating adaptation, it should not be considered equivalent to it.

That music therapists draw upon aspects of music to enhance health demonstrates that they are implicitly adapting an ethological approach, according to Dissanayake. Because music contributes to psychobiological well-being, this is considered as evidence that it is adaptive in a biological sense. This argument certainly can be challenged.

Dissanayake is saying that because music helps people, the only explanation is that it is adaptive. But just because music is beneficial to people does not make it adaptive in the biological sense; otherwise everything humans do and value must be explained biologically in the sense of how an activity facilitates adaption to physical and physiological circumstances. The reductive assumption here is that music represents a reactive adjustment to external considerations rather than being an external manifestation of an internal drive to self-actualization. Even if music originated as an adaptation in this sense—which is highly arguable—this does not imply that its functions in music therapy are limited to the adaptive ones.

One of the important strengths of Dissanayake's approach for music therapy is how it integrates the developmental and socio-cultural rationales into one theory. Equally important to the developmental aspects of her story about the origins of music is the weight placed on the ceremonial, ritual aspects. For Dissanayake, ceremonial rituals are collections of arts. She characterizes her own hypothesis about the origins of music as unique in considering "the first music to have consisted of simultaneously presented vocal, visual and kinesic ordinary behaviours that were to some degree altered—simplified or formalized, repeated, exaggerated, elaborated, and sometimes manipulated to delay (or otherwise confound) expectation—making them non-ordinary" (Dissanayake, 2009, p. 24).

According to Dissanayake, the three spheres of activity of early interaction, ceremonial ritual, and the conscious creation of art are all linked by a developmental progression from the former to the latter and they all rely on the same human capacities:

> Ceremonies composed of music and associated arts are the behavioural or expressive counterpart of religious doctrine and belief, providing something "special (shaped, embellished) to do for humans cognizant of and attempting to cope with the problems and uncertainties of mortal existence, whether past, present or future. In ceremonies, the temporal arts, based on the protoaesthetic operations of communicative musicality, could similarly coordinate and conjoin individuals, providing emotional reassurance that the group's efforts would prevail.
>
> (Dissanayake, 2009, pp. 24–25)

Rituals where music was central functioned primarily to establish feelings of community and to provide answers to the uncertainties of life, particularly regarding the existential concerns surrounding mortality. In this way, the original functions of music can be seen as still present in contemporary music therapy practice where the allaying of anxiety and establishment of communal feelings are common prominent goals. For Dissanayake, the very processes that enable us to form human connections and seek answers to fundamental human concerns are present in musicality and music. This recognition provides a powerful explanatory theory and rationale for music therapy.

But the language of Dissanayake's hypothesis, for example, "distilled music from protomusic," indicates an assumption that music was latent within protomusic rather than something that developed as an emergent property. This assumption raises the question of whether it is a more fruitful strategy to highlight the differences between music and musicality and seek for the efficacy of music therapy in those differences, or to minimize those differences and seek for the efficacy of music therapy in the commonalities.

For Dissanayake (2001), the inherent musicality of infants demonstrates that musicality is an essential aspect of human life. Musical interaction between an infant and a caring adult is required for health and development. This suggests that its analog in the "musical interaction between a compromised person and a therapist reprises not simply an individual's own maternal relationship but an evolved, adaptive encounter that has characterized human psychological development for at least two million years" (p. 171). Thus, Dissanayake goes well beyond psychoanalytic theorizing to suggest that we base psychotherapy theory not on the recapitulation of the individual's early development (ontogeny) but on a phylogenetic model. The similarity with psychoanalytic thinking is in suggesting the basing of music therapy theory on musicality rather than music.

Dissanayake acknowledges that the protomusical behaviors of mother–infant interaction must be artified and ritualized to become music. Music therapy takes place through music, that which is present after the process of artification and ritualization. It is thus not clear why the qualities of the evolutionary and ontogenetic precursor (the mother–infant interaction) would be relevant for understanding music because it has developed well beyond the mother–infant interaction qualities of relating from which it originated. It is fine to say that the basis of what made music possible originated in mother–infant interaction, and that the function of these protomusical bases was to bond individuals. The question becomes whether or not to base music therapy theory on the commonalities between musicality and music or their differences. In other words, is the value of music therapy to be located in its protomusical origins or in its identity as an art form?

It is clear that Dissanayake holds music in great esteem and her ideas are therefore tempting for music therapists, especially in light of the perspectives offered by theorists who are dismissive of music (Kennair) or who characterize it as subservient to other processes (Grinde). In asserting that "musicality is a psychobiological capacity that underlies all human communication, including music" (2009, p. 17), Dissanayake appears to elevate the status of musicality at the expense of diminishing the importance of music. This is in spite of her view that musicality "has evolved to become a universal characteristic of human nature . . . part of what makes us human" (p. 17).

In identifying musicality and music as essential to being human, Dissanayake creates a strong rationale for the provision of music therapy, one that is particularly well suited to music-centered rationales. However, by conflating musicality and music, these rationales obscure the important differences between the two and this really is the crux of the matter. By providing musicality with so much explanatory weight, there is insufficient room for the efficacy of music in its role as a creative and aesthetic art form. All of the theorists who emphasize early interaction and the evolutionary value of music as bases for music therapy stress the connections between musicality and music in order to provide health-promoting value to music. In contrast, my own view and that of related music-based theorists is that it is the differences between musicality and music that hold the real key to understanding the value of music therapy. Seeing music as something that may emerge from musicality—either ontogenetically, phylogenetically, or both—rather than as something reduced to it, means that one has to account for music as it is actually experienced and used qua music, rather than as merely an adult manifestation of early interaction.

A Response to the Critique from Biology and Ethology

The first assumption of ethological explanation[1] to be critiqued was stated by both Grinde and Dissanayake. This assumption has two facets: that the only explanation for widespread behaviors (such as music) is that they must be biologically advantageous and that affective experience and aesthetic preferences are mere reinforcements for biologically advantageous behaviors.

This just seems wrong on the face of it. It is just not true that every activity that is prevalent and that people are predisposed to engaging in is beneficial for their own well-being and promotes the species' survival. If it were true, anything pleasurable would be adaptive. But it is clear that many agreeable sensations can stem from maladaptive actions.

Moreover, individuals engage in altruistic behaviors that put their own well-being at risk. I once read about a man who was working in an upper floor on the World Trade Center who, after the initial attacks in 2001, made a few trips up and down the tower to lead people to safety. He was killed in the collapse of the tower. Clearly his altruistic behavior did not enhance this brave individual's capacity for survival and in fact it served the opposite function: it put his life in jeopardy. Here is an example of a behavior that exemplifies that which is most noble in human beings and its presence as a human trait cannot be explained by saying that it confers an enhanced survival value.

The presence of altruism within a species can promote its survival in competition with another species but it does not enhance the survival of the individual. Any one organism with altruistic tendencies is less likely to survive so its presence cannot be explained by processes of natural selection. If there is a genetic predisposition to altruism, these genes will be less likely to be passed on because those who possess these predispositions would have been more likely to place themselves in danger than those individuals without such predispositions. So here is an essentially human trait whose presence cannot be explained by the processes of natural selection upon which ethological explanation rests.

The basic deficiency of the biological/ethological perspective is that it denies any intrinsic value to music and explains its existence on purely pragmatic reasons related to its survival value. For example, in Grinde's (2000) view "our appreciation for music was designed by evolution primarily in order to improve brain structures involved in language" (p. 21). While the specifics of this claim have been disputed by both Christensen (2000) and Merker (2000), neither of these two authors argue against the belief that the presence of music must be explained by the way in which it enables some other type of behavior: they merely dispute the claim that it was language development that music was oriented toward facilitating.

This view is reminiscent of the discredited "Mozart effect" rationale for music education, that exposing children to quality music and musical experiences will enhance their performance in other areas such as mathematics. The value of music is that it exercises the brain for a related task. In an evolutionary perspective, one could hypothesize that tribes with communal music-making learned to cooperate better and therefore became better hunters as a group and therefore could survive better in harsh environments. The area of functioning that music is supposed to enhance varies, but the argument remains the same.

The problem is that creating music together will never be the most efficient way to learn to do math, become a better hunter, or engage in any number of other types of nonmusical behaviors. In response to Grinde, it would seem that it would be much more efficient if evolutionary processes endowed pleasurable sensations to language play directly rather than to music. Just as it seems both inefficient and indirect to use a nonlinguistic activity to prepare one for linguistic activity, engaging in music-related activity will never be the most efficient way to develop nonmusical skills. Musicians, music therapists, music therapy clients, and music lovers of all types know that the emotional concomitants of musical experience function primarily to encourage one to return to music itself.

There is also a problem with the logic of ethological explanation on the value of music and music therapy. It cannot explain why the enjoyment that music evokes emerged in the first place. Recall the logic of this type of explanation: It is that the gratification we experience in music is a creation of the brain to encourage certain behaviors. This seems like a reasonable explanation when applied to something such as the way that sexual pleasure encourages procreative activities. Yet it seems inadequate when considering activities without immediate survival value such as music. How could the human brain anticipate that the musical-social forms that humans would create would be beneficial for nonmusical areas of functioning, such as language development, hunting, and coexisting in social structures? In other words, musicing itself—unlike procreation—is without immediate survival value. It just seems illogical to assume that the brain would create enjoyable experiences for an activity that was so unrelated to immediate survival, especially when daily survival was such a pressing concern.

Both Grinde and Dissanayake have anticipated that music therapists will consider their views reductive in minimizing what many consider to be the qualities of music that endow it with therapeutic potential. Grinde (2000) anticipates this criticism in saying that "it should be pointed out that the present theory of musical appreciation does not require all music related behavior to be adaptive" (p. 24). He then acknowledges that "music may take on secondary functions such as the maintenance of social cohesion" and that "these functions may also have adaptive value" (p. 24). The problem is that the qualities that aesthetic theory in music therapy posits as being primary are relegated to being secondary, incidental qualities of music. The enhanced value to life that aesthetic experiences add cannot be reduced to a property that provides enhanced adaptation.

In a similar vein, Dissanayake (2001) claims that "an ethological view is not intended to 'explain away' music's felt profundities and complexities but rather to provide natural, rather than supernatural, bases for these in human biology and evolutionary history" (p. 172). But this nod to the "profundities and complexities" of music seems to be motivated more by sentiment than substance. Dissanayake's viewpoint undermines considering the profundities as profundities. Moreover, the choice she poses is a false one. Rejecting the reduction of music to biological imperatives does not mean one is embracing supernatural doctrine.

The ethological view is necessarily a reduction of this type because the affective, experiential concomitants of music become an artifact, something that motivates a person to engage in music but something without the ability to explain the efficacy of music therapy. And this is the primary deficiency of this perspective: the very factors that render music into a therapeutic medium are prohibited from functioning in an explanatory capacity as they become mere proximate causes of the interaction with music.

A Synthesis of Positions on the Brain, Evolution, Culture, Early Interaction, and Music Therapy

Brynjulf Stige (2002a) outlines a broad, general theory of music therapy that includes developmental, evolutionary, and other biological considerations. He says that while biological theory has a role in music therapy, the particular constraints of biology should not be transferred to music therapy because culture and other contextual considerations are as important as biological ones. The work of Trevarthen and Malloch (2000) and Dissanayake (2001) that utilize the concepts of *communicative musicality* and *protomusicality* as foundations for music therapy theory, while worthy of further exploration, should "not be taken as arguments for biology as the sole foundation of music therapy" (Stige, 2002a, p. 104). While biology does place some constraints on culture, "music as culture is more than a reflection of biology" (p. 104).

For Stige (2002a), the evolutionary and early developmental considerations present in the notion of protomusicality are relevant to clinical music therapy across many domains because "interaction through sound and movement is a basic human motivation" (p. 105). However, because these capacities are "cultivated in ontogeny" a complete theory of music therapy must include the "conventional and social aspects of musicking" (p. 105). While the biological notions speak to preconventional aspects of musicking, they cannot address the "*conventional and postconventional aspects* of music therapy musicking" (p. 105) necessary to provide a full accounting of the power of music in music therapy.

As Stige (2002a) observes, "even the most spontaneous of acts is channeled through some socially and culturally defined mode of expression in order to be comprehensible" (p. 105). Explanations regarding the therapeutic value of music in music therapy have to account for its value as an artified medium. Even when attempts are made to musically relate without any predetermined stylistic constraints, the resultant playing may better be thought of as postconventional rather than aconventional. In nonclinical domains of musicing such as free jazz, there are still certain conventions followed. And even those conventions deliberately ignored create a new convention by their prohibition. According to Stige, these social aspects are always relevant, even if by their negation. The necessary role of culture means that "it is impossible to go directly from phylogeny to ontogeny" (Stige, 2003, p. 157); the role of music in the evolution of humankind cannot be uncritically applied to the role of music in the development of the individual.

Stige articulates the relationship among phylogeny, ontogeny and culture, specifically as it is relevant for music therapy. He argues that if there is a specific musical predisposition that originated early in the human species, this means that every potential human is musical, something that presents a unique potential for music therapy:

> If *protomusicality* is music as human capacity, evolved in *phylogeny*, it will represent a potential for development in every human being. The potential will be more or less developed, and it will be shaped in different directions, depending upon the *ontogeny* of the individual, which again depends upon the *cultural history* of the groups and persons the individual gets in contact with.
>
> (Stige, 2003, p. 151)

Stylistic forms of music are not arbitrary constructions but instead are determined by the interaction of a variety of biological, cultural, and physical considerations. In adopting John Blacking's view on the evolution of music, Stige (2003) articulates a broad-based framework where the rules and structures of musical engagement "are closely linked to social and cultural life, to human biological capacities, as well as to individual experiences" (p. 153).

Stige agrees with the present author that music as music must be considered in creating music therapy theory. He does not think that the preconventional music processes can explain the music therapy process. It is true that these preconventional processes are relevant because music does not exist in their absence. However, it is the way that music reflects cultural considerations other than or in addition to its aesthetic identity that explains why the biologically-based ideas are insufficient to explain music therapy. They are necessary to consider, according to Stige, but not sufficient to account for all that happens in music therapy. Stige (2003) goes on to say that, because there will always be some genre of expression that music occurs within, it makes more sense to think of music in music therapy "as *postconventional* rather than as preconventional" (p. 171).

My own views on the proper limitations of biologically-based theory for music therapy have been critiqued by Stige, who correctly notes that one of the primary reasons I have been critical of biological perspectives is that they represent a reduction of the value of music to evolutionary factors. But Stige rightfully asks whether or not this type of reduction is inevitable. He does not believe that the drawbacks of present biological theory should weight against the value of biological theory in principle. Instead, it is possible to "think of biological perspectives as *necessary but not sufficient* perspectives of the understanding of human beings" (Stige, 2008a, p. 26). Rather than arguing whether or not biology is relevant to music therapy theory, it would be more fruitful to determine "which evolutionary informed perspective on music and music appreciation will best inform music therapy" (Stige, 2008a, p. 26).

Part of my rejection of biological theory as foundational for music therapy is due to the presentation of a false dichotomy in existing literature in which music is either seen as a direct target of natural selection or as something without consequence for human well-being. The conceit of existing biological perspectives on the origins of music is that unless it has survival value—reflected in being selected for—then it really is of no consequence or inherent value for humans. Music therapists have implicitly bought into this conceit in supporting those theories such as Dissanayake's that argue for the evolutionary value of music, particularly in ways intimately connected to ontogenetic human development. The idea is that if music has been selected for, it would provide a rationale for the value of music in general and for music therapy in particular.

The evolutionary perspective as a foundation for music therapy is misguided in two respects. First, by connecting music to biological survival and flourishing, the psycho-social aspects of the value of music in human life are diminished and reduced to incidental, secondary consequences. Those things that many writers believe explain the primary value of music are reduced to accidental by-products. Second, the biological perspective becomes privileged and music becomes something that is only of value because of its biological implications in terms of evolution and individual human development.

However, I agree with the position argued by the music philosopher, David Elliott (1995) who claims that musicing is a most valuable human experience. He asserts that self-growth, self-knowledge, and enjoyment are the primary reasons for making music. They underlie all others. The human engagement with music consists of activities that order and strengthen the self, and our goal as human beings is to engage in activities that reflect this desire. We find as enjoyable and meaningful those activities that are congruent with our fundamental drive toward self-development and the development of self comes primarily from activities *without* biological necessity.

Thus, it is not that music is portrayed as possessing biological value that I believe is mistaken; it is the *necessity* of demonstrating this value that I believe is incorrect. In applying biological thinking to music therapy it is necessary to find a perspective that can do so without having this necessity as a fundamental assumption.

The framework proposed by the neuroscientist Aniruddh Patel (2008) is just such a perspective. His analysis demonstrates that the dichotomy described above is a false one, that existing evidence does not demonstrate the selective value of music, and that, most importantly, this does not diminish the value of music for human beings.

It is difficult to say if there will ever be sufficient evidence to determine if the capacity for music was selected for or if music arose from the appropriation of abilities designed for other purposes. We may never know if it was selected for or what the nature of this selection value was, for example, sexual attraction, group cohesion, language preparation, etc. Patel's perspective shows that music therapists need not wait for answers to the evolutionary questions for two reasons: First, an answer may never be forthcoming, and second, the answer may be irrelevant to explaining the primary value of music.

Patel (2008) acknowledges that "from an evolutionary standpoint, language and music are peculiar phenomena, because they appear in only one species" (p. 355). However, just because music is universal and unique to humans does not mean that it necessarily emerged through processes of natural selection:

> The example of fire making teaches us that when we see a universal and unique human trait, we cannot simply assume that it has been a direct target of selection. In fact, from a scientific perspective it is better (because it assumes less) to take the null hypothesis that the trait in question *has not* been a direct target of selection. One can then ask if there is enough evidence to reject this hypothesis.
>
> (Patel, 2008, p. 356)

Patel's exhaustive examination of the literature leads him to conclude that the null hypothesis cannot be rejected.

Some authors note the specificity of loss of music function when very specific areas of the brain are damaged to argue that these brain systems are specific to music and that they emerged through selection. Patel says that the loss of musical abilities in this way does not in and of itself demonstrate the origins of music in selection processes. Just because this modularity of functioning illustrating a brain region dedicated to music is present does not prove that these functions are innate rather than something that developed through musical engagement because they "can be a product of development, rather than reflecting innately specified brain specialization" (Patel, 2008, p. 357).

In a novel and important perspective for music therapy, Patel describes music as a technology for self-transformation that humans created because of how it affords experiences highly valued by people. Patel's novel view is summed up in the title of one of his book chapters: *music is neither adaptation nor frill*. Patel asks rhetorically whether, if no evidence is discovered that human minds were designed specifically for musical capacities, it forces us to the conclusion that music is a frill in human existence. Is it then true that it functions purely to provide hedonistic diversions and can be easily dispensed with, without a great cost to humankind? Patel answers in the negative to this question:

> I would like to suggest that the choice between adaptation and frill is a false dichotomy, and that music belongs in a different category. *Homo sapiens* is unique among all living organisms in terms of its ability to invent things that transform its existence. Written language is a good example: This technology makes it possible to share complex thoughts across space and time and to accumulate knowledge in a way that transcends the limits of any single human mind . . . Music can be sensibly thought of in this framework, in other words, as something that we invented that transforms human life. Just as with other transformative technologies, once invented and experienced, it becomes virtually impossible to give up.
>
> (Patel, 2008, pp. 400–401)

Conceptualizing music as a transformative technology explains the ubiquity of music in human culture. Its universality owes to its capacity to afford experiences that are universally valued by humans. Patel (2008) refers to "emotional aesthetic experience and identity formation" (p. 401) as two examples of these types of experience.

Music is analogous to fire—also universally present in human cultures—because the control of fire similarly transforms human lives in ways that are deeply valued. And the direction of development of such transformative technologies—fire, music, and written language—is linear, not circular. Once present, the phenomenon does not disappear because even though humans can live without the particular technology, the experiences it affords are too highly valued to ever relinquish.

Patel's position that human bodies and brains have been shaped by natural selection for language skills but not for music is arrived at not dogmatically but by a rigorous analysis of existing evidence. He leaves open the possibility that as yet undiscovered evidence could change the status of music in this regard. But again, because he rejects the false dichotomy that music "is either a product of biological adaptation or a frill" (2008, p. 412), even if music is a human invention, this does not diminish its status or importance. In fact, Patel sees it as even more remarkable a phenomenon than the ability to control fire because it represents the human capacity for self-transformation. Music is not only "a product of our brain's mental capacities, it also has the power to change the brain. It is thus emblematic of our species' unique ability to change the nature of ourselves" (p. 412).

In this way, Patel positions music as something humans created as a reflection of our inner drive toward self-transformation. Rather than considering human beings as purely reactive organisms at the mercy of environmental pressures, in his view people are endowed with the capacity to play a role in the direction of our continued evolution. In this way, Patel's view of music is important as it is a biologically-grounded one that is nonetheless consistent with humanistic strains within music therapy practice and theory.

Note

1. This response was first presented in Aigen (2008).

PART VI

How is Music Therapy Theory Developing?

16

AN OVERVIEW OF CURRENT MUSIC THERAPY FRAMEWORKS

Theory: What is it Good For?

The conventional wisdom in music therapy has always upheld the importance of theory, identifying it along with research and clinical practice as one of three pillars of the discipline. The idea is that practice and research not guided by theory run the risk of being unsystematic and trivial, respectively. Clinical practice, which is not guided by theory, has no rationale for the procedures undertaken, and research unguided by theory has no means for ensuring its relevance to clinical applications.

However, as is common with the conventional wisdom in many social domains, there are flaws with these oft-repeated assertions. The three oldest and most well-known indigenous models of music therapy practice—analytical music therapy (AMT), guided imagery and music (GIM), and Nordoff-Robbins music therapy (NRMT)—evolved in highly pragmatic ways, primarily as forms of clinical practice without an overarching theory to dictate procedures and protocols[1]. These clinical models were developed experientially and have been implemented successfully in the absence of fully-developed theory. The theory that has been developed within both models is useful in understanding why the approaches can be effective in a post-hoc manner, yet it is clear that the practices have not been based on the theories.

The conventional view is that theory is necessary to generate hypotheses for testing in research. While this is certainly true for most forms of science, one glance at the quantitative literature base in music therapy research will show a great deal of research and very little theory. Moreover, theory has a much different and less prominent role in qualitative research as this form of inquiry focuses primarily on gaining insight into human experience.

Two contrasting visions of music therapy can be seen in the different attitudes toward theory. In the scientific vision of music therapy, "it is the function of theory to provide explanatory models and help develop a dynamic understanding of cause and effect relationships for phenomena under observation" (Thaut, 2000, p. 4). In the more artistic, music-based view, where cause–effect relationships are not necessarily sought, treatment is guided by exemplars. Theory has the alternative role of supporting social structures in music therapy by providing post-hoc rationales, an overall worldview and value system, and guidelines for the types of skills that are necessary for the successful education of music therapists (Aigen, 2005a).

Stages in Music Therapy Theory

In spite of these caveats and differences in relation to the conventional wisdom on theory, the development and application of theory has been part of music therapy since the inception of the modern discipline in the mid-1940s. It is possible to distinguish three stages of development in relation to music therapy theory. In each of these stages, theory has had a somewhat different relationship to clinical practice.

In the first stage, theories imported from clinical psychology tended to predominate, first psychoanalysis in the 1950s through to the late 1960s and then behavioral learning theory in the late 1960s and on. In some ways, it might be more accurate to say that there was no music therapy theory, *per se*, as these theorists gave primacy to constructs from psychology and interpreted music therapy theory through these modes of understanding. For example, in utilizing psychoanalysis, music was considered a tool for a therapeutically useful regression to an earlier developmental stage, and in behavioral music therapy, music was considered as a form of reinforcement. No novel mechanisms were suggested and no indigenous practices or ideas were promoted. Instead, music therapy was fitted into these pre-existing conceptual systems without any thought given to the idea that music therapy practice ought to force an accommodation in them.

In the second stage of development, during the years 1965–1981, four music therapy models were advanced that represented a qualitative difference from what had preceded them. In chronological order of their first appearance, Nordoff-Robbins music therapy (NRMT) (Nordoff & Robbins, 1971, 1977, 2007), analytical music therapy (AMT) (Priestley, 1975), guided imagery and music (GIM) (Bonny, 1978a, 1978b, 1980), and Benenzon music therapy (Benenzon, 1981) represented the first fully-developed models of music therapy including clinical practices, methods of training, and a supportive conceptual framework. While there

TABLE 16.1 Three Stages of Development in Models of Music Therapy and Associated Theory

Stage	Years	Characteristics
1	1945–1964	Ideas imported from psychology Little or no novel constructs Weak connection between theory and practice No specific educational/training method connected to theory
2	1965–1981	Treatment models developed in practice Original theory developed to support proprietary models of practice Stronger connection between theory and practice Specific training methods developed
3	1982–Present	Beginning of indigenous theory Theories that are imported originate primarily from social sciences, arts disciplines, and biological sciences Broad-based general theories relevant to multiple models and generic forms of practice

are significant differences among them, they had a number of important similarities: First, each model was created by a single individual or team working in close collaboration in a specific area of clinical practice; second, each model was developed pragmatically out of clinical practice—practice led theory rather than the reverse; third, each model took advantage of the intrinsic qualities of music and musical experience; fourth, the developers of each model put forth novel concepts originating in their clinical experiences as music therapists; and fifth, each model had specific clinical practices that defined it. In all of these ways, the four models represented a qualitative advancement over what had preceded them.

For a number of reasons, theory was not extraordinarily prominent in these models, except for perhaps the Benenzon approach. For the most part, their procedures were pragmatically developed within practice that was based on a few core principles and, in the case of AMT and GIM, self-experimentation by their originators. In the case of NRMT, Paul Nordoff and Clive Robbins had a fundamental belief that improvising music with disabled children could awaken dormant capacities; in developing GIM, Helen Bonny believed that listening to specially-designed musical programs in altered states of consciousness could evoke imagery and other experiences that facilitated psychological healing and development; and in AMT, it might be argued that there was an implicit theoretical foundation in that many AMT interventions were based on psychoanalytic reasoning, yet there was no pre-existing theory about how music could function in the analytical framework upon which Mary Priestley developed her approach.

Of course, this is not to say that theory played no role in these models. It is to say that theory played a subordinate role as it was developed after the fact, primarily to explain some of their underlying mechanisms. For example, Nordoff and Robbins developed the concept of the "music child"—an "individualized musicality inborn in every child (2007, p. 3)—to explain the extraordinary responsiveness to improvised music that they witnessed in otherwise unresponsive children. Mary Priestley developed the notion of the "resonator function" to explain how a music therapist "apprehends the clinical significance of the created music" (Langenberg, Frommer, & Tress, 1993, p. 61) by resonating to its latent content. However, these mechanisms came about from the post-hoc reflections on successful clinical practice. Theory reflected practice rather than dictating it.

In the third stage of development—which has only really fully emerged during the first decade of the twenty-first century—theory became much more prominent in music therapy as it has matured. However, with the exception of Thaut (2008), all of the ways of thinking about music therapy that have emerged during this stage have followed this ethic of putting forth theory that explains practice rather than theory that dictates it. This pragmatic approach— that prioritizes service to clients over fidelity to agendas dictated by abstract conceptual systems, pragmatic social concerns such as those related to funding, or narrowly defined epistemological positions on research and health care—is deeply rooted in the values of music therapy as a service profession. At the same time, it is an indication of the epistemology, philosophy of science, and broadly-based humanistic value system that has been embraced by a number of prominent theorists in music therapy.

The various orientations emerging during stage three are the focus of the present chapter.[2] The publications and authors emerging during this third stage of development are listed chronologically in Table 16.2.

In considering theories and models that do not fit neatly into these three stages, it is essential to examine the work of William Sears (1968, 2007a, 2007b) and Carolyn Kenny.

TABLE 16.2 Stage Three Music Therapy Orientations Presented Chronologically

Field of Play/Mythic Artery (Kenny, 1982, 1987, 1989, 2006)
Biomedical Music Therapy (Taylor, 1997)
Neurological Music Therapy (Thaut, 2000, 2008)
Culture-Centered Music Therapy (Stige, 2002a)
Aesthetic Music Therapy (Lee, 2003)
Community Music Therapy (Pavlicevic and Ansdell, 2004a)
Complexity-Based Music Therapy (Crowe, 2004)
Music-Centered Music Therapy (Aigen, 2005a)
Analogy-Based Music Therapy (Smeijsters, 2005)
Dialogical Music Therapy (Garred, 2006)
Feminist Music Therapy (Hadley, 2006)
Resource-Oriented Music Therapy (Rolvsjord, 2010)
Humanities-Oriented Music Therapy (Ruud, 2010)

Sears was a profound thinker with an expansive vision who retains relevance for contemporary theorists, even though he is rooted in the infancy of the modern profession of music therapy. Sears's relevance to subsequent theorists can be seen in the work of authors such as Kenny and Rolvsjord, the latter of whom observes that "Sears's list of categorizations resembles a manifesto for resource-oriented music therapy" (Rolvsjord, 2010, p. 6). He is not associated with a particular form of practice as the content and style of his thinking transcended distinctions of clinical models and scholarly disciplines. While his ideas will not be discussed in detail in the present chapter, in order to fully understand the context of contemporary thinking in music therapy it is important to detail the nature of his contributions.

Although Sears was a highly influential speaker and teacher, he has left very little in terms of a written record. In fact, his publication on "Processes in Music Therapy" (Sears, 1968) was one of the only works available until a collection consisting of the 1968 publication, a revision of it, and some previously unpublished works was made available in 2007 (Sears, 2007). It is the 1968 publication that bears some discussion in the present context.

Sears's works consists of a detailed taxonomy of what occurs in music therapy within three broad categories of experience: experience within structure, experience in self-organization, and experience in relating to others. While the content of his taxonomy is not comprehensive by contemporary standards, and although its terminology was to a significant extent affected by the behavioral approach that was gaining ascendancy at the time—notwithstanding Sears's own antipathy to behaviorism—there are some aspects of the way that Sears approached his work that suggest it as a meaningful precursor to later developments:

1. his expressed desire that the implications of ideas not be limited to particular psychological orientations, but that by virtue of their expression as a generic component of music therapy, they should be relevant to all the various orientations under which music therapy was practiced;

2. an emphasis on the importance of human experience as the element through which the benefits of music therapy must be conceived, a notion supported by the

predominance of contemporary orientations in music therapy, save those of Taylor (1997) and Thaut (2008);

3. a recognition that music has unique qualities and structures and that the benefits of music therapy stem from the structuring processes music evokes in individuals;

4. an emphasis on the interaction between music and the context in which musical experience occurs; and

5. a belief that an accurate model of music therapy should be non-linear and non-hierarchical, something that was stressed in the revision of his original model.

(Sears, 2007b)

All of these elements of Sears's thinking have been taken up to varying degrees by contemporary theorists. Before moving to a discussion of these trends, I would like to make a few comments on the notion of intellectual stages. The delineation of the development of thought into discrete stages is an abstraction, yet it is one that can help facilitate understanding. While authors in each stage share a number of essential characteristics, some theorists are more accurately considered as transitional figures whose constellation of ideas makes it difficult to accurately categorize them.

This is especially true for an author such as Carolyn Kenny. While the timing of her major publications throughout the 1980s corresponds to an earlier stage of development, the content of her ideas seems more appropriate to stage three. She is a seminal figure whose writings frequently pioneered new areas that subsequent authors have developed further. In fact, the only reason the beginning of stage three is set in 1982 is to accommodate Kenny's publication of that year. If her works were not being considered, the beginning of stage three could actually be placed 15 years later with the appearance of Taylor's (1997) book.

Kenny's contributions have encompassed a broad range of scholarly thinking and she is still making important contributions to contemporary music therapy theory. Her two major works (Kenny, 1982, 1989)[3] include important dimensions that solidify her position as a unique transitional figure in the music therapy literature. Kenny's first major publication focused upon articulating a formulation of music therapy that drew from the intrinsic qualities of music and musical experience, and it was one of the first music therapy publications that consciously attempted to move beyond conventional notions of health care, therapy, and science. Rather than formulating a rationale for music therapy as a treatment modality based upon clinical conditions and needs, she focused upon how music meets universal human needs for creative outlets, experiences of beauty, and a connection to communal wisdom through ritual. Her notion of health is a holistic one and she directs music therapists to the ways in which music activates resources within their clients. Her work was integrative in that it linked anthropological thinking on myth and ritual with musicological thinking on music in the Western classical tradition, showing that the same mythic forces were present in both areas.

Her second major work (Kenny, 1989) articulated a theoretical model for music therapy practice intended to apply to a broad range of clinical models and approaches. Called *The Field of Play*, this model comprises the "essential elements of the music therapy experience" (Kenny, 2006, p. 98), divided into seven fields, including three primary fields (the aesthetic, the musical space, and the field of play) and four secondary fields (ritual, state of consciousness, power, and creative process). Although it predates many of the publications in stage three by a number of years, its predominant characteristics support the inclusion of Kenny's work in this latter stage. These include its focus on description of existing practice as opposed to a

TABLE 16.3 Characteristics of Stage Three Orientations

	Reflecting Practice	No Clinical Model	Emphasis on Music	Integrative Focus	Critiques Medical Model	Emphasis on Context
Field of Play	✓	✓	✓	✓	✓	
Bio-Medical MT		✓	✓	✓		
Culture-Centered MT	✓	✓	✓	✓	✓	✓
Aesthetic MT		✓	✓		✓	
Community MT	✓	✓	✓	✓	✓	✓
Complexity-Based MT	✓	✓	✓	✓	✓	
Music-Centered MT	✓	✓	✓	✓	✓	
Analogy-Based MT	✓	✓	✓	✓		
Neurological MT		✓	✓			
Feminist MT				✓	✓	✓
Dialogical MT	✓	✓	✓	✓	✓	✓
Resource-Oriented MT	✓	✓	✓	✓	✓	✓
Humanities-Oriented MT	✓	✓	✓	✓	✓	✓

prescription for how to practice and its ability to be applied to a number of different clinical models. It provides a way of describing, conceptualizing, and explaining clinical practice that cuts across diverse forms of treatment. The one major similarity it has with stage two models—and therefore its one major difference with those from stage three—is its origin as the product of one individual's unique vision. This one difference is what makes Kenny a little more difficult to classify but in placing her in stage three I am putting more weight on the content of her ideas than on their origins.

Six factors are common to many of the stage three orientations and they are listed in Table 16.3. In the area of *reflecting practice*, 9 of the 13 contemporary orientations have as their focus providing a perspective or viewpoint on existing clinical practices and 11 approaches[4] offer *no new clinical model* for consideration. This is perhaps the clearest difference between the theories from stage two, all of which proposed clinical models comprising theory, interventions, and training methods. The *emphasis on music* and *music-based explanation* characterizes 12 of 13 orientations and this theoretical preference contrasts sharply with previous periods in music therapy where concepts from psychology predominate. An *integrative focus* that attempts to create either general or foundational theory that is applicable across a wide domain of existing practice is also a predominant characteristic of 11 of the orientations covered. A *critique of the medical model* as a foundation for music therapy practice characterizes 10 of the 13 orientations. And the consideration of *social context* characterizes 6 of the approaches.

A cursory examination of Table 16.3 reveals that nine of the orientations possess at least four of the six characteristics, and four of the orientations possess three or less of the shared characteristics. These four outliers are aesthetic music therapy, feminist music therapy, bio-medical music therapy, and neurological music therapy. The first of these approaches exists at one end of the theoretical spectrum as it is the most strongly arts-based of the orientations, and the last two approaches exist at the other end of the spectrum as they are most strongly aligned with traditional medical and natural science principles. Interestingly, the one characteristic shared by two of the most opposite approaches (aesthetic music therapy and neurological music therapy) is the emphasis on music.

Contemporary Music Therapy Orientations

So what exactly are these entities that constitute contemporary thought in music therapy? What is striking is that outside of Thaut's publication detailing his ideas about neurological music therapy, none of the other publications present clinical models of the type developed during the second stage of music therapy. The four treatment models in stage two contain specific procedures, techniques, goals, and theories, all of which function in a mutually-supportive way to give directions to clinicians in practical work. In considering the 12 orientations other than neurological music therapy, none of them are clinical treatment models in this sense. I call them *orientations* because they are tendencies of thought. They offer a mode of experiencing, describing, and explaining the value of existing music therapy practices. Comprising values, concepts, and overt philosophical foundations, they cannot be described merely as *theories*, although they do contain theoretical constructs; because they do not contain specific interventions, procedures and goals, the term *models* would not be appropriate. I have chosen the term *orientation* because they all represent perspectives from which a variety of existing practices can be viewed or new practices can be developed. In fact, their relative stances in relation to whether they (i) explain existing practice, (ii) provide foundations for new practices, or (iii) actually develop new practices, allows them to be categorized in this way.

Group One: Providing Support for Existing Practice

Aigen, Garred, Kenny, Pavlicevic and Ansdell, Rolvsjord, Smeijsters, and Stige

In the largest subgroup, each of these publications reflects ways of looking at existing clinical practice and each of them claims to be created in response to these practices. Smeijsters's focus on analogy came about from his empirical analysis of a large body of music therapy literature; my thinking on music-centered music therapy and Pavlicevic and Ansdell's conceptions of community music therapy exist to provide an explication and foundation for ways of working already prevalent in the field; Garred developed theory to support the *music as therapy* approach already present in the field; Kenny wants to develop a language and model to describe the music therapy experience in a way that accurately reflects the process as it has already existed and, in her early work particularly, she put forth rationales for the effectiveness of music therapy to accommodate what she had been experiencing in music therapy in a psychiatric setting; Rolvsjord's thoughts on resource-oriented music therapy bridge the gap between music therapy literature that has taken on a medical model conceptualization and actual practice that she asserts is more attuned to resource-oriented principles; and Stige's (2002a) stated intent in developing culture-centered music therapy is not to "promote specific new forms of practice . . . [but] to develop fresh new ways of understanding both new and established practices of music therapy" (p. 5).

Each of these orientations take a particular core construct or phenomenon—whether this is music, community, culture, analogy, or resource and empowerment—and develops an argument for the importance of the construct while detailing ways in which current practices can be supported conceptually through the ideas developed from the core construct. The plethora of orientations of this type suggests that for many years music therapy practice has developed in advance of music therapy theory. In spite of the development of the four models in stage two, the predominance of music therapists worldwide do not practice within one of these proprietary models, instead working in a more generic way that combines personal preference, skills, and orientations of the academic program where they trained. The proliferation of orientations whose purpose is to provide a foundation for existing practice—while also developing new ways of thinking about music therapy based on their conceptual elaborations—indicates both a strong need for theory and evidence that theory is finally catching up to practice.

Group Two: Providing Foundations for New Practices

Crowe, Hadley, Lee, Ruud, and Taylor

In contrast to the first group, this group of theorists all represent what they argue is a new conceptual approach to music therapy that, when implemented, will both support some existing practices and create new forms of clinical practice. They are all characterized by a desire to influence the development of clinical music therapy by providing conceptual support for new forms of practice based on a set of concepts, an underlying philosophy, and/or a particular value system. Crowe draws from systems theory in developing a new approach to music therapy—that she calls "music and soulmaking"—based on complexity science and chaos theory; Hadley compiles a variety of perspectives that all utilize principles of feminism and feminist therapy through which to critique existing practices and upon which to build new ones; although he acknowledges his debt to Nordoff-Robbins music therapy, Lee (2003) uses musicological ideas to "find a blueprint for a new approach to music therapy" (p. xvi) that has music-centered and humanistic facets; Ruud outlines a form of music therapy practice based on the humanities that emphasizes qualities such as respecting human dignity, empathy, and self-determination; and Taylor (1997) argues for a biomedical foundation for music therapy practice based on the idea of "the human brain as the basic domain of treatment and the primary focus for change in all music therapy applications" (p. 15). Adoption of the biomedical approach "carries with it numerous implications of change in the way music therapists explain the discipline, educate and train practitioners, practice clinical procedures, and conduct research" (p. 122).

It could be argued that practices according to the guidelines provided by Crowe, Lee, and Ruud already exist. In Crowe's case, the suggestion that complexity science will lead to a new form of therapy seems strongly colored by her consideration of typical practice in music therapy as an activities-based, behavioral form of music therapy that, while predominant in much of the United States, neither represents all of music therapy in the USA, nor is an accurate description of the international practice of music therapy. The elements of complexity music therapy—such as mindfulness, intuition, a decreased emphasis on a musically-prescriptive approach, a holistic understanding of the person, and greater attention to musical factors—all could be said to characterize a fair amount of existing clinical practice.

For Lee, the differences between his approach and Nordoff-Robbins music therapy are not that well delineated. Lee does mention that his ideas differ from NRMT in that he analyzes music therapy improvisations through an analytic, compositional perspective. It is an open question as to what degree this perspective leads to practices that would differ meaningfully from existing NRMT-influenced practice.

Similarly, it could be argued that there is already a great deal of music therapy practice undertaken within the perspective that Ruud articulates. Nevertheless, the intent of all these authors is to influence changes in the way that music therapy is practiced and it is this intention that links them and that distinguishes them from the orientations in group one.

Group Three: Providing Foundations for a New Clinical Model

Thaut

Thaut is alone in suggesting an entirely new direction for music therapy based upon his orthodox stance on science and health care, and his adherence to the precepts of the traditional medical model. He considers his work to herald a paradigmatic shift in music therapy from a predominant reliance on social science constructs to one dominated purely by neuroscience. Thaut (2008) believes that a limitation of the traditional view is that it "has created a diffuse, more ancillary, and complementary role for music therapy" (p. 114). His idea is that a more central role for music therapy can be carved out when it is based upon a neuroscientific framework that articulates how diagnosis-specific, functional therapeutic goals can be achieved through planned and systematic interventions that are based on what is known about music and the brain. The standardization of interventions based on these principles has coalesced into the model known as neurological music therapy (NMT). However, there are strong reasons to believe that Thaut's approach is not a model of practice in the same way as forms of practice such as AMT, GIM, and NRMT. While NMT is a training that takes place over days, the other forms of practice take years to learn over many hundreds of hours of experience. The types of skills comprising NMT appear to be more of a technology of application as opposed to the combination of musical, creative, and intuitive skills comprising the stage two models.

Integrative Focus of Contemporary Orientations

All but one[5] of the contemporary frameworks considered in the present chapter claim an integrative focus. In their own way, they each purport to establish connections among seemingly disparate practices and to provide conceptual support for clinical work in a way that cuts across traditional divisions such as client population, disabling condition, milieu of therapy, or intervention. Where they differ from one another is on how broadly they construe their implications and whether they view their area of emphasis in a restrictive way that limits practice, or in an open way that expands clinical practice. This broad-based agenda contrasts with the stage two music therapy theorists who were primarily concerned with theory oriented toward a specific clinical model.

Integration within Music Therapy

I have previously discussed these trends (Aigen, 2005a) where I made the distinction between foundational theory and general theory. *Foundational theories* are based upon a priori epistemological assumptions, meta-theoretical commitments, and pragmatic concerns that restrict clinical practice to those considered to be legitimate based upon traditional views of science and health care. *General theories* are more accommodative, endeavoring to provide an inclusive umbrella for existing practices. They are created in much more of a bottom-up procedure as theories are developed to accommodate practice. The opposite is true in foundational theories where theories are developed in more of a top-down mode. Kenny's notion that general theory involves balancing the complementary poles of generality and uniqueness supports the accommodative impulse of general theory.

Thaut (2000), the strongest advocate of a foundational approach, argues that his rational scientific mediating model (RSMM) represents the future of music therapy practice. For pragmatic and epistemological reasons, Thaut believes that music therapy practice must conform to—and be based upon—traditional notions of science that characterize the medical model. The focus of music therapy research should be to reveal the mechanisms involved in transferring musical responses to the nonmusical areas of functioning that he claims are the focus of music therapy. All theoretical models—and particularly those put forth as foundational in nature—have to be grounded in basic knowledge regarding "(a) music cognition, (b) music affective response, and (c) music and sensorimotor processes" (Thaut, 2008, p. 117).

The profession-wide implementation of Thaut's foundational theory would integrate the field of music therapy, but it would do so by becoming a monopolistic practice that would not leave room for other clinical approaches and sources of theory. Thaut puts forth his ideas as a means of helping music therapy to progress, but a strict adherence to these notions would create a degree of uniformity in the profession that is not advocated by any of the other authors and theorists, and that would serve to greatly limit the options of clinical services available to clients.

While Thaut's position is unabashedly foundational, Taylor's position is somewhat more ambiguous. He demonstrates the broad scope he intends for his theory in setting out the criteria that what is needed is a conception of music therapy "sufficiently inclusive . . . to the extremely wide variety of types of disabilities, illnesses, settings, and age groups with whom music therapists work" (Taylor, 1997, p. 5). He seems to be more accommodating to other positions in claiming that his work "is not intended to support, replace, or discredit any former theoretical position regarding the therapeutic value of music," and he anticipates "that it will provide a common foundation for diverse ideologies, a consistent link between the many disparate and seemingly incompatible theories" (p. viii).

Yet when he describes his approach in detail, Taylor (1997) says that "it will provide a practical and useful foundation for research and applications of music in medicine" (p. 15), thus seeming to carve out a more narrow scope. However, he also makes the contrasting, more general claim, that the biomedical theory of music therapy "systematically and objectively defines music therapy interventions in terms that are applicable to the full range of client populations" (p. 15). Taylor clearly believes in the primacy of brain science by arguing that the brain is the primary focus and domain of treatment in all the various music therapy applications. This exclusionary perspective marginalizes other forms of music therapy practice not based upon or reducible to neurological considerations. In sum, while Taylor's sentiment may be more toward the idea of general theory, the specifics of his theory function in an exclusionary way which is more characteristic of foundational theory.

The position of feminist music therapy on this topic is more difficult to discern. On the one hand, there is no effort in any of the feminist music therapy writings to suggest that feminist principles should be used to dictate appropriate forms of practice. In fact, this would be antithetical to one of its core principles regarding the empowerment of clients and the importance of allowing clients to choose how they engage with music therapy. On the other hand, Adrienne (2006) uses the feminist perspective to critique the entire social-clinical structure of music therapy as it currently exists, asserting that contemporary concepts of professional practice make a true feminist music therapy impossible:

> The professionalization of music therapy may actually be part of the reason it cannot be feminist in model . . . The construction of assessments, goals, objectives, evaluations, clinical notes, and insurance diagnoses, are all how we socially create what is necessary in order to legitimate our profession and to legitimate the need for our job.
>
> (Adrienne, 2006, p. 47)

In this view, contemporary music therapy is complicit in maintaining destructive social structures that disempower female clients. It actually prevents real and meaningful change by serving to acclimate clients to highly negative circumstances. Thus, a more radical reading of feminist music therapy is that the implementation of a feminist program would cause fundamental changes in the profession applicable to all clinical domains.

In contrast to these three approaches, all of the authors from the remaining frameworks, who address questions regarding the domain of the applicability of their ideas, articulate positions consistent with the idea of general theory.

Three different approaches can be discerned within those theorists who advocate for general theory. Crowe exemplifies an approach that seeks to unify all existing approaches into one grand, accommodative theory; Aigen, Kenny, and Stige put forth ideas that can be applied in a variety of existing models thus revealing commonalities among them, but without seeking to provide any type of integrative umbrella as is the case with Crowe; last, Garred and Smeijsters articulate a more circumscribed agenda, seeking to provide explanations for a particular area of music therapy practice: music-based practice in Garred's case and improvisational music therapy in psychotherapeutic applications for Smeijsters.

Crowe (2004) is overt in her interest in creating a unifying music therapy theory that "is inclusive of all the approaches and processes observed in the highly complex interactions of music and human functioning found in music therapy" (p. 334). Complexity science as a scientific paradigm—and music and soulmaking as its associated music therapy theory— constitute the broader and more balanced perspective that Crowe argues will allow for the integration of "all music therapy approaches and theoretical orientations" (p. 335).

I have argued that since all music therapy applications utilize music, a music-centered theory (Aigen, 2005a) is potentially applicable to all modes of working within music therapy. Music-centered thinking is also described as an all-encompassing perspective and as a temporary stance that can be inhabited when its tenets are particularly relevant for a given clinical milieu or client, a flexibility that supports its general applicability. Just as theories of personality support psychotherapy models, the idea here is that a theory of music should support music therapy models. Interestingly, although this approach is diametrically opposed to Thaut's in almost every other dimension, they share the primacy placed on music. The fact that "it is the nature of how music is experienced and conceptualized that is the element most common to all types of music therapy . . . makes a strong case for the viability of music-centered concepts as a source for general theory in music therapy" (Aigen, p. 164).

The elaborations upon Kenny's *Field of Play* operate in the area of general theory and it is "therefore not limited to specific populations" (Kenny, 2006, p. 125). Kenny's model focuses on fields of interaction and dynamic qualities that could be present in many different types of music therapy practice. Because its qualities are open ones that stimulate discovery, the model itself is accommodative in nature and can be applied across methods, clinical populations, and treatment milieus.

Similarly, Stige argues that culture is such a pervasive force in human experience and cognition that its influence must be considered in all music therapy applications. Instead of thinking about culture as something that humans live within, the influence of which can be considered at a distance, Stige's notion is that culture permeates the life of sentient beings. Simply put, we do not live within culture, culture lives within us. As such a pervasive, all-encompassing force, culture's influence must then be considered relevant to all applications.

Although the focus of his work is acknowledged to be improvisational music therapy, Smeijsters (2005) considers his theory of analogy to be a candidate for general theory because "it gives a general explanation of the question why music therapy works" (p. 31). Moreover, Smeijsters argues that "the time has come to research the nonspecific shared characteristics of different models of music therapy" (p. 37). The concept of *analogy* as the core construct of a general music therapy theory has come about from Smeijsters's investigation of the literature, although the title of his book suggests not a universal application but something relevant to uses of improvisation in music therapy. He does posit his theory as one that accommodates "music therapists working with diverse theoretical frameworks" while leaving "room for both the variation among individual clients and the variation among different methodological approaches" (p. 12). It can do this because each individual client's problem "has its own analogous processes in the music" (p. 12).

Garred (2006) also overtly posits his dialogical approach as capable of serving as a general theory of music therapy because it "may be applied to whatever modality of music is being used, whether improvised or structured, in individual, group, or community settings, and whether one is actively performing or just listening to music" (p. 317). Thus, it is not connected to any one model of music therapy.

Integration between Music and Clinical Domains

One important trend that is part of this integrative focus is the interest in creating theory that can establish links between music and domains of clinical interest, most often consisting of psychological phenomena. This effort can be understood as part of the perennial concern in music therapy to link the two words in its name: how does the *music* relate to the *therapy*?

For the theorists who believe that music therapy operates on the psychological level (as opposed to the neurological or behavioral), the challenge is to find a way to link musical phenomena with psychological phenomena. In music-centered thinking, the cognitive metaphor theory of Lakoff and Johnson (1980) is used to show how the basic schemas that underlie all human thought and cognition are present in, and actually necessary for, musical experience. Thus, schema theory provides the link between musical experience and basic, essential human needs.

In contrast, Smeijsters argues that the concept of *analogy* provides a stronger explanatory connection than is provided by *metaphor* because it offers a non-symbolic link between music and the psychosocial processes that interest music therapists. According to Smeijsters (2005), "when you express yourself in musical sounds, you are the sounds and the sounds are you" (p. 46). Music does not symbolize aspects of individuals—as might be the case in a more traditionally psychoanalytic perspective—but rather the sounds are enactments of the person. In musical forms, Smeijsters sees analogies of basic human social interaction, particularly those that characterize normal developmental patterns of infants and caregivers. It is through these interactional patterns that the link between music and psychology is achieved in his system.

Whereas Smeijsters and I draw from psychological concepts to link music and therapy, Garred chooses an approach grounded in philosophy, in particular the notion of *dialogue* as developed by Martin Buber. As a music-based theorist, Garred shares the challenge of authors such as Pavlicevic and Ansdell, Lee, and the present author, which is to find a way to explain the value of music based on the qualities of the medium itself. Buber's philosophy emphasizes reciprocity and mutuality as defining qualities of human relationship and Garred (2006) asserts the appropriateness of these qualities as a foundation for music therapy practice because they can "illuminate *dynamics of interrelation*" [italics in original] (p. 37) that are at the core of what occurs when people engage with music and with each other through music.

Garred's unique contribution is not in applying Buber's ideas to the interpersonal interactions that occur within music therapy as this was first suggested by Ansdell (1995). However, Garred takes this line of thinking further by applying the dialogical perspective both to the role of the music and to the interrelation between the role of music and the interpersonal connection. In other words, it is not just the interpersonal relationships (client–therapist, client–client) that can be characterized in the sense of Buber's "I–Thou" framework, but the client's relationship to music also has this quality.

The motivation to connect music therapy to other areas of human thought is one of the driving forces behind Kenny's *Field of Play* model. Her goal is to create a language and general model to describe and accurately reflect the music therapy experience, which also "can be understood and used by professionals in other fields" (2006, p. 82). In this way, Kenny's agenda is not overtly an explanatory one in the same sense of Aigen, Garred, and Smeijsters. Her goal is not necessarily to connect musical with clinical phenomena, but rather to create a framework that is broad enough to be intelligible to individuals with backgrounds in the arts and human well-being.

This agenda is reflected in the design of Kenny's (1987) original study where the research panel included a composer, an Eastern medicine practitioner, a psychiatrist, a neuro-psychologist, a philosopher, and a dance-movement therapist. Implied in this design is the idea that if individuals with an awareness of the arts and their relationship to health-related concerns could understand her model and grasp the subtleties of music therapy process—without having had the direct experience of the process of music therapists and their clients—then the model can serve as the basis for explanatory theory. Because only one element of Kenny's model—the musical space—is specific to music, it lends itself to multi-disciplinary understanding and to connecting phenomena in music therapy to universal human concerns and needs.

Integration as a Central Construct

The notion of *integration* is central to Pavlicevic and Ansdell's formulation of community music therapy. In traditional music therapy approaches—or those representing the *consensus model* as Pavlicevic and Ansdell (2004b) describe it—integration generally is considered to be an intrapersonal phenomenon as music facilitates the abilities of the various constituents of the personality to function more in concert. However, for these authors "the central organizing concept of [community music therapy] is musical *communitas*" [italics in original] (p. 28). The experience of *communitas*—adapted from the work of Victor Turner—is a special feeling of camaraderie and connection that is established among individuals who undergo particular types of rituals together. Thus the first level of integration is with smaller subgroups.

A fundamental focus of community music therapy is the integration of various communities with one another: circumstantial communities of individuals—such as those formed by individuals residing in a rehabilitation center, political refugees, or individuals who share a common psychiatric condition, just to name some common examples—are integrated within the larger social, political, and civic communities in which they are embedded. Integration in this sense is the driving force behind community music therapy.

And in feminist music therapy, a core principle is the belief that the personal is the political. Therapy must focus on internal and external domains simultaneously. Social change is a necessary focus for therapists because otherwise all that therapists are doing is helping women to adapt to a dysfunctional culture. Thus, the integration of the social and personal world is central in feminist music therapy.

No less important than the clinical focus on integration in this approach is the extensive multi-disciplinary activity that it has given rise to, something that functions to better integrate music therapy as a scholarly discipline with other areas of music studies. Community music therapy draws extensively from nonclinical musical domains such as the sociology of music, (e.g. DeNora, 2000), ethnomusicology (e.g. Charles Keil & Steven Feld, 1994), and the philosophy of music (e.g. Christopher Small, 1998), in building its theoretical foundations. This strategy is important because it suggests that the uses of music in therapy are continuous with how it is used outside of therapy and it reflects an underlying premise that the key to understanding music therapy lies in its everyday, naturalistic uses. These notions have two important implications in the present discussion. First, they foster the integration of the scholarly aspects of music therapy with other music disciplines, suggesting that music therapists can gain from drawing from these areas well as having something unique to contribute to these other areas. Second, implicit in suggesting that nonclinical theory is relevant to explain how music therapy functions is the notion that the way people with disabilities engage with music is no different from how people without disabilities engage with it. This belief reinforces the integration of individuals from various communities that is at the heart of community music therapy while it reduces the stigma attached to individuals with disabilities. Through this strategy, individuals with disabilities are no longer defined as "the other" or somehow different from people without disabilities.

Two of the most important issues facing music therapy (on a practical and theoretical level) are its relation to the medical model of practice and the fundamental way that the use of music is conceptualized. With the detailed portrait of the different approaches now in hand, it is possible to consider the various positions on these two vital issues within a broader context. This examination will occupy Chapter 17.

Notes

1. While the founder of AMT, Mary Priestley, did employ existing psychoanalytic theory to some extent, her actual practice was developed experimentally and pragmatically in a manner not so different from GIM and NRMT.
2. This chapter and the one that follows are not intended as comprehensive overviews of theory in music therapy. The works of the original stage-one authors are not being considered here nor are contemporary developments in music therapy theory that are primarily extensions of the stage one theorists' work. See the following references for contemporary developments in theory along these lines: For AMT, see Scheiby (2002, 2010); for GIM, see Bruscia (2002) and Summer (2002); for developments in cognitive behavioral approaches, see Baker, Gleadhill, and Dingle (2007) and Hilliard (2001); for NRMT, see Ansdell (1995), Aigen (1998), and Turry (1998). See Bruscia (2012) for a comprehensive overview of theory in music therapy.
3. Kenny's two major publications are from 1982 and 1989, both of which were included in an anthology (Kenny, 2006). When discussing Kenny's ideas in general, the original publications will be referenced to maintain the proper time perspective. When her work is quoted directly, the 2006 publication will be used for ease of access for interested readers.
4. While existing writings on feminist music therapy have not yet proposed a particular clinical or educational model, its critique of many aspects of music therapy as it is commonly practiced suggests that feminist thinking provides a foundation for such models.
5. The lone outlier is Lee's aesthetic music therapy, which in some ways is more akin to stage two theories as it represents a personalized variation of Nordoff-Robbins music therapy.

17

A COMPARATIVE ANALYIS OF CURRENT MUSIC THERAPY FRAMEWORKS

Views of Science and Values of Inclusion in Contemporary Music Therapy Theory

Throughout its modern history, the notion of what constitutes legitimate scientific activity—and what relationship clinical practice should have to this conception of science—has been a topic of discussion in the music therapy literature. For perhaps the first 40 years of this history, comprising the period 1945–1985, music therapists accepted a narrow, conventional notion of science inherited from behaviorism, along with the associated idea that clinical practice should rest upon a firm research foundation. This was evident in frequent published exhortations to meet the standards of medical practitioners dating back to the 1950s (Aigen, 1991b). The current arguments for meeting the standards of evidence-based practice are merely the latest manifestation of this position.

An interesting schism developed in which academic theoreticians argued for scientific-based methods while clinicians continued to develop forms of practice through pragmatic experience that were not based on the narrow guidelines of traditional science[1]. It was not until the early 1980s that music therapy scholars and theorists in academic settings began arguing for qualitative research methods supported by Kuhnian and other critiques of the logical positivist philosophy of science, along with more constructivist epistemologies.

Hence, it is not surprising that an important theme in some contemporary approaches is the inadequacy of the traditional scientific method in providing a comprehensive foundation for treatment. For example, Crowe (2004) describes how "it became clear to me that the tool for researching the complex, intricate process involved in music therapy, the empirical, scientific method, was neither appropriate nor adequate" (p. xiii). In highlighting the way that inferential statistics can be used in a biased manner, Kenny (1982) anticipated current critiques of the evidence-based practice movement and argued for a much broader epistemological foundation for clinical music therapy practice. And the present author (Aigen, 1991b, 2005a) argues overtly for a post-Kuhnian[2] philosophy of science that embraces functions for scientific theory that go beyond merely providing hypotheses for testing in experimental research designs.

A consensus has developed around the idea that music therapy will benefit from qualitative and quantitative research, employed both independently and in concert as in mixed-methods research, a position forcefully argued for by Ruud (2010), Smeijsters (2005), and Stige (2002a), among others. The general sentiment is that both approaches to research have benefits and that the choice of method should be determined by the questions being asked and the purposes to which the research is put rather than by rigid adherence to a particular research philosophy or epistemology. Tellingly, the authors advocating for this more inclusive approach are all more associated with qualitative research than with quantitative research.

Taylor (1997) and Thaut (2000, 2008), the two authors whose clinical models are firmly grounded in a traditional scientific paradigm, do not express support for the idea that methodological diversity is a strength, instead believing that the only valid clinical approaches are those based on the evidence-based practice hierarchy. For them, the problem is that qualitative research does not reveal the presence of "predictable therapeutic outcomes that would justify the inclusion of music therapy with other medical interventions in a clinical setting" (Taylor, 1997, p. 124). Other than Taylor and Thaut (and to a far lesser degree, Smeijsters) all of the other theorists do not consider music therapy to be primarily a medical intervention and therefore do not advocate that it should be constrained by criteria that pertain to medicine. It is because of this core idea that they are led to more expansive and inclusive values in developing their respective approaches to music therapy.

Relationship to the Medical Model and Conceptions of Health

Music therapists were challenging the appropriateness of a medical model for music therapy as early as the mid-1960s. Lester Glick (1966) likened the position of music therapy to that of clinical psychology in its relation to the medically-based discipline of psychiatry. In this vein, he asserted that the following sentiment—expressing the opinion of a psychologist addressing the American Psychological Association—was equally applicable to music therapy: "I insist that psychology will not come into its own until it has successfully confronted and dealt explicitly with the inappropriateness of the illness model as an explanation of behavioral deviations" (Albee as cited in Glick, p. 120). While a number of different positions are occupied by contemporary music therapy theorists in relation to traditional notions of health and medical practice, the predominance of contemporary music therapy theorists are seeking a framework for music therapy beyond that provided by an orthodox medical model.

As was previously noted, in contrast to many contemporaries, Taylor and Thaut both embrace a traditional medical model and formulate their approaches to fit this worldview. Their conceptions of music therapy are of a discipline whose elements should be identical to those of medical practice. For example, Taylor asks the following questions, somewhat rhetorically: "Is music therapy a professional discipline? Does it stand as an independently justifiable profession with the arena of medical practice?" (1997, p. 120). Two seemingly contradictory positions are implicitly being argued for here: First, support for the idea of autonomy for music therapy; and second, support for the notion of music therapy as a category of medical practice. The issue of the identity and status of music therapy as an autonomous discipline was discussed extensively in Chapter 1, so it will not be commented on here. However, Taylor's (1997) commitment to a conception of music therapy as facilitating "the enhancement of human capabilities through the planned use of musical influences on human brain functioning" (p. 120) means that he is fundamentally supportive of a view of music therapy congruent with principles of medical practice.

Similarly, Thaut's support for a conception of music therapy as consistent with medical practice has both epistemological and pragmatic dimensions. In the pragmatic dimension, Thaut argues that nonmedical conceptions of music therapy have impeded its development as an autonomous discipline. He asserts that conceptions of music therapy that contrast with his view, and that formulate the goal of music therapy in terms of nonmedically-defined goals such as well-being, have "created a diffuse, more ancillary, and complementary role for music therapy" (Thaut, 2008, p. 114). For music therapy to be elevated to the status of a primary treatment modality with a central role in health care, it is necessary to define it as a form of treatment characterized "by a focus on diagnosis-specific, functional therapeutic goals" (p. 114).

The importance of music therapy interventions being diagnosis-specific is also taken up by Smeijsters (2005), although the way he implements this belief puts him in a unique position. He accepts the precepts of traditional medical thinking while offering creative interpretations of this way of thinking so that a more progressive form of music therapy treatment can accommodate itself to these requirements. For Smeijsters, the use of theory for the legitimization of music therapy in the outside world is acceptable only if the framework chosen "does justice to the medium" (p. 5) of music therapy. Pragmatic considerations alone are not sufficient to warrant the application of any particular framework in music therapy.

Smeijsters splits the difference between the two other types of theorists in music therapy. Taylor and Thaut fully accept the conventional scientific-medical paradigm and argue that music therapy procedures must conform to its criteria. Aigen (1991b), Kenny (2006), Rolvsjord (2010), Stige (2002a) and others argue that a new conception of science and health care should be developed to accommodate the nature of the human engagement with music that has emerged through music therapy practice over the 60 years. Smeijsters is perhaps unique in articulating a vision that is completely consistent with the traditional mode of science and medicine, while developing methods for explaining how creative, improvisational, psycho-therapeutic music therapy practice can be implemented within these conventional modes.

The core of Smeijsters's (2005) approach is a set of criteria for indications for determining when music therapy should be used and how it should be implemented, a process of decision-making that conforms to contemporary standards of evidence-based practice. Five core criteria center on: (i) the nature of the client's problem, (ii) the goals appropriate to the problem, (iii) the suitability of music therapy for these goals, (iv) the presence of a music therapy theory based on psychological and psychotherapeutic models to explain the effects of music therapy in reaching that goal, and (v) the conditions required for successful treatment. Smeijsters offers examples of criteria that center on particular disabling conditions, their associated symptoms, and the possible benefits of music therapy in eliminating the symptoms. Hence, his overall framework is illness-based and his concept of music therapy is as a traditional medical intervention. But he does make a novel contribution in attempting to demonstrate how music therapy as practiced can find a place within conventional standards of health, health care, and science.

Kenny's early work—such as her 1982 publication—contains one of the first critiques of the medical approach for music therapy and many of the ideas that she developed were taken up by subsequent authors. Her view is that traditional medicine disempowers individuals, robbing them of autonomy and responsibility for their own well-being. Traditional medicine does not allow for a number of important qualities necessary for health, among them freedom, choice, self-determination, responsibility, self-expression, spiritual and philosophical realization, and opportunities for innovative thought and behavior. Music therapy, based on creative processes, offers the very experiences that traditional medicine denies. In considering some of the theorists who followed Kenny, there are a number who believe that the practice of music therapy does not comport well with a traditional model of medicine and it is possible to discern two different strategies taken by them.

Authors such as Crowe, Rolvsjord, Stige, and Ruud embrace modern critiques of medicine and show how music therapy practice can offer elements lacking in traditional medical approaches. Other authors—such as Aigen, Kenny, and Garred—formulate a conception of music therapy that envisions it as something different from a medical intervention.[3]

Crowe (2004) believes that the traditional scientific method—and, by extension, a conventional medical approach—is not adequate for gaining a comprehensive understanding of what happens in music therapy. The traditional scientific method is not wrong for music therapy, she asserts, it just provides an incomplete representation and she advocates for the perspective of complexity science to remedy the deficiencies of the conventional approaches.

The name of Crowe's (2004) work—music and soulmaking—is drawn from the work of James Hillman "who saw 'soul' as a perspective, a way of seeing the world, and the true province of psychology" (p. 341). Her approach toward health is fundamentally psychological in nature and incorporates "a harmonious relationship among all elements of human functioning" comprising "mind, emotion, body, and spirit" (p. 341). In the view from complexity science, "health is a nonlinear state of chaos" and healthy human functioning is portrayed as a "dynamical system in motion" (p. 341). This notion of health is not consistent with the traditional idea of health as the absence of disease; instead, health is defined as the process humans engage in to "function optimally in the face of change, trauma, and challenge" (p. 342).

Because health is an emergent property that only comes about on the level of the complex interactions of systems, it is more than the sum of its parts, a quality that Crowe (2004) also attributes to music and to music therapy. The traditional medical mode of understanding— based on an older model of empirical science—is an inadequate tool to understand how and why music therapy works: "The therapeutic effects of music therapy are a process of creative emergence, which cannot be reduced to component parts to re-create the emergent whole–health and healing benefits" (p. 347). The notion that interventions in music therapy will not affect every client consistently is based on complexity science principles that represent fundamental aspects of reality and how humans interact with music. Therefore, criteria of proof that require standardization of interventions and their effects are "impossible and unrealistic based on the real, complex nature of the world" (p. 347). In sum, it is necessary to move beyond traditional science and medicine in order to be responsive to the realities encountered in music therapy processes.

Stige, Ruud, and Rolvsjord share a common view on the nature of health. Stige challenges the medical tradition, built on the idea that health is merely a state of not being sick on a biological level. He asserts that health has psychological, social, and cultural-historical aspects as well. Stige expresses agreement with the definition of health developed by Uffe Juul Jensen as "a set of *personal qualifications for participation in a community*, connected to *care and communication between people*" [italics in original] (Stige, 2002a, p. 187). For Stige, then, health and quality of life are strongly related.

Being included in one's culture is a necessary component of quality of life and hence, health. Health requires the capacity for action, self-esteem, relationships to others, and a sense of one's life as meaningful. For Stige, "health is a *process*, not a state or condition" [italics in original] (2002a, p. 116). Because health, quality of life, and engagement in culture have an intimate relationship, working toward health goals can require social action to support the deinstitutionalization of individuals with disabilities.

Ruud (2010) concurs with the concept of health as an experience of "well-being and meaning in life" (p. 103). Health is a resource that allows people to achieve the goals that they have set for themselves. He also considers health as a process rather than a state, and he believes that different uses of music in music therapy implicate different conceptions of health as variously "curative, palliative, preventative, or health promoting" (p. 104). Individuals are the experts on their own use of music and Ruud supports this type of concept for music therapy as opposed to "pharmacological models imposed on music consumers" (p. 106) where music might be prescribed by an expert.

Ruud also cites Stige's discussion of *participation*—itself drawn from the anthropological literature—as an important component of health. Illness and disability isolate individuals from their communities, both spatially and temporally. Health requires a re-establishment of cultural participation. Health can be equated with quality of life, according to Ruud (2010). Health also has a necessarily relational component because to be healthy one must have a good relationship to oneself, to other people "and to important existential values" (p. 112).

The holistic approach to well-being that includes notions of quality of life is also relevant to Garred's thinking. For Garred (2006), in the dialogical rationale for his practice it is necessary to address the whole person. Because the arena of health promotion in society relies on the methods of natural science including predictability and scientific notions of evidence, the dialogical approach is not subsumable into this framework. As an "intuitive and creative practice" (p. 256) it cannot be operationalized into the type of technology required by a strictly scientific approach and it must partake of the qualities of arts activity.

Garred (2006) argues that a music-based approach to music therapy cannot invoke traditional concepts of assessment, diagnosis, and treatment because these activities stem from the medical model in which the authoritative practitioner engages in an objectification of the client/patient through such processes. Garred recognizes that some of these processes are necessary to do music therapy, but that "no such scheme of assessment or evaluation could be considered definitive or conclusive" (p. 258) and these objectifying activities must take a secondary role because "therapeutic change happens primarily in and through relational processes" (p. 258) whose outcome cannot be predicted.

A strong critique of the medical model is inherent to feminist perspectives where even use of the word *therapy* is contested. The basic dilemma of terminology in a feminist music therapy is described by McFerran and O'Grady (2006): "The label 'therapy' is extremely problematic when paired with feminist ideals, largely due to its inextricable and longstanding association with the patriarchal implications of the psychotherapeutic and medical models of therapy" (p. 77).

An element of the medical model that draws particular critique from a feminist perspective is the reliance on systems of referral, assessment, intervention, and evaluation. These procedures prohibit the clinical process to develop according to "where the client and the music lead" (McFerran & O'Grady, 2006, p. 65). Additionally, within feminist thinking the expert–patient dichotomy that puts the therapist in superior relation to clients is not adhered to and the emphasis on diagnosis and symptoms that is focused on in traditional psychotherapeutic and medical models is abandoned for a holistic focus on working with the healthy aspects of a person.

A fundamental issue is that the word *therapy* carries connotations at odds with feminist principles. It has traditionally implied that a person's difficulties lie within that person in an intra-psychic way. This approach overemphasizes individual autonomy and implies that the person is in need of help which disempowered individuals may not believe characterizes their position. At the heart of the matter is that if one party is in need of help this creates a skewed power differential that not only might not be necessary, but could actually work against the interests of clients.

Of all the theorists being considered, Rolvsjord (2010) makes the most sustained, far-reaching, and well-developed critique of the traditional medical model. Her analysis has political and epistemological facets as well as components more conventionally related to the concerns of music therapy. Its emphasis on the role of cultural, political, and social forces on health and the importance of considering health in these contexts expands upon views that have also been supported by Ruud and Stige, among others. However, Rolvsjord's critique of traditional thinking—and, therefore, the foundation of her approach—is most clearly articulated in opposition to the traditional approach.

This is true even though she does assert that research done according to the dictates of evidence-based practice based upon "the effects of various interventions in relation to various mental health problems, symptoms, and diseases . . . constitutes an important contribution to research into music therapy" (Rolvsjord, 2010, p. 4). However, the rationale for her framework is that the traditional approach obscures essential "aspects of music therapy concerned with the development of strengths, experiences of positive emotions, and social participation" (Rolvsjord, 2010, p. 4) in addition to the unique contributions made by clients to their own therapeutic outcomes. Notwithstanding her pluralistic sentiment, Rolvsjord's work serves as a powerful critique of the traditional approach to medicine and health care. Rolvsjord directs her analysis solely to mental health care, but her arguments have implications for broader areas as well.

Her resource-oriented approach holds that rather than being based solely on "fixing pathology and solving problems," therapy can focus equally on "nurturing resources and strengths" (Rolvsjord, 2010, p. 5). While psychotherapy has traditionally focused on the exploration of problems and trauma, Rolvsjord says that it is just as important to include opportunities "to explore strengths; to experience pleasure, joy, and mastery; and to try out ways of using music as a resource in everyday life" (p. 5). Therefore, the very essence of her framework exists in opposition to a traditional illness-based model of health and health care.

This traditional approach is characterized as an "illness ideology" (Rolvsjord, 2010, p. 18) that has powerful political, social, and economic forces behind it. A number of elements of the illness ideology come under attack in Rolvsjord's analysis. These include traditional diagnostic systems, the notion that interventions determine outcome, the tenets of the evidence-based practice movement, the excessive focus on problems, the overly individualistic focus of health, and power structures in psychiatric care that maintain the illness ideology. This illness ideology is a grand narrative or discourse that promulgates its particular philosophy through the hegemony of its language. As a result, a critique of it must begin with an examination of the discourse of illness and how this discourse is manipulated to privilege particular approaches to mental health care and music therapy.

One powerful example of Rolvsjord's original approach is her analysis of the word *intervention* as it is used in music therapy discourse. Although a seemingly neutral description of the therapist's role in the therapy process, Rolvsjord argues that placing priority on the therapist's interventions as the key element in the therapy process is embedded in, and reinforces, a conventional medical approach that does not well accommodate notions of equality and mutuality between client and therapist. Rolvsjord prefers notions of "collaborations, negotiations, and interactions when describing the process of resource-oriented music therapy" (2010, p. 23), rather than talking about an intervention that implies a unidirectional flow of causation from therapist to client.

Rolvsjord develops a very effective argument that meta-analyses of psychotherapy research contradict the notion that specific interventions are the primary causative factors in psychotherapy practice. She highlights the common factors approach to explanation, which holds that it is not the specific theoretical components of any psychotherapy model that leads to its effectiveness but rather the presence of factors common to all psychotherapy models that determines efficacy. These elements include the quality of the therapeutic relationship, the type of interaction that occurs, and the underlying ritual structure of psychotherapy.

However, because research according to the criteria of the evidence-based medicine movement focuses on evaluating interventions, its application in music therapy may be completely unwarranted and lead to a narrowing of legitimate practices based upon faulty assumptions. This is why Rolvsjord's analysis is so important for the future of music therapy. It simultaneously offers a critique of the medical model of practice in music therapy while it also demonstrates the folly of following the dictates of one of the strongest social forces now influencing music therapy.

Rolvsjord suggests that music therapists should focus their attention "away from the therapist and the music's capabilities and toward how clients make use of music and music therapy in their strivings toward health and quality of life, and even toward music and musical experiences and activities" (2010, p. 52). Clients possess a craft in how they engage with music in therapy and in everyday life and music therapists will have a better understanding of clinical processes if they include clients' own use of music.

This notion leads us into one of the basic premises of music-centered music therapy, the framework articulated by the present author: the uses of music in music therapy are, for the most part, continuous with how music is engaged in nonclinical settings. Clients in music therapy have the same essential human needs as other people and through music therapy they are actively supported in discovering how to use music to meet these needs. In this framework, music therapy is conceptualized as a specialized application of music (specialized only in the sense that some of the implicit functions of music are rendered more explicitly) rather than as a specialized medium of therapy.

Hence, the practice of music therapy cannot be subsumed to a medical model because many of the uses to which music is put—both in therapy and outside of therapy—are not addressing problems that can be accurately described by a medical framework. They cannot be conceptualized by an illness ideology that requires the action of an authoritative professional who bases the intervention on a particular problem, illness, or condition. In this way, music-centered thinking is very much aligned with the analysis provided Rolvsjord.

The music-centered perspective is built on the idea that "music is more than an art form, a means for communication, or even a vehicle for therapy. It is a way of being with other people that embodies particular values" (Aigen, 2005a, p. 77). The experiential states and forms of expression and relationship which are natural to music-making form the foundation for music therapy practice. By positing the various phenomena, processes, and experiences that emerge from the human engagement with music as the foundation for music therapy—rather than social or pragmatic needs as is invoked by supporters of an orthodox medical model—it can be argued that the music-centered approach is actually following a more scientific strategy. It is allowing the phenomena of interest to dictate the conceptualizations and explanations developed to account for what is observed rather than allowing a prior epistemological, social, or even financial concern to dictate its foundations and theories.

A truism in conventional approaches to music therapy defines it as the use of music to reach nonmusical (clinical) goals. Music-centered thinking supports the opposite notion that musical goals are a legitimate focus of music therapy. No one disputes that the goals of music education, music appreciation, and music theory, for example, are musical in nature. In music therapy, it is only the dictates of the medical framework that proscribe the use of musical goals, thus preventing it from being aligned with other music disciplines. However, it is inarguable that the majority of music therapy clients have musical goals: they want to play instruments, sing, and compose music. These are the reasons they come to music therapy and this is what motivates them. By grounding explanatory concepts in the naturalistic essence of music-making and in the core concerns of the clients for whom the discipline exists, the music-centered approach offers a strong counterargument to the notion of music therapy as primarily a medical endeavor.

Emphasis on Music in Contemporary Orientations

What is striking about the contemporary orientations taken as a whole is the universal argument presented for a stronger role for music and musical phenomena in music therapy theory and practice, something that indicates that the specific role of music in music therapy has historically not received adequate attention. This is true of the approaches that are overtly music-based, such as music-centered music therapy and dialogical music therapy, as well as those based on contrasting foundations, such as neurological music therapy. Although present in the Nordoff-Robbins approach since the early 1960s, the need for considering the unique contributions of music in music therapy first began being overtly argued for in the 1980s. Forinash and Gonzalez (1989) articulated this sentiment in arguing for a research method that does not explain musical forms of interaction through "non-musical models of human life" (p. 36). The conceptual developments in this area represent the response of theorists in music therapy to this need.

A variety of rationales are presented for the increased focus on music according to other methodological and/or epistemological commitments within each approach. However, something that just about all of the approaches have in common is formulating theory in music therapy based upon what music is and the way that it is engaged in, experienced, and cognitively and neurologically processed in nonclinical domains as well as in the clinical domain. In other words, the trend is to explain the value of music therapy based upon music's naturalistic identity as a nearly universal aspect of human culture and experience, rather than in its uniquely clinical dimensions. Again, the various frameworks seem to form three somewhat natural groupings according to the degree to which the qualities of music as music are drawn upon in an explanatory capacity.

Group One: Music as a Core Organizing Element

Aigen, Lee, Pavlicevic and Ansdell

The three approaches of aesthetic music therapy (Lee, 2003), community music therapy (Pavlicevic & Ansdell, 2004a), and music-centered music therapy (Aigen, 2005a) are the ones most fully grounded in music. While there are differences among them, they share the notion that music is an intrinsically valuable experience and that the human motivation for musical experience is a valid self-justification for music therapy treatment. In other words, they each believe that the experience of music as music is sufficient to explain the benefits of music therapy: Thus, there is neither a need for clients in music therapy to either verbally interpret, or have interpreted for them, the extra-musical significance of the musical experience for it to be considered valuable. There is no need in these approaches to move beyond musical discourse to fully understand the value of music and therefore music therapy.

Contrary to some critiques, the emphasis on music does not suggest that these approaches are anti-intellectual as they all draw upon different sources for conceptual foundations and for particular ways of better explaining the value of the essentially musical experience. The present author's definition of music-centered music therapy—itself expanding on an earlier notion of Ansdell's—delineates the perspectives through which music-centered thinking operates: "In music-music therapy, the mechanisms of music therapy process are located in the forces, experiences, processes, and structures of music" (Aigen, 2005a, p. 51). Each of these aspects reflects a different discipline through which music is considered: music philosophy considers ontological or metaphysical speculations on the nature of music, including the notion of forces in music; music psychology investigates questions of how music is experienced; the sociology of music and ethnomusicology look at the social and interpersonal processes and contexts involved in the creation of music; and musicology and music theory consider questions related to the structure of music.

Each of the three orientations in this group is oriented to one or more of these musical sub-disciplines. Music-centered music therapy draws upon aesthetic philosophies (such as Dewey, 1934), music metaphysics (Zuckerkandl, 1956), and cognitive schema theory (Lakoff & Johnson, 1980) in building the foundations and drawing the implications of music-centered thinking. Pavlicevic and Ansdell draw upon thinking in new musicology, the sociology of music (DeNora, 2000), and sociology, to explore how understanding the naturalistic use of music in context can form the foundations for music therapy practices. Lee stays primarily within ideas from Western musicology in exploring how the underlying musical form of the music created in music therapy holds the key to understanding its clinical value.

Yet what all of these approaches have in common is the recognition that musical experience and expression are inherently beneficial human activities that are legitimate ways to address the reasons for which people come to therapy. In this way, there is a fundamental distinction, both between these orientations and their precursors, and between these orientations and the other contemporary frameworks. To varying degrees, other orientations in music therapy have conceptual commitments that are equal to their commitments to music. This group is unique in making the commitment to musical experience the core aspect of their conceptual systems.

For example, in community music therapy, it is argued that music therapy demands community engagement because of the "ripple effect," a quality of music whereby "music naturally *radiates*, like dropping a pebble in a pond seeing the waves of energy spread out in concentric circles" (Pavlicevic & Ansdell, 2004b, p. 16). And in contrast to what is generally the case in music therapy, in aesthetic music therapy "musical form influences clinical form" so that the music in music therapy is considered "from a music analytic and compositional foundation first and foremost" (Lee, 2003, p. 9). A consequence of this commitment to music is that its use in therapy is more continuous with how it is used in nonclinical domains than is the case in other approaches to music therapy.

This group of approaches suggests that what gives music value in therapy are the same elements that give it value outside of therapy. While this commitment is also shared by Rolvsjord, Ruud, and Stige (from group three below), what differentiates the theorists in group one is a greater willingness to consider attributes of music itself, not just music as a socially-constructed entity, in explaining its clinical value.

Group Two: Music as an Important Element that Exists in Combination with other Equal Commitments

Crowe, Garred, Kenny, Taylor, and Thaut

In contrast to group one where the three orientations have a very strong mutual compatibility, this group comprises four theorists from quite different ends of the theoretical spectrum: Garred and Kenny advocate strongly for a conception of music therapy that includes musicological, philosophical, and sociological elements, while Taylor and Thaut are the strongest advocates for an orthodox medical framework. Crowe's approach appears to straddle these two domains, drawing as it does, from all areas of human thought.

In Kenny's earlier work, she "identified music as carrying implicit healing patterns for human development" (Kenny, 2006, p. 82), and in her later work, music remains a central part of her orientation as the musical space is one of three primary fields in the music therapy process. Yet the other primary elements of Kenny's model—such the aesthetic and the field of play—are less fundamental than is music.

Similarly, Garred's (2006) goal is to formulate a conception of "music therapy based on the qualities of the medium itself" (p. 29) as opposed to one reliant on psychodynamic theory. However, he clearly explains that he wants to go beyond purely music-centered thinking in order to provide a foundation for both the role of music and interpersonal relationships in music therapy. Hence, he invokes the relations that characterize Buber's dialogical philosophy in building his theory, thus giving it equal weight to any concerns indigenous to music studies.

Taylor (1997) argues that more than behavior, the mind or human emotions, the human brain is the "true domain of music therapy" (p. 18). He operationalizes his commitment to a medical model of music therapy through an argument that because music is processed by the brain, and because the processing of music incorporates unique patterns of cortical activity relevant to brain areas implicated in various clinical conditions, that the only way for music therapy to advance as a discipline is to ground its practices and explanations in brain science. In one sense, music is put in the foreground in his model because the therapeutic effects of music are considered to the exclusion of things such as interpersonal relationships, yet it is clear that his equally fundamental commitment is to brain science.

Similarly, Thaut (2000) asserts that "music intrinsically communicates . . . its own structure and patterns" in addition to the "values of the listener . . . [regarding] aesthetic quality, cultural meanings, and personal associations and experiences in the music" (p. 3). He critiques the practice of drawing theory from nonmusical domains in building music therapy theory because in so doing "the understanding of music as a therapeutic agent is predefined by nonmusical therapy models" and "the therapeutic effects of music can be misunderstood and misinterpreted" (2000, p. 6). Because "music therapy's unique contribution to rehabilitation and medicine is the use of music" (2000, p. 5), Thaut argues that the most useful and generalizable theory in music therapy is one that is able to explain how music influences psychological and physiological processes in therapeutic ways.

In his later work, Thaut (2008) builds upon the notion that music is "a biologically deeply ingrained function of the human brain [with] . . . neural circuitry that is dedicated to music" (p. viii). He creates a treatment framework built exclusively on the rhythmic aspects of music. Thus, in a way similar to that of Taylor, Thaut privileges musical phenomena (albeit the one element of rhythm) in his approach to music therapy, although also in a manner similar to Taylor, he envisions the brain as the focus of interventions.

Based on the premises of complexity science, Crowe (2004) argues for a much greater awareness about the role of music in music therapy. The premise of this argument is the focus in complexity science on how initial conditions in a field combined with small changes can lead to extraordinarily dramatic changes because "in nonlinear systems, small things can have big consequences" (p. 351). This means that therapists have to pay much greater attention to "the importance of certain intervals, melodic contours, and rhythmic patterns" (p. 351) in addition to elements such as timbre and dynamics, because these are the factors that can lead to major changes. This demands a much greater focus on music than in many previous music therapy theories.

Group Three: Music Requires Enhanced Attention but without a Particularly Unique Role

Hadley, Rolvsjord, Ruud, Smeijsters, and Stige

This group of authors investigates music from their respective viewpoints although music itself has no special or prominent role. Rolvsjord, Ruud, and Stige do not place a special emphasis on music but they share a common vision of music as a situated activity that affords different experiences according to the context of its engagement. This view is also held by Pavlicevic and Ansdell, with the one difference being that the intrinsic value of music is given somewhat more emphasis in community music therapy than in the perspectives comprising the present group, although the difference is merely one of emphasis. The concepts of J.J. Gibson (a psychologist studying perception), Christopher Small (a musicologist), and Tia DeNora (a sociologist of music) form a strong, mutually supportive belief system whose tenets are argued for by Rolvsjord, Ruud, and Stige.

In strong contrast to Taylor and Thaut, these authors use notions from Gibson in formulating a critique of the notion of music as an autonomous object with essential elements whose causal properties should be investigated. The proper question to explore is not what music causes—because when context is so important, the concept of concrete cause–effect relationships is not relevant—but what types of experiences and uses its properties afford, and what uses can be appropriated by those who engage with music. Small's (1998) notion of musicking that incorporates the idea of music as something humans do (rather than as an object or something they know) and that includes all activities associated with the sound-producing act, is consistent with the importance of context. And because the use of music in everyday life is considered to be continuous with the uses of music in music therapy, DeNora's (2000) investigations in this area also provide support for music therapy theory.

Stige (2002a) goes into the greatest detail in his exploration of the idea of music as a situated activity and draws from two current strains in musicology: First, music and biology, and second, music and culture. He describes how protomusicality developed in human phylogeny combined with the artifacts produced by human culture creates one's life history through music. He wants to specify "the biological basis for music-making in ways that are compatible with sensitivity for the importance of cultural learning" (2002a, p. 90).

Neither the feminist outlook presented by Hadley (2006), nor the stance advocated by Smeijsters, share the theoretical focuses and interests of this group. However they both want to move beyond some of the orthodox notions and concerns about musical meaning that are present in other forms of music therapy.

In this regard, Smeijsters (2005) wants to consider the nature of music as sound rather than as a referential language, and in this way he is moving past some of the more typical ways of thinking about music therapy through psychodynamic frameworks. His focus is on establishing a more immediate connection between music and the human psychological processes that are the focus of music therapy. He puts forth his theory of analogy, which he argues establishes a stronger, more direct, and more immediate connection between music and people than do other concepts such as metaphor.

For Smeijsters, musical forms are analogies of psychological processes. Hence, the specific attributes of music as music are more central to his approach than in previous psychodynamic theories, but the musical forms exist as they do not because they reflect any aspects of music *per se*—as would be the case in a music-centered approach—but because they reflect aspects of human experience such as the communicative patterns that constitute early social interaction between infants and their caregivers.

In some feminist approaches, using conventional music is considered countertherapeutic. Existing conventional music necessarily embodies oppressive gendered forms that maintain clients in the disempowered positions that brought them to therapy. As described by Adrienne (2006), every convention of music actually is embedded within sociological functions that sustain social structures. "Our tonal and timbral system of music helped construct the values required to build an industrialized, corporate, patriarchal society . . . Classical music is not neutral, safe, harmless, or innocent, but alienating to all but the bureaucratized norm" (p. 54).

Future Developments in Music Therapy Orientations

What does the future hold for music therapy theory? Will there be a proliferation of frameworks such as those described as part of the third stage of theory development, or will there be a return to the second stage type of thinking in which specific clinical models are developed? While it is impossible to know for certain, there are particular conditions which suggest that the era of grand narrative models that typified stage two will not return and that theoretical developments in music therapy will continue to proliferate along the lines that characterize stage three.

The models of AMT, GIM, and NRMT were largely developed by dedicated, pioneering individuals working outside of academic settings and structures. The original formulations resulted from the singular vision, creativity, and immersion in the experience that characterizes pioneers. Certainly these original formulations were not context-sensitive, a trait of many of the stage three frameworks. Yet this context-sensitivity is only possible once the purer forms of practice have been developed.

In contrast to the fact that the original models were developed outside of academic settings, all of the stage three frameworks have originated in and are being promulgated within the academic community. And a general characteristic of the modern academy—in North America, at least but likely in other contexts as well—is to support nonproprietary approaches and models of practice. Universities are expected to educate and train competent therapists as generalists prepared to work in a variety of clinical settings and with a variety of clinical tools. A well-educated music therapist is expected to have knowledge about—although not necessarily the ability to practice in—the great variety of approaches that exist in the field. Thus, it is rare to find university-based degree programs that are overtly dedicated to a particular proprietary model of practice.

It is possible to see the developments represented by the stage three frameworks as a natural consequence of the maturation of music therapy when the development of theory and practice moved primarily into academic settings. As this is the current status of music therapy, it suggests that future developments will continue to be influenced by the conventions and obligations of scholarly work. This includes an exposure to ideas from many disciplines, efforts to connect thinking in music therapy to theories and concepts from other areas of human inquiry, and a need to combine these scholarly concerns with the pragmatic dictates required to educate people in a specific profession with particular skills. All of these considerations suggest that the type of developments that characterize thinking in music therapy in the third stage will continue.

Notes

1. Behavioral music therapy is one prominent exception in this regard. See Aigen (1991b) for a critical analysis of the philosophy of science that guided the conduct of research in music therapy from approximately 1950 through the mid-1980s.
2. Thomas Kuhn (1970) was an historian of science whose work was highly influential in changing how progress in science was understood by philosophers.
3. A few of the theorists—such as Lee (2003) and Pavlicevic and Ansdell (2004b)—do not address this question directly, although in both cases an argument could be made that elements of both frameworks directly conflict with a conventional medical model.

CONCLUSION

I would like to conclude the present book with some more personal thoughts about the future of music therapy. I have had the good fortune to work closely with four seminal figures in this profession, two clinicians and two educators. As I move into the latter stages of my own career, I realize that those of us who worked directly with the pioneers in music therapy will also soon be moving on. As each of these four people have left an indelible mark on the way that I think about music therapy, I want to conclude the present book by sharing what I have learned from them as I believe that they all offer essential values for the next generation of music therapists, who will determine what its future will be.

As I write these words, Barbara Hesser is preparing for her fortieth year as head of the music therapy program at New York University (NYU). While this fact of longevity is certainly a testament to the power of her vision of music therapy education, more important than just longevity is her belief that creating an extended educational community with music at its core is the best way to develop effective music therapists. The communal spirit that permeates the music therapy staff, students, and alumni of NYU extends to the clients of all these clinicians. It demonstrates that for music therapy to continue to thrive, it is necessary to keep the spirit of music alive in all of the clinical, theoretical, educational, and research aspects of music therapy.

As early as the late 1950s, Florence Tyson was developing an in-depth approach to psycho-therapeutic music therapy that was based on psychoanalytic principles. The force of her vision enlisted supporters of all types and she successfully built an outpatient facility for individuals with mental illness that offered music, art, dance, drama, and poetry therapy. The Creative Arts Rehabilitation Center (CARC) was located on the third and fourth floors of a walk-up building in midtown Manhattan, just above a French bistro. To enter CARC, therapists and clients had to walk through the bar area of the bistro.

I once saw Florence sitting at the bar having a drink with a patient. In most conventional views of therapy—and especially in psychoanalytic ones within which Florence couched her work—such an act would be considered highly countertherapeutic, if not unethical. When I questioned her about it, Florence explained that she had worked 20 years in individual therapy with this particular client who, for the first time in her adult life, had successfully secured a job and was now earning a regular paycheck. According to Florence, to not acknowledge such a major life achievement in the way that the client preferred would be countertherapeutic and an abrogation of one's clinical responsibility.

The lesson from Florence was that the guidelines for what to do as a therapist can be influenced by common sense and our instinctual human reactions to the struggles and triumphs of our fellow human beings. In her theoretical leanings, Florence was as psychoanalytic as they come, but she did not allow a blind allegiance to this abstract conceptual system trump what she believed was the right thing to do in the moment with her clients.

The man to whom this book is dedicated, Clive Robbins, left a powerful impression on all those who met him. We worked together on a daily basis for 15 years and his impact on me was global, affecting the way that I think about and practice music therapy, as well as the way I interact with colleagues. However, one incident that affects how I play music stands out for me at the moment.

I was preparing some compositions to play at the piano that Clive wanted me to learn for a lecture-teaching trip to Japan, Australia, and New Zealand that we would take together. I was playing the song "Something is Going to Happen"[1] that he had composed together with Paul Nordoff. Although I was not a very technically skilled pianist, I had always felt that playing with feeling was a strength of mine and I expected Clive to be pleased with my rendition of the song.

As soon as I completed the song (it is relatively brief, nine measures long, played *andante*) I could see that not all was right. In a nonjudgmental but very direct way, Clive conveyed to me that my approach to the song was not what was needed. I was playing in far too sentimental a way, projecting my own concept of emotional expressiveness onto the music rather than allowing the inherent expressiveness of the music to reveal itself. The emotion was embedded and embodied in the composition. It did not require me to layer my own feeling onto it, something that made it sound sentimental rather than expressive. Clive's analysis made perfect sense to me and something about the clear, direct, and objective way he had of providing the feedback to me allowed me to hear it and take it in. I still remember this incident 16 years after the fact as it has forever changed the way that I play music. The lesson here for music therapists is to remember to get out of the way of the music in our work with clients.

In the early 1990s, I became president of the American Association for Music Therapy (AAMT) which, at the time, was involved with a variety of contentious issues with the National Association for Music Therapy (NAMT)[2]. In seeking guidance in negotiating these issues, I engaged in an ongoing correspondence with Kenneth Bruscia, a former AAMT President and someone who is recognized as the foremost scholar of music therapy internationally. The quality, breadth, depth, and impact of his writings, teaching, and lecturing, have been an enormous service to the field and I consider him to be "the teacher's teacher."

At the time, I felt that some of the political issues that I was dealing with owed to the fact that while the AAMT had a primarily humanistic orientation in its educational and clinical philosophy, the NAMT was guided more by the agenda of behaviorism in its educational, clinical, and research policies. Although I had not yet developed a personal relationship with Ken, because of his writings and from what I knew of his educational program at Temple University, I expected a sympathetic ear. What I received was much more valuable.

Ken's letters to me stemmed from one central point. Building on his view, that it was not right for a professional association to have *any* type of underlying philosophy that guided policy, whether this was covert or overt, Ken took pains to emphasize the central importance of a pluralistic outlook that valued diversity and inclusiveness. Once any viewpoint was excluded from the debate or from a seat at the table, the debate was already lost. While I wanted to frame the debate as one of humanistic versus behavioristic values, Ken's argument convinced me that the real debate was between the values of inclusion and diversity versus those of exclusion and enforced uniformity. Ken's argument swayed me and I am eternally grateful to him for it. The recurring plea for an acceptance of diversity throughout the present book owes to the force and passion of Ken Bruscia's thoughts on such matters.

In reflecting on the various positions I have supported throughout the present book, I can see the impact of these four individuals and the values that they manifested: the central importance of music, prioritizing the commitment to people over that of a conceptual system, letting the music do its work, and the inherent value of diversity. More important than any of the specific positions that I have argued for in the present book are these four values. Keeping them alive as essential aspects of the ongoing debate in music therapy will ensure that the profession continues to develop in a way that meets the needs and desires of the clients for whom it exists.

Notes

1. "Something is going to happen" © 1962 published in *The First Book of Children's Play-Songs*. Bryn Mawr, PA: Theodore Presser.
2. The two organizations resolved their differences and unified in 1998 to create the American Music Therapy Association.

REFERENCES

Aasgaard, T. (2000). "A Suspiciously Cheerful Lady": A study of a song's life in the paediatric oncology ward, and beyond . . . . *British Journal of Music Therapy, 14*(2), 70–82.

Aasgaard, T. (2005). Song creations by children with cancer: Process and meaning. In D. Aldridge (Ed.), *Case study designs in music therapy* (pp. 67–96). London: Jessica Kingsley.

Adrienne, J. (2006). A feminist sociology of professional issues in music therapy. In S. Hadley (Ed.), *Feminist perspectives in music therapy* (pp. 41–62). Gilsum, NH: Barcelona.

Aigen, K. (1991a). The voice of the forest: A conception of music for music therapy. *Music Therapy, 10*(1), 77–98.

Aigen, K. (1991b). *The roots of music therapy: Towards an indigenous research paradigm.* (Doctoral Dissertation, New York University).

Aigen, K. (1995a). Cognitive and affective processes in music therapy with individuals with developmental delays: A preliminary model for contemporary Nordoff-Robbins practice. *Music Therapy, 13*(1), 13–46.

Aigen, K. (1995b). The aesthetic foundation of clinical theory: A basis of Nordoff-Robbins music therapy. In C.B. Kenny (Ed.), *Listening, playing, creating: Essays on the power of sound* (pp. 233–257). Albany, New York: State University of New York Press.

Aigen, K. (1998). *Paths of development in Nordoff-Robbins music therapy.* Gilsum, NH: Barcelona.

Aigen, K. (1999). The true nature of music-centered music therapy theory. *British Journal of Music Therapy, 13*(2), 77–82.

Aigen, K. (2004). Conversations on creating community: Performance as music therapy in New York City. In M. Pavlicevic & G. Ansdell (Eds.), *Community music therapy* (pp. 186–213). London: Jessica Kingsley.

Aigen, K. (2005a). *Music-centered music therapy.* Gilsum, NH: Barcelona.

Aigen, K. (2005b). *Being in music: Foundations of Nordoff-Robbins music therapy.* Gilsum, NH: Barcelona.

Aigen, K. (2005c). *Playin' in the band: A qualitative study of popular music styles as clinical improvisation.* Gilsum, NH: Barcelona.

Aigen, K. (2006). Theoretical issues in considering music as a therapeutic medium: An essay on *Music as Therapy: A Dialogical Perspective. Nordic Journal of Music Therapy, 15*(2), 154–166.

Aigen, K. (2007). In defense of beauty: A role for the aesthetic in music therapy theory (part I): The development of aesthetic theory in music therapy. *Nordic Journal of Music Therapy, 16*(2), 112–128.

Aigen, K. (2008). In defense of beauty: A role for the aesthetic in music therapy theory (part II): Challenges to aesthetic theory in music therapy: Summary and response. *Nordic Journal of Music Therapy, 17*(1), 3–18.

Aigen, K. (2009). Verticality and containment in improvisation and song: An application of schema theory to Nordoff-Robbins Music Therapy. *Journal of Music Therapy, 46*(3), 238–267.

Aigen, K. (2012). Community music therapy. In G. McPherson & G. Welch (Eds.), *Oxford handbook of music education, Volume 2* (pp. 138–154). New York: Oxford University Press.

Aigen, K. (2013). Social interaction in jazz: Implications for music therapy. *Nordic Journal of Music Therapy, 22*(2).

Aluede, C.O., & Iyeh, P.M.A. (2008). Music and dance therapy in Nigeria: The task before the potential Nigerian music therapists in the twenty-first century. *Voices: A World Forum for Music Therapy, 8*(1). Retrieved December 19, 2012, from https://normt.uib.no/index.php/voices/article/view/446/364

American Music Therapy Association (AMTA). (2012). What is music therapy? Retrieved September 28, 2012, from www.musictherapy.org/about/quotes/

Amir, D. (1999). Musical and verbal interventions in music therapy: A qualitative study. *Journal of Music Therapy, 36*(2), 144–175.

Ansdell, G. (1995). *Music for life: Aspects of creative music therapy with adult clients.* London: Jessica Kingsley.

Ansdell, G. (1999a). Challenging premises. *British Journal of Music Therapy, 13*(2), 72–76.

Ansdell, G. (1999b). *Music therapy as discourse and discipline: A study of "music therapist's dilemma."* (Doctoral Dissertation, City University, London).

Ansdell, G. (2002). Community music therapy and the winds of change. *Voices: A World Forum for Music Therapy, 2*(2). Retrieved September 27, 2012, from https://normt.uib.no/index.php/voices/article/view/83/65

Ansdell, G. (2003). Community music therapy: Big British balloon or future international trend? In *Community, relationship and spirit: Continuing the dialogue and debate.* London: British Society for Music Therapy Publications.

Ansdell, G. (2004). Rethinking music and community: Theoretical perspectives in support of community music therapy. In M. Pavlicevic & G. Ansdell (Eds.), *Community music therapy* (pp. 65–90). London: Jessica Kingsley.

Ansdell, G. (2005). Being who you aren't; Doing what you can't: Community music therapy and the paradoxes of performance. *Voices: A World Forum for Music Therapy, 5*(3). Retrieved December 14, 2012, from https://normt.uib.no/index.php/voices/article/view/229/173

Ansdell, G. (2010). Where performing helps: Processes and affordance of performance in community music therapy. In B. Stige, G. Ansdell, C. Elefant, & M. Pavlicevic. *Where music helps: Community music therapy in action and reflection* (pp. 161–186). Farnham, UK: Ashgate.

Austin, D. (1991). The musical mirror: Music therapy for the narcissistically injured. In K.E. Bruscia (Ed.), *Case studies in music therapy* (pp. 291–307). Gilsum, NH: Barcelona.

Austin, D. (1996). The role of improvisational music in psychodynamic music therapy with adults. *Music Therapy, 14*, 29–43.

Austin, D. (2004). *When words sing and music speaks: A qualitative study of in-depth psychotherapy with adults* (Doctoral dissertation, New York University).

Austin, D. (2006). Response to "Music psychotherapy and community music therapy: Questions and considerations." *Voices: A World Forum for Music Therapy.* Retrieved December 14, 2012, from https://normt.uib.no/index.php/voices/article/view/208/152

Austin, D., & Dvorkin, J. (1993). Resistance in individual music therapy. *The Arts in Psychotherapy, 20*(5), 423–430.

Baker, F.A. (2013). Front and center stage: Participants performing songs created during music therapy. *The Arts in Psychotherapy, 40*, 20–28.

Baker, F.A., Gleadhill, L.M., & Dingle, G.A. (2007). Music therapy and emotional exploration: Exposing substance abuse clients to the experiences of non-drug-induced emotions. *The Arts in Psychotherapy, 34*, 321–330.

Barz, G. (2006). *Singing for life: HIV/AIDS and music in Uganda.* New York: Routledge.

Benenzon, R.O. (1981). *Music therapy manual.* Springfield, IL: Charles C. Thomas.

Berliner, P. (1994). *Thinking in jazz: The infinite art of improvisation.* Chicago, IL: University of Chicago Press.

Bonny, H. (1978a). *Facilitating GIM sessions*. Baltimore, MD: ICM Books.

Bonny, H. (1978b). *The role of taped music programs in the GIM process*. Baltimore, MD: ICM Books.

Bonny, H. (1980). *GIM therapy: Past, present and future implications*. Baltimore, MD: ICM Books.

Bonny, H. (2002). *Music consciousness: The evolution of guided imagery and music*. Gilsum, NH: Barcelona.

Borczon, R.M. (1997). *Music therapy: Group vignettes*. Gilsum, NH: Barcelona.

Boxill, E.H. (1985). *Music therapy for the developmentally disabled*. Rockville, MD: Aspen.

Brooks, D.M. (1998). *Anima experiences of men in Guided Imagery and Music* (GIM). (Doctoral Dissertation, Temple University).

Broucek, M. (1987). Beyond healing to "whole-ing": A plea for the deinstitutionalization of music therapy. *Music Therapy, 6*(2), 50–58.

Brown, S. (1999). Some thoughts on music, therapy, and music therapy. *British Journal of Music Therapy, 13*(2), 63–71.

Brown, S., & Pavlicevic, M. (1996). Clinical improvisation in creative music therapy: Musical aesthetic and the interpersonal dimension. *The Arts in Psychotherapy, 23*(5), 397–405.

Bruscia, K.E. (1989). *Defining music therapy*. Gilsum, NH: Barcelona.

Bruscia, K.E. (1998a). *Defining music therapy* (2nd ed.). Gilsum, NH: Barcelona.

Bruscia, K.E. (1998b). An introduction to music psychotherapy. In K.E. Bruscia (Ed.), *The dynamics of music psychotherapy* (pp. 1–15). Gilsum, NH: Barcelona.

Bruscia, K.E. (2002). Client assessment in the Bonny Method of guided imagery and music (BMGIM). In K.E. Bruscia & D.E. Grocke (Eds.), *Guided imagery and music: The Bonny Method and beyond* (pp. 273–295). Gilsum, NH: Barcelona.

Bruscia, K.E. (Ed) (2012). *Readings in music therapy theory*. Gilsum, NH: Barcelona.

Bunt, L. (1994). *Music therapy: An art beyond words*. London: Routledge.

Bunt, L., & Pavlicevic, M. (2001). Music and emotion: Perspectives from music therapy. In J.A. Sloboda (Ed.), *Music and emotion: Theory and research* (pp. 181–204). New York: Oxford University Press.

Chase, K.M. (2003). Multicultural music therapy: A review of literature. *Music Therapy Perspectives, 21*(2), 84–88.

Christensen, E. (2000). Music precedes language. *Nordic Journal of Music Therapy, 9*(2), 32–35.

Crowe, B. (2004). *Music and soulmaking: Toward a new theory of music therapy*. Lanham, MD: The Scarecrow Press.

Crowe, B.J., & Scovel, M. (1996). An overview of sound healing practices: Implications for the profession of music therapy. *Music Therapy Perspectives, 14*(1), 21–29.

Darrow, A., & Molloy, D. (1998). Multicultural perspectives in music therapy: An examination of the literature, educational curricula, and clinical practices in culturally diverse cities of the United States. *Music Therapy Perspectives, 16*(1), 27–32.

Day, T., Baker, F., & Darlington, Y. (2009). Beyond the therapy room: Women's experiences of "going public" with song creations. *British Journal of Music Therapy, 23*(1), 19–26.

DeNora, T. (2000). *Music in everyday life*. Cambridge: Cambridge University Press.

Dewey, J. (1934). *Art as experience*. New York: Wideview/Perigee.

Dileo, C. (1999). Introduction. In C. Dileo (Ed.), *Music therapy and medicine: Theoretical and clinical applications* (pp. 1–10). Silver Spring, MD: American Music Therapy Association.

Dissanayake, E. (2001). An ethological view of music and its relevance to music therapy. *Nordic Journal of Music Therapy, 10*(2), 159–175.

Dissanayake, E. (2009). Root, leaf, blossom, or bole: Concerning the origin and adaptive function of music. In S. Malloch & C. Trevarthen (Eds.), *Communicative musicality: Exploring the basis of human companionship* (pp. 17–30). New York: Oxford University Press.

Edwards, J. (2002a). Debating the winds of change in community music therapy. *Voices: A World Forum for Music Therapy*. Retrieved December 14, 2012 from http://voices.no/?q=content/re-debating-winds-change-community-music-therapy

Edwards, J. (2002b). "Music therapy by any other name would smell as sweet" or "community music therapy" means "culturally sensitive music therapy" in our language. *Voices: A World Forum for Music Therapy*. Retrieved December 14, 2012 from http://voices.no/?q=content/context-and-culture #comment-621

Elefant, C. (2010). Giving voice: Participatory action research with a marginalized group. In B. Stige, G. Ansdell, C. Elefant, & M. Pavlicevic, *Where music helps: Community music therapy in action and reflection* (pp. 199–215). Farnham, UK: Ashgate.

Elliott, D.J. (1995). *Music matters: A new philosophy of music education.* New York: Oxford University Press.

Ellis, A. (1995). Rational emotive behavior therapy. In R.J. Corsini & D. Wedding (Eds.), *Current psychotherapies* (5th ed.) (pp. 162–196). Itasca, IL: F.E. Peacock.

Epp, E. (2001). Locating the autonomous voice: Self-expression in music-centered music therapy. *Voices: A World Forum for Music Therapy*, 7(1). Retrieved December 12, 2012, from https://normt.uib.no/index.php/voices/article/view/463/372

Feld, S. (1994). Aesthetics as iconicity of style (Uptown title); or (Downtown title) "Lift-up-over sounding": Getting into the Kaluli groove. In C. Keil & S. Feld, *Music grooves* (pp. 109–150). Chicago, IL: University of Chicago Press.

Forinash, M., & Gonzalez, D. (1989). A phenomenological perspective of music therapy. *Music Therapy*, 8(1), 35–46.

Garred, R. (2006). *Music as therapy: A dialogical perspective.* Gilsum, NH: Barcelona.

Gaston, E.T. (1964). The aesthetic experience and biological man. *Journal of Music Therapy*, 1(1), 1–7.

Gaston, E.T. (1968). Man and music. In E.Thayer Gaston (Ed.), *Music in therapy* (pp. 7–29). New York: Macmillan.

Gfeller, K.E. (2012). Music as communication. In K.E. Bruscia (Ed.), *Readings in music therapy theory* (pp. 493–511). Gilsum, NH: Barcelona.

Glick, L.G. (1966). Music as therapy in community agencies. *Journal of Music Therapy*, 3(4), 120–125.

Gouk, P. (Ed.). (2000a). *Musical healing in cultural contexts.* Aldershot, UK: Ashgate.

Gouk, P. (2000b). Introduction. In P. Gouk (Ed.), *Musical healing in cultural contexts* (pp. 1–25). Aldershot, UK: Ashgate.

Grinde, B. (2000). A biological perspective on musical appreciation. *Nordic Journal of Music Therapy*, 9(2), 18–27.

Grinde, B. (2001). Response to the comments made by Bjørn Merker and Erik Christensen. *Nordic Journal of Music Therapy*, 10(1), 100–102.

Hadley, S. (2006). *Feminist perspectives in music therapy.* Gilsum, NH: Barcelona.

Henderson, H. (1991). Improvised song stories in the treatment of a 13-year-old sexually abused girl from the Xhosa tribe in South Africa. In K.E. Bruscia (Ed.), *Case studies in music therapy* (pp. 207–217). Gilsum, NH: Barcelona.

Hesser, B. (2001). The transformative power of music in our lives: A personal perspective. *Music Therapy Perspectives*, 19(1), 53–58.

Hesser, B. (2002). Music in psychotherapy. Unpublished paper.

Hibben, J. (Ed.). (1999). *Inside music therapy: Client experiences.* Gilsum, NH: Barcelona.

Hilliard, R.E. (2001). The use of cognitive-behavioral music therapy in the treatment of women with eating disorders. *Music Therapy Perspectives*, 19(2), 109–113.

Hodson, R. (2007). *Interaction, improvisation, and interplay in jazz.* New York: Routledge.

Horden, P. (Ed.). (2000a). *Music as medicine: The history of music therapy since antiquity.* Aldershot, UK: Ashgate.

Horden, P. (2000b). Introduction. In P. Horden (Ed.), *Music as medicine: The history of music therapy since antiquity* (pp. 1–3). Aldershot, UK: Ashgate.

Horden, P. (2000c). Musical solutions: Past and present in music therapy In P. Horden (Ed.), *Music as medicine: The history of music therapy since antiquity* (pp. 4–40). Aldershot, UK: Ashgate.

Jampel, P. (2006). *Performance in music therapy with mentally ill adults.* (Doctoral dissertation, New York University).

Janzen, J.M. (2000). Theories of music in African ngoma healing. In P. Gouk (Ed.), *Musical healing in cultural contexts* (pp. 46–66). Aldershot, UK: Ashgate.

John, D. (1995). The therapeutic relationship in music therapy as a tool in the treatment of psychosis. In T. Wigram, B. Saperston, & R. West (Eds.), *The art and science of music therapy: A handbook* (pp. 157–166). Chur, Switzerland: Harwood Academic Publishers.

Johnson, D.R. (1984). Establishing the creative arts therapies as an independent profession. *The Arts in Psychotherapy, 11*(3), 209–212.

Jones, C., Baker, F., & Day, T. (2004). From healing rituals to music therapy: Bridging the cultural divide between therapist and young Sudanese refugees. *The Arts in Psychotherapy, 31*, 89–100.

Keil, C. (1994). Participatory discrepancies and the power of music. In C. Keil & S. Feld, *Music grooves* (pp. 96–108). Chicago, IL: University of Chicago Press.

Keil, C. (1995). The theory of participatory discrepancies: A progress report. *Ethnomusicology, 39*(1), 1–20.

Keil, C., & Feld, S. (1994). *Music grooves.* Chicago, IL: University of Chicago Press.

Kennair, L.E.O. (2000). Developing minds for pathology and musicality. The role of theory development of personality and pathology in clinical thinking illustrated by the effect of taking an evolutionary perspective. *Nordic Journal of Music Therapy, 9*(1), 26–37.

Kennair, L.E.O. (2001). Origins: Investigations into biological human musical nature. *Nordic Journal of Music Therapy, 10*(1), 54–64

Kenny, C.B. (1982). *The mythic artery: The magic of music therapy.* Atascadero, CA: Ridgeview.

Kenny, C.B. (1987). *The field of play: A theoretical study of music therapy process.* (Doctoral dissertation, The Fielding Institute).

Kenny, C.B. (1989). *The field of play: A guide for the theory and practice of music therapy.* Atascadero. CA: Ridgeview.

Kenny, C.B. (1996). The dilemma of uniqueness: An essay on consciousness and qualities. *Nordic Journal of Music Therapy, 5*(2), 87–96.

Kenny, C.B. (2006). *Music and life in the field of play: An anthology.* Gilsum, NH: Barcelona.

Kestenberg, J. (1975). *Children and parents: Psychoanalytic studies in development.* New York: Jason Aronson.

Kigunda, B.M. (2003). Music therapy: A therapeutic force remains anonymous in Kenya. *Voices: A World Forum for Music Therapy, 3*(3). Retrieved December 19, 2012 from https://normt.uib.no/index.php/voices/article/view/131/107

Kigunda, B.M. (2004). Music therapy canning and the healing rituals of Catholic charismatics in Kenya. *Voices: A World Forum for Music Therapy, 4*(3). Retrieved December 19, 2012 from https://normt.uib.no/index.php/voices/article/view/186/145

Kovach, A.M.S. (1985). Shamanism and guided imagery and music: A comparison. *Journal of Music Therapy, 22*(3), 154–165.

Kuhn, T.S. (1970). *The structure of scientific revolutions* (2nd ed., enlarged). Chicago, IL: University of Chicago Press.

Lakoff, G., & Johnson, M. (1980). *Metaphors we live by.* Chicago, IL: University of Chicago Press.

Langenberg, M., Frommer, J. & Tress, W. (1993). A qualitative research approach to analytical music therapy. *Music Therapy, 12*(1), 59–84.

Lee, C. (1992). The need for professional questioning. *Journal of British Music Therapy, 6*(1), 23.

Lee, C. (1996). *Music at the edge: The music therapy experiences of a musician with AIDS.* London: Routledge.

Lee, C. (2003). *The architecture of aesthetic music therapy.* Gilsum, NH: Barcelona.

Legrenzi, P., & Umiltà, C. (2011). *Neuromania: On the limits of brain science.* Trans. by F. Anderson. New York: Oxford University Press.

Logis, M., & Turry, A. (1999). Singing my way through it: Facing the cancer, the darkness, and the fear. In J. Hibben (Ed.), *Inside music therapy: Client experiences* (pp. 97–118). Gilsum, NH: Barcelona.

McFerran, K. & O'Grady, L. (2006). Birthing feminist community music therapy: The progeny of community music therapy practice and feminist therapy theory. In S. Hadley (Ed.), *Feminist perspectives in music therapy* (pp. 63–80). Gilsum, NH: Barcelona.

McGuire, M.G. (Ed.). (2004). *Psychiatric music therapy in the community: The legacy of Florence Tyson.* Gilsum, NH: Barcelona.

McNiff, S. (1988). The shaman within. *The Arts in Psychotherapy, 15*(4), 285–291.

Maratos, A. (2004). Whatever next? Community music therapy for the institution. In M. Pavlicevic & G. Ansdell (Eds.), *Community music therapy* (pp. 131–146). London: Jessica Kingsley.

Maratos, A. (2005). Response to discussion paper on community music therapy. *Voices: A World Forum for Music Therapy*. Retrieved December 14, 2012, from https://normt.uib.no/index.php/voices/article/view/208/152

Marshman, A.T. (2003). The power of music: A Jungian aesthetic. *Music Therapy Perspectives, 21*(1), 21–26.

Mereni, A-E. (1996). "Kinesis und catharsis" The African traditional concept of sound/motion as music: Its applications in, and implications for, music therapy. *British Journal of Music Therapy, 10*(1), 17–23.

Mereni, A-E. (1997). "Kinesis und catharsis" The African traditional concept of sound/motion (music): Its applications in, and implications for, music therapy—part III. *British Journal of Music Therapy, 11*(1), 20–23.

Merker, B. (2000). A new theory of music origins: The language auxiliary hypothesis. *Nordic Journal of Music Therapy, 9*(2), 28–31.

Michel, D.E. (1976). *Music therapy: An introduction to therapy and special education through music.* Springfield, IL: Charles C. Thomas.

Monson, I. (1996). *Saying something: Jazz improvisation and interaction.* Chicago, IL: University of Chicago Press.

Moreno, J. (1988a). The music therapist: Creative arts therapist and contemporary shaman. *The Arts in Psychotherapy, 15*(4), 271–280.

Moreno, J. (1988b). Multicultural music therapy: The world music connection. *Journal of Music Therapy, 25*(1), 17–27.

Moreno, J.J. (1995a). Candomblé: Afro-Brazilian ritual as therapy. In C.B. Kenny (Ed.) *Listening, playing creating: Essays on the power of sound* (pp. 217–232). Albany, NY: State University of New York Press.

Moreno, J.J. (1995b). Ethnomusic therapy: An interdisciplinary approach to music healing. *The Arts in Psychotherapy, 22*(4), 329–338.

Nettl, B. (2005). *The study of ethnomusicology: Thirty-one issues and concepts.* Champaign, IL: University of Illinois Press.

Nolan, P. (1994). The therapeutic response in improvisational music therapy: What goes on inside? *Music Therapy Perspectives, 12*(2), 84–91.

Nolan, P. (2005). Verbal processing within the music therapy relationship. *Music Therapy Perspectives, 23*(1), 18–28.

Nordoff, P., & Robbins, C. (1971). *Therapy in music for handicapped children.* London: Victor Gollancz.

Nordoff, P., & Robbins, C. (1977). *Creative music therapy: Individualized treatment for the handicapped child.* New York: John Day.

Nordoff, P., & Robbins, C. (2004). *Therapy in music for handicapped children.* Gilsum, NH: Barcelona.

Nordoff, P., & Robbins, C. (2007). *Creative music therapy: A Guide to fostering clinical musicianship* (2nd ed., revised and expanded). Gilsum, NH: Barcelona.

O'Brien, E. (2006). Opera therapy: Creating and performing a new work with cancer patients and professional singers. *Nordic Journal of Music Therapy, 15*(1), 82–96.

O'Grady, L., & McFerran, K. (2007). Community music therapy and its relationship to community music: Where does it end? *Nordic Journal of Music Therapy, 16*(1), 14–26.

Patel, A.D. (2008). *Music, language, and the brain.* New York: Oxford University Press.

Pavlicevic, M. (1990). Dynamic interplay in clinical improvisation. *Journal of British Music Therapy, 4*(2), 5–9.

Pavlicevic, M. (1995). Interpersonal process in clinical improvisation: Towards a subjectively objective systematic definition. In T. Wigram, B. Saperston, & R. West (Eds.), *The art and science of music therapy: A handbook* (pp. 167–178). Chur, Switzerland: Harwood Academic Publishers.

Pavlicevic, M. (1997). *Music therapy in context: Music, meaning and relationship.* London: Jessica Kingsley.

Pavlicevic, M. (1999). Thoughts, words, and deeds. Harmonies and counterpoints in music therapy theory. *British Journal of Music Therapy, 13*(2), 59–62.

Pavlicevic. M. (2000). Improvisation in music therapy: Human communication in sound. *Journal of Music Therapy, 37*(4), 269–285.

Pavlicevic, M. (2001). Music therapy in South Africa: Compromise or synthesis? *Voices: A World Forum for Music Therapy, 1*(1). Accessed December 19, 2012, from https://normt.uib.no/index.php/voices/article/view/43/27

Pavlicevic, M. (2004). Learning from *Thembalethu*: Towards responsive and responsible practice in community music therapy. In M. Pavlicevic & G. Ansdell (Eds.), *Community music therapy* (pp. 35–47). London: Jessica Kingsley.

Pavlicevic, M. (2006). Worksongs, playsongs: Communication, collaboration, culture, and community. *Australian Journal of Music Therapy, 17,* 85–99.

Pavlicevic, M., & Ansdell, G. (Eds.). (2004a). *Community music therapy.* London: Jessica Kingsley.

Pavlicevic, M., & Ansdell, G. (2004b). Introduction: "The ripple effect." In M. Pavlicevic & G. Ansdell, (Eds.). *Community music therapy* (pp. 15–31). London: Jessica Kingsley.

Pavlicevic, M., & Ansdell, G. (2009). Between communicative musicality and collaborative musicing: A perspective from community music therapy. In S. Malloch & C. Trevarthen (Eds.) *Communicative musicality: Exploring the basis of human companionship* (pp. 357–376). New York: Oxford University Press.

Pelliteri, J. (2009). *Emotional processes in music therapy.* Gilsum, NH: Barcelona.

Priestley, M. (1975). *Music therapy in action.* London: Constable.

Priestley, M. (1987). Music and the shadow. *Music Therapy, 6*(2) 20–27.

Priestley, M. (1994). *Essays on analytical music therapy.* Gilsum, NH: Barcelona.

Priestley, M. (2012). *Music therapy in action* (2nd ed.). Gilsum, NH: Barcelona.

Rolvsjord, R. (2010). *Resource-oriented music therapy in mental health care.* Gilsum, NH: Barcelona.

Ruud, E. (1995). Improvisation as a liminal experience: Jazz and music therapy as modern "rites de passage." In C.B. Kenny (Ed.), *Listening, playing, creating: Essays on the power of sound* (pp. 91–117). Albany, NY: State University of New York Press.

Ruud, E. (1997). Music and identity. *Nordic Journal of Music Therapy, 6*(1), 3–13.

Ruud, E. (1998). *Music therapy: Improvisation, communication, and culture.* Gilsum, NH: Barcelona.

Ruud, E. (2004). Defining community music therapy. Voices: A World Forum for Music Therapy. Retrieved December 14, 2012 from http://voices.no/?q=content/re-debating-winds-change-community-music-therapy-1

Ruud, E. (2010). *Music therapy: A perspective from the humanities.* Gilsum, NH: Barcelona.

Schmais, C. (1988). Tread with care! *The Arts in Psychotherapy, 15*(4), 301.

Scheiby, B.B. (2002). Improvisation as a musical healing tool and life approach: Theoretical and clinical applications of analytical music therapy (AMT) in a short- and long-term rehabilitation facility. In J.T. Eschen (Ed.), *Analytical music therapy* (pp. 115–153). London: Jessica Kingsley.

Scheiby, B.B. (2010). Analytical music therapy and integrative medicine: The impact of medical trauma on the psyche. In K. Stewart (Ed.), *Music therapy and trauma: Bridging theory and clinical practice* (pp. 74–87). New York: Satchnote Press.

Schneider, E.H., Unkefer, R.F., & Gaston, E.T. (1968). Introduction. In E.T. Gaston (Ed.), *Music in therapy* (pp. 1–4). New York: Macmillan.

Sears W.W. (1968). Processes in music therapy. In E.T. Gaston (Ed.), *Music in therapy* (pp. 30–44). New York: Macmillan.

Sears. W.W. (2007a). Processes in music therapy. In M.S. Sears (Ed.), *Music: The therapeutic edge: Readings from William W. Sears* (pp. 1–15). Gilsum, NH: Barcelona.

Sears, W.W. (2007b). A re-vision and expansion of processes in music therapy. In M.S. Sears (Ed.), *Music: The therapeutic edge: Readings from William W. Sears* (pp. 16–41). Gilsum, NH: Barcelona.

Shapiro, N. (2005). Sounds in the world: Multicultural influences in music therapy in clinical practice and training. *Music Therapy Perspectives, 23*(1), 29–35.

Simpson, F. (2000). Speaking with clients: Perspectives from creative music therapy. *British Journal of Music Therapy, 14*(2), 83–92.

Small, C. (1998). *Musicking: The meanings of performing and listening.* Hanover, NH: University Press of New England.

Smeijsters, H. (1993). Music therapy and psychotherapy. *The Arts in Psychotherapy, 20*(3), 223–229.

Smeijsters H. (2003). Forms of feeling and forms of perception: The fundamentals of analogy in music therapy. *Nordic Journal of Music Therapy, 12*(1), 71–85.

Smeijsters, H. (2005). *Sounding the self: Analogy in improvisational music therapy.* Gilsum, NH: Barcelona.

Smeijsters, H. (2008). In defense of the person: Limitations of aesthetic theory of music therapy. *Nordic Journal of Music Therapy, 17*(1), 19–24.

Sobey, K. (1992). Relatedness in music therapy and psychotherapy. *Journal of British Music Therapy, 6*(1), 19–21.

Stige, B. (2002a). *Culture-centered music therapy.* Gilsum, NH: Barcelona.

Stige, B. (2002b). History and heritage: On tradition and innovation in creative music therapy. In B. Stige (Ed.), *Contemporary voices in music therapy: Communication, culture, and community.* Oslo: Unipub Forlag.

Stige, B. (2002c). The relentless roots of community music therapy. *Voices: A World Forum for Music Therapy, 2*(3). Retrieved December 14, 2012 from https://normt.uib.no/index.php/voices/article/view/98/75

Stige, B. (2002d). The "jambo" means "hello" in Africa syndrome. *Voices: A World Forum for Music Therapy.* Retrieved December 14, 2012, from http://testvoices.uib.no/?q=fortnightly-columns/2002-jambo-means-hello-africa-syndrome

Stige, B. (2003). *Elaborations toward a notion of community music therapy.* (Doctoral Dissertation, Faculty of Arts, University of Oslo).

Stige, B. (2004). On defining community music therapy. *Voices: A World Forum for Music Therapy.* Retrieved December 14, 2012, from http://voices.no/?q=content/re-debating-winds-change-community-music-therapy-2

Stige, B. (2008a). The aesthetic or multiple aesthetics? *Nordic Journal of Music Therapy, 17*(1), 25–29.

Stige, B. (2008b). Dancing the drama and singing for life: On ethnomusicology and music therapy. *Nordic Journal of Music Therapy, 17*(2), 155–171.

Streeter, E. (1999). Finding a balance between psychological thinking and musical awareness in music therapy theory: A psychoanalytic perspective. *British Journal of Music Therapy, 13*(1), 5–20.

Streeter, E. (2006). Response to "Music psychotherapy and community music therapy: Questions and considerations." *Voices: A World Forum for Music Therapy.* Retrieved December 14, 2012, from https://normt.uib.no/index.php/voices/article/view/208/152

Summer, L. (1995). Unsound medicine. In C.B. Kenny, (Ed.). *Listening, playing, creating: Essays on the power of sound* (pp. 59–64). Albany, NY: State University of New York Press.

Summer, L. (1996). *Music: The new age elixir.* Amherst, NY: Prometheus.

Summer, L. (2002). Group music and imagery therapy: Emergent receptive techniques in music therapy practice. In K.E. Bruscia & D.E. Grocke (Eds.), *Guided imagery and music: The Bonny Method and beyond* (pp. 297–306). Gilsum, NH: Barcelona.

Taylor, D. B. (1997). *Biomedical foundations of music as therapy.* St. Louis, MO: MMB Music.

Thaut, M.H. (2000). *A scientific model of music in therapy and medicine.* San Antonio, TX: IMR Press.

Thaut, M.H. (2008). *Rhythm, music, and the brain: Scientific foundations and clinical applications.* New York: Routledge.

Tønsberg, G.E.H., & Hauge, T.S. (2003). The musical nature of human interaction. *Voices: A World Forum for Music Therapy, 3*(1). https://normt.uib.no/index.php/voices/article/view/111/87

Toppozada, M.R. (1995). Multicultural training for music therapists: An examination of current issues based on a national survey of professional music therapists. *Journal of Music Therapy, 32*(2), 65–90.

Trevarthen, C., & Malloch, S. (2000). The dance of wellbeing: Defining the musical therapeutic effect. *Nordic Journal of Music Therapy, 9*(2), 3–17.

Turner, V. (1969). *The ritual process. Structure and anti-structure.* Chicago, IL: Aldine.

Turry, A. (1998). Transference and countertransference in Nordoff-Robbins music therapy. In K.E. Bruscia (Ed.), *The dynamics of music psychotherapy* (pp. 161–212). Gilsum, NH: Barcelona.

Turry, A. (1999). Performance and product: Clinical implications for the music therapist. *Music Therapy World.* Retrieved December 1, 2009, from http://musictherapyworld.net/

Turry, A. (2005). Music psychotherapy and community music therapy: Questions and considerations. *Voices: A World Forum for Music Therapy*, 5(1). Retrieved December 14, 2012, from https://normt. uib.no/index.php/voices/article/view/208/152.

Turry, A. (2010). Integrating musical and psychological thinking: The relationship between music and words in clinically improvised songs. *Qualitative Inquiries in Music Therapy*, 5, 116–172.

Turry, A. (2011). *Between music and psychology: A music therapist's method for improvising songs*. Colne, DE: Lambert Academic Publishing.

Tyson, F. (1981). *Psychiatric music therapy*. New York: Creative Arts Rehabilitation Center.

Tyson, F. (1982). Individual singing instruction: An evolutionary framework for psychiatric music therapists. *Music Therapy Perspectives*, 1(1), 5–15.

Tyson, F. (2004). Music and the primary relationship. In M.G. McGuire (Ed.), *Psychiatric music therapy in the community: The legacy of Florence Tyson* (pp. 7–11). Gilsum, NH: Barcelona.

Verney, R., & Ansdell, G. (2010). *Conversations on Nordoff-Robbins music therapy*. Gilsum, NH: Barcelona.

Viega, M. (2012). *"Loving me and my butterfly wings:" An arts-based study of songs written by inner city adolescents*. (Doctoral Dissertation, Temple University).

Wexler, M.M.D. (1989). The use of song in grief therapy with Cibecue White Mountain Apaches. *Music Therapy Perspectives*, 7, 63–66.

Wheeler, B. (1983). A psychotherapeutic classification of music therapy practices: A continuum of procedures. *Music Therapy Perspectives*, 1(2), 8–12.

Winn, T., Crowe, B., & Moreno, J.J. (1989). Shamanism and music therapy: Ancient healing techniques in modern practice. *Music Therapy Perspectives*, 7, 67–71.

Wood, S. (2006). "The matrix": A model of community music therapy processes. *Voices: A World Forum for Music Therapy*, 6(3). Retrieved September 28, 2012, from https://normt.uib.no/index.php/voices/article/view/279/204.

Wood, S., Verney, R., & Atkinson, J. (2004). From therapy to community: Making music in neurological rehabilitation. In M. Pavlicevic & G. Ansdell (Eds.), *Community music therapy* (pp. 48–62). London: Jessica Kingsley.

World Federation of Music Therapy (2011). What is music therapy? Retrieved May 14, 2013, from www.musictherapyworld.net/WFMT/About_WFMT.html

York, E. (2006). Finding voice: Feminist music therapy and research with women survivors of domestic violence. In S. Hadley (Ed.), *Feminist perspectives in music therapy* (pp. 245–265). Gilsum, NH: Barcelona.

Zharinova-Sanderson, O. (2004). Promoting integration and socio-cultural change: Community music therapy with traumatised refugees in Berlin. In M. Pavlicevic & G. Ansdell (Eds.), *Community music therapy* (pp. 233–248). London: Jessica Kingsley.

Zuckerkandl, V. (1956). *Sound and symbol Volume I: Music and the external world*. Trans. by W.R. Trask. Princeton, NJ: Princeton University Press.

AUTHOR INDEX

SUBJECT INDEX